Trans-Generational Family Relations

A volume in
Perspectives on Human Development
Dieter Ferring, Jaan Valsiner, and Conchita D'Ambrosio, *Series Editors*

Trans-Generational Family Relations

Investigating Ambivalences

edited by

Isabelle Albert
University of Luxembourg

Emily Abbey
Ramapo College of New Jersey

Jaan Valsiner
Aalborg University

IAP

INFORMATION AGE PUBLISHING, INC.
Charlotte, NC • www.infoagepub.com

Library of Congress Cataloging-in-Publication Data

A CIP record for this book is available from the Library of Congress
http://www.loc.gov

ISBN: 978-1-64113-082-0 (Paperback)
978-1-64113-083-7 (Hardcover)
978-1-64113-084-4 (ebook)

Printed and bound by CPI Group (UK) Ltd, Croydon, CR0 4YY

CONTENTS

Series Editor's Foreword ... ix

General Introduction: Looking at Relations Across Generations: Ambivalence in Context ... xiii

PART I

CONCEPTUAL ISSUES: AMBIVALENCE AND ITS STUDY

1 Tensegrity as Existential Condition: The Inherent Ambivalence of Development ... 3
Luca Tateo

2 The Research Act: Creating Knowledge From the Not (Yet) Known ... 21
Eugenia Gouvedari

PART II

LIFESPAN AND TRANSGENERATIONAL FOCUS

3 Multilevel Approach to Ambivalence in Family Sphere: Changing Structures, Roles, and Relationships ... 33
Kairi Kasearu, Kadri Raid, and Dagmar Kutsar

4 Ambivalence in the Family Transmission of Values: Assuming Similarity and Recognizing Differences 55
Daniela Barni and Silvia Donato

5 Anticipatory Recognition: Creating a Cycle of Flexible Meanings in Intergenerational Relations 73
Elsa de Mattos

6 Ambivalence Toward Parents During the Process of Individuation: Being Caught Between Autonomy and Relatedness? 99
Isabelle Albert and Dieter Ferring

7 Dynamic Relations Between Perceived Parental Responsiveness, Experiences of Ambivalence, and Self-Esteeem Development in Adolescence 121
Annekatrin Steinhoff and Marlis Buchmann

8 Emotional Ambivalence in Adult Children of Care-Dependent Older Parents: Heuristic Impulses From Cognitive-Motivational Emotion Theories 141
Thomas Boll

PART III

EXPERIENCING AMBIVALENCE: FOCUS ON PHENOMENA

9 Ambivalence When Family Values Change: Development of New Values in the Perspective of Sociocultural Global "Advancement" 179
Maliina Lyberth

10 Transgenerational Ambivalence in the Time to Come: How Meanings Regulate Being Pregnant and Facing Miscarriage 197
Vívian Volkmer Pontes and Lívia Mathias Simão

11 Saudade: A Unique Feeling Within the Lusitanian Soul 217
Stephanie Barros and Gaby Marinho Ribeiro

12 Desired Ambiguities and Dealing With Ambivalences in the Context of Social Work 247
Mogens Jensen

13 Your Duty Toward My Right: Ambivalent Traps of Rights and Duties 263
Kevin R. Carriere

PART IV

MEASURING AMBIVALENCE

14 Attachment Ambivalence: The Concept, Psychological Importance, and Measurement Issues 283
Katarzyna Lubiewska

PART V

GENERAL CONCLUSIONS

15 Transcending Ambivalence: Overcoming the Ambiguity of Theory and Practices 311
Jaan Valsiner, Isabelle Albert, and Emily Abbey

About the Contributors 333

SERIES EDITOR'S FOREWORD

As the title tells us, this book looks at relations across generations, with a focus on ambivalences that may be experienced in these relationships. One could put it more simply—but certainly not easier—and say that this book is about love. The editors are not afraid to state this in the first sentences of their introduction. Love is still a neglected topic within psychology—not to speak of the social sciences in general. This may still be considered a consequence of positivist models and their underlying motive to measure, calibrate, and chart the quality of human relationships. At the level of phenomena and their underlying needs and motives, only few needs seem so strong than the need for love. A sound analysis of this phenomenon cannot exclude that love in family (and other) relations is joined with other feelings and cognitions that may represent antagonists of such an emotion. This is where the concept of ambivalence comes into play. In the psychological view, ambivalence is about the coexistence of feelings and thoughts about a person or an object; the sociological perspective highlights ambivalence as an inherent characteristic of a social role.

The concept is thus shared by several theoretical approaches, and the editors rightly choose to analyze this phenomenon based on several disciplinary and methodological perspectives. The reader will find contributions elaborating perspectives of cultural and developmental psychology as well as sociological theories and social work on ambivalence. Moreover, she or he finds quantitative and qualitative approaches in the description and conceptual deconstruction of the phenomenon. The book also covers different periods of the life course, focusing on adolescence and youth,

Trans-Generational Family Relations, pages ix–ix

adulthood, and old age. This brief overview conveys that ambivalence happens throughout the human life course and constitutes a universal and basic experience of the human condition. Given all this, one may ask why this concept is not more prominent across social sciences, and this puts it into close relationship with the treatment that the phenomenon of love received in psychological theory and research.

My impression is that the study of these phenomena is neglected because it does not follow the linear logic that has become part of psychological theory-building and the basis of a corresponding methodology. In such a linear conception, factors or independent variables or predictors influence a criterion or dependent variable at a given time. This implies a unidirectional causal sequence that will allow us to change or modify dependent variables by changing the independent ones. Such an approach is not only linked to the experimental procedure; you will find it in nearly all research following a nomothetic approach. Although epistemologies highlight probabilistic and reciprocal dynamics underlying relationships, it seems to me that the linear approach still predominates in psychology theory. Ambivalence as the coexistence of feelings and cognitions that may even be antagonistic withdraws itself from such a linear logic. To feel ambivalence—at least in the beginning—may also withdraw from a conscious reflection and/or open communication both within and between persons.

A person may feel love and hate toward one person at the same time, whether he or she is a parent, child, or partner; at the same time, he or she may forbid her or himself to have this negative feeling because one "ought not" to feel this way. Thus, a person may tend to deny the experience of ambivalence following the paradoxical notion that you first have to perceive a phenomenon to deny it. Furthermore, a person will have difficulties expressing ambivalence to others given that he or she is motivated to deny or blunt this experience. This has evident consequences for research on ambivalence, and one may ask whether a phenomenon that a person is not aware of or that he or she denies can be assessed at all. It is not for nothing that ambivalence gets evident in therapeutic interactions and dialogues where both partners coconstruct and agree on the meaning of such an experience. All this has consequences for measurement and assessment as well, and the volume editors consequently address this notion and deliver further insights here.

Taking all this together, the present book captures a phenomenon that is an essential part of the human condition but substantial challenges theory and research. The editors and authors of this volume know about this, and they took up this challenge. This book thus contributes to theory-building and developing and broadening measurement in interpersonal relations. One of the best things one could say about a book contribution to an ongoing discourse is that it renders new insights and inspires new ideas. The editors of this volume have clearly achieved this goal by joining junior and senior researchers and giving them space to elaborate their ideas.

—Dieter Ferring
Luxembourg

GENERAL INTRODUCTION

LOOKING AT RELATIONS ACROSS GENERATIONS

Ambivalence in Context

Isabelle Albert, Emily Abbey, and Jaan Valsiner

We love our parents and our grandparents. We honor our ancestors. Our feelings about our families across generations may give us much strength in "feeling ourselves." Yet in everyday relations with our beloved family members, we may encounter misunderstandings, frustrations, and even explicit conflicts. We cannot understand how our parents and grandparents do not understand our contemporary needs, and they do not understand ours. Yet we keep loving them—and they us. The mutuality of transgenerational family relations is inherently ambivalent. We live it in our deep feelings.

The interest in the concept of ambivalence has grown considerably in the last years in family research, as documented by an increasing number of publications, workshops, and symposia around the topic. Scientifically used for the first time by the psychiatrist Eugen Bleuler in his work on schizophrenia (Bleuler, 1910, 1914; see also Tateo, Chapter 1, this volume, for a historical overview) and highly prominent in psychoanalysis (Freud, 1919; McGregor, 2010), the concept of ambivalence was introduced into family

Trans-Generational Family Relations, pages xiii–xxx

research mainly by Lüscher and Pillemer (1998). In their seminal article, they proposed it as "a new approach to the study of parent-child relations in later life" in response to the solidarity paradigm (see Bengtson & Roberts, 1991), which failed to acknowledge that positive and negative aspects in intergenerational relationships can occur at the same time.

THE CONCEPT OF AMBIVALENCE: ITS HISTORY AND STRUCTURE

The concept of ambivalence also has a long tradition in social psychological research, such as the approach-avoidance conflict as described by Lewin (1935), cognitive dissonance by Festinger (1957), or further works on attitudinal ambivalence (e.g., Kaplan, 1972). It has also been closely studied in the framework of cultural psychology in the last years (Abbey, 2004; Abbey & Valsiner, 2005). We are all familiar with the experience of ambivalences to some extent, as particularly inherent in human nature[1] due to the capacity of hypothetical thinking, imagination, anticipation, and perspective taking. However, conception and reception of ambivalence seem to vary considerably, and it might be more salient for some than for others. Ambivalence is a complex phenomenon that has been studied in different ways and is not always conceptually clear. Thus, what exactly do we mean by ambivalence?

Commonly, when we hear the word "ambivalence," we are tempted to think of a relationship comprised of polar opposites. However, as outlined herein, that is but one of an array of ways to conceptualize the term. Most basically, ambivalence can be defined as a tension produced by a system entailing a kernel and at least two vectors that are nonisomorphic in size and direction. In such a system, ambivalence can occur under all conditions except for the one where the vectors are exactly the same size and direction (see Figure I.1D). Figure I.1A represents the most typical understanding of ambivalence described previously, that is, the polar opposition of two equally strong forces pulling the individual in opposite directions. In the current framework, this could be referred to as the maximum degree of ambivalence. Figures I.1B and I.1C produce ambivalence that is weaker yet present nonetheless. In Figure I.1B, although the two forces are not completely opposing, they create a tension between two different orientations. Figure I.1C depicts the discrepancy in strength of forces that creates ambivalence. We could refer to these as moderate strengths of ambivalence.

This way of defining ambivalence created by vectors of different sizes and directions borrows from Lewin's (1936) topological psychology, in which he offers the notion of a life space filled with forces that are of different degrees of attraction and repulsion. Although Lewin focused his work on the description of forces that were either exclusively positive or negative,

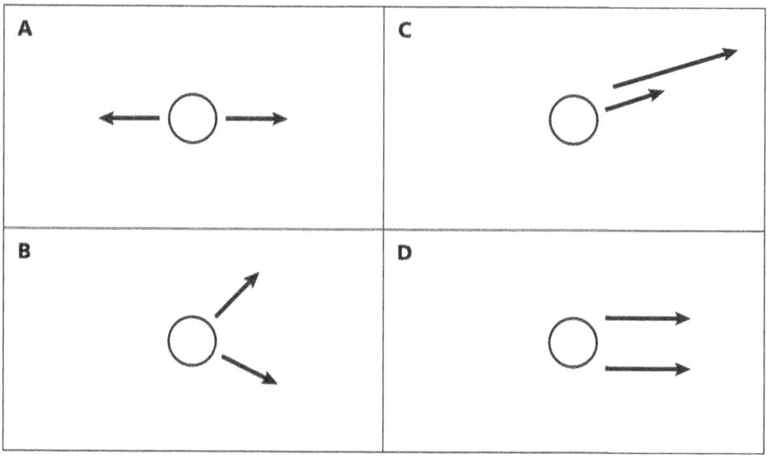

Figure I.1 Forms and strengths of ambivalence.

it is also possible to consider combining them to create the idea of ambivalence. In this latter case, the life space is composed of forces that pull him or her in differing if not outright opposing directions.

According to Lüscher and colleagues (2017), the ambivalence concept refers to "the experience of vacillating ('oscillating') between polar contradictions of feeling, thinking, wanting or social structures in the search for the meaning of social relationships, facts and texts, which are important for facets of the self and agency" (p. 41).

Whereas the polar contradiction of two forces that point exactly in opposite directions constitutes the constellation of maximum ambivalence that has been most often referred to when studying ambivalence, as outlined earlier further levels of ambivalence are possible (see also Abbey, 2012, in her semiotic analysis about the emergence of signs). In fact, apart from polarity between two opposite forces, one could also think of less strong contradictions that might be experienced as ambivalence. In a broader sense, one could consider A and non-A as a starting point for describing the field of ambivalence, implying the tension between what is and what could be.

A maximum level of ambivalence—two polar opposites—could, for example, entail love and hate toward a parent. As Abbey (2012) suggests, such a strong experience of ambivalence could be followed by a monologization (i.e., choosing either opposite) as the tension between both becomes too strong for the individual. The result would be the creation of strong signs that are more unambiguous, either love or hate, thus navigating toward a harmonious or conflicting relationship (see also Ferring, Michels, Boll, & Filipp, 2009, regarding the dynamic nature of intergenerational relationships). Another possibility would be that one leaves the situation as already described by Lewin, turning to the null condition in Abbey's words. This could mean that one dissociates from the parents altogether, reducing contact to a minimum, or that one leaves the situation temporarily. Although the latter could be a relief from tensions in the short run, it would probably entail a reappearance of ambivalences at the next encounter.

A moderate level of ambivalence would then refer to two forces that are in different directions but not in polar opposition. Ambivalence would again arise if these two forces are experienced as incompatible by the individual, in the sense that choosing one possibility would mean that you cannot choose the other (interestingly, in his lifespan developmental approach, Baltes, 1987, noted this interplay between gains and losses as inherent in developmental processes). However, in contrast to the first condition, because these vectors are not in polar contradiction, such incompatibility might be easier to overcome by finding a way to reconcile the two forces. An example could be a man who wants to be a good father and a good worker. These two aims might be experienced as incompatible even if not exactly opposed to each other. Different scenarios are thinkable here as to how this dynamic could evolve. One possibility would be that the man searches for a solution on how to reconcile both goals with a possible end state where he would find common ground and therefore not experience being a good father and a good worker as contradiction anymore. In contrast, such states of ambivalence might last longer (compared with the first condition of maximum level of ambivalence) because they could be easier to tolerate by an individual. In fact, the man might continue to oscillate between these two goals and thus continue to experience moderate levels of ambivalence (see also Lüscher and Hoff's, 2013, notion of captivation).

A further form of ambivalence could even contain two vectors that show in the same direction but are of different strength. For instance, in principle one might be willing to be a caring child and support aging parents but oscillate between possibilities regarding the amount of such support. One might also want to be a good mother but struggle with the decision as to how strongly to dedicate life to family and children.

All these constellations would be incompatible in the sense that when choosing A, one cannot choose not-A. However, this exclusiveness would have to be experienced as incompatible by the individual to create the experience of ambivalence that entails the oscillation or vacillation between different forces. As soon as one would find these different forces as compatible, they could become polyvalences, and the oscillation or vacillation between them would stop. Maybe, in fact, one idea on how to deal with ambivalences would be trying to turn ambivalence into polyvalence.

In summary, one common feature between the just described different levels of the experience of ambivalence might be its experience as being irreconcilable, and it could depend on the constellation between the two forces as to how strong the ambivalence is felt or perceived. Thus, ambivalence might refer to experienced contradictions of different strength within the same as well as between different areas of psychological functioning—cognitions, emotions, or behavioral tendencies. Examples are opposing ways of thinking about the same object (in the case of family relations; e.g., a parent) such as like and dislike, contradictory behavioral tendencies such as approach and avoidance, conflicting emotions such as love and hate, approaching behaviors accompanied by feelings of disgust, and so on. Importantly, the time perspective also seems to play a crucial role because there might be contradictions in past, present, and future imaginations of self and others (see e.g., Pontes & Simão, Chapter 10, this volume). In view of the different facets, it seems that a multidimensional conception and more fine-grained view of ambivalence(s) would make sense (see also Boll, Chapter 8, this volume; Gouvedari, Chapter 2, this volume).

Hereby, it should be made clear that ambivalence does not mean polyvalence, which would describe different meanings and valences of an object that would not be experienced as contradictory and incompatible. In the same way, ambiguity is not equal to ambivalence. Instead, ambiguity can be a precondition for the experience of ambivalence (see also Jensen, Chapter 12, this volume). In fact, we should distinguish between potentially ambivalent situations that create opportunities for the experience of ambivalence and the actual experience of ambivalence.

LEVELS OF AMBIVALENCE

Different levels of ambivalence have been described. A widely held distinction is the one between sociological (structural) and psychological ambivalence (for a summary, see Connidis, 2015). Sociological ambivalence refers to contradictions on the societal level, for instance, regarding role expectations that are difficult to reconcile. As said before, we might identify situations or contexts that are characterized by contradictory aspects bearing the potential of being experienced as ambivalent. These structural contradictions also might give rise to the subjective experience of ambivalences at the individual level, for instance, in the form of inner conflicts between internalized norms and personal wishes. As the world becomes more complex—especially in times of transition and social change—rules might be less clearly defined, and as a consequence more opportunities for ambivalences occur (Kasearu, Raid, and Kutsar, Chapter 3, this volume; Lyberth, Chapter 9, this volume).

Ambivalences might also derive from the family level as proximal context, in which interpersonal relations can be embedded. Specific family cultures generally entail rules and norms that are more or less shared by family members. Ambivalences might arise if family values are more cherished by some family members than by others (who could, however, feel obliged to follow them despite different personal preferences or needs) or if rules within the family are not clear. Because family bonds are, in principle, unsolvable and enduring, ambivalences can find a fertile ground because stopping these relations might not be an option (Lüscher & Hoff, 2013; also Van Gaalen, Dykstra, & Komter, 2010).

Ambivalence has often been said to occur in times of social or individual transition (see also Mattos, Chapter 5, this volume). To understand ambivalences inherent in these transitional phases, we could also make use of the concept of liminality, which describes the state of being in between, entailing disorientation but also new possibilities (see Hagestad, 2016; Turner, 1964). Ambivalence might serve as a catalyzer that helps dissolve the state of liminality and further develop in one direction or the other (Cabell & Valsiner, 2014; Carriere, Chapter 13, this volume).

AMBIVALENCE IN SOCIAL RELATIONS

Social relations in general—and probably family relations even more so—are particularly prone to the experience of ambivalences because of the dialectic tensions inherent in interpersonal relations and human communication (e.g., Baxter & Montgomery, 1996). Human communication is never unambiguous and entails the possibility of misunderstandings as the message passes through several filters—of the sender and the receiver—leaving much space for (mis)interpretations and changes in meaning during the processes of externalization and internalization (Kuczynski, Marshall, & Schell, 1997; Valsiner, 1997; see also Barni & Donato, Chapter 4, this volume). Certainly, expectations and misperceptions play a crucial role here. Further, the message of the sender might not be clear in itself, such as described by Bateson, Jackson, Haley, and Weakland (1956) with the term of double bind (i.e., an ambiguous way of communicating, where what the sender says is not compatible with how it is said; see also Abbey, 2004).

DIFFERENTIAL VIEW

As mentioned previously, one has to distinguish the potential of ambivalence as created by structural conditions that might set the stage for the occurrence of ambivalence, but how this is actually experienced also depends on the individual. In fact, some persons might be more sensitive to the experience of ambivalence than others depending on different personality traits, cognitive styles, expectations, meta-perceptions, and the like. In the end, ambivalences might occur either due to "objectively" ambiguous situations that are experienced as such or imagined ambiguities. In that sense, we might even think of situations where ambivalences are experienced, although the situation is not characterized by specific favoring features (actually, for some people, the experience of ambivalence could even become an automated reaction to certain cues, sometimes even pathological; see also rumination, e.g., Koster, Fang, & Marchetti, 2015) and, vice versa, of persons being completely unaware of potential ambivalences occurring around them (i.e., not getting any cue). Certainly, processes in the individual development of each person might play a role here, notably also early (and later) experiences within the family as primary socialization agent (see also Lubiewska, Chapter 14, this volume).

CONSEQUENCES OF AMBIVALENCE

Although ambivalence has had a rather negative connotation in the past, recent approaches have shifted to a more neutral view, which regards ambivalence rather as a catalyzer and, as such, inherent in all developmental processes (Cabell & Valsiner, 2014; see also Lüscher, 2016). It might thus trigger developmental processes and can be useful in decisional processes. However, if the experience of ambivalence is lasting too long—and we would still have to define the threshold—it might become a nuisance, hampering our achievements as it binds cognitive resources that might prolong our decisional processes and influence aspects of subjective well-being such as self-esteem (Steinhoff & Buchmann, Chapter 7, this volume).

On the cognitive level as well as regarding accompanying emotions, inter- and intraindividual differences may exist about how ambivalence is actually experienced. For some individuals, the experience of ambivalence might be rather unpleasant, whereas for others it might be more motivating or again something in between.[2] To illustrate this more closely, we might look at the phenomenon of *saudade*, a bittersweet feeling of suffering that is also pleasant and even searched for and can motivate further action (see Barros and Ribeiro, Chapter 11, this volume).

In summary, in contrast to earlier research and lay conceptions, we might not be able to say from the start whether ambivalences should be seen as positive or negative. Rather, most importantly, we should look at how ambivalences are dealt with because this might make the difference with regard to the impact on subjective well-being (see Jensen, Chapter 12, this volume).

DEALING WITH AMBIVALENCE IN FAMILY RELATIONS

With regard to family relations, different dynamics are possible depending on situational factors and opportunity structures as well as the stage in the family life cycle (see also Albert & Ferring, Chapter 6, this volume). Although some families with close and frequent contact might have recurrent opportunities for experiencing ambivalence, others might experience it especially in situations where they come together (exceptionally). In a dynamic perspective, when dealing with ambivalence, families might move from a rather ambivalent pattern to a more amicable or harmonious one, they might end up in conflict, or they might become more distant by reducing contact as a reaction to ambivalence. How ambivalent relations might be turned into other forms can be nicely illustrated following the earlier conceptualization of Abbey (2012) (see also Ferring et al., 2009). In this sense, ambivalence might serve as the previously mentioned catalyzer that helps the relationship to develop and, at best, mature. Lüscher and Hoff (2013) proposed a fourfold model to describe several strategies regarding the handling of ambivalences within family relations, namely, "solidarity" (i.e., underlining cohesion in the family by stressing commonalities in the relation and intergenerational support), "emancipation" (i.e., acknowledging ambivalences openly and negotiating the relationship while preserving relatedness), "captivation" (i.e., being captured in ambivalent relations without resolving them), or "atomization" (i.e., developing into tense and conflict-laden relations or even separation). Interestingly, one can also think of a temporary leaving of the relationship in which ambivalences are occurring, without actually dealing with them and separating completely from each other, namely, by leaving the situation in the sense of going out of the field (see also Lewin, 1935). Take, for example, an emerging adult who leaves the parental home—and a maybe highly ambivalent parent-child relation—to temporarily study in another city. This "break" in the relationship might be beneficial for the moment, but ambivalences might reoccur at the next meeting, say, during the Christmas holidays. In the same vein, when (young) adult children move, for whatever reason, back to the parental home after some time of (relative) independence, this seems to be fertile ground for the experience of ambivalence—even more so if coupled with the economic difficulties and problems young adults face when entering the job market, as recently described in particular for Southern European countries due to the economic crisis (see Coimbra, Ribeiro, & Fontaine, 2013).

In these cases, leaving the ambivalent parent-child relation temporarily might signify a "break" in the individuation process in which autonomy and relatedness are negotiated. If potential sources for ambivalence have not yet been tackled, then a reappearance and restart of the individuation process might reoccur when the relation is becoming closer again after a longer break, when these issues were simply not salient. This might partly explain why transitions that entail changes in intergenerational relations (e.g., when parents become old and frail, needing care) (see also Boll, Chapter 8, this volume) have often been described as particularly prone to ambivalence. In fact, taking into consideration the just outlined "break" in intergenerational relationship regulation, it seems that when relations become closer again after a longer period of independence, unresolved issues might come to the fore again, giving rise to the experience of ambivalence. This might then be a catalyzer that triggers further developmental processes, which can thus turn out to be positive for the relationship regulation; in other cases, it might be rather negative (see also Van Gaalen et al., 2010, who distinguish between positive and negative ambivalence).

MEASUREMENT

As already said, a differentiation should be made between the potential of ambivalence (i.e., structural conditions that may raise the possibility for the occurrence of ambivalences) and the actual experience of ambivalence. In a quantitative design, a closely related question is then whether direct or indirect measures should be used, the former asking explicitly for contradictory feelings or cognitions, the latter being based on the post-hoc combination (mostly done by researchers) of positive and negative ratings on different scales evaluating the same object. Further, in social psychological research, reaction times have been used as implicit measures for ambivalence (e.g., Mikulincer, Shaver, Bar-On, & Ein-Dor, 2010), and one could certainly think of further indicators such as different physiological markers, arousal state, and so on. Apart from these quantitative approaches, qualitative approaches might be helpful to get a deeper insight into context-specific aspects or developmental aspects, for instance, inferring ambivalences from narrations (Albert & Steinhoff, 2016). Rather than a mere variable, ambivalence might then serve as a "sensitizing concept" or heuristic guiding the analysis (see Lüscher, 2016).

Linked to these measurement issues is also the question of whether one actually needs to be aware of ambivalence occurring or whether it can be indirectly inferred (see also Lubiewska, Chapter 14, this volume). Finally, we could also ask when the ability to experience ambivalence starts (i.e., from which developmental age can ambivalence be experienced). More precisely, do we need the capacity for hypothetical thinking, perspective taking, and imagination? Not least, the individual life course phase in the family life cycle and cultural aspects need to be considered (Valsiner, 2007).

THE PRESENT VOLUME

The present volume has developed out of a workshop, Ambivalence in Intergenerational Family Relationships: New Perspectives on Methodology,[3] held in Remich, Luxembourg, in June 2014. The workshop brought together researchers on ambivalence from different disciplines and led to fruitful and vivid discussions around the topic. The present volume picks up this discussion and sheds further light on the concept and phenomena of ambivalence from different disciplinary perspectives, also taking into account qualitative and quantitative approaches alike. Focusing on ambivalences in intergenerational family relations, it combines rather theoretically oriented articles regarding conceptual issues, empirical studies (both quantitative and qualitative) that deal with ambivalences in different phases of the life course and transgenerationally, as well as specific phenomena and measurement questions.

Starting with conceptual issues, the first two chapters trace the roots of the concept of ambivalence back to early works aiming to answer how we can approach the concept of ambivalence and how we can define it.

In Chapter 1, "Tensegrity as Existential Condition: The Inherent Ambivalence of Development," authored by Luca Tateo, the concept of ambivalence is illuminated, starting with historical as well as current conceptions about ambivalence, thereby focusing mostly on works from psychology. Tateo states that ambivalence and uncertainty are basically inherent in all developmental processes. To capture this fact, he introduces the concept of tensegrity, substituting the more common homeostatic models of development. More precisely, he proposes to "reverse the picture and... assume that ambivalence is an existential condition of tension generated by the inherently ambiguous nature of experiencing." He also underlines that ambivalence might be regarded in terms of catalytic processes rather than causalities. In this view, if tension is a constitutive element of a system, then it might be more important to determine how to deal with ambivalences rather than trying to resolve them; in line with this, one might also ask how much ambivalence a system allows for.

In Chapter 2, "The Research Act: Creating Knowledge From the Not (Yet) Known," Eugenia Gouvedari shares the view of ambivalence as central in developmental processes and human agency. After summarizing the debate among scholars who advocate the ambivalence view or the solidarity-conflict model, she focuses from a meta-perspective on the process of research development as entailing ambivalence due to the "conscious striving to reach the not yet there." As she states, "researching ambivalences is indeed an ambivalent process itself." She also underlines that ambivalence is multifaceted. Hence, she prefers ambivalences in the plural form, which can take into account occurrences of ambivalence at different levels of experience and meaning making based on different theoretical and methodological approaches.

In the next part of this book, we take a lifespan and transgenerational perspective. Thus, in Chapter 3, "Multilevel Approach to Ambivalence in the Family Sphere: Changing Structures, Roles, and Relationships" by Kairi Kasearu, Kadri Raid, and Dagmar Kutsar, the view is shifted from a more general perspective on ambivalence to a specific context, namely, the family in which ambivalence might occur. The authors start again with a historical view on family, delineating how norms have determined the individual behavior in the past and how development turned toward more individualization coupled with increasing freedom and shrinking societal guidance. Starting with the concept of ambivalence as used in sociology in the early works, namely, as mostly referring to contradictory roles, the authors state that sociological and psychological ambivalence should be considered in a combined way, referring also to contradictions between social structures and the individual. With the example of changing family patterns, they outline that in contexts where norms become less clear, there is more room for ambivalence along with multiple possibilities. Thus, structural ambivalences at the macrolevel have an impact at the individual level due to interactions between structural opportunities and cultural values, personal needs, and preferences.

In Chapter 4, "Ambivalence in the Family Transmission of Values: Assuming Similarity and Recognizing Differences," Daniela Barni and Silvia Donato focus on the interesting question of how innovation and distinctiveness might be reconciled with connectedness among family members of different generations in the process of intergenerational value transmission. In general, the degree to which parents and their children give similar importance to certain values seems to be an important outcome for the value transmission process. However, the perception of such similarity may actually be rather biased or accurate, and the chapter focuses on this topic. Drawing on ideas from interpersonal perception research, the authors aim to introduce bias and accuracy as sources of ambivalence from the parents' perspective. Thereby, they advocate that, in line with the ambivalence framework, bias and accuracy might not be regarded in a dualistic but rather in a dialectical manner. In such a view, bias and accuracy give each other their meaning, and their coexistence enables negotiation between social partners and change in social relations.

After this more general look at intergenerational family relations, the next three chapters focus more explicitly on a specific time in the family life cycle, namely, adolescence and young adulthood. Claiming that adolescence and young adulthood are particularly prone for the experience of intergenerational ambivalences, we focus here on ambivalences occurring in relations between adolescents/young adults and significant others, drawing on empirical data from qualitative interviews as well as cross-sectional and longitudinal quantitative studies.

In Chapter 5, "Anticipatory Recognition: Creating a Cycle of Flexible Meanings in Intergenerational Relations," Elsa de Mattos concentrates on self-other relations and the dialogical self during adolescents' transition to adulthood. She suggests that the process of exploration during this transitional phase might entail breaks in adolescents' sense of continuity of the self, which trigger internal semiotic regulatory processes, such as a reorganization and (re)construction of identity. According to the author, ambivalences occurring within the self might be negotiated in the interaction with significant others. Drawing on the principle of linking lives, the author develops a semiotic-dialogical perspective of youth transitions, in which she describes how individuals are embedded in social relationships over the lifespan and how intergenerational relations support young people's life transitions. She introduces the concept of "anticipatory recognition" as part of intergenerational relations between young people and significant others that might promote a process of internal regulation and foster the emergence of flexible signs in the self-system of young people, thereby enhancing creative meaning-making and the integration of life experiences over time. She illustrates the reconfiguration of the self-system during transitions with the case example of a young woman who negotiates significant meanings of herself and her world over a developmental period of seven years.

In Chapter 6, "Ambivalence Toward Parents During the Process of Individuation: Being Caught between Autonomy and Relatedness?" Isabelle Albert and Dieter Ferring look at specific characteristics of the parent-child relation that might correlate with the experience of ambivalence from the perspective of late adolescents and emerging adults. Starting from the perspective of individuation theory, they focus on the roles of parental acceptance and control during the negotiation of autonomy and relatedness between youth and their parents. In their cross-sectional data, they find evidence for a link between parenting dimensions and ambivalences, which also differs depending on the phase in the developmental process, pointing to the importance of continued parental support but also parents' adaptation to autonomy needs of their children in the process of individuation.

In Chapter 7, "Dynamic Relations Between Perceived Parental Responsiveness, Experiences of Ambivalence, and Self-Esteem Development in Adolescence," Annekatrin Steinhoff and Marlis Buchmann make use of a longitudinal quantitative dataset to examine the antecedents of ambivalence in the parent-child relations as well as a supposed outcome, thereby focusing on self-esteem development. More precisely, they take ambivalence as an outcome of parenting characteristics and an antecedent of self-esteem development. Acknowledging the empirically shown link between ambivalence and self-esteem in cross-sectional studies, the authors suggest that theoretically outcomes of ambivalences might depend on the ways in which ambivalences are dealt with. Therefore, their aim is to study different trajectories of ambivalences in adolescence and their outcomes in a longitudinal perspective. As far as developmental trajectories are concerned, their findings confirm the hypothesis that ambivalences are rather prevalent in mid-adolescence but then decline. They also advocate the function of ambivalences as catalyzer and find evidence that ambivalences might, but do not necessarily have to, have a negative impact on self-esteem depending on whether adolescents remain in a permanent state of confusion.

In Chapter 8, "Emotional Ambivalence in Adult Children of Care-Dependent Older Parents: Heuristic Impulses From Cognitive-Motivational Emotion Theories" authored by Thomas Boll, we move further into the family life cycle. The author provides a fine-grained analysis of the emergence of ambivalent emotions of adult children toward the care situation for their older parents in a cognitive-motivational approach. Starting from a definition of emotional ambivalence as copresence of positive and negative emotions toward a multifaceted care situation, he takes a closer look at the problems an adult child might encounter in such situation and how this might influence the subjective appraisals with regard to the care situation, entailing comparisons of desires and beliefs. Desires that are fulfilled are supposed to lead to positive emotions, whereas desires that are seen as frustrated by an individual should lead to negative emotions; however, desires might also be perceived as fulfilled in some respects but not in others, or there might be conflicting desires, all of which can entail ambivalent emotions. After a more general outline of these mechanisms, the practical relevance is demonstrated by a closer look at a specific care transition, namely, the parent's moving into a nursing home. Ambivalence might also be inherent in specific phenomena, and these phenomena are the focus of Part III of the book.

Maliina Lyberth takes a closer look at times of social change in Chapter 9, "Ambivalence When Family Values Change: Development of New Values in the Perspective of Sociocultural Global "Advancement." Her example of Greenland as a rapidly changing society over the last years demonstrates impressively how value change affects individuals differently at different stages in their lifespan, and how these intergenerational differences are negotiated within families. Her ideas revolve around a case study of a mother-daughter dyad living in Greenland and their experience of and dealing with intergenerational ambivalences linked to changed family values. On the background of social representations theory, she develops a theoretical view of how family values change from one generation to the next and how individuals make sense of these transitions, thereby trying to preserve their intergenerational relatedness.

Chapter 10 by Vívian Volkmer Pontes and Lívia Mathias Simão, "Transgenerational Ambivalence in the Time to Come: How Meanings Regulate Being Pregnant and Facing Miscarriage," is dedicated to the phenomenon of ambivalences regarding pregnancy and miscarriage. They refer to unwritten rules in families, such as the importance of the status of being a mother, which might entail intergenerational ambivalences with regard to the I-Other-World relationship in the transition to motherhood. To discuss their theoretical outline, they present a case study of a woman whose trajectory to motherhood is marked by successive spontaneous abortions. For this woman, being a mother seems to be part of the "normal" pace of life (i.e., constituting a normative event in her subjective life course theory), and not becoming a mother becomes a nonevent that also raises conflicts with the partner. Thereby, past experiences are crucial for the interpretation of present events and imaginations of the future, and hence the prime importance of imaginations, temporality, as well as hypothetical thinking for the experience of ambivalence.

Elements of ambivalence can also be found in culture-specific phenomena and concepts. This is what Stephanie Barros and Gaby Marinho Ribeiro focus on in Chapter 11, "Saudade: A Unique Feeling Within the Lusitanian Soul." After outlining the cultural and historical origins of this culture-specific phenomenon, they examine the different emotional components of *saudade* in an empirical study to find out which features are linked to the phenomenon in the point of view of Portuguese immigrants living in Luxembourg, also comparing views of different generations, namely, born in the country of origin or host country. Thereby, they are able to shed light on aspects of the intergenerational transmission of the meaning of *saudade* as well as on the change in meaning from one migrant generation to the next.

Ambivalences might also occur in social relations between older and younger generations outside the family, and these are highlighted in Chapter 12, "Desired Ambiguities and Dealing With Ambivalences in the Context of Social Work." Mogens Jensen goes beyond intergenerational family relations and looks at relations of nonrelated adults and adolescents, namely, in the setting of social work. Ambivalence might be inherent in such relations as the social worker—who represents the social system that forces the adolescent into this situation—has to establish a relation toward the adolescent, who often has a relational history of neglect and disturbed attachment. Jensen draws on the establishment of mutual trust relations and looks at ambivalences as a part of the meaning-making process, being important for agency. He distinguishes between the cognitive aspects of mere ambiguity, which he characterizes as neutral, on the one hand, and ambivalence as containing contradictory feelings and behavioral tendencies, on the other hand. Most important, the dealing with ambivalences seems to make the difference regarding positive or negative outcomes, and he outlines along two case studies how ambivalence can be used to establish a dialogue or initiate relationship dynamics in relations that are stuck in negative aspects.

In Chapter 13, "Your Duty Toward My Right: Ambivalent Traps of Rights and Duties," Kevin Carriere starts from the theoretical perspective of semiotic cultural psychology and elaborates the mechanism of a "semiotic trap" when focusing on the negotiation between rights and duties in intergenerational family relations and the inherent ambivalences in this process using multiple illustrative examples. He finally suggests the idea of a mechanism-based cultural psychology, including mediators and regulators that allow for a clearer understanding of psychological processes.

This brings us to Part IV of the book focusing on measurement issues. In Chapter 14, "Attachment Ambivalence: The Concept, Psychological Importance, and Measurement Issues," Katarzyna Lubiewska outlines how attachment theory might provide explanations to the questions of how and why some individuals are more prone than others to the experience of ambivalence in their close relations. Starting with a close description of attachment theory and how ambivalence is conceptualized within this framework, she makes a strong point for a differential view of ambivalence, also pointing to differential outcomes depending on how ambivalence is dealt with. The author then focuses on the important question of how ambivalence might be measured, outlining both explicit and implicit ways of measuring ambivalence and discussing direct and indirect measurements. Thereby, she also raises the question of how far researchers might actually trigger ambivalent feelings when asking study participants about it.

In summary, the present contributions might help to clarify and further develop the concept of ambivalence by shedding further light at different aspects illustrated by case examples as well as by focusing on specific phenomena which contain ambivalences. Apart from different situations and constellations, such as times of transition and social change as well as life course-specific phases that might be more or less prone to the experience of ambivalence, differential psychological considerations are also provided with regard to the emergence of and dealing with ambivalences.

The authors use different approaches—quantitative and qualitative studies—and their different theoretical perspectives enrich the present book by highlighting different aspects of the concept of ambivalence to contribute to its clarification.

ACKNOWLEDGMENTS

This book was prepared in the framework of the IRMA-project ("Intergenerational Relations in the light of Migration and Ageing) which was funded by a grant from the Fonds National de la Recherche Luxembourg (FNR,

2013-2016; PI: Dr. Isabelle Albert; Supervisor: Prof. Dr. Dieter Ferring; Mentor: Prof. Dr. Jaan Valsiner).

NOTES

1. We might note here, however, that ambivalent reactions have also been described in Pavlov's experiments when exposing dogs to stress.
2. Notably, already Bleuler (1910) agreed with C. G. Jung that the guiding force would not be the ambivalence but the affectivity.
3. This workshop was co-sponsored by The Leir Luxembourg Program-Clark University (LLP-CU); Integrative Research Unit on Social and Individual Development (INSIDE), Université du Luxembourg; and the Niels Bohr Centre of Cultural Psychology, Aalborg Universitet, Denmark.

REFERENCES

Abbey, E. (2004). Circumventing ambivalence in identity: The importance of latent and overt aspects of symbolic meaning. *Culture & Psychology, 10*(3), 331–336.

Abbey, E. (2012). Ambivalence and its transformations. In J. Valsiner (Ed.), *The Oxford handbook of culture and psychology* (pp. 989–997). New York, NY: Oxford University Press.

Abbey, E., & Valsiner, J. (2005). Emergence of meanings through ambivalence. *Forum: Qualitative Social Research, 6*(1). Available at: http://www.qualitative-research.net/index.php/fqs/article/view/515/1114

Albert, I., & Steinhoff, A. (2016). Intergenerationelle Ambivalenz in Eltern-Kind-Beziehungen im Jugend- und jungen Erwachsenenalter: Theoretische Reflexionen und Möglichkeiten der quantitativen Analyse [Intergenerational ambivalence in parent-child relationships during adolescence and young adulthood: Theoretical reflections and possibilities of quantitative analysis]. *Zeitschrift für Soziologie der Erziehung und Sozialisation* [*Journal for Sociology of Education and Socialization*], *36*(2), 178–194.

Baltes, P. B. (1987). Theoretical propositions of life span developmental psychology: On the dynamics between growth and decline. *Developmental Psychology, 23*, 611–626.

Bateson, G., Jackson, D. D., Haley, J., & Weakland, J. (1956). Toward a theory of schizophrenia. *Behavioral Science, 1*(4), 251–254.

Baxter, L. A., & Montgomery, B. M. (1996). *Relating: Dialogues and dialectics*. New York, NY: Guilford.

Bengtson, V. L., & Roberts, R. E. L. (1991). Intergenerational solidarity in aging families: An example of formal theory construction. *Journal of Marriage and Family, 53*, 856–870.

Bleuler, E. (1910). Vortrag von Prof. Bleuler über Ambivalenz. Aus Vereinen und Versammlungen. Ordentliche Winterversammlung des Vereins schweizerischer

Irrenärzte in Bern. 26–27 November 1910. *Zentralblatt für Psychoanalyse (1911), 1*, 266–268.
Bleuler, E. (1914). Die Ambivalenz [Ambivalence]. In U. Zürich (Ed.), *Festgabe zur Einweihung der Neubauten* (pp. 94–106). Zürich, Switzerland: Schultheiss.
Cabell, K., & Valsiner, J. (2014). *The catalyzing mind: Beyond models of causality.* New York, NY: Springer.
Coimbra, S., Ribeiro, L., & Fontaine, A. (2013). Intergenerational solidarity in an ageing society: Socio-demographic determinants of intergenerational support to elderly parents. In I. Albert & D. Ferring (Eds.), *Intergenerational relations: European perspectives on family and society* (pp. 205–222). Bristol, England: Policy Press at the University of Bristol.
Connidis, I. A. (2015). Exploring ambivalence in family ties: Progress and prospects. *Journal of Marriage and Family, 77*(1), 77–95.
Ferring, D., Michels, T., Boll, T., & Filipp, S.-H. (2009). Emotional relationship quality of adult children with ageing parents: on solidarity, conflict and ambivalence. *European Journal of Ageing, 6*, 253–265.
Festinger, L. (1957). *A theory of cognitive dissonance.* Stanford, CA: Stanford University Press.
Freud, S. (1919). *Totem and taboo* (A. A. Brill, Trans.). London, England: Routledge. (Original work published 1913).
Hagestad, G. (2016). *Her and his? Exploring gender in intergenerational patterns.* Keynote at the 8th Congress of the European Society on Family Relations (ESFR), August 31–September 3, 2016, TU Dortmund University, Germany.
Kaplan, K. J. (1972). On the ambivalence-indifference problem in attitude theory and measurement: A suggested modification of the semantic differential technique. *Psychological Review, 77*, 361–372.
Koster, E. H. W, Fang, L., & Marchetti, I. (2015). Self-regulation through rumination: Consequences and mechanisms. In G. H. E. Gendolla, M. Tops, & S. L. Koole (Eds.), *Handbook of biobehavioral approaches to self-regulation* (pp. 371–383). New York, NY: Springer Science+Business Media.
Kuczynski, L., Marshall, S., & Schell, K. (1997). Value socialization in a bidirectional context. In J. E. Grusec & L. Kuczynski (Eds.), *Parenting and the internalization of values: A handbook of contemporary theory* (pp. 227–256). New York, NY: Wiley.
Lewin, K. (1935). *A dynamic theory of personality.* New York, NY: McGraw-Hill.
Lewin, K. (1936). *Principles of topological psychology.* New York, NY: McGraw-Hill.
Lüscher, K. (2016). Sozialisation und Ambivalenzen. Bausteine eines Vademecums [Socialisation and ambivalences]. *Zeitschrift für Soziologie der Erziehung und Sozialisation [Journal for Sociology of Education and Socialization], 36*(2), 118–136.
Lüscher, K., & Hoff, A. (2013). Intergenerational ambivalence: Beyond solidarity and conflict. In I. Albert & D. Ferring (Eds.), *Intergenerational relations: European perspectives on family and society* (pp. 39–64). Bristol, England: Policy Press at the University of Bristol.
Lüscher, K., & Pillemer, K. (1998). Intergenerational ambivalence: A new approach to the study of parent–child relations in later life. *Journal of Marriage and the Family, 60*, 413–425.
Lüscher, K., Hoff, A., Klimczuk, A., Lamura, G., Renzi, M., de Salles Oliveira, P., Sánchez, M., . . . Canatan, A. (2017). *Generations, intergenerational relationships,*

generational policy: A multilingual compendium [White paper]. Universität Konstanz. Retrieved from http://www.generationen-compendium.de/downloads/Kompendium_12sprachig_05-04-2017.pdf

McGregor, I. (2010). Ambivalence. *Cosini Encyclopedia of Psychology*, pp. 1–2.

Mikulincer, M., Shaver, P. R., Bar-On, N., & Ein-Dor, T. (2010). The pushes and pulls of close relationships: Attachment insecurities and relational ambivalence. *Journal of Personality and Social Psychology, 98*, 450–468.

Turner, V. W. (1964). Betwixt and between: The liminal period in rites de passage. In J. Helm (Ed.), *The Proceedings of the American Ethnological Society: Symposium on New Approaches to the Study of Religion* (pp. 4–20). Seattle, WA: American Ethnological Society.

Valsiner, J. (1997). *Constructing identity: A theoretical problem for social sciences.* Presentation at the Workshop "Identitätsdiskusionen in der Psychologie," in the framework of the Graduiertenkolleg "Identitätsforschung" of Martin-Luther-Universität Halle-Wittenberg, April 18, 1997.

Valsiner, J. (2007). *Culture in minds and societies: Foundations of cultural psychology.* Thousand Oaks, CA: SAGE.

Van Gaalen, R., Dykstra, P. A., & Komter, A. E. (2010). Where is the exit? Intergenerational ambivalence and relationship quality in high contact ties. *Journal of Aging Studies, 24*(2), 105–114.

PART I

CONCEPTUAL ISSUES: AMBIVALENCE AND ITS STUDY

CHAPTER 1

TENSEGRITY AS EXISTENTIAL CONDITION

The Inherent Ambivalence of Development

Luca Tateo
University of Aalborg

Childrearing tends to be imperfect because with each of its particular acts it must serve two opposed tendencies: freeing and binding.
—Simmel (1918/2010, p. 177)

"Will you pay with cash or credit card?" This is a simple and familiar question we are often asked by a shop clerk. Apparently, it is a simple choice that we make after briefly considering how much cash we have in our wallet, what our monthly purchase limit on the credit card is, maybe if one method is more suitable according to the shop's reputation, and so on. Yet once the choice is made, we cannot completely avoid that irritating feeling of having paid a stiff price for the good we have just purchased. Nevertheless, we should feel relief because we have reduced uncertainty and made a decision, fulfilling our need for closure. We exit the shop still reckoning on that uncomfortable feeling, until, after few steps, we suddenly realize that

Trans-Generational Family Relations, pages 3–20

the question "Will you pay with cash or credit card?" was actually an apparent choice. What was at stake was indeed the fact that we had no choice but paying the imposed price, and the clerk was not even questioning such an assumption. Now, with our good in the shopping bag, we experience that mixed feeling of happiness because we got what we desired and disappointment for the stiff price. Continuing our shopping, we think about the pros and cons of the purchase until we reach an agreement with ourselves, probably that the good was expensive but worth the price. Nevertheless, every time we wear that article of clothing (let's imagine we bought an Italian model dress), we think about the purchase, and the cycle resumes.

A simple situation like the one just described implies different levels of experience. The more superficial one is that of a micro decision-making process, in which a person is required to answer a question by comparing alternative courses of action. At a closer look, one finds that such a micro decision is framed in a more complex process. I deliberately skipped the history preceding the payment situation. Probably, a former moment occurred in which we realized that we needed a new dress or we were just walking in a shopping center and our gaze focused on something in the shop window. We formed the decision to enter the shop and try on the dress. At every single step, we could have being considering whether we really needed that dress or it was just an impulsive decision, you name it. What I want to stress here is the lack of clarity in the experience and the fact that such clarity is persisting after the event. Rather than a plain process of decision formation, the shopping example looks more like a dilemmatic situation. By dilemmatic, I mean a condition that cannot be described in terms of a decision tree, but rather in terms of a field of different overlapping potential courses of action (or nonaction) that immediately evoke their counterpart. Besides, this field is multidimensional, including the affective dimension (feeling glad, disappointed, satisfied, etc.), the ethical dimension (was worth buying, was a waste of money, was the price honest, etc.), and the cognitive dimension (how the question about payment framed the elaboration of the choice, the meta-cognitive process of reevaluating after leaving the shop). All these additional dimensions evoke their counterparts, too. Another difference between a tree- and dilemma-like situation is that although in the former the correct course of action can be established a posteriori with respect to some gains and losses, in the latter there is no correct choice in absolute terms because the alternative course of action maintains some degree of presence even after a long time. Clarity, definition of mutual excluding alternatives, binary logic, causality, directionality, and closure are all features of a tree-like process. A dilemmatic situation is instead characterized by fuzziness; contemporary presence of cognitive, affective, and ethical dimensions; mutually defining alternative courses of action; and persistence over time.

Let's consider another example of dilemmatic situation in everyday life. Many people decided to enroll in a university program. One can remember how it was a cognitive task also involving affective and ethical issues, fears, desires, expectations, pressures, and requirements. Even if one felt made for medicine, it was not easy to contemplate and compare alternative courses. The fact of inclining toward one choice called into existence the opposite choices. Becoming a doctor means not becoming a lawyer, an engineer, and so on. The family background, the peers, and the partner all played a role in interpreting the situation and making sense of the different options. Significant others were involved as a source of comparison, suggestions, and guidance. In some specific moment, one experiences the dilemma of the field elements calling each other ("I can do [or be] it but won't do [or be] it"; "I cannot do [or be] it but will do [or be] it"; "I cannot do and won't do it"; "I can do it and will do it"; "I cannot do it now but..."; "I could do it now but..."; "I could do like (someone else) but..."; "I cannot do like (someone else) but..."; etc.). As the beginning of the academic year approaches, one has to make up one's mind and decide to enroll in the medical program. Even if it seems that once the choice is made, the dilemma is dissolved: the nonactualized alternatives no longer exist, and another aspect emerges. As a medical student, one is no longer (not yet) something else and one is no longer (not yet) like someone else. For the rest of the person's life, he or she will experience, at different degrees, the presence of the absent choice, not necessarily in terms of regret but rather in terms of codefinition of alternatives. In the field-like dilemmatic situations, the value is not attached to the choice alone, in terms of gains and losses, but rather is defined by the system of relationships between the elements of the field. What one becomes acquires value in relationship to what one has not become, could have become, or would have become, or what other people became.

Up until now, I have intentionally avoided the term *ambivalence*, although the examples I provided could easily recall it. This is why the term is somehow charged with a halo of negativity and irrationality, to the extent that the normative model of human in psychology is still valuing rationality as the term of comparison for the other dimensions (Smelser, 1998). The concept of rationality combined with the idea of agency (Swindell, 2010) establishes a hierarchy of psychological processes that structures a sharp distinction between opposite fields. On the one hand, there is the idea that humans strive for equilibrium, clarity, consistency, reduction of uncertainty, fulfillment, and moral good, which can be attained through rationality and reflectivity. On the other hand, the opposite field is populated by emotions, irrationality, vagueness, dissonance, ambivalence, you name it. This leads to an idea of rationality in itself, detached from the real person (the so-called epistemic agent in philosophy). When this abstract model, which has an epistemic function to understand the psychological and social processes, is imposed on the single individual or group, it tends to naturalize, generating the idea of a biased and limited human nature that is always directed to a perfection that will never be able to attend. As Georg Simmel (1918/2010) wisely summarized in one of his aphorisms, "One can elevate the man to the idea, but one cannot lower the idea to the man" (p. 171). It seems like psychology tends to forget that an abstract model of agent is nothing but an epistemological tool to describe a process, and a different theoretical model can describe it in a different way. When a theoretical model becomes a normative model, advancement of knowledge is inhibited.

An alternative model for understanding the human psychological condition should consider dilemmatic situations and ambivalence as the characteristic feature of human condition, rather than the pathology, without diminishing humans as irrational organisms. Instead, the opposition between rationality and irrationality must be overcome to understand how complex and multifaceted any psychological experience is.

> It is communicated in various dichotomies freedom versus constraint, independence versus dependence, autonomy versus dependence, maturity versus infancy, and more but whatever the dichotomy, the dilemma appears to be insoluble. Neither pole is a separate state or condition. Neither freedom nor dependence can be realized in a full or exclusive form, because one is part of the other. Human beings long and strive for both, but, when they achieve a measure of either, the other reasserts itself. As in the nature of ambivalence itself, we want both sides at once, but cannot fully satisfy either side. (Smelser, 1998, p. 15)

Experiencing, as the object of psychological science, is indeed a complex configuration of cognitive, affective, and ethic dimensions. The person experiences the "world" by affectively knowing and anticipating, loving and hating before deceiving, ambiguously doing and ethically accounting, actively looking for experiencing even before it happens. Pure and unambiguous cognitive or emotional acts are theoretically superimposed models (Tateo, 2015a). Besides, experiencing is characterized by uniqueness and similarity, the never accomplished eternal (re)formation of the self that is contextualized in the collective and cultural dimension of life-forms (Simmel, 1918/2010):

> the uniqueness of my inner experience and my agentive capability of making distinction between what happens, or used to happen, to me and what relates to others. When I produce a discourse about my feeling guilty or anguished, I can say that I feel "like" Rodion Raskolnikov in Dostoyevsky's novel "Crime and punishment". I can also say that I feel "like" my friend felt once. But at the same time, I am conscious that my feeling is a unique event that is not per-

> fectly framed in a pre-formed fashion or captured by the same signs already used by myself or by others in the past. "Humans consist of present, future, and past; sign, interpretant, and act; I, you, and me; and all the overlap, and connectedness, and solidarity among these elements" (Wiley, 1994, p. 216). (Tateo & Marsico, 2013, p. 5)

Experiencing is thus never attained because it is a developing self-feeding process. An alternative theoretical model able to look at experiencing without neglecting the complex, variform, and developmental aspects requires replacing concepts such as equilibrium and consistency with more dynamic ones. In the following sections, I first outline some of the historical and current conceptions about ambivalence in psychology, and then I try to draw a perspective based on the dilemmatic nature of experience and the idea of *tensegrity* as a more productive way to describe the self, replacing the homeostatic models.

AMBIVALENCE IN PSYCHOLOGY

The introduction of the term *ambivalence* in psychiatry is usually ascribed to Eugen Bleuler in his study on schizophrenia (Bleuler, 1911/1950). He described ambivalence as one of the four main symptoms of schizophrenia, as the "tendency to endow the most diverse psychisms with both a positive and negative indicator at the same time" (Bleuler, 1911/1950, p. 53). In Bleuler's theory, we relate to the objects that have inherently dual aspects, such as the rose and the thorn: "pleasant and unpleasant feelings simultaneously accompany the same experience" (Graubert & Miller, 1957, p. 458). Usually people are able to construct a set of associations in thoughts to evaluate the good and the bad and react quickly to the object in the most appropriate way. Due to a loosening in their capacity to form emotionally loaded associations, schizophrenics become unable to resolve the relationship with the object. Bleuler also noted that attaching opposite emotions to the object is a feature of normal people, who are nevertheless able to cope with them when the situation requires it. He also distinguished three dimensions of ambivalence: affective ambivalence, ambivalence of the will, and intellectual ambivalence. In the former, opposing feeling can be related to the same object, such as hating and loving the partner at the same time. Ambivalence of the will implies the desires of both doing and not doing a certain thing at the same time. Later, Otto Rank's theory will develop this idea by assuming that those two polarities are always in a relationship of complementarity (Menaker, 1998). Finally, intellectual ambivalence was considered a disorder of thought in which one idea is accompanied by its opposite. Bleuler's theory of ambivalence was extremely interesting because it took into account both normal and pathological relationships to objects, stressing the dualistic nature of human relationship with the object of thought and because he understood "ambivalence by co-existence at different levels of consciousness" (Graubert & Miller, 1957, p. 458). Thus, the issue was not ambivalence as a condition of experience but rather the way people are able to cope with it in the construction of self. The complexity of Bleuler's idea was developed in selective ways by the later psychologists who mainly reduced the several dimensions of ambivalence, preferring from time to time one of the dimensions.

For instance, Sigmund Freud (1938) developed a theory of ambivalence that will become a point of reference for all the following debates on the topic. He considers ambivalence at the level of affects and ideas. His theory of drives implies that the components share the same energy and are developed in pairs, with one polarity displaced into the unconscious without being completely resolved. This distribution is crystallized and subject to the culturally developed collective mechanism of elaboration. Nevertheless, it is always possible that in the development of the drive, its antagonist reappears from the repressed and persists, leading to ambivalence. At the drive content level, instead, the same object (e.g., the loved person) can be invested of coexisting drives, as in the case of love and hate (Graubert & Miller, 1957). A complete discussion of the role of ambivalence in Freud's theory falls outside the scope of this chapter and would require an adequate space for the relevance it assumed in psychoanalysis and psychotherapy. Nevertheless, what I want to stress here is that Freud's idea of ambivalence is applied to a more restricted and specific field than Bleuler's. Besides, in Freud's conception, ambivalence is an attribute of the drives' system, where opposite tendencies always coexist. The psychic work is that of finding an equilibrium between the two manifestations of energy, by operating a cultural led choice between the two. The eternal return of the repressed is the fate of the human being, whose existential condition is that of struggling with a constellation of opposing drives. Whether such a condition can result in creative or disruptive outcomes, it is a matter of the complex interaction between the individual self-development and the cultural system of regulation, such as in the case of ambivalence in motherhood, which is "rendered unmanageable by the snowballing interaction of cultural representations of good and bad mother with the particular emotional meanings motherhood maintained" (Parker, 1997, p. 21).

The role of the significant Other in the concept of ambivalence has been extensively developed in attachment theory (Ainsworth, Blehar, Waters, & Wall, 1978; see also Lubiewska, chapter 14, this volume). Also in this case, the concept of ambivalence is framed into a homeostatic model, in which opposite drives—exploration and security—are experienced by the child–mother pair, assuming that balance is the desirable outcome. In fact, anxious-ambivalent attachment style is understood as a problematic type of relationship. As we will see in the follow paragraphs, such a homeostatic view of psychological processes will always imply that ambivalence is understood as a perturbation regardless of whether it is located at the level of individual system of drives, as in the case of Freud and Ainsworth, at the level of logical inconsistency, or at the level of communication and intersubjectivity. In his phenomenological study on ambivalence, Harrist (2006) stresses how the rationalist assumptions in psychology have reinforced, also in common sense, the idea that experiencing ambivalence is bad. In his view, ambivalence is a condition of life in which "multiple feelings lead to experiences of ambivalence moving from background, to disorientation, exploration, resolution and back again" (Harrist, 2006, p. 110).

Instead, the ambivalence at the level of the will and the intellectual ambivalence have been the focus of cognitive philosophy and psychology. For instance, Swindell (2010) discusses ambivalence at two levels. It can be difficult to form a position in identifying the individual will (e.g., establishing a hierarchy or priority between diverging desires) or the moral stance toward a desire (e.g., deciding whether a desire is legitimate or outlaw). Ambivalence can also occur at the level of forming a will, that is, taking a decision of action after having identified the right order of her desires. At each level, different desires are invested with an affective charge. Ambivalence can present itself at different degrees, which goes from a difficulty or slowing down in forming the decision or enacting it to the paralyzing ambivalence of being completely unable to form a hierarchy of preferences.

Cognitive psychology has often conceptualized ambivalence in relationship to attitudes. In this context, ambivalence is defined in terms of (a) objective ambivalence that "represents the actual presence of conflicting evaluative reactions within a given person (i.e., having both positive and negative reactions towards the same object)" (DeMarree, Wheeler, Briñol, & Petty, 2014, p. 6); and (b) subjective ambivalence, that is, "the experience of evaluative conflict, including a sense of being conflicted, confused, torn, and mixed with regard to the attitude object" (DeMarree et al., 2014, p. 6). The issue of ambivalence soon emerged when research on attitudes showed that two-dimensional models of attitude scales were unable to grasp the phenomenon. Attitude toward an object could not be simply measured in terms of positive–negative polarities (see also Lubiewska, chapter 14, this volume). Thus, Kaplan (1972) then proposed to split the traditional attitude scales into two different subscales, each measuring the positive and negative polarities of each object. At this point, it was clear that the problem was not that of dealing with a bipolar coexistence of reactions toward an object, but rather a system of different levels of organization with respect to the expected reaction. Thus, ambivalence implied a cognitive level with mixed reactions, an affective level of conflicting feelings, and a behavioral level of decision making (DeMarree et al., 2014). Because the dominant epistemological model in cognitive psychology was the homeostatic principle of consistency and balance, the affective and behavioral levels have been reduced to the cognitive level, attributing the disquieting and contrasting feeling and the difficulty in action to the need for a correct and consistent appraisal of the situation (Albarracin, Zanna, & Blair, 2005). People experience ambivalence because of the difficulty in creating a consistent account of the object and their own relationship to it or reducing the dissonance or incongruence between the perceived and expected situations. Thus, individual differences in the capability of coping with uncertainty and incongruence lead to the different behavioral outcomes.

A step forward in the direction of the inherently ambivalent nature of experience is that of Bateson's double-bind theory (Bateson, 1972; Bateson, Jackson, Haley, & Weakland, 1956). The double bind is not related to ambivalence as a concept but rather to a specific interpersonal situation in which the individual is unable to resolve a communication conflict based on the confusion among different logic levels (Bateson et al., 1956). Although pathogenic, the double-bind concept is related to the impossibility of escaping from a situation that is ambivalent in itself (Bateson, 1972). It is ambivalent at the level of the message (opposite injunctions of a different order and polarity), of the power relationship (one participant must have some power of constriction over the other as well as an affective relation), at the level of logic inconsistency (the injunctions lead to incompatible outcomes), at the affective level (feelings of attraction and repulsion), and at the level of meaning (it is impossible to make sense of the situation and elaborate a solution). Interestingly, in the familiar context, the double bind situation can be functional "to the family homeostasis" (Bateson et al., 1956, p. 252). In contrast with the ideas on ambivalence discussed so far, for Bateson, ambivalence is an attribute of the whole situation rather than an incapability of the individual to resolve inner conflicts between opposite feelings. Thus, the only way to make sense of it and escape the meaning trap is to make explicit the ambiguity of the situation.

Several definitions of ambivalence emerged so far in this limited overview of the literature. Because Bleuler's first formulation is a "tendency to endow the most diverse psychisms with both a positive and negative indicator at the same time" (Bleuler, 1911/1950, p. 53), it has been defined as the conflict between two currents localized in the subject's mind in such a manner that they cannot come up against each other (Freud, 1938). Cognitive psychology defines it as either "mixed evaluative reactions whether they stem from explicit or implicit discrepancies" (DeMarree et al., 2014, p. 5), "a function of the amount of conflict within an attitude, whereas evaluative-cognitive consistency is a function of the magnitude of the difference between evaluations" (Albarracin et al., 2005, p. 332), or, finally, "a structure of the will in which there is either a difficulty in forming second order positions (identifying or outlawing) or a difficulty ordering second order desires (willing), that necessarily typically causes the agent to feel torn" (Swindell, 2010, p. 32). Personally, I think these definitions share a common understanding of ambivalence as a feature of the subject's limited psychological nature. Ambivalence is thus an attribute of the subject because of the peculiar structure of his perceptual, cognitive, affective, and instinctive characteristics. Thus, the task of development becomes a process of learning to cope with these limitations to reduce ambivalence to a reasonable degree. The underlying conception is that of the homeostatic nature of psychological processes that tend to equilibrium unless an external stimulus coming from the world is not altering it, requiring counteraction. Instead, what if we try to reverse the picture and assume that ambivalence is an existential condition of tension generated by the inherently ambiguous nature of experiencing?

An example of this condition is represented in Simmel's aphorism opening the chapter. The childrearing activity is not just an interpersonal relationship constructed between a developing person and her caregivers; rather, it is inscribed in a system of value-oriented practices that contain contradictory elements as an integral part of the process. In every form of social organization (e.g., family, school, group of peers, political parties) in which the individual develops, he or she can find such complex dilemmatic fields of contrasting values that generate tension and ambivalence. In formal education, for instance, one can easily find ambivalent messages such as "become independent" and "obey your teacher." These are not pathological forms of miscommunication, as in the double bind case; rather, they are ordinary examples of how ambivalence constitutes experiencing. In the next section, I will try to argue that this new picture can foster new ideas for psychology.

FROM A CAUSAL TO CATALYTIC VIEW OF FUTURE-ORIENTED PSYCHOLOGICAL PROCESSES: TENSEGRITY

The homeostatic model considers the self as a system in equilibrium unless external forces do not alter it, requiring a reestablishment of equilibrium at a higher level of systemic organization (Tateo, 2014; Tateo & Marsico, 2013). Nevertheless, the ambivalence-related phenomena show that conceptualizing the interaction with the world in terms of temporary perturbation of the system equilibrium cannot fully account for the inclusion of ambivalence in the self that persists for a long time. Besides, one cannot consider the individual in isolation because ambivalence in organizations (e.g., family and school) makes them behave like a near-equilibrium open system, in which the system organization and functioning define at the same time the range of acceptable structural indeterminacy and the boundaries of the system with respect to the environment (Sawada & Caley, 1985). The double bind example helps to see how the problem of ambivalence is related to the fact that the feature of interpersonal and social situations follows a cogenetic logic (Herbst, 1976). That is, the situation of ambivalence can be rephrased in terms of a systemic organization in which the alternatives and their opposites are called to existence at the same time. In the relationship with the Other, the rules and the violation of the rules are both evoked at the same time. Thus, the system creates within a single circumstance the condition for functioning and the acceptable range of uncertainty and ambiguity that the system can tolerate without being affected. For instance:

> Certain sorts of deviant behavior are highly valuable, others are not. The former is usually called creative and is supported (in normal times) as long as it remains within bounds; the latter is called destructive. If we assume that the highest educational priority is placed on creativity, then special environments within which to pursue creativity must be constructed (recognized as open systems); otherwise the stabilizing forces of "normal" schooling will "normalize" (destroy) emerging creativity. (Sawada & Caley, 1985, p. 17)

At the same time, the double bind is an example of the normal functioning of a systemic relationship and the potential pathology that emerges when the range of acceptable indeterminacy is lowered to zero. In a "normal" condition, ambivalence is part of the system because it is based on the codetermination of the positive meaning and the evoked countermeaning. In abstract terms, it makes no difference whether the ambivalence is generated by the environment, the other or the person's drives. As in the example of the university choice illustrated in the introduction, every alternative immediately evokes the opposite alternatives in the dilemmatic field. Thus, tension in the field is the inherent condition of the experience rather than its pathological manifestation. The double bind situation paradoxically defines the extreme situation in which the conditions of respecting and violating the primary and secondary injunctions through setting to zero the possibility of deviating with the tertiary injunction (Bateson et al., 1956).

In equilibrium-based models, tension can be conceptualized in terms of a force exerted on the system by a pressure to adaptation (Tateo & Marsico, 2013). In the psychological theories that adopt this assumption, only two possible answers of the system to (re)establish a higher order equilibrium are available: adaptation or rupture. Both answers lead to a change in the system, which can be understood in terms of continuity or discontinuity of the system identity (Tateo & Marsico, 2013).

Nevertheless, people show a wide range of ways to cope with tension. Resilience resources and tolerance to uncertainty and ambiguity, as well as maintenance of ambivalence over time, are not just a matter of individual

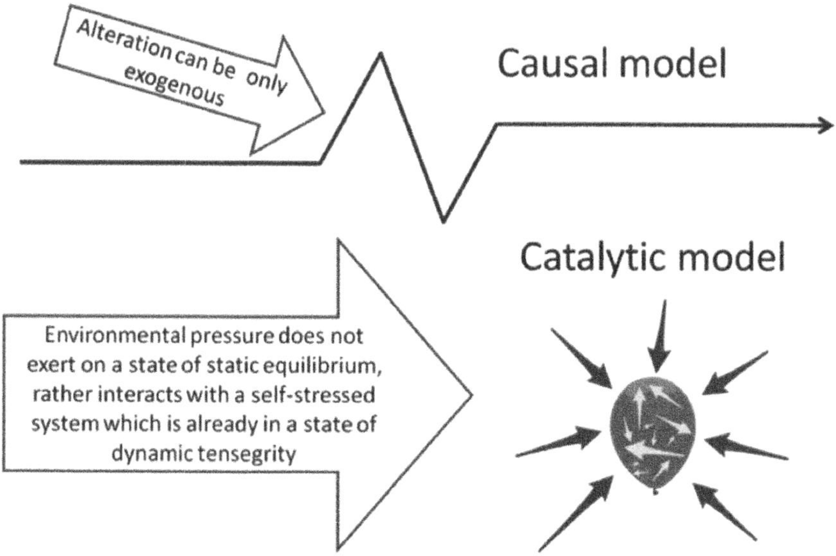

Figure 1.1 Catalytic versus Causal model.

differences in bearing ambivalence, as the cognitivist approach postulates, but can also vary according to the changing conditions. Tateo and Marsico (2013) argued that these arguments lead to a different theoretical view of experiencing and of the Self. If we assume that ambivalence and uncertainty are an existential condition of the self, then we can understand experiencing as a catalytic process rather than causal (Figure 1.1).

The idea of tension as a constitutive element of a system has been initially elaborated in the design of innovative architectural structures (Fuller, 1961). This principle was named tensegrity, a contraction for "tensional integrity." The idea is that tension is not a pathology of a system but rather one of its constitutive elements of identity, stability, and integrity.

> Our bodies provide a familiar example of a prestressed tensegrity structure: our bones act like struts to resist the pull of tensile muscles, tendons and ligaments, and the shape stability (stiffness) of our bodies varies depending on the tone (prestress) in our muscles. (Ingber, 2003, p. 1158)

Every system, natural or artificial, is made of subparts that are in a hierarchical relationship of continuous tension and discontinuous compression, which is called "self-stress" or "prestress." In this sense, we can reconceptualize the Freudian idea of opposing drives in terms of systemic tensegrity rather than dramatic struggle. "As the term 'tensegrity system' implies, the interplay between the tension and compression elements may be interpreted as a whole as systemic behavior unpredictable from the behavior of the parts considered individually" (IUED, 1978, p. 261). In the same way, we can use the concept of tensegrity to understand the dilemmatic nature of experiencing, in which the sense-making process is not just a *reductio ad unum* of several opposite alternatives that cannot be fulfilled at the same time but rather the construction of a dilemmatic field in which the different subelements cogenerate and coexist even after a specific choice is made (or avoided) and a specific action is taken (or inhibited). The dilemmatic field, a concept elaborated following topological psychology (Tateo, 2014), defines at the same time the range of acceptable structural indeterminacy and the boundaries of the system with respect to the environment in parametric rather than binary terms. Few are the situations in which we are confronted with clear and neat choices, even when they are opposites. According to Abbey and Valsiner (2005), this "null situation" can occur only in the case of a complete indifference of the person toward a new object. In all other cases, ambivalence is a "tension produced by a system entailing a kernel and at least two vectors that are non-isomorphic in size and direction" (Abbey & Valsiner, 2005, p. 4). In fact, conceptualizing ambivalence in terms of opposition between two polarities (e.g., loving and hating an object at the same time) is a form of structuring that necessarily evokes a dialectical overcoming, that is, a resolution of tension. That is why I strongly suspect that the dyadic representation of ambivalence in terms of opposing feelings, thoughts, or will is an oversimplification. However, in a homeostatic model of representation of psychic life could not be otherwise. In dilemmatic situations, instead, oppositions are catalyzed by the specific conditions of mutual organization of elements that the person is experiencing in her orientation toward the future. In this sense, the tensegrity model implies that tension is never resolved because it is a structural feature of the organism. In other words, tension is resolved by the fact that the organism is maintaining its structural organization. A choice acquires its value in relation to the person's continuous striving for what's next rather than the satisfaction of a need for closure and resolution. Of course, an excessive degree of tension provoked by too much ambivalence is unbearable by the organism and can bring to its disruption. The latter can be considered a special case of null situation, in which no further change is triggered but the end of the system because a completely chaotic condition would not allow any further choice. Otherwise, tensional integrity is ensured to maintain the system, with the environment providing scaffolds that the organism can use to guide the ambivalence within certain parameters. Without constraints, there would be no dilemmas. One could say that the person is "in tension" because of "intention," that is, a goal-oriented directionality toward a particular object of experience that become meaningful also by virtue of the social constraints attached to it. Such a direction of existence is always dealing with the uniqueness of experience and the cultural guidance that frames it (Tateo & Marsico, 2013). In the next section, I will try to apply the idea of tensegrity to the developmental processes.

THE INHERENT AMBIVALENCE OF DEVELOPMENT

In general terms, psychological processes are characterized by an inherent ambivalence at cognitive affective and ethical levels. In particular, during the developmental age, the individual/culture relationship is guided by specific institutions (e.g., family and school) that behave like near-equilibrium open systems, codefining the range of acceptable structural indeterminacy and the boundaries of the system with respect to the environment (Sawada & Caley, 1985). This context of guided development generates dilemmatic situations, a set of ambivalences that the individual is negotiating and making sense of, while developing his own self and personal culture. For instance, educational contexts are constructing situations in which ambivalent sets of guidelines are continuously produced (be independent but follow the rules, be mature enough but can't do whatever you want, be sociable but don't speak in classroom, etc.). In the inherent tension of the self, these sets of suggestions and constraints constitute the cultural framework for the elaboration of the personal trajectory.

Individuals are required to keep their unique self-construction process within acceptable boundaries, for instance, by fulfilling performance standards or age steps (Figure 1.2). Of course, not every situation is dilemmatic at the highest level (Tateo, 2015b). The ambivalent and dilemmatic nature of experience especially emerges in "the way in which human beings should be treated" (Amsterdam & Bruner, 2000, p. 6). The general values underneath this process are continuity and consistency with respect to the cultural

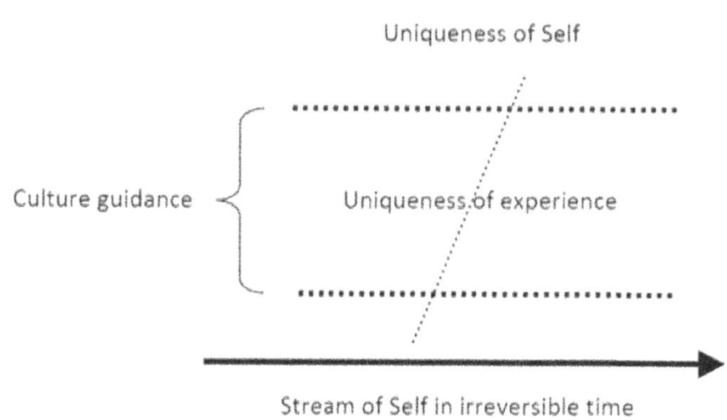

Figure 1.2 Ambivalence and tension in development.

community. The process of developing the Self while fulfilling contradictory cultural expectations is one of the most relevant developmental tasks related to ambivalence. The person is experiencing dilemmatic situations in which ambivalence can be never resolved because it is part of the system.

Thus, development can be conceptualized as a form of tensegrity between continuity and discontinuity: in every adolescent dwells a potential adult, and in every adult dwells a former adolescent. The ambivalent nature of developmental processes is also related to the progressive movement of the developmental horizon over time (Tateo, 2014) and among contexts (Marsico, Komatsu, & Iannaccone, 2013). It can be said that the distinction between continuity and discontinuity in development are related to the fact that experiences are unique because they happen at the temporal horizon and the contextual border of the Self. Each organization in which development takes place (e.g., school, family, peers, etc.) acts as a value-driven near-equilibrium system, defining the range of objectives, boundaries, and deviance that define an acceptable—for the community—developmental outcome.

Transgenerational family relationships provide an example of such value-driven forms of development, taking place, for instance, in the dilemmatic field of parental models. As an example, I will use an excerpt from the famous novel *Sons and Lovers*, published in 1913 by D. H. Lawrence. The novel tells the family story of the young artist Paul Morel, and Lawrence began writing it in the period of his mother's illness, often referring to her through the female protagonist Gertrude Morel. The plot describes the story of a couple, Gertrude, coming from a good bourgeois family and Walter, a poor miner. After a first phase of passion, the couple falls apart because of the different expectations and background, with Walter ending up at the pub every day and becoming at times violent with the kids whom he somehow likens to the mother. The attention of Gertrude progressively shifts to their two children, William and Paul, establishing an ambiguous relationship that will mark their adult lives. Gertrude is the portrait of a refined woman who can only run after her passions, first for the husband and later for her kids. As young adults, William and Paul both try to escape the ambivalent relationship with the mother/lover. But only William will succeed moving to another town, whereas Paul will remain unable to establish satisfactory relationships with other women and spends the rest of his life alone after the mother's death. Nevertheless, both of them will carry the mark of the mother's ownership on their souls.

I have selected an interesting excerpt from Chapter 3, "The Casting Off of Morel: The Taking on of William." At this point of the novel, a third child is born:

> Meanwhile another infant was coming, fruit of this little peace and tenderness between the separating parents. Paul was seventeen months old when

the new baby was born. He was then a plump, pale child, quiet, with heavy blue eyes, and still the peculiar slight knitting of the brows. The last child was also a boy, fair and bonny. Mrs. Morel was sorry when she knew she was with child, both for economic reasons and because she did not love her husband; but not for the sake of the infant.

They called the baby Arthur. He was very pretty, with a mop of gold curls, and he loved his father from the first. Mrs. Morel was glad this child loved the father. Hearing the miner's footsteps, the baby would put up his arms and crow. And if Morel were in a good temper, he called back immediately, in his hearty, mellow voice:

"What then, my beauty? I sh'll come to thee in a minute."

And as soon as he had taken off his pit-coat, Mrs. Morel would put an apron round the child, and give him to his father.

"What a sight the lad looks!" she would exclaim sometimes, taking back the baby, that was smutted on the face from his father's kisses and play. Then Morel laughed joyfully.

"He's a little collier, bless his bit o' mutton!" he exclaimed.

And these were the happy moments of her life now, when the children included the father in her heart.

Meanwhile William grew bigger and stronger and more active, while Paul, always rather delicate and quiet, got slimmer, and trotted after his mother like her shadow. He was usually active and interested, but sometimes he would have fits of depression. Then the mother would find the boy of three or four crying on the sofa.

"What's the matter?" she asked, and got no answer.

"What's the matter?" she insisted, getting cross.

"I don't know," sobbed the child.

So she tried to reason him out of it, or to amuse him, but without effect. It made her feel beside herself. Then the father, always impatient, would jump from his chair and shout:

"If he doesn't stop, I'll smack him till he does."

"You'll do nothing of the sort," said the mother coldly. And then she carried the child into the yard, plumped him into his little chair, and said: "Now cry there, Misery!"

And then a butterfly on the rhubarb-leaves perhaps caught his eye, or at last he cried himself to sleep. These fits were not often, but they caused a shadow in Mrs. Morel's heart, and her treatment of Paul was different from that of the other children. (Lawrence, 1994, pp. 55–56).

The birth of the new child is described by Lawrence as an ambivalent event. The first element that catches the eye is the enormous presence of emotional up and downs. In Lawrence's description, all the family members seem characterized by an idiosyncratic ambivalent polarity in the expression of their feelings. Both parents express ambivalent feelings and behavior with respect to Arthur. The birth acts as a catalyzer of the parents' feelings, fostering responses that are neither completely positive nor completely negative. The dilemma here is: (a) how do we deal with the newborn in the context of a disrupted marriage, and (b) how do we reorganize the family system formerly structured around the ambiguous relationships between husband and wife and mother and children?

CONCLUSIONS

There is a proper time and way to develop what is culturally defined while developing through generations and can be understood as a dilemmatic field with its inherent ambivalences. At the same time, defining parameters cogenerate the range of nonparameters. For instance, defining what is meant by "behaving like an adult" or what is "homework" complementary defines what is "not behaving like an adult" or "behaving quasi like an adult or what is "not homework." At the same time, it also defines what "an adult should behave like" and what "homework should be." Thus, we can see that the person is not confronted with a simple opposition between "childhood" and "adulthood" or between "homework" and "play" but enters a complex dilemmatic field in which the elements acquire meaning with respect to each other. This requires a continuous negotiation of meaning in which the desired and the acceptable, the familiar and the new, the injunction and the alternatives are articulated in an ambivalent way, including the fact that under specific catalytic conditions, an adult can go back and behave like a child or the other way round.

We will continue to think about the expensive dress we purchased as well as the choice of becoming a doctor in relation to the fact that we want to learn from our experiences and do the best choice next time, but also because we are made of our dilemmas, of the choices we didn't make and the mistakes we still regret. The concept of tensegrity allows us to make sense of this way in which the past acquires a specific value in relation to the horizon of development, and at the same time ambivalence is part of the experience of life as an unsolvable dilemma. The proposed theoretical model could help to look at developmental phenomena under a new angle. Rather than a sequence of equilibrium states and crises, development could be seen as a self-feeding process of dynamic tensegrity between the organism oriented toward the future goals and its environment (Marsico & Tateo,

2017; Tanggaard & Tateo, 2017). Studying education and transgenerational family relationships by looking at the elements of ambivalence and tension as systemic features would then account for a wider range of phenomena. In fact, antinomies, ambivalences, and idiosyncrasies, not surprisingly, co-exist in the life course and across generations (Tateo, 2015b), representing both the discomforts and resources of our being humans always striving for transcending our present condition.

ACKNOWLEDGMENTS

This work has been funded by the Marie Curie IEF-2012 grant "EPICS: Epistemology in psychological science, the heritage of Giambattista Vico and the cultural psychology" at Aalborg University (Denmark).

REFERENCES

Abbey, E., & Valsiner, J. (2005). Emergence of meanings through ambivalence. *Forum Qualitative Sozialforschung/Forum: Qualitative Social Research, 6*(1), Art. 23. Retrieved from http://nbn-resolving.de/urn:nbn:de:0114-fqs0501231

Ainsworth, M. D., Blehar, M. C., Waters, E., & Wall, S. (1978). *Patterns of attachment: A psychological study of the strange situation.* Hillsdale, NJ: Erlbaum.

Albarracin, J., Zanna, D., & Blair, M. (2005). *The handbook of attitudes.* Mahwah, NJ: Erlbaum.

Amsterdam, A. G., & Bruner, J. (2000). *Minding the law.* Cambridge, MA: Harvard University Press.

Bateson, G. (1972). *Steps to an ecology of mind: Collected essays in anthropology, psychiatry, evolution, and epistemology.* Chicago, IL: University of Chicago Press.

Bateson, G., Jackson, D. D., Haley, J., & Weakland, J. (1956). Toward a theory of schizophrenia. *Behavioral Science, 1*, 251–264.

Bleuler, P. E. (1911/1950). *Dementia praecox or the group of schizophrenias* (J. Zimkin, Trans.). New York, NY: International Universities Press.

DeMarree, K. G., Wheeler, S. C., Briñol, P., & Petty, R.E. (2014). Wanting other attitudes: Actual–desired attitude discrepancies predict feelings of ambivalence and ambivalence consequences. *Journal of Experimental Social Psychology, 53*, 5–18.

Freud, S. (1938). Totem and taboo. In *Basic Writings of Sigmund Freud* (A. A. Brill, Trans.). New York, NY: Modern Library, Random House. Fuller, R. B. (1961). Tensegrity. *Portfolio and Art News Annual, 4*, 112–127.

Graubert, D. N., & Miller, J. S. A. (1957). On ambivalence. *The Psychiatric Quarterly, 31*(1–4), 458–464.

Harrist, S. (2006). A phenomenological investigation of the experience of ambivalence. *Journal of Phenomenological Psychology, 37*(1), 85–114.

Herbst, D. P. G. (1976). *Alternatives to hierarchies.* Leiden: Martinus Nijhoff.

Ingber, D. E. (2003). Tensegrity I. Cell structure and hierarchical systems biology. *Journal of Cell Science, 116*, 1157–1173.

IUED (Institut Universitaire d'études du developpement) (Eds.). (1978). *Transcending duality through tensional integrity. Part II: A lesson in organization from building design. Transnational Associations, 5*, 258–265.

Kaplan, K. J. (1972). On the ambivalence-indifference problem in attitude theory and measurement: A suggested modification of the semantic differential technique. *Psychological Bulletin, 77*, 361–372.

Lawrence, D. H. (1994). *Sons and lovers* (H. Baron & C. Baron, Eds.). London, England: Penguin. (Original work published 1913)

Marsico, G., Komatsu, K., & Iannaccone, A. (2013). *Crossing boundaries: Intercontextual dynamics between family and school.* Charlotte, NC: Information Age.

Marsico, G., & Tateo, L. (2017) Borders, tensegrity, and development in dialogue. *Integrative Psychological and Behavioral Science, 51*(4), 536–556.

Menaker, E. (1998). Otto Rank's conception of the will. *Journal of Religion and Health, 37*(1), 9–14.

Parker, R. (1997). The production and purposes of maternal ambivalence. In W. Hollway & B. Featherstone (Eds.), *Mothering and ambivalence* (pp. 17–36). London, England: Routledge.

Sawada, D., & Caley, M. T. (1985). Dissipative structures: New metaphors for becoming in education. *Educational Researcher, 14*(3), 13–19.

Simmel, G. (2010). *The view of life. Four metaphysical essays with journal aphorisms* (J. Andrews & D. Levine, Trans.). Chicago: University of Chicago Press. (Original work published 1918)

Smelser, N. J. (1998). The rational and the ambivalent in the social sciences: 1997 presidential address. *American Sociological Review, 63*(1), 1–15.

Swindell, J. S. (2010). Ambivalence. *Philosophical Explorations: An International Journal for the Philosophy of Mind and Action, 13*(1), 23–34.

Tanggaard, L., & Tateo, L. (2017). Unity of the real and the non-real: Imagination in action and talk. *Nordic Psychology*, 1–10. doi:10.1080/19012276.2017.1362991

Tateo, L. (2014). Beyond the self and the environment: The psychological horizon. In K. R. Cabell & J. Valsiner (Eds.), *The catalyzing mind: Beyond models of causality. Series: Annals of theoretical psychology* (Vol. 11, pp. 223–237). New York, NY: Springer Science+Business Media.

Tateo, L. (2015a). Gulliver's eggs: Why methods are not an issue of qualitative research in cultural psychology. *Integrative Psychological & Behavioral Science, 49*(2), 187–201.

Tateo, L. (2015b). Let's frankly play: Ambivalence, dilemmas and imagination. In G. Marsico (Ed.), *Jerome S. Bruner beyond 100: Cultivating Possibilities* (pp. 30–44). New York, NY: Springer.

Tateo, L., & Marsico, G. (2013). The self as tension of wholeness and emptiness. *Interacções, 24*, 1–19.

Wiley, N. (1994). *The semiotic self.* Cambridge, MA: Polity Press.

CHAPTER 2

THE RESEARCH ACT

Creating Knowledge From the Not (Yet) Known

Eugenia Gouvedari
University of Luxembourg

The present chapter is a meta-reflective exercise on the concept of ambivalence—the central concept of the book. The centrality of a concept in a research endeavor can be inspiring, but it also gestates two risks: one is to take the concept for granted, reify it, and go ahead to study or measure "it" in essentialistic terms. In other words, the object of research can acquire an unquestioned self-evidence of an everyday object (Daston, 2000). In contrast, the risk is to be enmeshed in endless loops of self-reflexivity and never arrive at another working definition of what your concept is and how it guides your research. Despite this double riskiness, I hope my meta-perspective will enable reflection on the concept of ambivalence that will expand and transform its conceptualizations.

In this chapter, I will explore the concept of ambivalence from the perspective of cultural psychology (Valsiner, 2014), and I will make a statement about the centrality of ambivalence in developmental processes. Selecting a concept

Trans-Generational Family Relations, pages 21–29

as pivotal in the study of psychological phenomena has many implications and is integrated within a complex web of assumptions, axioms, intuitions, and theoretical and methodological perspectives. The whole conception of phenomena is differentially refracted depending on the guiding concept.

To take the example of research in intergenerational relations, ambivalence has become a key concept while also triggering debates as to its utility and relevance. Thus, certain researchers in intergenerational relations (e.g., Connidis & McMullin, 2002; Lüscher, 2002; Lüscher & Pillemer, 1998) have seen ambivalence as a pivotal concept that provides an escape from what they see as problematic polar juxtapositions of solidarity versus conflict that prevailed in previous research. They argue that intergenerational relations are ambivalence generating, allowing for the coexistence of opposites. Ambivalence for them allows for a more dynamic view of having solidarity and tension at the same time (Lüscher, 2011), instead of either longing for the static idealized picture of the harmonious stability or deploring the inevitability of generational conflicts. Lüscher and Pillemer (1998) trace this change back to a postmodern and feminist influence as intergenerational studies started to share their "distrust of dualistic thinking, and instead deal explicitly with contradiction and paradox in social relations" (p. 6). Ambivalence is not seen as something negative to be eradicated but as a basic condition to live and cope with productively related to many levels of experience. More specifically, Connidis and McMullin (2002) have developed the concept of sociological ambivalence that is embedded in social structures, and they connect family life to individual agency and social policy and change through negotiation by focusing on processes and not steady states.

On the other side of the debate, scholars such as Bengtson, Giarrusso, Mabry, and Silverstein (2002) prefer to remain advocates of the well-established solidarity framework that they have dialectically complemented with conflict on several dimensions. However, they concede that ambivalence is a useful concept that can be accommodated within solidarity and conflict as a concomitant of these disjunctures. The advocates of the solidarity model are against the adoption of ambivalence as the key concept because for them solidarity exists before ambivalence is generated (Bengtson et al., 2002).

Therefore, the way a concept transforms the study and interpretation of a phenomenon cannot be explained in isolation but is enmeshed within a complex web of philosophical, theoretical assumptions and academic traditions and viewpoints. The introduction of ambivalence has provoked a fruitful dialogue and enriched the theoretical explorations in the field of intergenerational relations.

In the same way and on a meta-level, I will discuss the process of research development as ambivalence generating. Researching ambivalences is indeed an ambivalent process, just like any other research process. Thus, my focus will be rather on ambivalence in intertransdisciplinary research relations. Steering away from relations of either conflict or solidarity with quantitative or qualitative research methods, the present book is indeed a concrete example of ambivalence in research aspiring to bridge qualitative and quantitative research projects.

AMBIVALENCE IN DEVELOPMENT OR THE INEXORABILITY OF OSCILLATION

From the cultural psychology perspective (Valsiner, 2014), ambivalence is embedded in developmental processes and is not considered a condition contingent on problematic situations. Looking at development not as a predetermined transition from one stage to the other but as an open-ended process entails the indispensability of ambivalence and puts an end to determinism (Bauman, 2013). Development in cultural psychology is seen as time embedded and hence inextricably related to the notion of irreversibility of time. Time is asymmetrically conceived between the past and the future; the future looms uncertain and is constructed out of multiple potentialities. There is oscillation between alternatives, and the tension and ambivalence is temporarily resolved through the selection of one trajectory among multiple.

Within this dialectical process, a bidirectional exchange occurs between the individual and the context, of the past and the anticipated future. There is a tension of centrifugal and centripetal processes (Stern, 1938) that both constrain and enable. Within this Heraclitean[1] flux of emergence and the coexistence of opposites, no definitely predetermined trajectories of development exist.

Indeed at a high level of philosophical abstraction, ambivalence has been seen as a liberating, enabling concept central to the human agency and free will and thus is at the center of nondeterminism (Bauman, 2013; Lüscher, 2011; Smelser, 1998). It captures the dialectic tension, duality, and simultaneity of A and non-A, between autonomy and dependence, freedom and constraint. If to be nonambivalent is comfortable, then it is also oppressive. If to be ambivalent is stressful, then it is also the vehicle of free meaning and decision making. It is at the heart of agency and enablement. It embodies the cultural psychological axiom that culture has no agency and cannot definitely determine, although it guides unique becomings.

AMBIVALENCE: THE END OF CERTAINTY OR TO BRIDGE? AND WHAT TO BRIDGE?

The irreversibility of time and the open systemic nature of developmental phenomena entail this open-ended potentiality and the end of certainty

(Prigogine, 1997) that enables envisioning in different modalities. Initial conditions do not guarantee specific outcomes, and this unpredictability excludes certainties and gives space for potentialities. Ambivalence is time-embedded, and its exploration should dynamically involve the invisible dimension of the not yet actualized potentialities. The absent, not yet there, the in-between, as if can take up the modalities of as it should be, as it must be, as I want it to be, as it could be, or go back as a meta-reflection to what could have been (Valsiner, 2011). The as if envisioning acts as a scaffold (Vaihinger, 1935), and this is where ambivalence also acts as a scaffold to reach the stability of the as is in the eternal process of becoming. In development, a leap exists between the known and the not yet known, and this in-between is the less tangible part where the future emerges.

This is the reason that ambivalence is such a recalcitrant and fascinating concept to research. It is in between. It lies in the invisible as if, not yet actualized potentialities. In *Incomplete Nature*, Deacon (2013) talks about the importance of what is not yet there. He argues that in the study of conscience, meaning and values that matter most is what is absent, what he calls "absential features." According to him, what is envisioned cannot be totally materially grounded in the here and now, but "there is something present that makes this curious intrinsic relation to something absent" (Deacon, 2013, p. 8). This idea of incompleteness of concepts, ideas, and meaning is pertinent for the study of ambivalence as it promotes through the absence of the *not yet there* methodologies related to emergent dynamics and unrealized potentials (Deacon, 2013).

Vaihinger (1935) sees fictions as useful instruments not verifiable but justifiable in relation to the purpose they serve. In the philosophy of the as if, he views the as if fictions as auxiliary constructs that have to be discarded when they have completed their function and as "scaffolding afterwards to be demolished" (p. 87). However, he argues that the fictions cannot be fully discarded because they are integrated in the final as is decision making and are constitutive of the "reality." Indeed the importance of the imagination in development is more and more recognized as it has become prominent that the visible constituents of the here and now are not sufficient to give a full account of life courses: "Imagination in life is thus a constant process of expansion of the present along three dimensions-time, space and degrees of reality" (Zittoun et al., 2013, p. 3).

The image of the bridge is pertinent here as a visual conceptualization of this process. The bridge is the nonambivalent finality. However, it surreptitiously encloses a precedent oscillation so as to anticipate the arrival on the "other end" of the constructed bridge on certain grounds. Simmel's (1994) philosophical reflection on the bridge captures its elusive quality. To build the bridge means to suspend ambivalence, suspend the as if, and come momentarily to the as is.

What is a visible construction presupposes an invisible as if oscillating preceding process. The whole process of development can be viewed—in Simmel's (1994) terms—as an analog to building a bridge—from the past to the future, from the known to not (yet) known, from the "I" to the "Other":

> the bridge symbolizes the expansion of the sphere of our will over space. Only for us are the banks of the river not only in different places, but "divided". If we did not link them together first in our needs and our imagination, our concept of separation would have no meaning. (Simmel, 1994, p. 2)

Opening the "black box" of the envisioning of the bridge unfolds the oscillations as to *what* to connect and *how*. The finalized monodrome has been attained first through the envisioned, ambivalent, "absential" connection. Smelser (1998) calls these momentary resolutions of ambivalence "truce points" in the eternal process of temporarily resolving ambivalence, bringing in the example of the elections or survey results where the former ambivalence of the voters is presented as absolute univalent preference. We need to and finally build the bridge and suspend the as if clause; otherwise we will die like Buridan's ass (the donkey that died of starvation because it could not decide which of the two equidistal stacks of hay to eat) (Valsiner, 2011)[2] or end up schizophrenic (Bateson, 1972).

CATALYSIS OR MY ENVISIONED BRIDGE

Within this conception of development as dynamic, uncertain, irreversible, and, of course, ambivalent, the concept of catalysis (Cabell & Valsiner, 2013) coming from chemistry and the life sciences resonates well with a conception of causality toward the construction of a specific future trajectory. The catalytic conception of causality accounts for the in-between, absent, not yet actualized potentiality. Catalysis takes psychology away from a mechanistic conception of causality of a direct cause-effect relation (Cabell & Valsiner, 2013). The catalyst creates the conditions under which certain processes are constrained or enabled, but it does not fully determine developmental processes that are individually constructed but at the same time socially and culturally directed and guided. Kull (2014) argues that, contrary to chemical catalysis that refers to quantities of energy, semiotic catalysis refers to qualitative relations and involves the meaning-making process when there is incompatibility in a situation. When the individual is ambivalent, there is a cultural, societal guidance or even canalization to a specific direction. However, the individual reconstructs and reconstrues in a unique way the future resolving ambivalence by actively selecting or serendipitously encountering the relevant catalysts.

This dialectic tension between dependence and autonomy, freedom and constraint has been a "thema" that has preoccupied the "scientific imagination" (Holton, 1978) in several ways, and it is always at the heart of the relation of the individual with the context. It has been pivotal in theorizing about ambivalence (Bauman, 2013; Lüscher, 2011; Smelser, 1998). Stern (1938) has described the human personality and experiencing as the dialogue between centripetal and centrifugal processes. Juarrero (2002) explores the idea of the constraint as both constraining and at the same time enabling, closing off alternatives and creating new possibilities. In the same way, the philosophers of chemistry saw in catalysis the potential to capture more philosophically this tension between determining and being determined. They extrapolated catalytic processes into higher human functions and saw catalysts as both free and conditioned, as being determining and determined, with freedom and bondage being complementary and impossible to exist separately (Farber, 1966). I propose their bridging in searching to unfold their tensions and resonances.

CONSTRUCTING NONAMBIVALENT BRIDGES IN AN AMBIVALENT PSYCHOLOGY

Research is a developmental process par excellence, where self-reflection on the ambivalences and conscious striving to reach the *not yet there* is inherent. The researcher is faced with dilemmas, emergent questioning reaching bifurcations toward the *not yet there.* Within this oscillation between reproduction and transformation, I would agree with Polanyi (1962):

Scientific discovery reveals new knowledge, but the new vision that accompanies it is not knowledge. It is less than knowledge, for it is a guess; but it is more than knowledge, for it is a foreknowledge of things unknown and at present perhaps inconceivable. (p. 135)

Following Abbey and Valsiner (2005), we can distinguish several levels of increasing or decreasing ambivalence that affect the meaning-making process. Thus, the "null condition" of no ambivalence at all does not initiate any meaning construction. The null condition in the research process can be limiting. Fixed certainties and blind allegiances block the exploration of new syntheses and transformations. Creating or even deliberately provoking ambivalence is the moving force for introducing new concepts, encouraging new theoretical encounters, and envisioning the design of new bridges. Creating ambivalence takes us qualitative and quantitative researchers out of the "I don't care" about the other side of the river attitude and puts us into the oscillating face of maximum ambivalence, which can lead to synthesis, fusion, rejection, or bridging.

Indeed, ambivalence has been characterized by Lüscher (2011), a "bridging construct" between "disciplines as well as between research, theory and, not least, practice" (p. 202). In the process of doing research, the construction of bridges can be seen as the creation of research synergies. It can also be theoretically manifested in the metaphorical introduction of concepts from other disciplines, such as the concept of catalysis discussed earlier that has been metaphorically introduced to psychology from chemistry and the life sciences. Ambivalence can be the scaffold for new theoretical encounters and for designing new bridges that will help us cross well-established boundaries.

The next question is whether there is always space for ambivalence. The idealized, highly abstracted picture of ambivalence as liberating and essential to agency does not always find its place in cases where space for ambivalence is limited and decisions have to be taken instantly, such as, for example, in an emergency hospital room. However, in self-reflective practices such as research, there can be *potentially* maximum space for ambivalence. Ambivalence is in the in-between, where things can get in a muddle and get back tidy again while the rules of the game are rediscussed (Bateson, 1972). Ambivalence can be the heuristic power that can initiate a check on our epistemologies and urge us to ask new or old questions in novel ways (Toomela, 2009).

Within this ambivalent space, the dynamics of centripetal and centrifugal processes of being determined and determining the academic context is not always symmetrical, and they depend on a whole complex of power dynamics in the academic community, personal interests, and orientations and issues of values and validity. As Lüscher (2011) points out, the "oscillations can be asymmetrical, imbalanced, and reflect the impact of powers" (p. 197).

Thus, in the process of research emergence, there is ambivalent tension between what is already there in the research tradition and what is not yet there. Researchers actively and serendipitously select the catalysts that lead to the final research trajectory, which can lead to reproduction, creative synthesis, or outright resistance or transformation.

FROM AMBIVALENCE TO AMBIVALENCES

Ambivalences in the plural implies that there is no unifying way of seeing the concept because it is experienced and studied in many ways with different ontological and epistemological presuppositions. The present book is an embodiment of this multiplicity because it incorporates studies on ambivalence in different layers of meaning making, on different levels of experience and psychological reality, as well as reposing on diverse theoretical and methodological approaches.

Knorr-Cetina (2008) argues that epistemic objects are always incomplete, generating new questions and not finalized. She points out that, although they are multiply manifested, they are "lacking," unfolding, changing, and open ended. In the same way, abstract concepts such as ambivalence are constantly transformed. The way it is conceptualized and stabilized in each research project is integrated within a whole constellation of theoretical and methodological assumptions and relevant research questions. Through the present book, the various ambivalences can generate new questions and ways of exploring psychological phenomena.

NOTE

1. The ideas of the continuous flux and the unity of opposites is traced back to the 6th-century BC Greek philosopher Heraclitus, who captured them in the image of the ever-flowing river and with his famous aphorism that you cannot step into the same river twice.
2. The philosophical paradox of Buridan's ass is used to show how unlike the hypothetical donkey that died out of inability to make a decision, in human meaning-making, there is overdetermination of meaning, and the occasional immobilizing indecision and ambivalence is resolved through signs and mediating artefacts (e.g., Vygotsky's example of tossing a coin in a moment of indecision).

REFERENCES

Abbey, E., & Valsiner, J. (2005). Emergence of meanings through ambivalence. *Forum Qualitative Sozialforschung/Forum: Qualitative Social Research, 6*(1), Art. 23. Retrieved from http://nbn-resolving.de/urn:nbn:de:0114-fqs0501231

Bateson, G. (1972). *Steps to an ecology of mind: Collected essays in anthropology, psychiatry, evolution, and epistemology.* Chicago, IL: University of Chicago Press.

Bauman, Z. (2013). *Modernity and ambivalence.* New York, NY: Wiley.

Bengtson, V., Giarrusso, R., Mabry, J. B., & Silverstein, M. (2002). Solidarity, conflict, and ambivalence: Complementary or competing perspectives on intergenerational relationships? *Journal of Marriage and Family, 64*(3), 568–576.

Cabell, K. R., & Valsiner, J. (2013). *The catalyzing mind: Beyond models of causality.* New York, NY: Springer Science+Business Media.

Connidis, I. A., & McMullin, J. A. (2002). Ambivalence, family ties, and doing sociology. *Journal of Marriage and Family, 64*(3), 594–601.

Daston, L. (2000). *Biographies of scientific objects.* Chicago, IL: University of Chicago Press.

Deacon, T. W. (2013). *Incomplete nature: How mind emerged from matter.* New York, NY: W. W. Norton.

Farber, E. (1966). From chemistry to philosophy: The way of Alwin Mittasch (1869–1953). *Chymia*, pp. 157–178.

Holton, G. J. (1978). *The scientific imagination: Case studies.* New York, NY: Cambridge University Press.

Juarrero, A. (2002). Complex dynamical systems and the problems of identity. *Emergence, 4*(1–2), 94–104.

Knorr-Cetina, K. K. (2008). *Objectual practice: Knowledge as social order: Rethinking the sociology of Barry Barnes, 83.* Retrieved from http://www.google.com/books?hl=en&lr=&id=KuFwKZ43Mr0C&oi=fnd&pg=PA83&dq=knorr+cetina+objectual+practice+&ots=cDzTmZW2fP&sig=_vKBHGQYkaA0kKugFGAWTgvskk8

Kull, K. (2014). Catalysis and scaffolding in semiosis. In K. R. Cabell & J. Valsiner (Eds.), *The catalyzing mind* (pp. 111–121). New York, NY: Springer Science+Business Media.

Lüscher, K. (2002). Intergenerational ambivalence: Further steps in theory and research. *Journal of Marriage and Family, 64*(3), 585–593.

Lüscher, K. (2011). Ambivalence: A "sensitizing construct" for the study and practice of intergenerational relationships. *Journal of Intergenerational Relationships, 9*(2), 191–206.

Lüscher, K., & Pillemer, K. (1998). Intergenerational ambivalence: A new approach to the study of parent–child relations in later life. *Journal of Marriage and the Family,* pp. 413–425.

Polanyi, M. (1962). *Personal knowledge: Towards a post-critical philosophy.* Chicago: University of Chicago Press.

Prigogine, I. (1997). *The end of certainty.* New York, NY: The Free Press.

Simmel, G. (1994). Bridge and door. *Theory, culture & society, 11*(1), 5–10.

Smelser, N. J. (1998). The rational and the ambivalent in the social sciences. *American Sociological Review, 63,* 1–16.

Stern, W. (1938). *General psychology from the personalistic standpoint.* University Microfilms.

Toomela, A. (2009). How methodology became a toolbox—and how it escapes from that box. In J. Valsiner, P. C. M. Molenaar, M. C. D. P. Lyra, & N. Chaudhary (Eds.), *Dynamic process methodology in the social and developmental sciences* (pp. 45–66). New York, NY: Springer. Retrieved from http://link.springer.com/chapter/10.1007/978-0-387-95922-1_3

Vaihinger, H. (1935). *The philosophy of "as if": A system of the theoretical, practical and religious fictions of mankind* (2nd ed.). London, England: Routledge.

Valsiner, J. (2011). Constructing the vanishing present between the future and the past. *Infancia Y Aprendizaje, 34*(2), 141–150.

Valsiner, J. (2014). *An invitation to cultural psychology.* London, England: SAGE.

Zittoun, T., Valsiner, J., Salgado, J., Gonçalves, M. M., Vedeler, D., & Ferring, D. (2013). *Human development in the life course: Melodies of living.* Cambridge, England: Cambridge University Press.

PART II

LIFESPAN AND TRANSGENERATIONAL FOCUS

CHAPTER 3

MULTILEVEL APPROACH TO AMBIVALENCE IN FAMILY SPHERE

Changing Structures, Roles, and Relationships

Kairi Kasearu, Kadri Raid, and Dagmar Kutsar
University of Tartu

Family as a social institution and a unity of family generations has gone through remarkable changes in time and space. In the words of Beck and Beck-Gernsheim (2002), going back to Western preindustrial societies, the family institution could be defined as a "community of need" held together by an "obligation of solidarity." In the beginning of the 20th century and beyond, the family was unanimously defined as a married couple with their child(ren) and/or close relatives who lived in the same household and shared family-related tasks (Hansson, 2011). People contracted their marriages at an early age, thus entering into adulthood and family life (Amato et al., 2008). The fact of getting married marked a man and woman becoming

Trans-Generational Family Relations, pages 33–54

part of an institution that overwhelmed their individual preferences—the whole family life was framed by social norms, and it was assumed that the individual would sacrifice personal interests for the sake of the family union (Coontz, 2005). Family members were bound together by interdependence in a socially determined normative framework of family tasks and roles in the context of economic survival, also keeping family generations together in an extended family unit.

From the mid-20th century, along with intensive urbanization, scholarization, and emancipation of women, the family institution was more often represented by nuclear family unions and a dramatic increase of divorces, especially in the urban setting. In the 1970s, hot debates started over the survival of a traditional marriage-based family model in the Western World inspired by a search for alternative family forms. Sussman and Cogswell (1972) related this family institutional change with "the continuous struggle of human beings for self-fulfillment and their search for meaningful identities" (p. 7). Destabilization of family unions, broadening cohabitation without marriage, and diversification of family structures led to a shift from traditional to a companionship orientation of family structure and attention to the quality of relationships (see e.g., Spanier & Lewis, 1980), the latter serving as a guarantee of family stability. The accompanied weakening of the intergenerational bonds led to the acknowledged need for development of family support services (see e.g., Cogswell & Sussman, 1972) to compensate for the loosening intergenerational solidarity.

By the 21st century, the Western family institution had entered into a new era: strict external norms that controlled one's family life had lost their power, and people had achieved more freedom in making their own family-related decisions. These developments have been directed toward individualization, thus affecting both the further diversification of family formation and family-related behavior (Beck & Beck-Gernsheim, 2002; Cherlin, 2004; Giddens, 1991), the latter being strongly embedded in the social context where individual actors or actor groups make their decisions. The family as a union of interdependent members with externally determined homogeneous interests and positions was replaced by family unions of individuals with their own expectations and interests that do matter. Men and women have become more visible as separate persons, each experiencing different opportunities and burdens (Beck & Beck-Gernsheim, 2002). These changes also could be described as a "privatization" of family behavior (Ditch, Barnes, Bradshaw, Commaille, & Eardley, 1994). Paraphrasing Sussman and Cogswell (1972), human beings have won the struggle "for self-fulfillment and search for meaningful identities," however, paying the cost with growing ambivalence, as discussed later.

The condition of postmodernity is characterized by a dramatically accelerated pace, and it occurs on an enormous scale in Western societies. These developments have had a major impact on human relationships: almost disappeared societal guidance about carrying out relationships and weakened family bonds are serving as major sources of ambivalence (Lüscher & Pillemer, 1998). Our interest is in binding together the changing family behaviors and the theoretical perspective of ambivalence. Connidis (2015) emphasizes that ambivalence is more visible in relations that are different from traditional family behavior and therefore less established, such as preferring unmarried cohabitation over marriage contract, postponing childbearing, and choosing intentional childlessness. We also relate the emergence of ambivalence to family dissolutions and blended families. We argue that changes at the societal level lead to changes in the family institution, also shaping the relations between family members and increasing individual ambivalence in family behavior. Moreover, we also suppose that there are reverse effects of solving individual ambivalence with uncustomary individual actions, thus gradually launching wider changes in the family institution and societal conditions (norms, values, statuses). In the current article, we bring some examples from Estonia, which has witnessed dramatic and overwhelming changes in its political, economic, and social environments since the 1990s after the collapse of the Soviet Union (see e.g., Kutsar & Kärner, 2010), has reached a deep age gap in people's values when the transitions were over by the 2000s (Raudsepp, Tart, & Heinla, 2013), and is currently practicing diverse family forms and structures.

WHAT IS AMBIVALENCE?

The concept of ambivalence is not new; it has been applied in psychiatry, psychoanalysis, psychotherapy, and family therapy for more than 100 years (Lüscher, 2002) and recently has been widely discussed in family and intergenerational studies (Connidis, 2015). Scholars (e.g., Connidis, 2015; Lüscher, 2002) suggest ambivalence to be a suitable approach for explaining changed family life and its implications on relations as it rejects traditional beliefs of feelings being either positive or negative and brings in the assumption of "mixed feelings," enabling us to understand contradictions that individuals face in contemporary family life. Because ambivalence might emerge from different levels (individual, group, society), the main distinction is made between psychological and sociological approaches to ambivalence.

Robert K. Merton was one of the first scholars who brought the concept of ambivalence to sociology. Previously, this concept was mainly used in psychiatry and treated as a phenomenon that emerges on the individual level, meaning simultaneously held opposing feelings based on countervailing normative expectations and ideas about how individuals should act. Thus, the sociological approach to ambivalence points out that these "mixed feelings" are responses to structural social relations expressed with the ongoing negotiation of contradictions. It means that the sociological approach to ambivalence turns attention to the potential external or societal sources of ambivalence. According to Merton (1976), ambivalence "focuses on the ways which ambivalence comes to be built into the structure of social statuses and roles. It directs us to examine the processes in the social structure that affect the probability of ambivalence turning up in particular kind of role-relations" (p. 5).

Merton (1976) differentiated among six sources of ambivalence that are initiated by structural conditions. First, the core type of ambivalence is described as "incompatible normative expectations incorporated in a single role of a single social status" (Merton, 1976, p. 6). For instance, the role of a stepmother in a blended family can be defined as a contradiction between the norms dictating that she should offer parental warmth and support to the stepchild similarly to the biological mother. However, by popular belief, she can never fully replace her.

The second source of ambivalence is the contradiction between different statuses and roles that an individual carries, causing mixed feelings and compromise behavior. For instance, performing both full-time mother and full-time employee roles is an example of sociological ambivalence.

The third source of ambivalence is found in the conflict between roles associated with a particular status. In our case, the stepmother can carry multiple roles in the family, such as having a career, being a wife, and being a mediator of concerns between the stepchild and school.

The fourth kind of sociological ambivalence is drawn from contradictory cultural values that are not related to particular statuses but are normative and generally expected to be followed by the society members. For instance, being a tolerant person and expressing the value of zero tolerance where particular behaviors are concerned are contradictory.

The fifth source of ambivalence is the contradiction between cultural and social structures. This ambivalence could be found in the situation where culturally prescribed aspirations (e.g., aspiring for success) are not supported by socially structured opportunities (e.g., limited or no access to necessary resources that could pave the way to success).

The sixth source of ambivalence is emerging in the case of different sets of cultural values (e.g., in the case of migration, your own cultural values vs. values of the new home society can cause ambivalence). We suggest that different sources of ambivalence are interrelated and can function simultaneously: the ambivalence may result from controversies in cultural values or competing statuses and roles, and thus they can magnify the effect of the perceived ambivalence. For instance, cultural values and norms may presuppose that women should care for children and stay on parental leave;

however, they are also expected to take care of their career. Thus, the ambivalence is embedded in the (gendered) social structure. Moreover, the ambivalence can result from contradictions of old (traditional) and new (postmodern) values, norms, and social practices.

Although Merton's (1976) original approach emphasizes the importance of structure and pays less attention to human agency, more recent developments in defining ambivalence have focused on the interplay between social structure and individual action. It is argued that, although differences between psychological and sociological approaches to ambivalence exist, these approaches should be combined and not treated separately. Connidis and McMullin (2002b), borrowing the core ideas of the symbolic interactionism approach, claim that people create and are subjects to social order at the same time, which means that social structure and individual action are not independent; rather they interplay with each other. This dialectical combination, which supposes that the conditions of the social structure shape and condition the individual responses, might counteract and bring gradual structural changes. The basic notion here is that social roles are not static; they are gradually changing, and to some extent individuals can disrupt the expectations related to the role without sanctions (Connidis & McMullin, 2002b). Moreover, the social structure creates differences on the basis of gender, ethnicity, educational level, socioeconomic status, and ability to exercise agency in resolving ambivalence. This experience of ambivalence may be crystallized at the group level, and thus the ambivalence acts as a catalyst generating awareness and a response of organized collective action (Hillcoat-Nallétamby & Phillips, 2011). Thus, the human agency plays an important role in dealing with structural sources of ambivalence by reacting to the external signals in a selective way and applying solutions in one's individual life. Resolving the structural ambivalence related to family relations can thus contribute to the wider changes in the family institution, where the human agency can serve as a catalyst for societal change.

As highlighted earlier, family relations are influenced by social structural forces. When social structural arrangements, which distribute opportunities, rights, and privileges differently, collide with their attempts to exercise agency when negotiating relationships, individuals experience ambivalence (Connidis & McMullin, 2002a, 2002b). The terms *structured ambivalence* (see Connidis & McMullin, 2002a, 2002b) and *structural ambivalence* (Lorenz-Meyer, 2004) are applied to describe these structural contradictions inherent in institutional structures. Therefore, it can be said that contradictions individuals encounter in their family relationships are often socially determined. In the contemporary world, people are forced to take responsibility for, and often cope alone with, things that used to be handled collectively before (Beck & Beck-Gernsheim, 2002). Thus, we assume that more sources for the appearance of ambivalence in family relations exist than ever before; however, its determining factors are extremely diverse and come from different levels of social action. By drawing ideas from cognitive behavioral approach in psychology, according to which thoughts determine feelings and behavior (see e.g., Albert Ellis), we suppose that a cognitive appraisal of the perceived contradictions in norms, values, or statuses can solve the ambivalence. Further, if the individual family-related behavior diverts from the most customary, it feeds the emergence of new family forms, thus also causing further diversification of norms, values, and statuses at the societal level. As individuals differ by acknowledging ambivalence, individual appraisal and coping with it also differ.

We suppose that diversification of family forms and accompanied changes in structural conditions (values, norms, statuses) also determine changes in intergenerational relationships and solidarity. For example, the family taking care of their elderly relatives was a strict norm in earlier times in Estonia, which meant that they might experience less ambivalence because of clearly defined obligations as behavior prescriptions. Nowadays, when family networks are weaker and partly compensated by services, the appropriated norm to take care of elderly family members is not so clear-cut. Therefore, the norm of solidarity has weakened as well: the one who has to contribute more than expected to helping his or her elderly might experience higher ambivalence. Going back to the case of Estonia, compared with Nordic countries, such as Finland and Denmark, the provision of eldercare services is less developed, and the main responsibility for eldercare is still left according to the Family Law on close relatives (Tarum & Kutsar, 2015). Even more, as research evidence shows, the lack of eldercare services in Estonia refers to the mindsets of both policymakers, who could develop services, and individual caregivers, who could choose working instead of caring, intervening with deeply seated traditional norms and stereotypes of providing informal family care at a cost to the caregiver's career (Kutsar, Kasearu, & Trumm, 2015). Because working is an acknowledged norm in Estonian society, it does create ambivalence when choosing between working and providing informal care to the fragile close relative. Consequently, we assume that ambivalence in individual decision making can be higher in Estonia compared with the previously mentioned Nordic countries.

We have introduced different approaches of ambivalence and demonstrated how emergence and resolution of ambivalence take into account social structure and individual actors with their contradictory feelings and cognitions that are products of structural ambivalence (Connidis & Walker, 2009). By linking these different approaches in family studies, we can connect internal dynamics of ambivalence with mixed feelings and cognitions and contradictory behavior of family members, on the one hand, and reactions to the contradictions of social, cultural, political, and economic arrangements, on the other hand (Connidis, 2015, 2010; Connidis

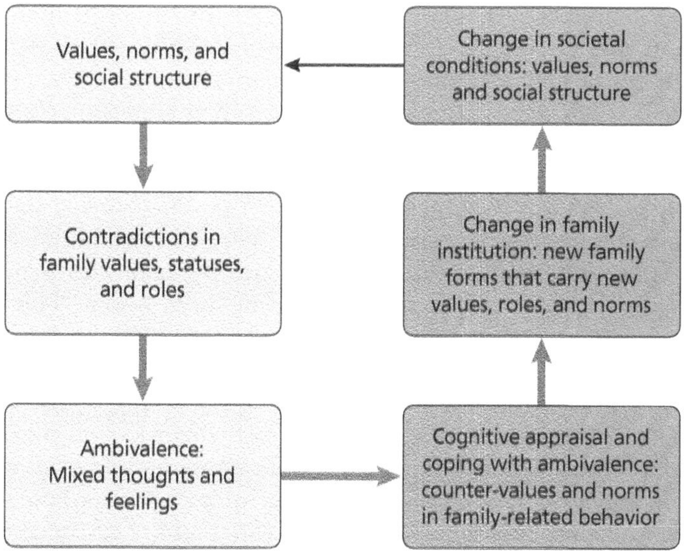

Figure 3.1 Multilevel approach to ambivalence.

& McMullin, 2002a, 2002b; Lüscher & Pillemer, 1998). Therefore, in the current article, we agree with Connidis (2015) that multilevel treatment of ambivalence should be central in family studies. We agree that what happens inside the families relates to what happens outside, and the key premise is that the ongoing negotiations of contradictions in family matters are a result of how life is organized and structured on the societal level. In turn, individuals, while negotiating their family ties, influence the social world beyond them. This kind of multilevel approach refers to interconnectedness and interrelatedness of the levels of social action by understanding ambivalence in family formation and behavior (see Figure 3.1).

CHANGING PATTERNS OF FAMILY LIFE: THE WAY TO STRUCTURAL AMBIVALENCE

According to Beck and Beck-Gernsheim (2002), a new stage in family history began with the gradual development of the welfare state. A series of social security mechanisms were introduced to guarantee minimum existence beyond the family union. This step gave the individual an opportunity to function without a family and also has reshaped the social norms guiding family life. Therefore, one's life course became less determined by the family and local community. This also supports the idea of an individualization hypothesis, whereby people have more choices and opportunities to lead their lives. These changes have affected family formation pathways to become more diverse (Amato et al., 2008). However, the life course is still quite standardized through institutionalization; many aspects of life are continually framed by the state (Shanahan, 2000), such as education. In Estonia, it is compulsory to attend school until age 17; after that individuals can decide whether to continue their education. Also, entry into and exit from the labor market are continually framed by the state—serviceable age is fixed, and after that one has a right to retire. The more institutionalized life domains that individuals have to combine with the family formation have become more flexible and less determined by social norms. This change increases individuals' freedom to create a personal life path (e.g., choosing to be committed to education and career first and thus postponing family formation or forming the family first and focusing on the personal career development later). The choice increases the risk of making choices that lead to a "wrong" or less successful path. Consequently, every decision or options carries potentials for ambivalence growth. We suppose that the multiplicity of choices in family-related behavior patterns has created a new social context for the emergence of structural ambivalence.

Family formation patterns in Western countries have altered; unmarried cohabitation as a prelude to or replacement of marriage has become widespread since 1970s, especially in the last decades (Kasearu & Kutsar, 2011; Kiernan, 2001; Katus, Puur, Põldma, & Sakkeus, 2007). As stated by Hatch (2015), one can distinguish among four types of unmarried cohabitation: (a) living together as a step in the marriage process, (b) being single and living alone, (c) a substitute or alternative to marriage, and (d) opposition to marriage. Mäenpää (2009) has indicates that only a fraction of modern couples marry without cohabiting first. For instance, in 2013 in Estonia, 74% of newlyweds reported that their previous relationship status was unmarried cohabitation (Statistics Estonia, 2015). This percentage refers to the widespread trend of cohabitation, which has had a notable influence on the evolution of family norms. On the one hand, the variation of family events has increased enormously, and on the other hand, this change has notably weakened the effect of traditional family norms, especially among younger cohorts (Cherlin, 1988; Elzinga & Liefbroer, 2007; Ravanera, Rajulton, & Burch, 2004; Beck & Beck-Gernsheim, 2002).

With the spreading evidence of cohabitations across Europe, the share of extramarital births has also increased enormously in past decades. For instance, in Estonia in recent years, more than 60% of children are born outside marriage. This social practice demonstrates that being married is not considered so important when having children. According to the most recent Civil Census in 2011, 61% of children in Estonia who live with both parents have married parents, and the rest have cohabiting parents, whereby younger children live more often with cohabiting parents and older children live with married ones (Laes, Krusell, Reinomägi, & Toros, 2013). This finding shows that marriage is still valued, but it has freed up space for other options of being related.

In addition to changed preferences of cohabiting forms, family formation behavior has also changed. Beck and Beck-Gensheim (2002) characterize contemporary family life as an effort to tie together threads of different rhythms that do not match. According to present considerations, birth reducing and other factors, such as the decreasing living standard together with appearing children, reconstruction of leisure time, commitment costs, and rising demands on the role of parents, influence people's decisions (Eckhard, 2014). Therefore, the postponement of family formation is taking shape and is evident by the increasing age at childbirth in all European countries (Gustafsson, 2001). For instance, since 1990, in some postsocialist countries (e.g., Estonia), women's mean age at the birth of a first child has increased by more than seven years (Statistics Estonia, 2015). In addition to postponing family formation and childbearing, one might make a deliberate choice not to have children at all (Tanturri & Mencarini, 2008). People calculate whether to start a family, questioning whether it fits with their future visions and ambitions and answering the questions "how" and "when"; children might be seen as an obstacle for personal achievements, and the decision not to have children can be taken. Also contemporary societies set up conflicting expectations, especially for women. In Western countries, approximately 10% to 20% of women born in the 1960s do not have children (Rowland, 2007), and the share of child-free individuals in younger cohorts is expected to increase (Tanturri et al., 2015). However, it is important to mention that not all so-called child-free individuals are voluntarily or intentionally childless; other factors might determine the situation, such as age, medical conditions, and so on.

Wager (2000) points out that childless women rarely decide that they do not want to have children; rather, they choose or value other things in their lives, such as their career and socializing with friends, over children. Nor can they believe in successful reconciliation of family life and other life domains. Tanturri and Mencarini (2008) emphasize that childlessness is often a consequence of postponing childbearing or disruption of a relationship. However, there is not a single reason or pathway to childlessness; rather, we can speak about various pathways toward it. However, when looking at preferences and attitudes about family formation behavior in European youth, most adolescents still prefer to have children and form a family in the future. The proportion of adolescents who do not want to have children is according, to the study of "Value of Children and Intergenerational Relations," approximately 10% in Germany and much lower in Poland, Russia, and France (Mayer & Trommsdorff, 2012). The difference between people who do not plan to have children and those who are voluntarily childfree uncovers two important aspects: (a) the status of being childfree or childless develops over the lifecourse and is a dynamic process rather than a clear-cut decision, and (b) it is taking place within different sociocultural contexts and opportunity structures, which may induce structural ambivalence to different degrees.

In addition to the previously mentioned changes, new family types have emerged. In the postmodern era, happiness in family relations and marriage is evaluated according to its contribution to self-development and satisfaction of deep psychological needs (Beck & Beck-Gernsheim, 2002). Therefore, the importance of the structural elements of marriage has decreased, and family as a union has turned into a formation where partners constantly have to negotiate norms, values, and preferences. When counterparts feel that the relationship does not satisfy their needs, they can step out of it and start the new one. Therefore, because of increasing divorce and dissolution rates, single-parent and blended families have become common (Therborn, 2004). Recent empirical evidence confirms that in countries where the poverty rate of single-parent families is lower and enrollment in child care is higher, the acceptance of divorce when young children are involved is higher (Rijken & Liefbroer, 2012). This finding suggests that structural conditions might have an influence on social norms guiding family behavior. The change of previously dominant social norms will lead to the redefinition of parental roles (e.g., psychological vs. physical absence of the parent). Although social norms are changing, their influence on individual behavior remains. For instance, the social approval of divorce still diverges across countries. For instance, Kalmijn and Uunk (2007) indicate that the association between divorce and the weakening of social contacts after divorce varies across countries according to the general attitude toward divorce. In countries where the general attitude toward divorce is rather negative, men and women after divorce will lose more social contacts than in societies with more tolerant attitude toward the family breakup. Consequently, the context for the emergence of ambivalence in family relations differs across countries, families, and individuals. Due to these changes, the reconstituted (blended) family is the fastest growing family form in Western countries; however, societies remain critical toward it when acknowledging its fragility as a union (Greeff, Vansteenwegen, & Smets, 2008). Björklund, Ginther, & Sundström (2007) claim that by age 15, some 30% of Swedish and 40% of U.S. children have experienced parental separation; moreover, nearly one out of five children have lived with a stepparent at some point during the childhood. According to the last Civil Census (2011), in Estonia about 21% of all children live in one-family households with a lone parent, meaning that almost all have experienced parental separation or divorce. The older the children, the more likely they are to live in a lone parent arrangement (17% of children under age 3 and

29% of children ages 12–17), or they have to adapt to a stepparent (2% of children under age 3 and 14% of children ages 12–17) (Laes et al., 2013). As described by different studies, dynamic family arrangements entail several sources of ambivalence for all people involved: the division of resources between stepchildren and blended children (Henretta, Van Voorhis, & Soldo, 2014), uncertainties about relationships and family membership boundaries (Stewart, 2005), mixed feelings regarding filial responsibilities (Ganong & Coleman, 2004), expectations and experiences of stepfather's authority (Mitchell, 2013), and even grandparental support to grandchild and/or step grandchild (Tanskanen, Danielsbacka, & Rotkirch, 2014).

To conclude, in the postmodern era, individually designed lives have gained a central position, which means that everyone is less bound to diverse societal norms, values, and statuses and thus can be freer to make individual decisions, including his or her own family affairs. However, this shift brings more fragility into family formation and functioning. In the next section, we study in more detail the interplay between the changing family institution and emerging ambivalence in the family spheres.

AMBIVALENCE IN THE FAMILY SPHERE

The traditional family model has changed from a primarily family- to an individual-focused model, the latter designed for individual needs (Eckhard, 2014). Stability of family life is not determined by external normative pressures anymore but by the quality of the couple's relationship and the extent to which the family union can contribute to its members' self-development. Therefore, the union can stay firm until it satisfies the deepest psychological needs of its counterparts. When traditional roles inside family and pair relationship were clear-cut, people had a prescription for how to act according to their role. In contrast, in contemporary societies, there is a continuous need to negotiate over needs, preferences, values, and norms of the family members. Together with acceptance of children's rights, being a normative frame of interaction with a child on the one side and new parenting ideas on the other, children have become an equal party in the negotiation process and, thus in principle, share ambivalence in family matters.

Ambivalence occurs in the case of conflicting options in the decision-making process and conflicts that might emerge when an individual feels confused about the roles he or she has taken or does not know how to act according to them. For instance, the rise of unmarried cohabitation could be seen as a free and reasoned choice of both partners (Hatch, 2015). However, our qualitative studies have indicated that even in Estonia, where unmarried cohabitation is widespread (see Kasearu & Kutsar, 2011), female partners especially have mixed feelings toward their family/marital status.

On the one hand, they do not see big differences between marriage and cohabitation in their everyday routine. However, they still admit to having a dream about a wedding in a beautiful white dress and are waiting for a proposal to marry someday (Jürisoo, 2007). Cohabiting partners are accepting their status, but they emphasize the symbolic value of the marriage contract (Jürisoo, 2007; Raid, 2013). This demonstrates how social norms have weakened and norms have become more diverse. People do not feel strong external pressure to marry, yet the traditional values are still embedded in mental structures and even romanticized: a woman can decide and make a proposal to have a child, but a marriage proposal still has to be initiated by a man (Jürisoo, 2007). The latter is seen as a sign of commitment and deepest love, thus serving as a source of ambivalence. A Civil Partnership Act was passed in Estonia in 2014. With this law, the legal norm of living together without marriage and forming one's family was established as a social norm besides the marriage. This law acknowledged living together as legal alternative to the traditional marriage-based union. We assume that this policy decision can ease the cognitive appraisal of societal values and norms, reduce the emergence of mixed feelings, and solve the ambivalence in concordance of people's individual preferences when standing at the crossroads of finding their own ways of forming family. Moreover, by introducing this law, the state demonstrates the will to adapt to changing social practices of family formation even when in some cases these new relationships are not truly negotiated.

What are the consequences of the rise of unmarried cohabitation on intergenerational relations? It has been suggested that new union types may challenge the pattern of intergenerational relations, although differences are found among countries depending on the spread of unmarried cohabitation. For instance, in the United States, where cohabitation unions as alternatives to marriage are not broadly spread, cohabiting and married individuals differ by intergenerational exchange of support, the latter showing tighter intergenerational bonds (Eggebeen, 2005). On the contrary, in Norway, where the cohabitation rate is high, the union type has no effect on intergenerational solidarity between parents and their grown-up children (Daatland, 2007). More recently, Hogerbrugge and Dykstra (2009) revealed that cohabiting people in the Netherlands have less contact with their families of origin than the married ones and explained this mostly by different sociodemographic background characteristics of the cohabiting and married individuals. The cohabiting individuals were more likely to have divorced parents, lived further away from parents, and were less religious. Also, Nazio and Saraceno (2008) relying on Italian data, brought out the proximity factor, namely, cohabiting couples are living farther away from their homes of origin compared with married couples, which puts limits on the helping activities in everyday chores. However, the evidence shows transformation patterns of helping activities from physical to psychological. Living elsewhere and relying on welfare service provisions, people can more often give psychological support and save feelings of togetherness by using new communication forms, such as Skype and the internet (Kasearu & Kutsar, 2013).

Even less information is available on the intergenerational relations between cohabiting partners and their partners' parents. On the basis of data from the Estonian Social Survey, we found that cohabiting partners receive and give less support to their partner's parents compared with married couples (see also Chesley & Poppie, 2009). This finding is explained by the institutional approach: cohabitation is seen as a fragile, uncertain, or temporary union, and the family network around the cohabiting couple can be less developed and ready to help. In that case, they are less institutionalized compared with the married couples (Nock, 1995). Thus, the parents of cohabiting partners may feel fewer obligations to offer support because of the perceived ambiguity and estimated uncertainty of the cohabitation union (Eggebeen, 2005; Hogerbrugge & Dykstra, 2009). Moreover, cohabiting couples may see cohabitation as a temporary phase in their lives and apologize for contributing to a lesser extent to the bonding of kinship ties. The unanswered question is, when does the union become certain for the partners' parents? Would this be a moment when they acquire biological bonding with the union as ancestors? We claim that cohabitation as a new type of union contains a source of ambivalence—toward cohabiting partners' positions, obligations, and rights in wider kinship structure. It could be seen as twofold: how the cohabiting partners perceive their relationship and how they are perceived by the kinship from both sides. This leads us to agree with Lowenstein and Daatland (2006) and their idea of affection and choice as binding generations together into helping relationships. However, in countries that have passed the Civil Partnership Law, and thus cohabitation union has been acknowledged as a legal union with mutually shared responsibilities and rights (e.g., Estonia), this political act may also bind together generations, decrease ambivalence in decision-making situations, and restore intergenerational family solidarity to some extent.

The picture gets more undefined in the case of remarriage or recohabitation, especially when children are involved. Many divorced or separated people marry or cohabit with a new partner who also might have been married before and have children of their own. Children of these families commute between two or more family worlds. They may have a so-called everyday parent, who lives with a new partner, and the weekend parent, who lives separately from the child and also might have formed a new family. A child has received two homes and might enjoy the new "richness"; however, it is accompanied by (and increasing) ambivalence. Children learn norms and values during their socialization process. As active social actors, they are not merely passive receivers of socializing interventions, but they do actively appropriate societal norms, values, and statuses and perform as mediators of change to the next generation of adults (see e.g., Corsaro, 1997). In general, children are normative in their behavior: they try to be socially adequate companions in social interactions. However, when children from blended families try to follow norms, they may face acute emotional dilemmas and ambivalence: who is my mother, the "biological" who lives apart and I visit her or the "obtained" who loves me and takes daily care of me? Am I socially "adequate" when children are supposed to love their mother the most while I probably love my stepmother even more? Also, parents of a family as a network of old and new bonds face ambivalence. For instance, isn't it in the best interest of the child to have both parents in his or her life after the parents' separation? Is the negotiated visiting scheme meeting that acknowledged right?

The formation of a blended family leads to a complex relationship structure because the family boundaries cannot be clearly identified anymore, and there might be more than one family, at least for a child. Also, the cohabitant partners of children's parents when obtaining roles of everyday mothers or fathers, or those who host the visiting children of their partners, experience ambivalence: who actually belongs to my family and who does not? How do I best perform the new role? Together with the lost clear-cut identification of the marriage-based family union, today we can find a number of definitions. Every person, including the children, in a family group can have different identifications of the family union, and these definitions can change over time. Personal preferences have become important, and external pressures no longer should be the main determinants of the family bond. Today, people create kin by actively establishing relationships. Therefore, family ties and relations can no longer be taken for granted (Beck & Beck-Gernsheim, 2002). In the process of the interplay of old and new values, norms, and statuses and family change in a generational perspective, children's agency plays a mediator's role by carrying changes from the current generation of adults to the next one and also impacting the next generation of children. In this process, children are determined by normativity and thus may experience the highest level of ambivalence when navigating from one family structure to another and trying to make the divide between the wrong and right. Regarding intergenerational relations, we believe otherness plays a role in the intergenerational bonding between a partner or a spouse who has child(ren) from the former relationship(s) and the older generation. This otherness may be the decisive factor in determining the types and levels of intergenerational exchange of support and care, thus carrying both ambivalence and keys to solve it.

SOCIETAL CONTEXT DETERMINING AMBIVALENCE: ARE POSTSOCIALIST COUNTRIES MORE VULNERABLE THAN THEIR CAPITALIST COUNTERPARTS?

As stated by Weigert (1991), change is the soil for ambivalence. Revolutionary periods of social and political change expose high social risks and upheavals in family-related behavior (Kutsar & Tiit, 2003). Conditions that foster the emergence of ambivalence will broaden, and the latter could also be seen as a characteristic of contemporary societies. After the collapse of the Soviet Union, the postsocialist countries went through ideational changes as their societies started to move toward Western values: rising individualism, self-actualization, autonomy, self-reliance, and so on (Lauristin, 1997; Sztompka, 2003). This process is described as developmental idealism (Thornton & Philipov, 2009), whereby Western values and ways of living were perceived as desirable and a sign of a higher level of development. Moreover, the rapid economic, social, and political changes altered the institutional context, and new opportunities and risks (e.g., unemployment, poverty) emerged (Kutsar, 1997). As a consequence of these transformations, rapid demographic changes occurred: fertility and marriage rates decreased, and the number of divorces and unmarried cohabitations increased (e.g., Aassve, Billari, & Spéder, 2006; Kantorova, 2004; Katus et al., 2007; Kohler & Kohler, 2002). Thus, life in the 1990s became more self-determined, mobile, and flexible, but it also meant taking more social and welfare risks (Weyman, Sackmann, & Wingens, 1999). These contradictions embedded in the process of societal change could be described as permanent tensions between structure and agency (Lauristin, 1997) and sources of structural ambivalence.

According to Kutsar and Tiit (2003), structural changes (cohabitation, divorces, births out of wedlock) of families in Estonia have taken place slightly before the collapse of the totalitarian system in parallel to the rest of the Nordic countries, where all these new features of family life were the most widely spread in Europe. However, the deinstitutionalization processes collected speed after the economic and political turn in the early 1990s, thus also impacting changes in relations between family members (Kasearu, 2010).

We propose that in postsocialist countries, structural ambivalence has multiple roots. First, it could be seen as the outcome of rapidly transforming cultural values in a society, which means a mixture of previous social norms and newly emerged counternorms push forward earlier emerging trends. For instance, it is suggested that the socialization patterns of young people before and after the collapse of the Soviet Union vary, although the age difference between these cohorts is not so big (Nugin, 2013), and the age gap in values has increased (Raudsepp, Tart, & Heinla, 2013). This finding suggests that in family relations, the younger and older generations might have different expectations toward each other's role as a parent, child, or grandparent. Moreover, our studies have shown that individuals are holding contradictory family-related values. There is high acceptance that marriage should be life-long, but at the same time they do not disagree that, "for the sake of children, it is better to avoid divorce" (Kasearu, 2009). Ambivalence regarding the family institution can also be observed in children. Studies among teenagers in Estonia (Heinma, 2014; Roots, 2010) have demonstrated that, on the one hand, adolescents still carry old norms regarding contracting marriages; however, they value good family relations and happiness over the marriage contract. This finding supports the idea of norms and counternorms, which in turn results in the further change of family behavior, at least when the next generation of adults is concerned. Second, we believe that the roots of structural ambivalence are embedded in the interplay between the structural opportunities and life values/expectations, which was called the fifth source of sociological ambivalence by Merton (1976). For instance, Ghodsee and Bernardi (2012) point out that after the collapse of communism in Bulgaria, the number of child births decreased due to economic reasons and lack of formal child care. At the same time, the prevailing ideal of two children still prevails. Bulgarian couples cope with this situation by having their first child in their early 20s but markedly postponing the birth of a second child. This means that structural opportunities restrict the fulfillment of ideals or planned behavior.

The next example describes how at the societal level, values, ideals, and standards of a good life will determine our individual preferences and actions. Many new European Union (EU) member states are confronted with a new social phenomenon, namely, children left behind by their parents who are leaving their country of origin for their jobs (Kutsar, Darmody, & Lahesoo, 2014). After regaining independence and going over to a market-based economy, the postsocialist societies and families in these countries face the extra pressure to catch up with the living standard of the old EU countries, although the structural opportunities are limited. At the same time, there are no structural barriers for working in other EU countries, where the wage level is higher than in the homeland. Kutsar et al. (2014) conclude that, due to temporary disruptions in face-to-face interactions, symbolic family membership (Derby & Atkins, 2012) starts to prevail: children need to feel that they are part of a family that remains together, but symbolic membership cannot compensate it on a daily basis even when the family's economic situation has improved. Structural ambivalence shapes children's everyday lives and causes distress. However, besides negative aspects, children are also clever to find the positive sides of the situation, such as increased independence (e.g., more freedom, more time to spend with friends, or the liberty to take actions following their own choices). The positive sides of parents' transnational migration can engine a change in societal values of this rather new social phenomenon, at least in Estonia and other CEE countries, and impact the decisions of the next generation of adults.

Also, parents who transnationally commute by job experience high ambivalence when putting together new roles as a parent and an employee or keeping parenting real not only symbolic. Our qualitative studies (Raudsepp, 2014) with fathers working abroad and whose families were left behind indicated that to cope with ambivalent feelings, they define and reason their choice as the best solution for their family and emphasize the father's role as a breadwinner. These new phenomena have become part of family life quickly and unexpectedly. Thus, society does not know how to cope with them yet. However, family generations should be able to find their own way.

In conclusion, postsocialist countries are additionally vulnerable due to extensive changes in the societal context. In a way, belonging to the EU sets standards that we want to correspond and creates a vision of Estonia as a small European country. Moreover, the socialist past has left its trails, and therefore roots of ambivalence are multifaceted and deep. Thus, more contradictions and possible conditions for ambivalence occur in the family sphere, at least in the case of Estonia as a postsocialist country compared with Western societies.

CONCLUDING REMARKS

In general, it has been argued that ambivalence is an inescapable feature of postmodern society (Beck, 1994; Giddens, 1990; Weigert, 1991). Thus, structural ambivalence could be seen as a wider concept, which characterizes all social relations, whereas the social norms are not so strict anymore. According to individualization theory, individuals will abandon the old traditional family ties to integrate into a modern differentiated society (Beck & Sopp, 1997), which means that a reconstruction of relations, norms, and roles is taking place. On the one hand, richness of societal conditions shaping family-related decisions gives more opportunities for human agency in a more flexible and less controlled social setting; on the other hand, increasing personal freedom and decreasing influence of social and behavioral scripts are likely to cause new contradictions and ambivalent situations that impact the lives of all family members, including children. Moreover, the high speed of changes in the postsocialist countries can carry an extra load of contradictions and thus ambivalence while uncovering the challenges of navigating through and within the complexities in their lives and family affairs.

We suggest that by assessing the experience of ambivalence in family relations, we can become aware of the sociocultural context in which the family institution is embedded. Thus, we assume that for understanding the sources for ambivalence in the family sphere, the answers to the following questions are crucial: What are the dominant norms and counternorms that define the statuses and roles in a society? What are the social conditions, opportunities, and support systems for the families? We claimed that the conditions for the emergence of structural ambivalence are formed at macro-level by the interaction between structural opportunities and cultural values that confront active social actors with their individual mindsets of choosing new solutions to meet their individual needs and preferences.

ACKNOWLEDGMENT

The writing of this chapter was supported by the Estonian Research Council (grant PUT499 and PUT1530) and by the University of Tartu (grant PSHSS13911).

REFERENCES

Aassve, A., Billari, F. C., & Spéder, Z. (2006). Societal transition, policy changes and family formation: Evidence from Hungary. *European Journal of Population, 22,* 127–152.

Amato, P. R., Landale, N. S., Havasevich-Brooks, T. C., Booth, A., Eggebeen, D. J., & McHale, S. M. (2008). Precursors of young women's family formation pathways. *Journal of Marriage and Family, 70,* 1271–1286.

Beck, U., & Beck-Gernsheim, E. (2002). *Individualization.* London, England: SAGE.

Beck, U., & Sopp, P. (1997). *Individualisierung und Integration: Neue Konfliktlinien und neuer Integrationsmodus?* Opladen: Leske + Budrich.

Björklund, A., Ginther, D., & Sundström, M. (2007). Family structure and child outcomes in the USA and Sweden. *Journal of Population Economics, 20,* 183–201.

Cherlin, A. J. (1988). *The changing American family and public policy.* Washington, DC: Urban Inst. Press.

Cherlin, A. J. (2004). The deinstitutionalization of American marriage. *Journal of Marriage and Family, 66,* 848–861.

Chesley, N., & Poppie, K. (2009). Assisting parents and in-laws: Gender, type of assistance, and couples' employment. *Journal of Marriage and Family, 71,* 247–262.

Cogswell, B. E., & Sussman, M. B. (1972). Changing family and marriage forms: Complications for human service systems. *Family Coordinator, 21*(4), 505–516.

Connidis, I. A. (2010). *Family ties and ageing* (2nd ed.). Thousand Oaks, CA: SAGE.

Connidis, I. A. (2015). Exploring ambivalence in family ties: Progress and prospects. *Journal of Marriage and Family, 77,* 77–95.

Connidis, I. A., & McMullin, J. A. (2002a). Ambivalence, family ties, and doing sociology. *Journal of Marriage and Family, 64,* 594–601.

Connidis, I. A., & McMullin, J. A. (2002b). Sociological ambivalence and family ties: A critical perspective. *Journal of Marriage and Family, 64,* 558–567.

Connidis, I. A., & Walker, A. J. (2009). (Re)visioning gender, age, and aging in families. In S. A. Lloyd, A. L. Few, & K. R. Allen (Eds.), *Handbook of feminist family studies* (pp. 147–159). Thousand Oaks, CA: SAGE.

Coontz, S. (2005). *Marriage, a history: From obedience to intimacy, or how love conquered marriage*New York, NY: Viking Penguin.

Corsaro, W. A. (1997). *The sociology of childhood.* Thousand Oaks, CA: Pine Forge Press.

Daatland, S. O. (2007). Marital history and intergenerational solidarity: The impact of divorce and unmarried cohabitation. *Journal of Social Issues, 63,* 809–825.

Derby, J., & Adkins, T. (2012). The strength of family ties: How US migration shapes children's ideas of family. *Childhood, 19*(2), 169–187.

Ditch, J., Barnes, H., Bradshaw J., Commaille J., & Eardley T. (Eds.). (1994). A synthesis of national family policies 1994. In *European observatory on national family policies.* University of York.

Eckhard, J. (2014). Theoretical explanations of increasing childlessness: Divergent approaches and the integrating potential of the frames selection theory. *Comparative Population Studies, 29,* 49–72.

Eggebeen, D. J. (2005). Cohabitation and exchanges of support. *Social Forces, 83,* 1097–1110.

Elzinga, C. H., & Liefbroer, A. C. (2007). De-standardization of family-life trajectories of young adults: A cross-national comparison using sequence analysis. *European Journal of Population, 23,* 225–250.

Ganong, L. H., & Coleman, M. (2004). *Stepfamily relationships: Development, dynamics and interventions.* New York, NY: Kluwer Academic.

Ghodsee, K., & Bernardi, L. (2012). Starting a family at your parents' house: Multigenerational households and below replacement fertility in urban Bulgaria. *Journal of Comparative Family Studies, 43,* 439–459.

Giddens, A. (1990). *The consequences of modernity.* Cambridge, England: Polity Press.

Giddens, A. (1991). *Modernity and self-identity.* Cambridge, England: Polity Press.

Greeff, A. P., Vansteenwegen, A., & Smets, I. (2008). Resilience in reconstituted families. In J. K. Quinn & I. G. Zambini (Eds.), *Family relations: 21st century issues and challenges.* New York, NY: Nova Science Publishers.

Gustafsson, S. (2001). Optimal age at motherhood: Theoretical and empirical considerations on postponement of maternity in Europe. *Journal of Population Economics, 14,* 225–247.

Hansson, L. (2011). Towards a definition of the family? In L. Farrer & W. Lay (Eds.), *Spotlights on contemporary family life.*

Hatch, A. (2015). Saying "I don't" to matrimony: An investigation of why long-term heterosexual cohabitors choose not to marry. *Journal of Family Issues,* pp. 1–24.

Heinma, G. (2014). *Asenduskodus elavate laste suhtumine samasooliste paaride lapsendamisõigusesse* [Attitude of the children living at the municipal substitute home towards adoption rights of the same-sex couples]. Unpublished manuscript, University of Tartu.

Henretta, J. C., Van Voorhis, M. F., & Soldo, B. J. (2014). Parental money, help to children and stepchildren. *Journal of Family Issues, 35*(9), 1131–1153.

Hillcoat-Nallétamby, S., & Phillips, J. E. (2011). Sociological ambivalence revisited. *Sociology, 45,* 202–217.

Hogerbrugge, M. J. A., & Dykstra, P. A. (2009). The family ties of unmarried cohabiting and married persons in the Netherlands. *Journal of Marriage and Family, 71*, 135–145.

Jürisoo, K. (2007). *Kooselupaaride nägemus abielust. Estonian Social Science Online.* Retrieved from http://oeiax4.nw.eenet.ee/esso4/20603.pdf

Kalmijn, M., & Uunk, W. (2007). Regional value differences in Europe and the social consequences of divorce: A test of the stigmatization hypothesis. *Social Science Research, 36*, 447–468.

Kantorova, V. (2004). Education and entry into motherhood: The Czech Republic during state socialism and transition period (1970–1997). *Demographic Research, 3*, 246-273.

Kasearu, K. (2009). *Muutuv perekond muutuvas Eestis.* Tartu: Tartu Ülikool, Rahvastikuministri büroo.

Kasearu, K. (2010). Intending to marry ... students' behavioral intentions toward family forming. *Trames. Journal of Humanities and Social Science, 14*, 3–20.

Kasearu, K., & Kutsar, D. (2011). Patterns behind unmarried cohabitation trends in Europe. *European Societies, 13*, 307–325.

Kasearu, K., & Kutsar, D. (2013). Intergenerational solidarity in families: Interplay between the family and the state. In I. Albert & D. Ferring (Eds.), *Intergenerational relations: European perspectives in family and society* (pp. 25–38). Bristol, England: The Policy Press.

Katus, K., Puur, A., Põldma, A., & Sakkeus, L. (2007). First union formation in Estonia, Latvia and Lithuania: Patterns across countries and gender. *Demographic Research, 17*, 247–300.

Kiernan, K. (2001). The rise of cohabitation and childbearing outside marriage in Western-Europe. *International Journal of Law, Policy and the Family, 15*, 1–21.

Kohler, H. P., & Kohler, I. (2002). Fertility decline in Russia in the early and mid-1990s: The role of economic uncertainty and labor market crises. *European Journal of Population, 18*, 233–262.

Kutsar, D. (1997). Multiple welfare losses and risk of social exclusion in the Baltic States during societal transition. In A. Aasland, K. Knudsen, D. Kutsar, & I. Trapenciere (Eds.), *The Baltic countries revisited: Living conditions and comparative challenges* (pp. 79–104). Fafo: Forskningsstiftelsen Fafo.

Kutsar, D., Darmody, M., & Lahesoo, L. (2014). Borders separating families: Children's perspectives of labor migration in Estonia. In S. Spirou & M. Christou (Eds.), *Children and borders* (pp. 261–275). New York, NY: Palgrave Macmillan.

Kutsar, D., Kasearu, K., & Trumm, A. (2015). Local policy making: The playground of ideas, mindsets, strategies and roles. In D. Kutsar & M. Kuronen (Eds.), *Local policy making in European cities* (pp. 87–100). New York, NY: Springer.

Kutsar, D., & Kärner, A. (2010). Exploration of societal transitions in Estonia from the threshold concepts perspective of teaching and learning. In J. H. F. Meyer, R. Land, & C. Baillie (Eds.), *Threshold concepts and transformational learning. Educational futures rethinking theory and practice* (pp. 383–398). Rotterdam, The Netherlands: Sense Publishers.

Kutsar, D., & Tiit, E.-M. (2003). Changing family structures and alternative paths to family formation in Estonia. In M.-T. Letablier & S. Pennec (Eds.), *Changing family structures in Europe: new challenges for public policy* (pp. 52–59). Loughborough: Loughborough University, European Research Centre.

Laes, T.-L., Krusell, S., Reinomägi, A., & Toros, K. (2013). Laps eri ekskkondades [The child in different environments]. In D. Kutsar (Ed.), *Laste heaolu [Child well-being]* (pp. 13–41). Tallinn: Eesti Statistika.

Lauristin, M. (1997). Context of transition. In M. Lauristin, P. Vihalemm, K. E. Rosengren, & L. Weibull (Eds.), *Return to the western world: Cultural and political* perspectives *on the Estonian post-communist transition* (pp. 25–40). Tartu: Tartu University Press.

Lowenstein, A., & Daatland S. (2006). Filial norms and family support in a comparative cross-national context: Evidence from the OASIS study. *Ageing and Society, 26*, 203–223.

Lorenz-Meyer, D. (2004). The ambivalences of parental care among young German adults. In K. Pillemer & K. Lüscher (Eds.), *Intergenerational ambivalences: New perspectives on parent-child relations in later life* (pp. 225–252). New York, NY: Elsevier.

Lüscher, K. (2002). Intergenerational ambivalence: Further steps in theory and research. *Journal of Marriage and Family, 64*, 585–593.

Lüscher, K., & Pillemer, K. (1998). Intergenerational ambivalence: A new approach to the study of parent-child relations in later life. *Journal of Marriage and Family, 60*, 413–425.

Mäenpää, E. (2009). Cohabiting partners' socioeconomic characteristics and the transition to marriage in Finland. *Finnish Yearbook of Population Research Marriage and Family, 66*, 848–861.

Mayer, B., & Trommsdorff, G. (2012). Cross-cultural perspectives on adolescents' religiosity and family orientation. In G. Trommsdorff & X. Chen (Eds.), *Values, religion, and culture in adolescent development* (pp. 341–369). New York. Cambridge University Press.

Merton, R. K. (1976). *Sociological ambivalence and other essays.* New York, NY: The Free Press.

Mitchell, J. M. (2013). *A qualitative investigation of young adult stepchildren's experiences of stepfather's authoirty.* Unpublished doctoral dissertation, Auckland University.

Nazio, T., & Saraceno, C. (2008). *Does cohabitation provide weaker intergenerational bonds than marriage? A comparison between Italy and the United Kingdom.* Paper presented at the meeting of the EQUALSOC, Berlin, Germany.

Nock, S. L. (1995). A comparison of marriages and cohabiting relationships. *Journal of Family Issues, 16*, 53–76.

Nugin, R. (2013). Individualism and its different faces: Some cases from post-socialist Estonia. *Journal of Youth Studies, 16*, 809–829.

Raid, K. (2013). *Kuidas meist sai perekond: Kooselupaaride pereloomelised narratiivid.* Retrievedfromhttp://dspace.utlib.ee/dspace/bitstream/handle/10062/31657/raid_kadri.pdf?sequence=1. Unpublished manuscript, University of Tartu.

Raudsepp, M. (2014). *Välismaal töötavate isade käsitlused kaugisaks olemisest* [Perceptions of fathers working abroad about the role of distance father]. Unpublished manuscript, University of Tartu.

Raudsepp, M., Tart, I., & Heinla, E. (2013). Post-socialist dynamics of value patterns in Estonia. *Studies of Transition States and Societies, 5*(2), 35–52.

Ravanera, Z. R., Rajulton, F., & Burch, T. K. (2004). Patterns of age variability in life course transitions. *Canadian Journal of Sociology, 29,* 527–542.

Rijken, A., & Liefbroer, A. C. (2012). European views of divorce among parents of young children: Understanding cross-national variation. *Demographic Research, 27,* 25–52.

Roots, M. (2010). *Perepiirid laste käsitluses* [Family boundaries: The children's perspectives]. Unpublished manuscript, University of Tartu.

Rowland, D. T. (2007). Historical trends in childlessness. *Journal of Family Issues, 28,* 1311–1337.

Shanahan, M. J. (2000). Pathways to adulthood in changing societies: Variability and mechanisms in life course perspective. *Annual Review of Sociology, 25,* 667–692.

Spanier, G. B., & Lewis, R. A. (1980). Marital quality: A review of the seventies. *Journal of Marriage and Family, 4,* 825–940.

Statistics Estonia. (2015). Retrieved from www.stat.ee

Stewart, S. D. (2005). Boundary ambiguity in stepfamilies. *Journal of Family Issues, 26,* 1002–1029.

Sztompka, P. (2003). *The sociology of social change.* Oxford: Blackwell Publishers.

Sussman, M. B., & Cogswell, B. E. (1972). The meaning of variant and experimental marriage styles and family forms in the 1970s. In M. B. Sussman (Ed.), *Non-traditional family forms in the 1970s* (pp. 7–13). Minneapolis, MN: National Council on Family Relations.

Tanskanen, A. O., Danielsbacka, M., & Rotkirch, A. (2014). Multi-partner fertility is associated with lower grandparental investments from in-laws in Finland. *Advances in Life Course Research.*

Tanturri, M. L., & Mencarini, L. (2008). Childless or childfree? Paths to voluntary childlessness in Italy. *Population and Development Review, 34,* 51–77.

Tanturri, M. L., Mills, M., Rotkirch, A., Sobotka, T., Takács, J., Miettinen, A., & Nasiri, D. (2015). State-of-the-art report: Childlessness in Europe. *Families and Societies.* Working Paper Series 32.

Tarum, H., & Kutsar, D. (2015). The impact of the policy framework on the integration of informal carers into the labour market in Tartu, Estonia. In D. Kutsar & M. Kuronen (Eds.), *Local policy making in European cities* (pp. 195–208). New York, NY: Springer.

Therborn, G. (2004). *Between sex and power: Family in the world 1900–2000.* London, England: Routledge.

Thornton, A., & Philipov, D. (2009). Sweeping changes in marriage, cohabitation and childbearing in Central and Eastern Europe: New insights from the developmental idealism framework. *European Journal of Population, 25,* 123-156.

Wager, M. (2000). I. Childless by choice? Ambivalence and the female identity. *Feminism and Psychology, 10*(3), 389–395.

Weigert, A. J. (1991). *Mixed emotions: Certain steps toward understanding ambivalence.* Albany, NY: State University of New York Press.

Weyman, A., Sackmann, R., & Wingens, M. (1999). Social change and the life course in East Germany: A cohort approach to inequalities. *International Journal of Sociology and Social Policy, 19,* 90–114.

CHAPTER 4

AMBIVALENCE IN THE FAMILY TRANSMISSION OF VALUES

Asumming Similarity and Recognizing Differences

Daniela Barni
LUMSA University of Rome

Silvia Donato
Catholic University of Milan

Over the past few decades, intergenerational relations have received increasing attention because of demographic transformations and changes in family and individual lifestyles (Trommsdorff, 2009). Indeed, in recent years, the field of psychosocial research has seen growing interest in the transmission of values across generations because of the relevance of this process for individual development and for societal functioning (Barni, 2009; Ranieri & Barni, 2012). Viewed as desirable and transsituational goals that serve as guiding

Trans-Generational Family Relations, pages 55–72

standards in life, values are used to characterize individuals and societies, understand the motivational bases of attitudes and behaviors, and explain cultural persistence or change over time (Schwartz, 2005).

One important outcome of the process of value transmission—beyond intergenerational negotiation and mutual influence (Kuczynski & Knafo, 2013)—is the value similarity between parents and their children, i.e., the degree to which parents and children attribute similar importance to several values. Thus, intergenerational transmission can be regarded as the parents' efforts to socialize children with their values and children's perception and acceptance or rejection of these values (Barni, Ranieri, Scabini, & Rosnati, 2011; Grusec & Goodnow, 1994). Parents' influence on children is mediated by parents' and children's complex interactions as agents and it is moderated by changed interpretative processes and relationships (Kuczynski & Parkin, 2007). The parents' choice regarding which values they hold onto and which they allow to be dropped, as well as the child's processing of parental messages, ensure that what the child internalizes is an innovative interpretation rather than a direct copy of the parents' message. Moreover, it is worthwhile noting that beyond parents' efforts, other socialization influences (e.g., horizontal transmission between members of the same generation, such as peers) as well as genetic and environmental influences affect adolescents' value development (e.g., Knafo & Spinath, 2011).

Parents' judgments about their children's attributes influence parenting beliefs and behaviors as well as their effectiveness in socializing children (Barni, Ranieri, Donato, Tagliabue, & Scabini, 2017; Rubin, Nelson, Hastings, & Asendorpf, 1999). In judging their children, parents can be biased as well as accurate. On the one hand, bias in judgments may be beneficial because the belief that one's child is consistent with oneself or one's ideals—no matter how similar to the self or the ideals the child actually is (i.e., assumed similarity)—may foster a higher relationship quality (e.g., Wenger & Fowers, 2008). On the other hand, parents who are accurate in judging their children should be able to match their teaching efforts to their children's cognitive and emotional states, that is, to tailor their disciplinary interventions to the particular states of their children at the time (e.g., Hastings & Grusec, 1997).

Although most studies focus on children's judgments of their parents' values and assess how much they are or are not consistent with parents' reports of their own values (e.g., Knafo & Schwartz, 2009), parents' judgments of their children's values have not received adequate attention thus far. Parents, indeed, may be able to function effectively on a "day-to-day basis" by adjusting bias and accuracy according to their motivations and the state of their relationships. The present chapter will focus specifically on assumed similarity and accuracy in the parents' perspective.

The main goal of this chapter is straightforward: We suggest that bias, in terms of assumed similarity, and accuracy in parents' judgments of their children's values may imply psychological ambivalence,[1] which consists of the parents' individual evaluative tension[2] between assumption of similarity and recognition of possible differences, and intergenerational ambivalence, in terms of the effects of bias and accuracy on the parent–child relationship. The effects of bias and accuracy in fact bear the potential to simultaneously promote and hinder parent–child value transmission. The assumption of similarity can make parents and children feel closer but may diminish parents' motivation to transmit something they feel is already transmitted. Accuracy, in contrast, can guide parents' socialization efforts but can also generate a sense of distance in case of recognized differences between parents and their children. In brief, our innovative proposal is to introduce insights deriving from the interpersonal perception[3] literature into the field of ambivalence research and to document sources of ambivalence (i.e., bias and accuracy) that were not considered by prior ambivalence models.

PARENT–CHILD (VALUE) SIMILARITY IN AMBIVALENCE RESEARCH

Parents and children always share a certain degree of similarity due to biological inheritance and socialization processes (Grusec & Kuczynski, 1997; Lüscher, 1998). Parent–child similarity has been shown to be important in understanding the development and maintenance of close relationships throughout the life course: Parents tend to have closer and more supportive relationships with children who share their social structural positions (Kaufman & Uhlenberg, 1998; Pillemer & Suitor, 2002) and values (Pillemer & Suitor, 2002; Suitor & Pillemer, 2006). Parent–child value similarity reduces value-related conflict, anxiety, and feelings of rejection, and it is likely to enhance parents' and children's well-being (Knafo & Assor, 2007). In fact, such similarity is one of the core components of model of intergenerational solidarity discussed by Bengtson (2001).

Ambivalence research was traditionally interested in parent–child (value) similarity because it can generate a paradox between closeness and distance: "The similarity is also reinforced by the intimacy of mutual learning processes. They contain a potential for closeness (. . .). At the same time, especially by growing older, the similarity is also cause of and reason for distancing (. . .)" (Lüscher, 1998, p. 15). In Lüscher's (2002) heuristic model, at the micro level, each family can be conceived as an emotional unit that contains the potential for closeness and subjective identification, reinforcing similarity between children and their parents. On the one hand, similarity and closeness are psychologically gratifying; on the other hand, they can also be experienced by family members as a threat to individuality. Thus, family members are motivated to keep the unit's cohesion, but they also seek separation and individuality. In value transmission, especially from adolescence, parents need to permit children to form their own separate views while communicating and reinforcing the values and perspectives parents endorse (Barni et al., 2011).

In our opinion, however, ambivalence research—and sometimes value transmission research as well—has oversimplified the issue of parent–child value similarity. For instance, it has not distinguished between parent–child actual similarity and assumed similarity, although the "relational meaning" of them can be different. In addition, it has never analyzed the mechanisms underlying judgments and potentially leading to similarity versus differences.

BIAS AND ACCURACY

In general, the term *interpersonal perceptions* refers to the relation between partners' judgments of one another (Sillars & Scott, 1983). Whereas person perception involves the study of one person's judgment of another, interpersonal perception involves the study of a relation between judgments. For example, although parents' judgment of the values their children hold as important refers to the parents' personal perception of their children's values, the degree of similarity between the parents' judgment and their children's self-reported values is a measure of parents' interpersonal perception (in this case, of parents' accuracy in perceiving children's values).

Bias in interpersonal perceptions has been defined in different ways, with different meanings and measures. In particular, two broad types of bias have mainly been investigated in the literature: the so-called directional bias and the concept of bias as variable (West & Kenny, 2011). Directional bias (or mean-level or positivity bias; Kunda, 1990) refers to how attracted judges are toward one end of the judgment scale. For example, we show a directional bias if we judge our partners as more attractive than he or she considers him or herself to be (Boyes & Fletcher, 2007).

Although research has documented significant levels of directional bias in intimate relationships across several domains of judgments (e.g., Fletcher & Kerr, 2010), in this chapter, we are not going to focus on this type of bias but instead focus on the second broad category of bias: bias as variable, that is, bias as the association between the individual's judgment of a close other's attribute or behavior and any factor influencing such a judgment, other than what is supposed to be the other person's true attribute or behavior. The judge's own attributes/behaviors, for example, are one of the most common factors influencing his or her judgment of close others. Research has shown in fact that we tend to project our own attributes/behaviors onto our partners, judging them as more similar to ourselves than they actually are (e.g., Kenny & Acitelli, 2001). Moreover, parents tend to project their attributes onto their children regardless of the level of actual similarity (Whitbeck & Gecas, 1988), and children judge themselves as more similar to their parents than to other nonsignificant adults (Ward & Day, 1969).

Overall, projecting the self onto a relationship partner seems to offer a way for people to affirm their positive views about themselves (Taylor & Brown, 1988) while also feeling closer to the other (Aron, Aron, Tudor, & Nelson, 1991). It is important to note that projection or assumed similarity is considered a bias only when exceeding actual similarity and that assumed similarity can also lead to accuracy. That is, if parents assume that they are similar to their children when in fact they are similar, their judgments of their children will be accurate.

Accuracy is normally defined in the interpersonal perception literature as the association, typically a correlation, between a judgment (or set of judgments) and a relevant benchmark for reality/truth (or set of benchmarks). The most frequent benchmarks used in the literature are target's self-reports of the attributes or behaviors judged by the perceiver[4] (Gagné & Lydon, 2004; Iafrate, Bertoni, Barni, & Donato, 2009), and this is the truth criterion most frequently used in studies on parent–child accuracy as well (Barni, Ranieri, Ferrari, Danioni & Rosnati, 2016; Knafo & Schwartz, 2003b).

Different types of accuracy have been investigated in the research on interpersonal perceptions. A relevant distinction in the literature is the one between what is called stereotypical accuracy and unique accuracy (Cronbach, 1955; Kenny & Acitelli, 1994). This means that accuracy due to the fact that one knows how people generally are or behave in some situations should be distinguished from accuracy due to the fact that one actually knows how his or her specific relationship partner is or behaves in some situations. For example, a parent's judgment of his or her child as a kind person may match the one of the child (may be accurate), not only because that parent knows his or her child's specific kindness (unique accuracy), but also because the parent has some knowledge of how kind children are in general (in his or her cultural context) (stereotype accuracy). Another distinction is between perceptive and expressive accuracy (Biesanz, 2010), that is, accuracy due to the fact that the judge is good at recognizing the others' attributes (he or she has motivations and skills to do so) is distinct from accuracy due to the fact that the other is a particularly good target (e.g., he or she expresses his or her emotions quite openly or communicates explicitly his or her feelings and thoughts).

Most literature on interpersonal perceptions has focused on the issue of the relation between bias and accuracy in close relationships and the consequences of bias and accuracy for the relationship. Translated into the ambivalence research, such issues refer, on the one hand, to the existence of a psychological ambivalence in parents' judgments of their children and the

TABLE 4.1 Bias and Accuracy: Motives and Effects

	Definition	Motive	Effect
Bias (Assumed similarity)	Tendency for judges (e.g., parents) to assume that the target (e.g., children) is similar to themselves or to their ideals.	Parents' need to maintain or enhance positive beliefs about the self, the child, or the relationship (esteem needs).	Overly positive judgments of one's children are the hallmark of strong and satisfying relationships.
Accuracy	Correspondence between a judgment (e.g., by parents) and a truth criterion (e.g., the children's self-report).	Parents' need to accurately understand the child to make predictions or important decisions or to understand or control a relational phenomenon (epistemic needs).	Children are happier in their relationships when they believe their parents know their true selves yet accept them nonetheless.

motives underneath such ambivalence and, on the other hand, to the existence of an intergenerational ambivalence in parent–child transmission of values, driven by the effects that bias and accuracy have on the parent–child relationship (Table 4.1).

PSYCHOLOGICAL AMBIVALENCE: MOTIVES TO BIAS AND ACCURACY IN CLOSE RELATIONSHIPS

With regard to psychological ambivalence, parents are both biased and accurate when judging their children's attributes. Although bias and accuracy cannot be directly compared, bias usually appears to be larger than accuracy (West, 2008). As interdependence is a key aspect of close relationships and close relationship partners' outcomes are interconnected (Tagliabue & Lanz, 2014), parents need to project a positive image of themselves by construing a positive view of their children and their relationship. Close relationship partners should then be motivated to see their close ones in the best light and to protect them by overestimating their good qualities and underestimating their faults. For example, research has shown that romantic partners are actually positively biased in the judgments of their partners and their relationship, as they, routinely rate the chances of their own marriages failing as considerably less than their judgments of the population base rates (Fowers, Lyons, Montel, & Shaked, 2001), or they tend to see their relationship as better than the one of the average other (e.g., Martz et al., 1998). In addition, parents tend to assume much greater similarity between themselves or their ideals and their children than in fact exists

(Gecas & Schwalbe, 1986). In their study involving parents and adolescents and relying on Schwartz's (1992) value theory, Barni and colleagues (2016) showed that parents' judgments of their children's values were largely related to and explained by the values parents would like to find in their children (i.e., socialization values).

Parents, however, are also reasonably accurate when judging their children (Barni et al., 2016). A broad array of empirical evidence suggests that lay judgments of close others and relationships are firmly tied to reality. Studies using a range of external criteria or benchmarks (including target's self-reports, observer ratings of interactive behavior, and the predicted future or recalled past states of the relationship) reveal quite good levels of accuracy in relationship and partner judgments (for a review, see Fletcher & Boyes, 2008; Fletcher & Kerr, 2010). For example, parents (especially mothers) were found to predict their children's responses to problem checklists with accuracy greater than chance (Glascoe & Dworkin, 1995; Wakefield, 1970). Parents' reports of their children's development problems are predictive of developmental delays and the use of parent-completed questionnaires is a useful way to monitor children's development (Bricker & Squires, 1989).

In summary, bias cannot be simply equated with inaccuracy so that accuracy is to be considered the absence of bias and vice versa. Rather, people can be both biased and accurate. In fact, several theoretical and empirical reviews have demonstrated that this is often the case (Fletcher & Kerr, 2010; Luo & Snider, 2009). Moreover, bias and accuracy may show changeable associations: they may be negatively correlated in some circumstances but positively correlated or independent in other cases. For example, in close relationships, closeness motivates judges to see their partners in the best possible light or to view them as similar to themselves and to want to understand their partners (Gagné & Lydon, 2004; Murray, 1999); that is, it motivates them to be biased and accurate at the same time. However, lack of information or threat can affect bias and accuracy in opposite directions, leading them to be negatively correlated. In threatening situations, for example, when the self or the relationship is at stake, bias may be negatively related to accuracy and then more bias may be associated with less accuracy and vice versa. Consider, for example, a study by West and Kenny (2011) in which mothers were judging their children's cheating behaviors at school. In cases where mothers reported they would be particularly hurt by discovering such behaviors in their children (in case of high threat), they were more biased in seeing their children as less cheating than they actually reported to be and were less accurate in their judgment of their children's cheating behaviors.

Indeed, bias and accuracy are subject to different types of evaluative motives—one more esteem-regulatory (theory-driven) and the other more epistemic (data-driven) in nature—that can be activated by different situations (Gagné & Lydon, 2004). According to close relationship lay theories (see Fletcher & Fitness, 1996), when individuals are motivated by esteem needs (i.e., the need to maintain or enhance positive beliefs about the self, target, or relationship), their evaluations may be more biased. A bias can represent an attempt by a judge "to fill in the blanks" when there is not enough information to make a judgment. Alternatively, a bias can represent a motive or goal that the judge has and that is imposed on reality. Differently, when individuals have access to information and are motivated by epistemic needs (i.e., need to accurately understand the target to make predictions or important decisions), their evaluations should be more accurate.

INTERGENERATIONAL AMBIVALENCE: EFFECTS OF BIAS AND ACCURACY IN CLOSE RELATIONSHIPS

A paradox exists in the formula for a healthy, functioning relationship. On the one hand, evidence demonstrates that bias can be the hallmark of strong and satisfying relationships. Some argue, in fact, that optimistic judgments are necessary to maintain a sense of conviction and security within couple relationships (Murray, Holmes, & Griffin, 1996) and that seeing the partner in a positive light is important for relationship functioning (e.g., Murray, Holmes, Bellavia, Griffin, & Dolderman, 2002; Wenger & Fowers, 2008). Assumed similarity in particular was found to promote feelings of connection between caring partners, the belief that the other will be there for them in times of need (Lemay, Pruchno, & Field, 2006). Partners more prone to project their own responsiveness onto the partner are also more likely to evaluate the partner positively, be supportive toward him or her, and be more satisfied with their relationship (Lemay & Clark, 2008; Lemay, Clark, & Feeney, 2007). Assumed similarity between parents and children was also found to be higher in well-adjusted dyads than in maladjusted ones (Manis, 1958), and it is likely to enhance relationship functioning, especially (but not exclusively) for parents. Adolescents' judgment of similarity with parents was also found to be positively related to their reported closeness to parents (Knafo & Schwartz, 2003a).

However, researchers have often hypothesized that higher accuracy should be associated with more relationship satisfaction. Accurately perceiving the partner's qualities, in fact, can be important to enhance couples' felt understanding (Murray, 1999) and relationship satisfaction (Iafrate, Bertoni, Donato, & Finkenauer, 2012), and it is a practical necessity for communication in everyday life (Wilhelm & Perrez, 2004). In parent–child relationships, accuracy of communication was generally found to be positively related to children's cognitive development (Dickson, 1980), and children are happier in the relationship when they believe their parents know their true selves and yet accept them nonetheless (Wenger & Fowers, 2008).

Overall, without positive bias, it could be difficult for parents to maintain the conviction that the relationship is good and worth pursuing. Assumed similarity creates the foundation for the basic ingredients of intimacy. After all, people are less likely to argue about differences if they feel the differences as less serious than they are. Conversely, ignoring epistemic needs for accuracy may lead to poor decision making, poor communication, and lack of understanding between parents and children. Failure to realistically consider and make use of disagreements and negative feedback about the relationship could set people up for disappointment and regret in the long run.

BIAS AND ACCURACY IN PARENTS' JUDGMENTS OF CHILDREN'S VALUES

What happens in the transmission of values between parents and children? To what extent are parents biased in judging their children's values? And accurate? In the first study attempting to answer these questions, Whitbeck and Gecas (1988) reported a considerable degree of misperception on the part of parents as well as of children, given their propensity to assume similarity between their reciprocal values. Interestingly, assumed similarity enhanced parental behaviors of support and inductive control (i.e., parents' use of reasoning or discussion about behaviors with the intent of obtaining children's voluntary compliance), which in turn affected similarity to parents' values assumed by children but not their actual similarity. In other words, bias alone appears to be insufficient to ensure value transmission, but it turns out to be positively related to good interactions between parents and their children. Parent–child value transmission was instead supported by children's accurate reports of parents' values, which thus turned out to be more effective in actual transmission than parents' and children's biases did. No data, however, were collected about parents' accuracy in judging their children's values.

Parents' accuracy in judging their children's values was instead measured in one of our recent studies (Barni, Ranieri, Rosnati, & Ferrari, 2014), carried out on a large sample of Italian family triads (i.e., composed of the father, mother, and one adolescent child ages 14–18) and based on Schwartz's (1992) value theory. The study analyzed parents' judgments of their adolescent children's values and aimed to reveal the extent to which parents' assumed similarity and accuracy were related to effectiveness in value transmission (i.e., parent–child value actual similarity) and children's behavioral difficulties (i.e., conduct problems; Goodman, 1997). On average, fathers and mothers were quite accurate in reporting their children's values. In fathers' and mothers' judgments, their children gave the greatest importance to self-transcendence values (i.e., universalism and benevolence), which emphasize concern for the welfare and interests of others, followed by conservation values (i.e., tradition, conformity, and security) and self-determination. The least important value was power, which emphasizes the control or dominance over people and resources at the expense of interpersonal relationships. Both parents, however, were guided in their judgments more by their own personal values than by their children's actual values, that is, children were judged as having values similar to those of parents. Thus, parents were both biased and accurate in judgments of their children's values, although more biased than accurate.

Bias and accuracy had specific relations with the outcome of value transmission and children's adjustment (Barni et al., 2014). In particular, both bias and accuracy enhanced parent–child value similarity. However, assumed similarity, measured in terms of correspondence between parents' own personal values and their perceptions of their children's values, was slightly stronger in promoting actual similarity between parents' and children's values than accuracy was. As far as children's adjustment—as rated by parents—was concerned, assumed similarity was more strongly associated with this outcome: The more parents judged their children's values as being close to their own personal values, regardless of the actual similarity, the less children were judged by parents as having behavioral difficulties (Table 4.2).

Thus, from Barni and colleagues' (2014) study, it emerged that parents were motived in value transmission mainly by the need to maintain a positive view of themselves, their children, and their relationship. This finding was also highlighted by Whitbeck and Gecas (1988). Parents could receive a confirmation of themselves as "being good parents" and of the relationship with their children as satisfying by judging "similar-to-them children" as better-adjusted (Human & Biesanz, 2011). In other words, in the value transmission, parents negotiate the dialectical motives of wanting to feel good in the relationship with their children and wanting to understand their children's values, generally fulfilling their esteem needs more than

TABLE 4.2 Zero-Order Correlations Between Parents' Assumed Similarity, Accuracy, Parent–Child Value Similarity, and Children's Behavioral Difficulties

	Parent–Child Value Similarity	Children's Behavioral Difficulties
Fathers' assumed similarity	.38*	–.39*
Fathers' accuracy	.24*	–.08
Mothers' assumed similarity	.36*	–.38*
Mothers' accuracy	.22*	–.21*

* $p < .01$

their epistemic needs. From an intergenerational perspective, both assumed similarity and accuracy give their positive contribution to transmission by promoting value similarity, although it is mostly assumed similarity by parents to sustain their perceptions of children's well-being.

CONCLUSIONS

In this chapter, we focused on parents' bias (i.e., assumed similarity) and accuracy in judging their children's values as possible sources of psychological and intergenerational ambivalence. Parents, indeed, experience competing needs in judging their children, as both bias and accuracy have effects on the parent–child relationship. The perception of value similarity can make parents and children feel closer but may diminish parents' motivation to transmit something they feel it is already transmitted. Accuracy, in contrast, can make parents' socialization efforts more effective, but it can also generate a sense of distance in case of recognized differences between them and their children.

The ambivalence framework specifically contributes to recognition of the need to stop thinking of bias and accuracy in a dualistic manner and to start thinking about them in a dialectical fashion (Baxter & Montgomery, 1996). Oppositional tendencies presuppose the existence of the other for its meaning, and the interplay between opposing forces is what distinguishes a dialectical perspective from a dualistic perspective.

At the same time, the interpersonal perception literature contributes to specify the role of ambivalence in family relationships. Bias and accuracy coexist in the judgment of others, and the concept of bias is meaningful only because accuracy exists and vice versa. The coexistence of bias and accuracy creates the potential for change in social reality. If judges were totally biased or totally accurate, then the change would be impossible: Thanks to bias and accuracy between parents and children, a continuous negotiation occurs as to what the target (or the relation with him or her) is like. This finding is consistent with contemporary research on value transmission: Transmission is an ongoing and bidirectional process that involves more than a simple reproduction of parents' personal values in their children. Parents and children are assumed to have inherent capacities for initiating action, making sense of their interactions with each other, and choosing (for a review, see Kuczynski & Navara, 2006).

Parents heavily invest in transmitting values to their children, and most parents want their children to develop values similar to their own. From their part, children can influence their parents and accept or reject parents' values, but they always need to feel that their parents respect their attempts to form values in exploratory and autonomous ways (Knafo & Assor, 2007).

Thus, in this specific area, the judgments of the other's perspective become critical, and difference is often thought to provide the most potential for conflict (Brehm, 1992). At the same time, however, the assumption of similarity between parents and children creates the relational prerequisites, in terms of closeness and acceptance, for conflict resolution. We believe that the tension between bias and accuracy in this context is functional to allow both continuity and innovation.

Extending the analysis of bias and accuracy to other "objects," beyond values, may be of interest for ambivalence research in the future. For example, given and received support are usually subject to bias: Parents and children tend to overreport given help and underreport received help, especially where there are strong feelings of family obligations (Madenmakers & Dykstra, 2008). Parents may do so to maintain a positive view of their relationship, whereas children may do so to self-enhance or contrast their sense of dependency from parents. Relationship partners, however, are also motivated to judge their given and received support accurately. Partners' reported support behaviors, in fact, were found to be accurately reflected, even beyond the effect of bias, in the other partner's perception of the support he or she received (Donato et al., 2015). Relationship partners may do so to facilitate coordination in their interactions and to feel confident about the predictability of the other's behaviors.

Moreover, because ambivalence research has always been interested in later-life families and caregiving, future research should analyze the effects of bias and accuracy by adopting a lifespan development perspective. Near the end of life, people indeed often become too old or sick to make their own decisions; in many cases, a surrogate decision maker, usually the partner or an adult child, is called on to make decisions using the judgment of the partner/parent's needs and wanting as standards for substituted judgment and, at the same time, is called on to take care of the relationship (Hopp, 2000).

"Ambivalence refers to experiences that occur while searching for the significance of facts, events, other persons, social relationships (. . .) These experiences thereby oscillate temporarily or permanently between polar contradictions in feeling, thinking, wanting (. . .)" (Lüscher & Hoff, 2013, p. 54), and we can now add "in judging close others." The trade-off between bias and accuracy in the parent–child relationship contains tendencies for ambivalences and, at the same time, is a rather sophisticated way to deal with them by activating permanent negotiation processes.

NOTES

1. We refer here to the potential occurrence of ambivalence rather than to the actual subjective experience of ambivalence. Both meanings are used in the

ambivalence literature (e.g., DeMarree, Wheeler, Brinol, & Petty, 2014), and it could also be that sources of ambivalence may lead to the subjective experience of ambivalence.

2. Consistent with the notion of bidirectionality in value transmission (e.g., Pinquart & Silbereisen, 2004), both parents' and children's judgments are likely to be subject to a similar tension. Throughout the chapter, we focus on the parents' perspective and judgments, which were the least investigated in the relevant literature. However, interest is growing in parents' perceptions of their children, such that these perceptions have been cited by researchers as evocative influences on parenting beliefs and behaviors, as well as on the parent–child relationship (Rubin et al., 1999). We are aware that in intergenerational relations, different goals and motivations exist depending on the generational position of family members (see e.g., the intergenerational stake hypothesis; Bengtson & Kuypers, 1971), and therefore the same evaluative tension in children (vs. parents) may have different sources and effects. For example, Albert, Ferring, and Michels (2013) found different results depending on the mothers' or daughters' perspective with regard to interconnections of value similarity with other aspects of intergenerational solidarity. This is, however, beyond the scope of the present chapter, which is especially focused on parents' perspective for the reasons mentioned previously. Future work should be devoted to compare sources and effects of psychological and intergenerational ambivalence in children and parents.
3. In the present chapter, we use the term *interpersonal perceptions* with reference to the individual's judgments about another person's attributes. We are aware that perceptions and judgments are not synonyms and that judgments involve an additional level of cognitive elaboration of stimuli than perceptions. Nonetheless, we kept the use of interpersonal perceptions whenever referring to the relevant literature, given the widespread and common use of such a term (e.g., Kenny, Kashy, & Cook, 2006).
4. Although the target's self-reports can be biased as well and therefore be a less-than-ideal truth criterion, other apparently more objective benchmarks also have their own faults: Third-party observations (family and friends), for example, can be biased because people tend to protect their relationships by undervaluing others. Trained coders can be biased because of lack of knowledge on specific meanings of interactions and exposure to a limited amount of targets' behaviors (Gagné & Lydon, 2004). Experimental tasks cannot be informative of the veracity of people's judgments in everyday life. Depending on the theory and truth criterion used, different types of accuracy questions can be formulated. When using the target's self-reports as criteria for the truth, for example, the question we are interested in is the judge's ability to detect the target's subjective experience.

REFERENCES

Albert, I., Ferring, D., & Michels, T. (2013). Intergenerational family relations in Luxembourg: Family values and intergenerational solidarity in Portuguese immigrant and Luxembourgish families. *European Psychologist, 18*(1), 59–69.

Aron, A., Aron, E. N., Tudor, M., & Nelson, G. (1991). Close relationships as including other in the self. *Journal of Personality and Social Psychology, 60*(2), 241–253.

Barni, D. (2009). *Trasmette re valori. Tre generazioni familiari a confronto* [Transmitting values. A comparison among three family generations]. Milano: Unicopli.

Barni, D., Ranieri, S., Donato, S., Tagliabue, S., & Scabini, E. (2017). Personal and family sources of parents' socialization values: A multilevel study. *Avances en Psicología Latinoamericana, 35*(1), 9–22.

Barni, D., Ranieri, S., Ferrari, L., Danioni, F., & Rosnati, R. (2016). Parents' perceptions of their adolescent children's personal values: Truth or bias? *Journal of Family Studies.* Advance online publication. doi:10.1080/13229400.2016.1259120

Barni, D., Ranieri, S., Rosnati, R., & Ferrari, L. (2014, July 15–19). *"Not me, but like me": Parents' accuracy and projection in perceiving adolescent children's values.* Paper presented at the XXII International Congress of IACCP, Reims.

Barni, D., Ranieri, S., Scabini, E., & Rosnati, R. (2011). Value transmission in the family: Do adolescents accept the values their parents want to transmit? *Journal of Moral Education, 40*(1), 105–121.

Baxter, L. A., & Montgomery, B. M. (1996). *Relating: Dialogues and dialectics.* New York, NY: Guilford Press.

Bengtson, V. L. (2001). Beyond the nuclear family: The increasing importance of multigenerational bonds. *Journal of Marriage and Family, 63*(1), 1–16.

Bengtson, V. L., & Kuypers, J. A. (1971). Generational difference and the developmental stake. *Aging and Human Development, 2*(4), 249–260.

Biesanz, J. C. (2010). The social accuracy model of interpersonal perception: Assessing individual differences in perceptive and expressive accuracy. *Multivariate Behavioral Research, 45*(5), 853–885.

Boyes, A. D., & Fletcher, G. J. O. (2007). Meta-awareness of bias in intimate relationships. *Journal of Personality and Social Psychology, 92*(2), 286–306.

Brehm, S. S. (1992). *Intimate relationships.* New York, NY: McGraw Hill.

Bricker, D., & Squires, J. (1989). The effectiveness of parental screening of at risk infants: The infant monitoring questionnaires. *Topics and Early Childhood Special Education, 9*(3), 67–85.

Cronbach, L. J. (1955). Processes affecting scores on "understanding of others" and "assumed similarity." *Psychological Bulletin, 50,* 456–473.

DeMarree, K. G., Wheeler, S. C., Brinol, P., & Petty, R. E. (2014). Wanting other attitudes: Actual-desired attitude discrepancies predict feelings of ambivalence and ambivalence consequences. *Journal of Experimental Social Psychology, 53,* 5–18.

Dickson, W. P. (1980). Accuracy versus style of communication in parent–child interaction. *International Journal of Psycholinguistic, 7*(1–2), 119–130.

Donato, S., Parise, M., Iafrate, R., Bertoni, A., Finkenauer, C., & Bodenmann, G. (2015). Dyadic coping responses and partners' perceptions for couple satisfaction: An actor–partner interdependence analysis. *Journal of Social and Personal Relationships, 32*(5), 580–600.

Fletcher, G. J. O., & Boyes, A. (2008). Is love blind? Reality and illusion in intimate relationships. In J. Forgas & J. Fitness (Eds.), *Social relationships: Cognitive, affective and motivational processes* (pp. 101–114). New York, NY: Cambridge University Press.

Fletcher, G. J. O., & Fitness, J. (Eds.). (1996). *Knowledge structures and interaction in close relationships: A social psychological approach.* Hillsdale, NJ: Erlbaum.

Fletcher, G. J. O., & Kerr, P. S. G. (2010). Through the eyes of love: Reality and illusion in intimate relationships. *Psychological Bulletin, 136*(4), 627–658.

Fowers, B. J., Lyons, E., Montel, K., & Shaked, N. (2001). Positive illusions about marriage among married and single individuals. *Journal of Family Psychology, 15*(1), 95–109.

Gagné, F. M., & Lydon, J. (2004). Bias and accuracy in close relationships: An integrative review. *Personality and Social Psychology Review, 8*(4), 322–338.

Gecas, V. L., & Schwalbe, M. L. (1986). Parental behavior and adolescent self-esteem. *Journal of Marriage and Family, 48*(1), 37–46.

Glascoe, F. P., & Dworkin, P. (1995). The role of parents in the detection of developmental and behavioral problems. *Pediatrics, 95*(6), 829–836.

Goodman, R. (1997). The strengths and difficulties questionnaire: A research note. *Journal of Child Psychology and Psychiatry, 38*(5), 581–586.

Grusec, J. E., Goodnow, J. J. (1994). Impact on parental discipline methods on the child's internalization of values: A reconceptualization of current points of view. *Developmental Psychology, 30*(1), 4–19.

Grusec, J. E., & Kuczynski, L. (1997). *Parenting and children's internalization of values: A handbook of contemporary theory.* New York, NY: Wiley

Hastings, P., & Grusec, J. E. (1997). Conflict outcomes as a function of parental accuracy in perceiving child cognitions and affect. *Social Development, 6*(1), 76–90.

Hopp, F. (2000). Preferences for surrogate decision makers, informal communication and advance directives among community-dwelling elders: Results from a national study. *The Gerontologist, 40*(4), 449–457.

Human, L. J., & Biesanz, J. C. (2011). Target adjustment and self-other agreement: Utilizing trait observability to disentangle judgeability and self-knowledge. *Journal of Personality and Social Psychology, 101*(1), 202–216.

Iafrate, R., Bertoni, A., Barni, D., & Donato, S. (2009). Congruenza percettiva nella coppia e stili di coping diadico [Perceptual congruence within the couple and dyadic coping styles]. *Psicologia Sociale, 1,* 95–114.

Iafrate, R., Bertoni, A., Donato, S., & Finkenauer, C. (2012). Perceived similarity and understanding in dyadic coping among young and mature couples. *Personal Relationships, 19*(3), 401–419.

Kaufman, G., & Uhlenberg, P. (1998). Effects of life course transitions on the quality of relationships between adult children and their parents. *Journal of Marriage and Family, 60*(4), 924–938.

Kenny, D. A., & Acitelli, L. K. (1994). Measuring similarity in couples. *Journal of Family Psychology, 8*(4), 417-431.

Kenny, D. A., & Acitelli, L. K. (2001). Accuracy and bias in the perception of the partner in a close relationship. *Journal of Personality and Social Psychology, 80*(3), 439–448.

Kenny, D. A., Kashy, D. A., & Cook, W. L. (2006). *Dyadic data analysis.* New York, NY: Guilford Press.

Knafo, A., & Assor, A. (2007). Motivation for agreement with parental values: Desirable when autonomous, problematic when controlled. *Motivation and Emotion, 31*(3), 232–245.

Knafo, A., & Schwartz, S. H. (2003a). Culture-appropriate parenting and value transmission in families of Israeli-born, Soviet-born adolescents in Israel. In T. Horowitz, S. Hoffman, & B. Kotik-Friedgut (Eds.), *From pacesetters to dropouts: Post-Soviet youth in comparative perspective* (pp. 69–88). New York, NY: The Rowan and Littlefield Publishers.

Knafo, A., & Schwartz, S. H. (2003b). Parenting and adolescent's accuracy in perceiving parental values. *Child Development, 74*(2), 595–611.

Knafo, A., & Schwartz, S. H. (2009). Accounting for parent-child value congruence: Theoretical considerations and empirical evidence. In U. Schönpflug (Ed.), *Cultural transmission: Psychological, developmental, social, and methodological aspects* (pp. 240–268). New York, NY: Cambridge University Press.

Knafo, A., & Spinath, F. M. (2011). Genetic and environmental influences on girls' and boys' gender-typed and gender-neutral values. *Developmental Psychology, 47*(3), 726–731.

Kuczynski, L., & Knafo, A. (2013). Innovation and continuity in socialization, internalization and acculturation. In M. Killen & J. G. Smetana (Eds.), *Handbook of moral development* (2nd ed., pp. 93–112). New York, NY: Taylor and Francis Publishers.

Kuczynski, L., & Navara, G. S. (2006). Sources of innovation and change in socialization, internalization and acculturation. In M. Killen & J. G. Smetana (Eds.), *Handbook of moral development* (pp. 299–327). Mahwah, NJ: Erlbaum.

Kuczynski, L., & Parkin, M. (2007). Agency and bidirectionality in socialization: Interactions, transactions, and relational dialectics. In J. E. Grusec & P. Hastings (Eds.), *Handbook of socialization* (pp. 259–283). New York, NY: Guilford Press.

Kunda, Z. (1990). The case for motivated reasoning. *Psychological Bulletin, 108*(3), 480–498.

Lemay, E. P., & Clark, M.S. (2008). How the head liberates the heart: Projection of communal responsiveness guides relationship promotion. *Journal of Personality and Social Psychology, 94*(4), 647–671.

Lemay, E. P., Clark, M. S., & Feeney, B. C. (2007). Projection of responsiveness to needs and the construction of satisfying communal relationships. *Journal of Personality and Social Psychology, 92*(5), 834–853.

Lemay, E. P., Pruchno, R. A., & Field, L. (2006). Accuracy and bias in perceptions of spouses' life sustaining medical treatment preference. *Journal of Applied Social Psychology, 36*(10), 2337–2362.

Luo, S., & Snider, A. G. (2009). Accuracy and biases in newlyweds' perceptions of each other: Not mutually exclusive but mutually beneficial. *Psychological Science, 20*(11), 1332–1339.

Lüscher, K. (1998, July). *A heuristic model for the study of intergenerational ambivalence.* Paper presented at the XV Biennial Meeting International Society for the Study of Behavioral Development, Berne.

Lüscher, K. (2002). Intergenerational ambivalence: Further steps in theory and research. *Journal of Family and Marriage, 64*(3), 585–593.

Lüscher, K., & Hoff, A. (2013). Intergenerational ambivalence: Beyond solidarity and conflict. In I. Albert & D. Ferring (Eds.), *Intergenerational relations: European perspectives in family and society* (pp. 39–63). Bristol: Policy Press.

Madenmakers, J. J., & Dykstra, P. A. (2008). Discrepancies in parent's and adult child's reports of support and contact. *Journal of Marriage and Family, 70*(2), 495–506.

Manis, M. (1958). Personal adjustment, assumed similarity to parents, and inferred parental-evaluations of the self. *Journal of Consulting Psychology, 22*(6), 481–485.

Martz, J. M., Verette, J., Arriaga, X. B., Slovik, L. F., Cox, C. L., & Rusbult, C. E. (1998). Positive illusion in close relationship. *Personal Relationships, 5*(2), 159–181.

Murray, S. L. (1999). The quest for conviction: Motivated cognition in romantic relationships. *Psychological Inquiry, 10*(1), 23–34.

Murray, S. L., Holmes, G. J., Bellavia, G., Griffin, D. W., & Dolderman, D. (2002). Kindred spirits? The benefits of egocentrism in close relationships. *Journal of Personality and Social Psychology, 82*(4), 563–581.

Murray, S. L., Holmes, J. G., & Griffin, D. W. (1996). The benefits of positive illusions: Idealization and the construction of satisfaction in close relationships. *Journal of Personality and Social Psychology, 70*(1), 79–98.

Pillemer, K., & Suitor, J. J. (2002). Explaining mothers' ambivalence toward their adult children. *Journal of Marriage and Family, 64*(3), 602–613.

Pinquart, M., & Silbereisen, R. K. (2004). Transmission of values from adolescents to their parents: The role of value content and authoritative parenting. *Adolescence, 39*(153), 83–100.

Ranieri, S., & Barni, D. (2012). Family and other social contexts in the intergenerational transmission of values. *Family Science, 3*(1), 1–3.

Rubin, K. H., Nelson, L. J., Hastings, P., & Asendorpf, J. (1999). The transaction between parents' perceptions of their children's shyness and their parenting styles. *International Journal of Behavioral Development, 23*(4), 937–957.

Schwartz, S. H. (1992). Universals in the content and structure of values: Theoretical advances and empirical tests in 20 countries. In M. P. Zanna (Ed.), *Advances in experimental social psychology* (Vol. 25, pp. 1–65). New York, NY: Academic Press.

Schwartz, S. H. (2005). Basic human values: Their content and structure across countries. In A. Tamayo & J. B. Porto (Eds.), *Valores e comportamento nas organizações* (pp. 21–55). Petrópolis, Brazil: Vozes.

Sillars, A. L., & Scott, M. D. (1983). Interpersonal perceptions between intimates: An integrative review. *Human Communication Research, 10*(1), 153–176.

Suitor, J. J., & Pillemer, K. (2006). Choosing daughters: Exploring why mothers favor adult daughters over sons. *Sociological Perspectives, 49*(2), 139–160.

Tagliabue, S., & Lanz, M. (2014). Exploring social and personal relationships: The issue of measurement invariance of non-independent observations. *European Journal of Social Psychology, 44*(7), 683–690.

Taylor, S. E., & Brown, J. D. (1988). Illusions and well-being: A social psychological perspective on mental health. *Psychological Bulletin, 103*(2), 193–210.

Trommsdorff, G. (2009). Intergenerational relations and cultural transmission. In U. Schönpflug (Ed.), *Cultural transmission: Psychological, developmental, social, and methodological aspects* (pp. 126–160). New York, NY: Cambridge University Press.

Wakefield, W. M. (1970). Awareness, affection, and perceived similarity in the parent-child relationship. *The Journal of Genetic Psychology: Research and Theory on Human Development, 117*(1), 91–97.

Ward, W. D., & Day, C. R. (1969). Perceived similarity to parents as compared to perceived similarity to other adults. *Perceptual and Motor Skills, 29*(3), 739–742.

Wenger, A., & Fowers, B. J. (2008). Positive illusions in parenting: Every child is above average. *Journal of Applied Social Psychology, 38*(3), 611–634.

West, T. V. (2008). *Four principles in the study of bias and accuracy in close relationships.* Unpublished doctoral dissertation. Retrieved from http://digitalcommons.uconn.edu/dissertations/AAI3325630

West, T. V., & Kenny, D. A. (2011). The truth and bias model of judgment. *Psychological Review, 118*(2), 357–378.

Whitbeck, L. B., & Gecas, V. (1988). Value attributions and value transmission between parents and children. *Journal of Marriage and Family, 50*(3), 829–840.

Wilhelm, P., & Perrez, M. (2004). How is my partner feeling in different daily-life settings? Accuracy of spouses' judgments about their partner's feelings at work and at home. *Social Indicators Research, 67*(1–2), 183–246.

CHAPTER 5

ANTICIPATORY RECOGNITION

Creating a Cycle of Flexible Meanings in Intergenerational Relations

Elsa de Mattos
Universidade Federal da Bahia, Salvador

Young people's development to adulthood is one of the most critical moments in the life course, when several changes and psychosocial transformations simultaneously pervade the person and his or her context (i.e., entering high school, vocational planning, finding a job, beginning sexual relationships, among others). As young people develop, they begin to navigate new spheres of experience that can bring significant ruptures to their sense of self continuity (Zittoun, 2006a, 2007, 2011). As pointed out by Zittoun (2006), ruptures demand reorganization in the form of identity (re) construction, learning, and meaning making. The person is confronted with perceptions that contradict those that were congruent up until then, allowing tensions and ambivalences to emerge. Many of these conflicting perceptions are negotiated in interactions with significant others located in different contexts. For example, tensions and ambivalences may emerge when a young person enters the world of work and starts to question what

Trans-Generational Family Relations, pages 73–98

she is able to do, her position in relation to others in the new contexts, as well as her identity and the meaning of her actions. In these situations, the young person may confront perceptions of colleagues and supervisors with those held by parents or teachers and vice versa. Tensions among contexts also become highlighted. This process gives rise to the negotiation of multiple and conflicting versions, positions, and projected possibilities (Taylor, 1994) and demand a person's capacity for self-organization. Therefore, this phase in the life course provides a significant window for the study of the construction of regulatory processes and, more specifically, of internal semiotic regulatory processes and a better understanding of the role of intergenerational relations in supporting young people's life transitions.

A traditional approach to the study of youth transition comes from the perspective of *Life Course*, developed by Elder (1998), who argues for a study of developmental transitions that is more "sensitive to the interlocking nature of human lives and generations, as well as an informed awareness of individual choice makers and agents of their own lives" (p. 4). One of the main principles highlighted by researchers on this perspective is the linking of lives. They regard transitions as interdependent through generations. According to Elder (1998):

> Human lives are typically embedded in social relationships with kin and friends across the life span. Social regulation and support occur in part through these relationships. [...] More generally, the principle of linking lives refers to the interaction between individual's social worlds over the life span. (p. 4)

This notion of linking lives is extremely relevant when thinking about social regulation between generations and to begin to understand how intergenerational relations may impact personal transitions. However, this view tends to emphasize the reproductive life cycle of intergenerational processes as they experience macrohistorical change and think about the interweave of generations in relation to historical change. Much still has to be understood about how intergenerational relations contribute to the construction of internal processes of regulation and how linking lives influences personal reorganization during life transitions.

In this chapter, I will advance the idea that linking lives can be seen in terms of dialogical relations between self and other, and I will develop a semiotic-dialogical perspective of youth transitions. Moreover, I will elaborate on the dynamics of linked lives, showing that a special kind of intergenerational relation between young people and significant others (hereafter called "anticipatory recognition") may foster a process of internal regulation and provide the emergence of flexible signs in the self-system of young people, promoting creative meaning-making and continued integration of life experiences over time.

This article is divided into three sections. The first section draws on the perspectives of cultural psychology and dialogism to propose a new understanding of youth developmental transitions, highlighting both the dialogical and semiotic nature of processes of self-regulation that characterize transitions. It also discusses recent approaches to the notion of recognition in the Social Sciences. The second part presents a case example that illustrates how a young woman—throughout a developmental period from ages 16 to 23 years negotiates significant meanings of herself and her world. Moreover, this part aims to describe how the participant builds dialogical relations with significant others that anticipate the creation of a new version of herself in the future—as a responsible person. The third section demonstrates and elaborates on the dynamics underlying anticipatory recognition and the processes of self-regulation by the action of flexible signs, leading to a reconfiguration of the self-system during transitions.

A SEMIOTIC-DIALOGICAL APPROACH TO YOUTH TRANSITIONS

Young people's development to adulthood is regarded as a critical juncture in the life course, when they are confronted with significant psychosocial changes (e.g., more complex ethical choices, expansion of social networks, entrance into the world of work, identification of a vocational path, among others). Departing from cultural psychology, we want to highlight developmental transitions as semiotic processes (i.e., as processes mediated by the production of signs). Semiotic mediation allows for human beings to synthesize new meanings, in both the reflexive (i.e., through generalizations from the meaning of words) and affective domains (Valsiner, 2008). Developmental transitions involve the capacity to question what is, to imagine a possible future to be (as if), and to continuously project oneself in that imaginary meaning field to orient one's life trajectory (Abbey & Valsiner, 2004).

According to Zittoun (2006a, 2007), the developing person actively participates in his or her process of development, using symbolic resources, appropriating signs that are available in the collective culture, as well as re-creating signs from his or her own personal experience. Transition processes are triggered by ruptures or discontinuities that occur when people face situations that question what they take for granted, their existing operating meaning fields (Zittoun, Aveling, Gillespie, & Cornish, 2012). Therefore, a semiotic dynamic is created to help the person overcome ruptures and reduce uncertainty. This will further help the person deal with emerging feelings, as he or she negotiates, modifies, and transforms cultural and shared meanings in a personal way, creating new meaning fields to organize and (re)structure his or her personal path in life, knitting past and future in the present (Zittoun, 2012). In this way, as young people face significant ruptures, they semiotically construct and reconstruct themselves, shape and reshape their life trajectories (Zittoun et al., 2012).

In this movement, the self is regarded as a regulatory system that produces innovation by transforming its own elements and seeking integration across time, orienting the person toward the future while allowing for and restricting the emergence of new meanings, as well as exerting flexible control over the way he or she positions him or herself at every moment (Valsiner, 2008, 2014). These dynamics of regulatory processes are related to how a person deals with tensions and ambivalences that emerge throughout his or her experience (Cabell, 2010; Cabell & Valsiner, 2011; Valsiner & Cabell, 2012). According to Abbey (2012a), ambivalences are at the core of a person's production of new meanings. Meanings emerge out of a person's attempt to overcome ambivalences that appear in his or her relations with the world. Ambivalences can therefore be regarded as a motor for transformations in the boundary zone between the present and the future, allowing for the emergence of a preadaptation to the future. This process entails the notion that the field of experience is built out of tensions between opposing or alternative perspectives that are inherently linked, as they exist on the basis of one another.

Along these lines, Abbey (2012a, 2012b) and Valsiner (2006) suggest that for a better understanding of how people create meanings, it is necessary to consider how they deal with the levels of the tension emerging between alternative perspectives. Abbey (2012a) proposed three levels of ambivalence: (a) when the level of ambivalence is null, the person does not engage in meaning construction; (b) when the level of ambivalence is moderate, the person constructs meanings on an erratic basis (i.e., emerging meanings are fragile and allow for guiding actions toward changing future conditions); and (c) when ambivalence reaches the maximum level of tension, the person constructs either strong signs that bring rigidity to the meaning system or abandons the process of meaning construction altogether. However, we still need to look at how people engage in these levels of meaning construction in dialogical relations, and more specifically in dialogical relations that become relevant when young people face transitions.

Another fruitful use of a dialogical approach can also be to understand processes of meaning construction that emerge in youth transitions. Dialogical perspectives presuppose that self and other are in mutual interdependence, and "through this mutuality they co-develop" (Marková, 2003, p. 250). This kind of mutuality entails joint communication and meaning-making activities. Researchers such as Marková, Linell, Grossen, and Orvig (2007) suggest that:

> The limits of the self are not within the I, but within the relationship with the other, "I and thou". Every individual makes his/her world in terms of others by dialogically constructing and re-constructing the social world as a set of multifaceted and multivoiced realities situated in culture. (p. 8)

Dialogism has also been associated with dynamic and multivocal movements of construction and reconstruction of meaning inside the self-system (Hermans, 2002, 2001). The perspective of dialogical self theory describes the self-system as multifaceted and complex, endowed with multiple voices and different positions that coexist and hold different perspectives about the world (Hermans, 2001; Ribeiro & Gonçalves, 2010; Salgado & Gonçalves, 2007). The idea is that these voices represent the various facets within the individual, interacting in a dialogical way. This process can lead to tensions that need to be solved by finding compromises, prioritizing, or, if this is not possible, simply enduring them (Hermans & Kempen, 1993; Hermans & Hermans-Jensen, 2003; Salgado & Hermans, 2005). This framework can also be used to situate the dialogical self within a set of social relations and examine self-reconfigurations that emerge through repositionings (i.e., positionings and counterpositionings) in interpersonal relations, as well as through different contexts (i.e., spheres of experience) in which the person navigates. This movement allows for the emergence of novelty, as well as the promotion of a qualitative reorganization of the self-system (Cunha, Gonçalves, & Valsiner, 2011; Hermans & Hermans-Konopka, 2010).

The notion of the dialogical self suggests variability within the self. The self is social and emerges through relational encounters with multiple alterities in different spheres of experience. Dialogical encounters with multiple "others" become progressively internalized in the form of I-positions. The self is, therefore, a "space" or, as suggested by Hermans (2001), a "landscape," composed of relations among I-positions, which are more than merely socially expected roles. They refer as well to reflexive meanings and affective states (Hermans, 2001). Therefore, a specific I-position is an emerging structure in a meaning field of possible/alternative ways in which the individual positions him or herself in a given context. Thus, the notion of the dialogical self emphasizes the fluidity of voices in a field of self-relations (Hermans & Hermans-Konopka, 2010). As a dynamic multiplicity, the self is permeated by tensions between voices that coexist and move along with changes that occur simultaneously in the diverse spheres of experience the person navigates (Cunha & Gonçalves, 2009; Cunha et al., 2011; Salgado & Gonçalves, 2007; Salgado & Hermans, 2005; Zittoun et al., 2012). Dealing with life's uncertainties sometimes leads to an overcoming of the tensions and production of a new synthesis, but other times it may lead to cyclical relation characterized by a quick return to dominant—and sometimes negative—voices in a process called *mutual-in-feeding* (Ribeiro & Gonçalves, 2011; Valsiner, 2002).

In this chapter, we regard youth transitions as semiotic-dialogical processes leading people to search for self-continuity after multiple changes that emerge as they participate in diverse spheres of experience (i.e., different contexts or domains of experience in which the person is involved; e.g., home, school, work, etc.) (Zittoun & Grossen, 2012). These processes, canalized by possibilities and affordances present in the sociocultural field, are characterized by self-reconfigurations by building of new meanings around constellations of I-positions and/or meta-positions (or by maintaining older ones) that orient people's actions toward the future. The idea that I want to put forth here is that, to understand youth transition processes, it is necessary to take into consideration the system of I/Other relations (intersubjective dimension), as well as human capacity for reflexivity (intrasubjective dimension) (i.e., both dialogical inter- and intrapersonal relations within the self, as movements of positions and counterpositions that orient the developing person toward the future). Besides, one has to consider the person's movement among different spheres of experience.

A DIALOGICAL VIEW OF RECOGNITION

According to Marková (2003), one of the fundamental principles of dialogism is a struggle for recognition. The latter entails the capacity to acknowledge the other as a human and to be acknowledged by the other in the same way. The term *recognition* has its roots in philosophical and political thought. It has been conceptualized as a form of identification, such as when we "recognize" a friend in the street, and as the act of acknowledging or respecting another being, such as when we "recognize" someone's status, achievements, or rights (Inwood, 1992). Along these lines, Taylor (1994) developed a theory of recognition, stressing that human beings are shaped through intersubjective relations and define what they are through their interactions with others. Moreover, Taylor argues that identity is partly shaped by recognition or its absence. He sees nonrecognition or misrecognition as a form of dominance or oppression and suggests that recognition can be regarded as a vital human need. The author used his insights to construct a politics of recognition of difference, stressing that people struggle with the recognition of their difference (i.e., of what is unique to certain people and groups of people).

Along the same lines, Honneth (1995, 2007) complements the ideas of Taylor (1994), arguing that recognition is essential to self-realization. He identifies the mechanics of how this is achieved, suggesting that there are patterns of recognition necessary for an individual's development of a positive relation to self. The patterns identified by the author are love, rights, and solidarity. It is beyond the scope of this chapter to explore these patterns more deeply. However, it is fruitful to notice that Honneth (2007) ascribes an expectation of recognition to humans and suggests that a failure of such expectations may bring negative emotional experiences to the person.

As Marková (2003) points out, social recognition is based on mutuality and reciprocity as well as tension and asymmetry. Dialogues entail communion and consensus with the other as well as dispute and negotiation over antinomies. For our purposes here, it is useful to retain that recognition implies a form of "active empathizing" with the other that involves, not a passive submersion or fusion of the self in the other's perspective, but rather a "struggle with Alter, with the strange" (Marková, 2003, p. 257) through patterns of recognition that need to be further explored and clarified.

These processes might be more prominent during times when the young person confronts new spheres of experience that challenge previous self-configurations of dominant positions developed over time within the family or at school—his or her most prevalent spheres of experience during childhood. Following this line of reasoning, I suggest that youth transitions involve a process of self-positioning and repositioning in which individuals seek to develop new meanings of themselves and the world as they participate in increasingly diverse spheres of life presented by their social-historical context. This process brings ambivalence and tensions between I-positions, demanding reconfigurations in the self-system. Youth transitions imply a movement of searching for specific forms of semiotic regulation and temporal reorganization of the self-system. In youth transitions, significant others may help bring multivocality to the self-system, increasing its flexibility and dialogicality as well as fostering development, and these might be achieved through specific patterns of recognition.

Dialogical relations with significant others—especially intergenerational relations—need further investigation. Forms of dialogical relations that involve specific patterns of recognition seem to influence young people's transitions. Sociopolitical recognition are concepts emerging from the fields of sociology and political science. Previous research emphasizes the value of recognition as a normative sociopolitical principle, as a form of public legitimizing and validation by significant others of a person's or group's rights or achievements (e.g., merits, services, virtues, etc.). It refers to the ways in which a community and/or an institutional structure feeds back to the person what the community values (or does not value) (e.g., comments, celebrations, certifications, awards, punishments, etc.). However, further study is needed to clarify psychosocial aspects of recognition.

In this chapter, I will elaborate on the notion of "anticipatory recognition"—a form of recognition by significant others that occurs in advance, before the person takes action or produces meanings. It is a form of dialogical relation in which the significant other perceives, recognizes, and validates qualities and characteristics of the self that have not yet been manifested or expressed. In "anticipatory recognition," significant others may facilitate the emergence of regulatory processes in the self-system capable of promoting transitions, through anticipating possible becomings or projecting the young person's self-system into alternative futures. These processes give rise to cycles of production of innovation and create hierarchies of meanings—they involve the emergence of promoter signs able to overcome—integrate and differentiate—ambivalent positions in the field of self. The created hierarchies of meanings exert a flexible control over other self-positions and produce a new self "version" projected into the future as a form of "being-in-becoming."

In the next section, I will focus on a case study, mapping the emerging tensions between I-positions and showing how these tensions evolve over time. Moreover, the role of significant others in the overcoming of ambivalences will be highlighted. An ideographic overview is the best methodological approach to reveal the dialogical tensions and the movement of overcoming these tensions through semiotic mediation. I suggest that new promoting positions emerge after dialogical encounters—intergenerational relations—that take the form of anticipatory recognition. My aim is to show how microgenetic regulatory processes, occurring between self and other, in specific moments of rupture in a developmental trajectory may facilitate the emergence of novelty and the shaping of alternative trajectories in a longitudinal perspective. The following case study refers to reconstructed experiences that were internalized into the self-system and subsequently externalized through the narrative process. Thus, my analysis departs from the idea that it is the person's (re)construction of experiences that drives change rather than experiences as they happened. I will elaborate on how a young woman, Jane, constructs and negotiates her self-meanings while shaping her future, making explicit the mechanisms through which a significant rupture—such as entering the world of work—resonates in her self-system and activates a process of reconfiguration of her patterns of action, thinking, and feeling that may lead to flexibility of her meaning system, after anticipatory recognition in intergenerational relations.

METHOD

The present study was designed as a longitudinal qualitative study of multiple cases (Stake, 2005). It was structured in three rounds of in-depth individual interviews with six afro-descendant youths who participated in a youth apprenticeship program developed by a nongovernmental organization (NGO) in Salvador, Bahia, Brazil. The program was designed to help youth with few educational opportunities. During the first round of data collection the youth were ages 18 to 19 years, in the second round they were ages 20 to 21, and in the third round ages 22 to 23. We will report the case of Jane, who participated in all three rounds of interviews, and focus on her experiences between ages 18 and 23 years, including her recollections of her former apprentice years (between ages 15 and 18 years). This particular case study was chosen among others in our sample because it showed the unfolding of "anticipatory recognition" by significant others in the spheres of family and work as a way to foster the emergence of new patterns of acting, thinking, and feeling that progressively led to more flexible self-meanings. Furthermore, it exemplifies the dialogical semiotic approach to youth transitions, emphasizing self-configuration strategies and negotiations of self-positions in different spheres of experience and across time.

Interviews took place at the NGO headquarters and lasted about two hours each. Data were digitally recorded and subsequently transcribed. Primary themes explored during the interviews were: (a) significant changes and challenges experienced, (b) work experience and family relations, and (c) educational experiences. The present analysis focuses primarily on youth relations in the dimensions of family and work because these significant spheres of experience are established in the literature concerning Brazilian youth in this age range (Dayrell, 2010; Sarti, 2004). Following the presentation of the case, we will articulate the analysis with theoretical perspectives.

CASE EXAMPLE

Jane's Case Synopsis in Three Times

Jane is an afro-descendent young woman who lives with her parents and sister in a poor inner-city neighborhood located on the outskirts of the city of Salvador. Her father is an auto mechanic in a car company, and her mother is a housekeeper. Before entering the NGO-run apprentice program, Jane had no previous paid work experience. When she began participating in the program, she was 16 years old, in her first year of high school, and was at that time hired as the apprentice of a library attendant and a receptionist at a private college.

Time 1: Ambivalences at Work and in the Family

At the moment of the first interview, Jane had just turned age 18 and told us about the rupture she had faced about two years before when she began working as an apprentice at a private college. When Jane was around 16 years old, her father was severely injured in a work accident and had to stop working for a while. Her family went through a lot of financial hardship, and in face of these events, Jane searched for a way to contribute to support her family. That is how she sought an apprentice program at an NGO and started working at a private college. She regarded this event as a turning point in her life because the survival of her family depended almost exclusively on her earnings as an apprentice and on the help of her grandmother.

At the beginning, when Jane entered the work environment as an apprentice, much the same way as other apprentices in our study, she reported that she "sat there with nothing to do and [...] just had to pay attention to what other people were doing." Moreover, she faced a critical moment as she felt discriminated by her coworkers. She thought that being an "apprentice" was not a valued position. She was confronted with a work environment permeated by conflicting discourses. On the one hand, employers were eager to hire apprentices and begin a new apprenticeship program in the company. On the other hand, people did not trust young people's ability to take on the new tasks and responsibilities of the job. As Jane says:

> I think that people [co-workers] made a distinction because I was an apprentice. They didn't treat me as a real worker. When someone from outside asked who I was, they said that I was a "young apprentice." They didn't consider me as an employee. As for myself, I thought I wouldn't be able to do all the work I had to do.

Tensions started to rise, and Jane felt "discriminated" by her coworkers. She thought people didn't treat her as a real employee at the company. They always referred to her as a young apprentice, and she felt unease and discomfort. As seen in Table 5.1, two conflicting positions emerged in Jane's work sphere: accepted-apprentice and unskilled youth. However, as time passed, Jane sought adult support in an older employee, Elena, who worked in the Human Resources Department, and they built a strong mentor-like relationship. Every time she had a problem or doubt, Jane turned to Elena, who encouraged her and gave her support and advice to overcome these challenges. Elena helped Jane to solve problems and clarify doubts, and she always encouraged Jane to perform new tasks and try new things, anticipating that Jane would succeed in her new tasks. Jane felt that Elena "trusted [her] more than [she] trusted her own self." These dialogical encounters with Elena were initially circumvented by Jane's lack of trust in herself and her feeling of discrimination. Although progressively, with time, the feeling of discrimination was turned into confidence as she began to internalize Elena's voice and started to perceive herself as competent and able to take on more complex job responsibilities. In this process, she gained social recognition from her supervisor and coworkers.

Through her dialogical relation with Elena, Jane was able to build self-confidence and position herself as a responsible worker. At this time, Jane developed a personal sense of responsibility, regarded as:

> An ability to commit to something that I was doing, knowing that what I was doing was something important, something that was helping me grow, which would influence my future.

TABLE 5.1 Synthesis of Jane's Positions in Time 1

Self-Positions	Description	Anticipatory Recognition
Accepted Apprentice × ***Unskilled Youth*** (mutual in-feeding) + ***Dependent Daughter*** × ***Provider*** *Negative affective field of discrimination* *Emergence of a new sign* "***responsible worker***"	Father's work accident and beginning to work as apprentice. Confronts *conflicting discourses*: acceptance × disqualification of apprentices. Ambivalence rises. *Mutual in-feeding* between opposing voices, maintenance of conflicting voices. Emergence of negative feeling of "*discrimination*." Starts *dialogical relation* with Elena, from the Human Resources Dept.—anticipatory recognition begins. In the family sphere, there is *ambivalence* between: being supported by parents × becoming the only household provider. She is the only money provider in the family but gives all the money she earns to her mother, who decides what to do with it (her mother manages home expenses).	Dialogical relation with Elena leads to an internalization of competence and responsibility at the work domain. Elena recognizes Jane in anticipation as responsible, competent and able to perform complex tasks at work and take on more responsibilities, even before Jane actually starts to perform more complex tasks. Initially Jane did not trust herself as Elena did. Emergence of a new sign "***responsible worker***."

In the family sphere, however, as seen in Table 5.1, Jane also felt ambivalence rising. Her father was sick, and she started to work and earn money to help overcome financial hardship. However, she gave all the money she earned as an apprentice to her mother, who was better able to manage home expenses. Her mother took the responsibility for buying goods, cooking, cleaning the house, going to the supermarket, paying taxes, and making the main decisions related to where and how the money should be spent. Jane remained as a dependent daughter inside the family sphere, being taken care of and supported by her parents. She thought her mother "knew better [than herself] what to do with the money," but she felt unease as she was becoming the only household provider. Therefore, as seen in Table 5.1, two conflicting self-positions also emerged in the family sphere as dependent daughter and provider.

Time 2: Escalation of Ruptures and Ambivalences

With the passage of time, Jane internalized Elena's voice and started to feel more confident. She began to value her own accomplishments and "commit" to what she was doing. When her apprentice contract terminated (at age 18), she was hired by the university to work at the Administration's Office. Through this experience, she "learned what responsibility mean[s]" and explained that she understood responsibility as the capacity "to commit to something... to know that what I am doing is something important, something that is making me grow, that will influence my future."

Jane started to take on more responsibilities at work and began to trust her new abilities. She took on a new function at a secretarial level and started to perform more complex tasks. By this time, Jane regarded herself as "one of those people with more responsibilities in the department." She believed she was doing a good job and felt more adjusted to work. Progressively, Jane built a sense of autonomy and felt she had become more independent from the influence of older people. She was "acting with more freedom," beginning to "do things for [herself]," not relying as much as she used to on the "advice and opinions of adults." She stopped doing what "adults told [her] to do."

At work, Jane said she began to feel that she "was not only responsible for [her]self but also for others." Therefore, a new sense of responsibility emerged deeply rooted within the dynamics of Jane's interactions within the work environment, which began to guide and orient her conduct.

However, when Jane was about 21 years old, another rupture happened in her family life, but her new sense of responsibility, acquired at work, did not transfer to her home context. Jane's mother got very sick, requiring Jane to manage her family money and home expenses—tasks her mother used to take care of. Her newly acquired job position and related responsibilities at work did not help her to cope with the problems and difficulties emerging in her family life. Even after perceiving herself as more autonomous from the influence of older people in the work sphere, Jane was not able to manage her new tasks at home.

As she said:

> I started to have money problems. I had a lot of debt in my credit card. I tried to manage the money in my family, because everything I earned I gave to support my family. I had to manage everything, and this was a lot of work! And debts started to pop-up.

Although Jane had a steady job and was the main contributor to the family budget, when she tried to manage the family expenses, she realized she was not able to perform this task with the same effectiveness her mother used to present or with the same competence and responsibility that she showed in her job. She spent the money she earned on unnecessary consumer goods that were not for the house. As a result, her parents criticized her and regarded her as irresponsible, questioning her capacity to take on her tasks at home. As seen in Table 5.2, a strong tension existed between the two main positions she occupied in the central spheres of her life. Her position as a responsible worker was confronted with her position in the family as a dependent daughter (who used to rely on her mother to take home decisions) and irresponsible for managing the home. Jane started to feel anxious and desperate as she confronted her new, emergent position of responsibility and autonomy (at work) with the old position of dependency (at home), and she was not able to integrate them.

As ambivalence grew and became maximized, Jane started to feel "desperate and swamped in financial debt." She developed psychosomatic symptoms such as hives and foreboding dreams. During this difficult time, Jane got closer to her grandmother, a powerful old woman who was the central figure in her family as well as a religious leader in her community. Her grandmother was a "mother-of-saint,"[1] a priestess of the Brazilian African-oriented religion *Candomblé.* Jane revealed during our interview that, sometime before, she was suffering from hives and forebodings that she "didn't know the meaning of." Her grandmother interpreted her symptoms and gave meaning to them. She told Jane that these symptoms could be regarded as a "calling from the Saint."[2] As Jane explained, her grandmother gave voice to the Saints who were calling Jane to convert to her grandmother's

TABLE 5.2 Synthesis of Jane's Positions in Time 2

Self-Positions	Description	Anticipatory Recognition
Responsible Worker (competent) × ***Irresponsible Money Manager*** (incompetent/ in debt) ***Generalized negative affective-filed*** (*fear and despair*) ↓ ***Emergence of the new sign*** "*initiated*"	Progressive internalization of Elena's voice (*responsible worker*) guides Jane to change job functions and become recognized by others as a responsible worker. Tensions emerge in the family when Jane's mother gets sick. Jane has to control home expenses (a function her mother used to take), but debts with credit cards start to appear, and she feels desperate and swamped. Body symptoms start to emerge (hives) as well as foreboding dreams (she gets terrified). Jane is regarded by parents as irresponsible. Proximity with grandmother, mother-of-saint (priestess of *Candomblé* religion). Grandmother recognizes Jane as "chosen by the Saints to follow the Religion." Emergence of a new sign "*initiated*" in the sphere of religion (*Candomblé*), which begins to integrate previous tensions in the self-system and differentiate Jane's self-configuration.	Dialogical relation with grandmother gains prominence. Grandmother gives meaning to somatic symptoms. Grandmother recognizes Jane as "*chosen by the Saints to follow the Religion.*" Proximity with *Candomblé* religion. Participation in rituals and leaning of religious values. Emergence of a new sign "*initiated*," answering the "call of the Saints" to convert to *Candomblé* and become responsible for performing religious obligations.

religion. She had to be initiated in *Candomblé* to face a new level of responsibility (i.e., religious responsibility) and "take responsibility not only for herself but also for others," as Jane's grandmother did.

Jane started to visit her grandmother's temple often and take part in religious rituals. As she deepened her dialogical relation with her grandmother, she started to learn new values and religious principles, and she began to take part in the religious ceremonies, although she was not a formal member of the religious community. As time passed, Jane started to feel that she was being "initiated" into the religion by her grandmother. She started to develop another level (as seen in Table 5.1) of responsibility that involved religious obligations, not only toward herself and proximal others, but also toward the broader religious community and the Gods.

Time 3: Overcoming of Main Tensions

As time passed, Jane increased her religious engagement, generating a significant change in her life. Gradually, she started to see herself as "initiated" in the religious community. She learned new religious values and participated more actively in religious rituals. For instance, she took care of the decorations and preparation of food that was served in different festivities, together with more experienced religious practitioners.

She explained that a new "sense of responsibility" emerged for her, and she began to take "responsibility, not only for [her]self, but also for others," referring to a kind of spiritual responsibility for the well-being of people belonging to the religious community[3]—the same kind of responsibility she attributed to her grandmother. In her own words, she remarked:

> I am not only responsible for myself, I am responsible for others too, for helping others, feeling that not only your own life depends on you, but the lives of others can also depend on you.

At home, some relevant changes also happened, as she "learned to organize [her] finances." She learned to deal with her finances more competently: She paid off all her debts and started to limit her expenses. She learned "to do everything the right way" and thought she gained her "own space." She also started taking care of her mother's money and opened a sort of savings account for her mother. Therefore, regarding management of family money, the mother and daughter positions reversed. Her mother started to trust her ability to manage the family money. Jane felt she could act based on her own decisions and could "take on the responsibility for her own mistakes," but she felt that this confidence was "difficult to achieve." As Jane puts it:

> Now I am learning to manage my money. I paid off all my debts. I cut up all my credit cards. [...] I think I can take charge of my own life now.

TABLE 5.3 Synthesis of Jane's Positions in Time 3

Self-Configuration	Description	Social Recognition
Flexible sign ***Initiated*** (in *Candomblé*) ↓ Promotes Cycle of production of innovation ↓ Weaving together ***Responsible Worker*** + ***Responsible Student*** + ***Responsible Money Manager/Provider*** ↓ ***Responsible Person*** (being-in-becoming)	Increase of religious engagement. The flexible sign "***initiated***" acts as promoter sign, knitting a "sense of responsibility" across time (past–future) and space (different spheres of experience), guiding Jane's actions and decisions in the direction of future goals. Jane gains more stability at work, studies hard and passes the public university exam, and changes her relationship in the home, especially with her mother. She gets more autonomy regarding her mother's opinions and takes care of the family money and even her mother's own money (reverse positions).	As Jane internalized the position of "initiated" and took on more responsibility in different spheres of her life, significant others started to recognize her new way of acting and praise these transformations. Jane's mother began to trust Jane's ability to manage the money and allowed her to take care of her personal savings account. Jane also passed a difficult exam to enter the public university.

As Jane explained, as time passed, she developed a new sense of self and of the surrounding world. A new self-configuration emerged, integrating positions at work and at home, with the support of significant adults, like her grandmother. Jane gained more stability at work. She wanted to continue her education, so she studied hard and passed the difficult exams to enter the public university.

As can be seen in Table 5.3, a new flexible sign in the form of the new emerging position as "initiated" acted as promoter sign, knitting past and future (times), as well as different spheres of experience (spaces), guiding Jane's actions and decisions in the direction of future goals. Such meaning-making movements, growing out of her interactions at work and in the family context, led Jane to reconfigure herself and create alternative life paths toward the future.

DISCUSSION

Self-Regulation Through Flexible Signs: The Role of "Anticipatory Recognition"

In this chapter, I wanted to advance the idea that semiotic regulation may lead to processes that facilitate a reconfiguration of the self-system through the emergence of flexible signs (i.e., signs that bring flexibility and increase dialogicality to personal meaning systems). Moreover, I suggest that the emergence of flexible signs is facilitated by an anticipatory recognition by significant others—a specific dialogical relation with significant others that becomes progressively internalized into the self-system and may help promote self-transformation. Jane's case illustrates the operation of anticipatory recognition and the creation of a cycle of flexible meanings in a longitudinal time frame.

Jane's transitions show how the process of self-regulation can bring flexibility and dialogicality into the self-system through the emergence of flexible signs that help overcome ambivalences in different spheres of life. Jane's life experience highlights the conditions under which semiotic regulation may lead to the creation of a cycle of flexible meanings. It shows how tensions among ambivalent positions within the self-system may escalate across time, leading sometimes to the emergence of psychosomatic symptoms. To deal with ambivalence, Jane increased dialogical relations with significant others in different spheres of experience (i.e., engaging in a special kind of dialogical relation). These exchanges facilitated the emergence of flexible signs, allowing for the creation of alternative meanings. These meanings became later internalized, bringing alternative ways of thinking, acting, and feeling to Jane. Here I call this pattern of meaning construction a "cycle of creation of flexible meanings," which in a longitudinal time frame may become a trajectory of flexible meaning construction.

To understand this process of semiotic regulation leading to the emergence of flexible meanings, I will focus on two significant bifurcation points in Jane's trajectory and look for the conditions for semiotic regulation to occur, leading to a particular pattern of development. The first bifurcation point emerges when Jane's father suffered an accident at work and she entered the work world as an apprentice. The second bifurcation point involves the escalation of ruptures within the family, when Jane's mother got sick.

As shown in Figure 5.1, at the time of the first bifurcation point in Jane's trajectory, when her father got sick, Jane had to find work as an apprentice to contribute to the family income. Several tensions emerged in her self-system after this significant moment. Initially, she confronted ambivalent discourses prevailing at the workplace that tended, on the one hand, to exclude young people from the work sphere as "inexperienced" or "unskilled," and, on the other hand, to include them by giving an opportunity to prove themselves as competent, giving them tasks that are regarded as challenges. Jane then oscillated between positions of apprentice (skilled) that is, the position she occupies in the sphere of work (Figure 5.1A), and unskilled youth, that is, the position she is seen/recognized by others (Figure 5.1B). To resolve these tensions, she started to adopt a mutual-in-feeding strategy (Valsiner, 2002), alternating between (opposing) positions of skilled and unskilled that did not lead to an overcoming of tensions—it did not allow for the elaboration of new meaning complexes. Instead, it

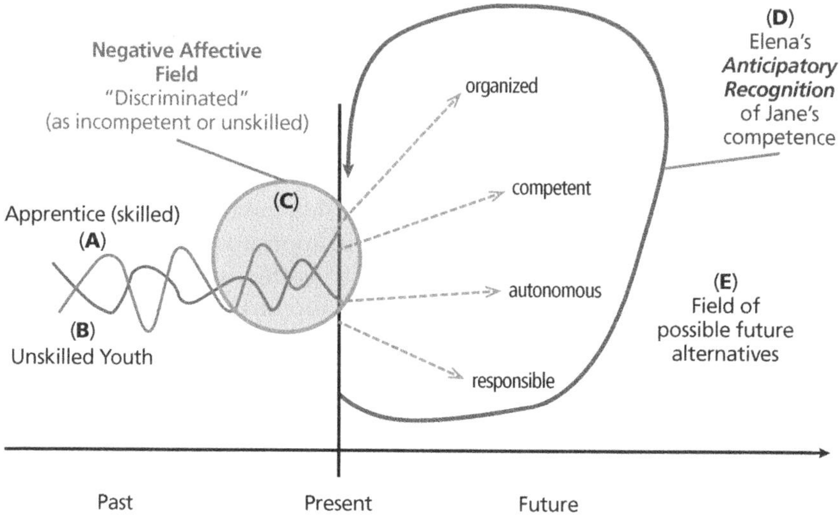

Figure 5.1 Jane's first bifurcation point.

resulted in an escalation of a dominant negative feeling of being discriminated against by her coworkers (Figure 5.1C).

At this time, as Jane felt increasingly devalued by her immediate supervisor and coworkers, a negative affective field of feeling discriminated against grew. Jane was trapped into a situation where, on the one hand, people seemed not to care much about her presence, and, on the other hand, gave her tasks below her level of expertise. As she explained, they considered her "just as a young apprentice." However, she wanted to be recognized as an "employee" in the company, leaving her expectations unfulfilled.

Jane could not deal positively with these ambivalent positions, which contributed to the escalation of anxiety and the rise of a negative feeling of being "discriminated," which started to organize and regulate her actions as well as her thinking in the workplace. The emerging feeling of being "discriminated" and "underprepared" to perform her tasks temporarily blocked the creation of alternative meanings and the imagination of alternative possibilities for her future (for a more complete description of this process, see Mattos & Chaves, 2013).

It is necessary to acknowledge that Jane endured and did not become paralyzed by these negative feelings. She looked for external help to overcome these tensions. Jane started to visit Elena from the Human Resource Department, looking for support. Elena seemed to demonstrate confidence in Jane, anticipating that she could perform successfully. Therefore, even before Jane could recognize these qualities in herself, Elena always told her that she was organized and competen, and could act more autonomously as well as take on more responsibilities (Figure 5.1D). The emergence of Elena's alternative voice—resulting from a dialogical relation characterized by anticipatory recognition of Jane's qualities—brought more dialogicality into Jane's self-system. Elena established a trustful relationship with Jane and anticipated Jane's ability and skill in performing new tasks. She encouraged Jane to take on more responsibilities in her job and oversaw qualities that Jane could not recognize in herself, indicating that she would overcome the challenges she was facing as an apprentice. With time, Elena contributed to Jane's development of a more positive overlook on herself. As Jane acknowledged and accepted Elena's support, she progressively internalized Elena's voice, and a new form of self-regulation emerged.

As shown in Figure 5.2, the initial strategy of self-regulation through mutual-in-feeding (Valsiner, 2002) was circumvented as Elena's anticipatory recognition was gradually internalized into Jane's self-system. The initial movement of alternating between opposing positions of skilled apprentice and unskilled youth was overcome, and the negative feeling of "discrimination" disappeared. The internalization of Elena's alternative voice led to the elaboration of a new meaning complex around the position of responsible worker, and Jane developed new routines and procedures that brought confidence in her own capacity to perform well. The position of responsible worker brings more dialogicality into Jane's self-system and orients a new trajectory in her work life. She acquired new skills and was hired as a company employee after the apprentice contract terminated, gaining more recognition from her coworkers.

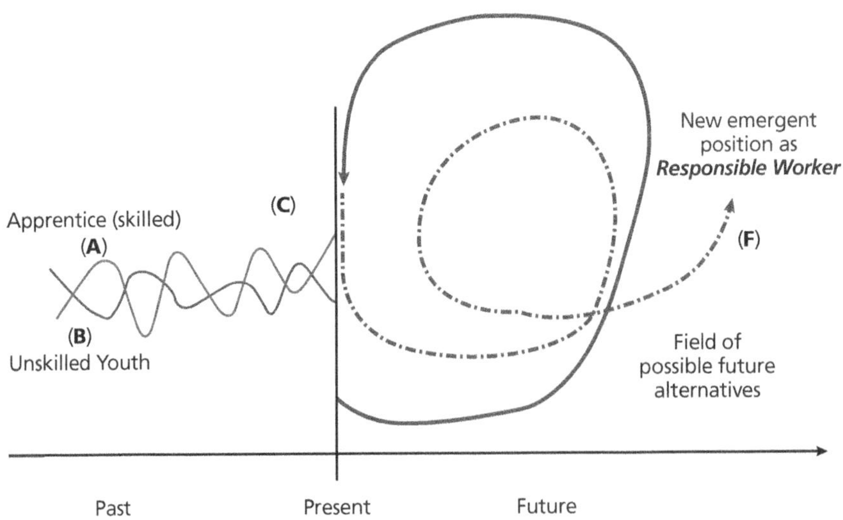

Figure 5.2 Emergence of a new position: Responsible worker.

Later, however, new ruptures emerged in Jane's life experience, forcing her to face a new bifurcation point. A new cycle of meaning construction started when Jane was around 21 years old. As a matter of fact, with the illness of her mother, Jane had to manage home expenses, taking over tasks that her mother used to perform. She constructed new meanings of herself and the world (i.e., self-positions) to overcome these tensions.

Figure 5.3A represents a moment in Jane's life before she started to work. Figures 5.3B and 5.3C and Figures 5.3B′ and 5.3C′ represent her relationship with coworkers and in the family, respectively, after she started to work as an apprentice. Through her dialogical relations within the work sphere, Jane ends up positioning herself as responsible worker. This I-position was consolidated in her work environment but could not be transferred to her family life. In the family sphere, Jane kept operating mostly from the position of dependent daughter. However, when her mother got sick, new demands emerged in the family sphere. Jane accrued several credit card debt and started to feel "desperate and swamped in financial debts." A startling contrast between the positions of responsible worker (at work) and irresponsible money manager (in the family sphere) can be highlighted here, putting Jane in a state of greater dependency on her parents at a time when she was expected to show greater autonomy from them. As ambivalence grew and Jane could not overcome tensions between the two main spheres of her

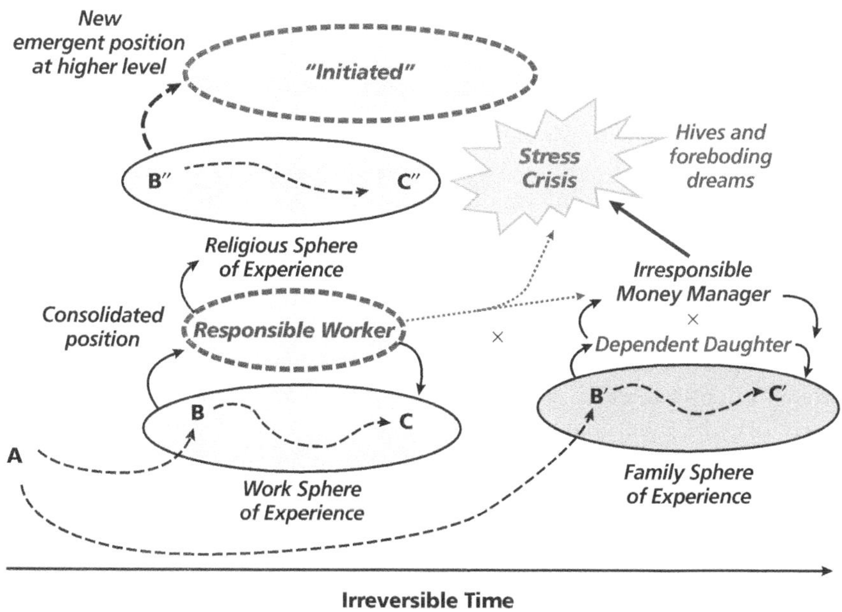

Figure 5.3 Jane's construction of new meanings.

life, she felt exhausted and overwhelmed, her body becoming the ultimate locus for change. She began to suffer psychosomatic symptoms like hives, to have dreams and forebodings that she "didn't know the meaning of."

During this difficult time, Jane sought and found external help to overcome these tensions from her grandmother. Jane started to visit the *Candomblé* temple more often and to take part in religious rituals. Through dialogical relations between Jane and her grandmother (Figure 5.3B″ and 5.3C″), the latter anticipated that Jane could be "initiated" in the religion, learning religious principles and values, and performing tasks in the preparation of rituals. Her grandmother "created" new meanings for Jane's condition, interpreting her physical symptoms (i.e., hives and bad dreams) as a "calling from the Saint."[4] Jane's grandmother suggested that Jane had to take religious responsibility (i.e., "to take responsibility not only for herself but also for others," just as she did herself). By doing so, the grandmother also anticipated a possible future for Jane as a religious leader. When Jane internalized this amplified meaning of being "initiated" into the religious sphere, a significant change occurred in her life. She "became more responsible" and "learned to organize [her] finances." She started to deal with her finances more competently: She paid off all her debts and controlled her expenses. She found out how "to do everything the right way," and she gained her "own space." Therefore, she could "take charge of [her] own life."

How Does a Flexible Sign Operate?

In another paper (Mattos & Chaves, 2013a), I have shown that cyclical movements between opposing meanings in mutual in-feeding may become intolerable and lead to the emergence of signs that inhibit the production of new meanings, bringing rigidity to the self-system. In Jane's case, however, the cycles meaning construction led to the production of promoter signs (i.e., responsible worker and initiated) that bring more flexibility and dialogicality to the self-system. How do these signs operate? Three important characteristics of flexible signs should be highlighted. First, they allow for distancing from the here-and-now flux of experience, distancing from the stream of contradictory discourses the person experiences (e.g., in Jane's trajectory, the emergence of responsible worker allowed for overcoming growing tensions between skilled apprentice and unskilled youth). Second, flexible signs are described as a differentiation from past experience, leading to a possible alternative (e.g., Jane could see her position as responsible worker emerging as a differentiation from her previous position as apprentice and leading to new job functions). Third, flexible signs allow for changes in the self-system when the context demands it (i.e., repositioning when changes take place in the context).

Therefore, flexible signs open an imaginary space of new possibilities for the person and allows for a generative construction of future alternatives. The meanings conveyed promote the emergence of alternative future possibilities and facilitate the construction of bridges between the person's past and future meanings of him or herself. Along these lines, I suggest an amplified view of flexible signs because, as highlighted by Abbey (2012), they allow for a generative preadaptation to either the present context in which the person is currently involved or to her future possibilities. Moreover, flexible signs weave together meanings coming from different life spheres (i.e., work, family, study, and religion).

In Jane's trajectory, she progressively constructed a hierarchy of flexible signs (Mattos & Chaves, 2013b). In the first bifurcation point, a cycle of meaning construction produces the flexible sign responsible worker, operating mainly in the work sphere of Jane's life. Later, another cycle of meaning construction takes place at the second bifurcation point. Here, the position as initiated created more differentiation in Jane's self-system, and a new amplified sense of responsibility was enabled. Every time she tried a new meaning loop—as a way to overcome current ambivalences—Jane entered a special form of dialogical relation with significant others. Anticipatory recognitions by others were turning points in Jane's trajectory, as she could internalize new meanings for herself that could orient her transitions. She ended up building new, higher level meanings that amplified her meaning field and brought more dialogicality into her self-system.

New flexible meanings emerged that allowed for integrating her past and future. She projected herself into alternative future goals, improving study and work performance and solving money problems. She was empowered by becoming "spiritually responsible."

As Figure 5.4 shows, meaning making operates through Cycles of Production of Innovation (Valsiner, 2008). Each time Jane reaches for new meanings that allow for a preadaptation to her life experiences, a new level in the hierarchy of meanings is built. Her first meaning loop operates in the work sphere (Figures 5.4A, B, and C) and leads to the emergence of the powerful position as responsible worker (for an overview of the meaning of "responsibility" in Jane's trajectory, see Mattos & Branco, 2014). Through a special type of dialogical relationship, Elena displays anticipatory recognition of Jane's ability to succeed in performing more complex job tasks. These dialogical relations (Figure 5.4A, B, and C) become progressively internalized, and Jane starts to build a new position for herself, integrating and differentiating former tensions in her self-system. However, new tensions grew in the family sphere (Figure 5.4A, B′, C′), leading to the emergence of a position as irresponsible money manager at home. Tensions grew within the dialogical relation between Jane (Figure 5.4B′) and her mother (Figure 5.4C′), who did not trust Jane's ability to manage the home

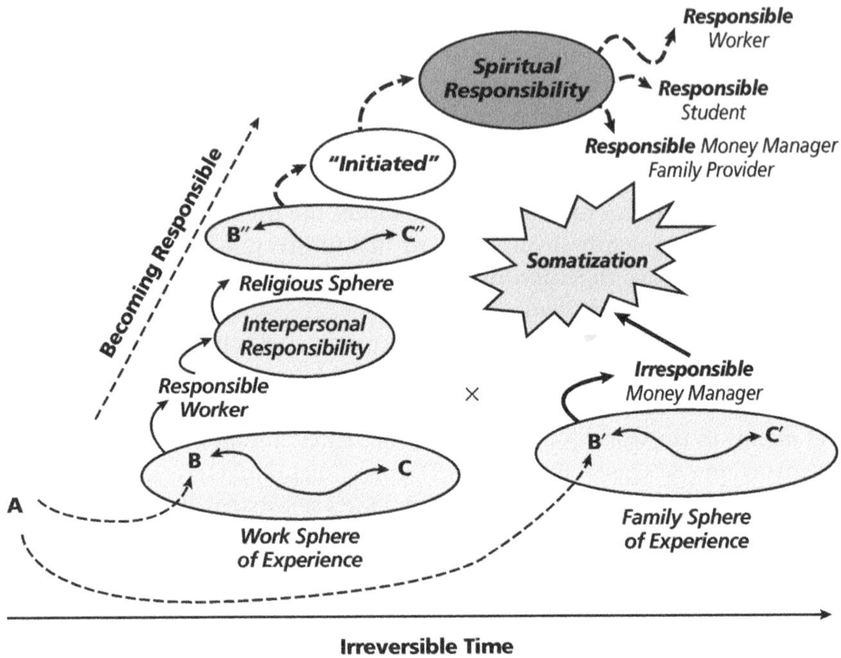

Figure 5.4 Cycles of meaning construction in Jane's trajectory.

expenses. Jane reached for a new meaning loop but could not integrate her new emerging position as responsible worker to family life. As ambivalences became more and more intolerable, she developed psychosomatic symptoms. Jane's grandmother offered a new interpretation for her symptoms. Thus, a new anticipation was developed, through Jane's (Figure 5.4B″) dialogical relations with her grandmother (Figure 5.4C″). This new meaning loop (Figure 5.4A, B″, and C″) allowed for the emergence of another powerful sign in a higher level of generalization of meanings. As Jane perceived herself as "initiated," she created a hierarchy of self-meanings knitting past with futures meanings.

CONCLUDING REMARKS

In this chapter, I have explored the processes taking place within the self-system of young people, highlighting how a special kind of dialogical relation with significant others—anticipatory recognition—may contribute to the operation of cycles of meaning construction leading to the emergence of flexible signs and producing new perspectives for the self and the world. I have also explored how emerging tensions and ambivalence can be resolved through the creation of new meanings in the self-system. The idea was to contribute to the understanding of self-regulatory processes through semiotic mediation. A case study was used to illustrate the condition of self-regulation in which flexible signs *are built out of anticipatory recognition by significant others and these anticipated qualities become progressively internalized and allow for more dialogicality and imagination.* New synthesis in the self-system is promoted by the action of such flexible signs, and Jane could preadapt for uncertainties of the future.

Expanding previous ideas on the role of significant others in young people's trajectories (Mattos & Chaves, 2014), here I suggest that significant others may anticipate new meanings for the self-system, promoting the emergence of new processes of internal regulation. They can provide anticipated recognition of a possible becoming (of the self) in the future and therefore facilitate the emergence of flexible signs/positions, as well as promote the emergence of positive feelings. At the same time, they validate or legitimize new meanings that are produced in the field of self into a broader context. These ideas expand previous research on recognition (Honneth, 1995; Taylor, 1994), especially Marková's (2003) notion that recognition implies a form of "active empathizing" with the other, involving not a passive submersion or fusion of the self in the other's perspective, but a "struggle with Alter, with the strange" (p. 257), as for "recognition" can be regarded as a form of trust. In our view, anticipatory recognition can also be regarded as a form of trust, in the sense that the initial struggle with the other (with the strange) is turned into trust, as the self progressively internalizes the other's perspective. Results shows that dialogical relations with significant others, especially intergenerational relations and patterns of recognition that involve anticipatory recognition of future becoming by significant others, seem to play a positive role in young people's transitions.

Flexible signs that emerge in anticipatory recognition by significant others allow for a distancing from the here-and-now flux of experiences, facilitate differentiation, and allow bringing changes to the self-system when the context requires it. Flexible signs enable the construction of alternative future self versions, a being-in-becoming or a coming-into-being that projects the person into the future. What results from this semiotic regulation process—operated by flexible signs—is therefore an integration of personal time, of past and future in the present (i.e., a meaning bridge that would frame the person's historicity), and an integration of personal life spaces (i.e., the different life spheres).

NOTES

1. A "mother-of-saint"—the translation of *mãe-de-santo*—is a priestess of the Brazilian afro-religion Candomblé. The word comes from the title Ialorixá in Yo-

rubá (African Language), where Iyá means mother and Orixá means a deity or ancestral spirit. Lalorixás run temples where several rituals and cults take place throughout the year (Matory, 2005).

2. Implying that one of the divinities of *Candomblé* wanted to be praised and honored by Jane.
3. The religious community to which Jane and her grandmother belonged was *Candomblé,* a religion with African-Brazilian origins, developed by the slaves who came from Africa to Bahia in Colonial time. In this religious tradition, the higher priest and religious leader is a female—called the *mother-of-saint.* Jane's grandmother was a *mother-of-saint.*
4. Implying that one of the divinities of *Candomblé* wanted to be praised and honored by Jane.

REFERENCES

Abbey, E. (2012a). Metaconceptual frameworks and the study of human infant category construction. *Integrative Psychology and Behavioral Science, 46,* 196–204.

Abbey, E. (2012b). Ambivalences and its transformations. In J. Valsiner (Ed.), *Oxford handbook of cultural psychology* (pp. 989–997). New York, NY: Oxford University Press.

Abbey, E., & Valsiner, J. (2004). Emergence of meanings through ambivalence. *Forum Qualitative Sozialforschung/Forum: Qualitative Social Research, 6*(1), Art. 23. Retrieved from http://nbn-resolving.de/urn:nbn:de:0114-fqs0501231

Cabell, K. (2010). Mediators, regulators, and catalyzers: A context-inclusive model of trajectory development. *Psychology & Society, 3*(1), 26–41.

Cabell, K., & Valsiner, J. (2011). Affective hypergeneralization: Leaning from psychoanalysis. In T. Zittoun & S. Salvatore (Eds.), *Cultural psychology and psychoanalysis: Pathways to synthesis* (pp. 87–113). Charlotte, NC: Information Age.

Cunha, C., & Gonçalves, M. M. (2009). Commentary: Accessing the experience of a dialogical self: Some needs and concerns. *Culture & Psychology, 15,* 120–133.

Cunha, C., Gonçalves, M., & Valsiner, J (2011). Transforming self-narratives in psychotherapy: Looking at different forms of ambivalence in change process. In R. Jones & M. Marioka (Eds.), *Jungian and dialogical self-perspectives* (pp. 43–66). New York, NY: Palgrave Macmillian.

Dayrell, J. (2010). Juventud, socialización y escuela. *Archivos de Ciencias de la Educación, [Archives of Educational Science], 4,* 15–34.

Elder, G. H. (1998). The life course as developmental theory. *Child Development, 69,* 1–12.

Hermans, H. J. M. (2001). The dialogical self: Toward a theory of personal and cultural positioning. *Culture & Psychology, 7,* 243–281.

Hermans, H. J. M. (2002). The dialogical self as a society of mind: Introduction. *Theory & Psychology, 12*(2), 147–160.

Hermans, H. J., & Hermans-Jansen, E. (2003). Dialogical processes and development of the self. In J. Valsiner & K. Connolly (Eds.), *Handbook of developmental psychology* (pp. 534–559). London, England: SAGE.

Hermans, H., & Hermans-Konopka, A. (2010). *Dialogical self theory: Positioning and counter-positioning in a globalizing society.* New York, NY: Cambridge University Press.

Hermans, H. J. M., & Kempen, H. J. G. (1995). Body, mind and culture: The dialogical nature of mediated action. *Culture & Psychology, 1,* 103–114.

Honneth, A. (1995). *The struggle for recognition: The grammar of social conflicts.* Cambridge, England: Polity.

Inwood, M. (1992). *A Hegel dictionary.* Oxford: Blackwell.

Marková, I. (2003). Constitution of the self: Intersubjectivity and dialogicality. *Culture & Psychology, 9*(3), 249–259.

Marková, I. (2006). On the inner alter in dialogue. *International Journal for Dialogical Science, 1*(1), 125–147.

Marková, I. (2009). A dialogical approach in psychology: An alternative to the dualism of theory of mind. In I. Leudar & A. Costall (Eds.), *Against the theory of mind* (pp. 209–220). London, England: Palgrave Macmillan.

Markova, I., Linell, P., Grossen, M., & Orvig, A. S. (2007). *Dialogue in focus groups: Exploring socially shared knowledge.* London, England: Equinox Publishing.

Mattos, E., & Branco, A. (2014). Exploring the intersection of personal and collective meanings: "Responsibility" in the transition to adulthood. *Psychology & Society, 6*(1), 11–27.

Mattos, E., & Chaves, A. M. (2013a). Semiotic regulation through inhibitor signs: Creating a cycle of rigid meanings. *Integrative Psychological and Behavioral Science, 47*(1), 95–122.

Mattos, E., & Chaves, A. M. (2013b). The architecture of self-in-motion: Exploring young people's construction of "becoming." *Interacções* [Interactions], *24,* 106–136.

Mattos, E., & Chaves, A. M. (2014). Exploring the role of catalyzing agents in the transition to adulthood: A longitudinal case study with Brazilian youth. In K. Cabell & J. Valsiner (Eds.), *Catalyzing minds: Beyond models of causality. Annals of Theoretical Psychology* (pp. 167–189). New York, NY: Springer.

Ribeiro, A. P., & Gonçalves, M. M. (2010). Innovation and stability within the dialogical self: The centrality of ambivalence. *Culture & Psychology, 16*(1) 116–126.

Ribeiro, A. P., & Gonçalves, M. M. (2011). Maintenance and transformation of problematic self-narratives: A semiotic-dialogical approach. *Integrative Psychology and Behavioral Science, 45,* 281–303.

Salgado, J., & Gonçalves, M. M. (2007). The dialogical self: social, personal, and (un)counscious. In J. Valsiner & A. Rosa (Eds.), *The Cambridge handbook of social cultural psychology* (pp. 608–621). Cambridge, England: Cambridge University Press.

Salgado, J., & Hermans, H. (2005). The return of subjectivity: From a multiplicity of selves to the dialogical Self. *E-Journal of Applied Psychology: Clinical Section, 1*(1), 3–13.

Sarti, C. A. (2004). A família como ordem simbólica [The family as symbolic order]. *Psicologia USP, 15*(3), 11–28.

Taylor, C. (1994). The politics of recognition. In A. Gutmann (Ed.), *Multiculturalism: Examining the politics of recognition* (pp. 25–73). Princeton, NJ: Princeton University Press.

Valsiner, J. (1997). *Culture and the development of children's actions: A theory of human development.* New York, NY: Wiley.

Valsiner, J. (2002). Forms of dialogical relations and semiotic autoregulation within the self. *Theory & Psychology, 12*(2), 251–264.

Valsiner, J. (2006). Ambivalence under scrutiny: Returning to the future. *Estudios de Psicologia, 27*(1), 117–130.

Valsiner, J. (2007). *Culture in minds and societies: Foundations of cultural psychology.* Thousand Oaks, CA: SAGE.

Valsiner, J. (2008). Open intransitivity cycles in development and education: Pathways to synthesis. *European Journal of Psychology of Education, 23*(2), 131–147.

Valsiner, J. (2014). *Invitation to cultural psychology.* London, England: SAGE.

Valsiner, J., & Cabell, K. (2012). Self-Making through synthesis: Extending dialogical self theory. In H. J. M. Hermans & T. Gieser (Eds.), *Handbook of the dialogical self* (pp. 82–97). New York, NY: Cambridge University Press.

Zittoun, T. (2006a). Dynamics of interiority: Ruptures and transitions in the self-development. In L. M. Simão & J. Valsiner (Eds.), *Otherness in question: Labyrinths of the self* (pp. 187–214). Charlotte, NC: Information Age Publishing

Zittoun, T. (2006b) *Transitions: Development through symbolic resources.* Charlotte, NC: Information Age.

Zittoun, T. (2007). Symbolic resources and responsibility in transitions. *Young, 15,* 193–211.

Zittoun, T. (2008) Editorial introduction: Transitions in the process of education. *European Journal of Psychology of Education, 23*(2), 121–130.

Zittoun, T. (2011). Meaning and change in psychotherapy. *Integrative Psychological and Behavioral Sciences, 45*(3), 325–334.

Zittoun, T. (2012). On the emergence of the subject. *Integrative Psychological and Behavioral Sciences, 46*(3), 259–273.

Zittoun, T., Aveling, E., Gillespie, A., & Cornish, F. (2012). People in transition in worlds in transition: Ambivalence in the transition to womanhood during WWII. In A. C. Bastos, K. Uriko, & J. Valsiner (Eds.), *Cultural dynamics of women's lives* (pp. 59–78). Charlotte, NC: Information Age.

Zittoun, T., & Grossen, M. (2012). Cultural elements and continuity in the self. In M. César & B. Ligorio (Eds.), *Interplays between dialogical learning and the dialogical self* (pp. 99–126). Charlotte, NC: Information Age.

CHAPTER 6

AMBIVALENCE TOWARD PARENTS DURING THE PROCESS OF INDIVIDUATION

Being Caught Between Autonomy and Relatedness?

Isabelle Albert and Dieter Ferring
University of Luxembourg

The concept of ambivalence has gained considerable research interest in the last years in the study of intergenerational relationships. Lüscher and colleagues (2010) define the experience of ambivalence as an oscillation between (temporarily or permanently) irreconcilable, contradictory emotions, thoughts, wishes, and behavioral tendencies that individuals may experience in identity- and agency-relevant social relationships. Such dynamics can include simultaneous conflicting tendencies of "autonomy and dependence," "freedom and control," or "closeness and distance" (Lüscher & Hoff, 2013). Because intergenerational family relations are in general relatively close over the whole lifespan and not easily dissolvable,

Trans-Generational Family Relations, pages 99–120

they are—according to these authors—particularly predisposed to experiences of ambivalence.

It is further assumed that ambivalences may especially occur during phases of transition that imply transformations in relationships. Having originated as a response and a complement to the solidarity–conflict model, which refers to adult child–parent relations (Bengtson & Roberts, 1991), previous research within the intergenerational ambivalence approach has typically concentrated on transitional situations in adulthood, such as when old parents become frail and need increasing support by their middle-age children (e.g., Ferring, Michels, Boll, & Filipp, 2009; Fingerman, Pitzer, Lefkowitz, Birditt, & Mroczek, 2008; Pillemer et al., 2007). Instead, the study of child–parent ambivalences in the earlier transitional phases of adolescence and emerging adulthood has been widely neglected to our knowledge (see also Albert & Steinhoff, 2016). One of the few studies that took ambivalence into consideration focused on individuation patterns in adolescence in relation to mothers and (step)fathers (Kruse & Walper, 2008). The authors of that study identified an ambivalent insecure individuation pattern that was described as asymmetrical with inconsistencies regarding closeness and search for support as well as avoidance, fear of rejection, and intrusion. Another study focused on attitudinal and motivational ambivalence in romantic relations of young adults and its link with attachment anxiety (Mikulincer, Shaver, Bar-On, & Ein-Dor, 2010). However, this conceptualization of ambivalence differs somewhat from our approach to ambivalence. In the just mentioned study, attachment anxiety referred to the coexistence of desires for security and closeness with fears of rejection and abandonment, whereas in the present study, we assume that a main theme in the experience of ambivalences between adolescents/emerging adults and their parents might refer to the balancing of autonomy and relatedness. It is highly plausible that different themes are prevalent in parent–child relations compared with peer and partner relations.

AMBIVALENCE TOWARD PARENTS IN ADOLESCENCE AND EMERGING ADULTHOOD

The lack of specific research on ambivalence in adolescent/emerging adult–parent relations is astounding. First of all, it is widely acknowledged that earlier experiences of family relations are relevant for parent–child relations later in the lifespan, thus it is of high interest to study possible antecedents of later experiences of ambivalence (see e.g., Shemmings, 2006; Silverstein, Parrott, & Bengtson, 1995). Second and maybe more important, adolescence and emerging adulthood are explicit transitional phases in which the relations between children and parents are renegotiated, for instance, with regard to their relative power in the relationship (see e.g., Furman & Buhrmester, 1992; Noack & Buhl, 2005). Finally, adolescents live mostly in the same households as their parents (or with one of their parents) and are generally financially dependent on them. This is also often valid for emerging adults, at least in several Western countries, where the age of leaving the parental home has increased along with longer times of education and difficulties entering the labor market in the last years (Seiffge-Krenke, 2009). These constellations limit adolescents' and emerging adults' possibilities to actively "leave" the relationship or reduce contact with their parents. As described by Van Gaalen, Dykstra, and Komter (2010), missing "exit options" (i.e., when the relationship between parents and their children is determined by missing alternatives rather than by voluntary choices) might especially favor the experience of—as they call it—negative ambivalence. Thus, adolescence and emerging adulthood also might be specifically prone to the experience of ambivalences for structural reasons (see also King, 2010, regarding the structural ambivalence of intergenerational relations in adolescence).

Ambivalence in the Process of Individuation

A major developmental task during the process of individuation refers to the balancing of two fundamental needs: relatedness and autonomy. The former might be defined as a continued need for parental approval, support, attachment, and loyalty, whereas the latter refers to the need to act and think independently (without feeling forced) in relations with parents (Grotevant & Cooper, 1985; Youniss & Smollar, 1985; see also Kagitcibasi, 2005). The renegotiation of these developmental needs in the individuation process may constitute a particularly fertile ground for the occurrence of simultaneous positive and negative emotions and contradictory action tendencies (e.g., feeling simultaneously close to and choked by the parent; oscillating between approaching and withdrawing from aparent).

Given that adolescence and emerging adulthood represent transitional phases, one may ask whether ambivalences occur more frequently during these periods. We agree with Lüscher et al. (2017) that not all relations are (at any time) ambivalent. In this vein, Kruse and Walper (2008) found that of the adolescents participating in their study, roughly one third belonged to the ambivalent insecure cluster with regard to relations with their mothers and 17.9% regarding the relations with their (step)fathers. Apart from that, the authors found a secure, an avoidant, as well as—in the case of (step)fathers—an uninvolved/disengaged individuation pattern.

Consequently, one has to identify those factors in the parent–child relationship that may foster (or prevent) the adolescents' experience of ambivalences in the individuation process. Ambivalences might especially occur when adolescents and emerging adults experience the needs of autonomy and relatedness in the relation to their parents as incompatible. This should depend not least on adolescents' perceptions and interpretations of their parents' parenting behaviors as (a) fostering or impeding their freedom to think, feel, and act autonomously; and (b) granting or withdrawing emotional support and closeness (Fuligni & Eccles, 1993; Grolnick, Gurland, DeCourcey, & Jacob, 2002; Smetana, Campione-Bar, & Metzger, 2006; Youniss & Smollar, 1985). Therefore, the present study focuses explicitly on the role of perceived parenting for the experience of ambivalence toward mothers and fathers in adolescence and emerging adulthood.

Parenting and Ambivalence

For a long time, typological approaches to parenting have dominated the research literature (Baumrind, 1971). However, later dimensional views on parenting became more prominent. Within this context, a distinction between the dimensions of parental warmth (also called acceptance or support) and two kinds of control—behavioral and psychological—has been proposed (see e.g., Barber, Stolz, & Olsen, 2005). Parental warmth and acceptance have generally been associated with positive effects (Khaleque & Rohner, 2002), whereas the effects of control have to be regarded in a more differentiated view (Barber et al., 2005).

Based on the relevant parenting literature, we assume here that warm and supportive parenting reduces adolescents' and emerging adults' experiences of ambivalence toward parents because it gratifies their age-specific needs of individuation regarding a secure base (of approval and support) from which they can explore autonomy and to which they can return for support if needed (Allen et al., 2003).

Behavioural control in the sense of providing structure and guidance seems to have positive effects on adolescents' developmental outcomes, whereas a lack of rules in the family has often been associated with externalized problems of adolescents (Barber, Olsen, & Shagle, 1994). Nonetheless, high levels of behavioral control may be experienced as patronizing and a restriction for adolescents' behavioral autonomy or as an invasion in their private domain (Arım, Marshall, & Shapka, 2010; Kakihara & Tilton-Weaver, 2009). This might apply especially for older adolescents. With growing age, adolescents tend to spend more time with their peers with whom they establish more balanced relationships regarding relative power. Thus, they also strive for more autonomy and power in their relations with their parents (Fuligni & Eccles, 1993; Steinberg & Silverberg, 1986), and they define more and more issues as their private matters (Smetana, 1988; Trommsdorff, 2006). Parents may differ in how far they adapt their authority demands, grant more autonomy, and include adolescents in decision-making processes and in discussions in line with these changed needs. Therefore, we suppose that with growing age of adolescents, their parents' use of high behavioral control could be a source for experienced ambivalence because adolescents may lack the possibility to renegotiate their relationships with their parents. These adolescents and emerging adults might move back and forth between compliance with parental requests and striving for autonomy or between the search for parental assistance and—at the same time—feeling oppressed.

We expect the strongest positive relation between psychological control and the experience of ambivalence because we presume that this form of control allows for the fulfillment of the respective needs of relatedness and autonomy only at the expense of each other. Psychological control refers to parental intrusion by criticizing, withdrawing love, or inducing guilt when the adolescent acts against the parent's will and has typically been related to internalizing problems (Barber et al., 1994). Adolescents with highly psychologically controlling parents may feel torn between their striving for autonomous exploration on the one hand and anxiety of losing parental approval and support on the other hand. In this case, we suppose that the individuation process is hampered because autonomy and relatedness appear to be incompatible for the adolescent. In a similar vein, psychologically controlling parenting was related to problems in the process of separation–individuation of emerging adults in a study by Kins, Soenens, and Beyer (2012). Therefore, we suppose here that when adolescents perceive their parents as psychologically controlling, balancing between the needs of autonomy and relatedness might seem impossible, and this should create a typical condition for the experience of ambivalence.

RESEARCH QUESTIONS AND HYPOTHESES

To summarize, we expect that parental warmth is negatively and psychological control positively related to ambivalence, independently of age, whereas parental control is increasingly positively related to ambivalence the older the study participants are.

We distinguish further between fathers and mothers as well as between sons and daughters to check for gender effects on both generational levels—parents and offspring. Although the importance of both mothers and fathers for child and adolescent development is widely acknowledged, mothers and fathers have been found to fulfill different roles in many studies (for an overview, see e.g., Lamb & Tamis-Lemonda, 2004). Several authors have described the relations with mothers (in particular of daughters) as more intimate compared with those with fathers; also, in general, fathers seem to spend less time with their offspring compared with mothers (e.g., Youniss & Smollar, 1985). Even though time spent with children has increased during the last years, there is still a gap between fathers and mothers (Dotti Sani & Treas, 2016). With regard to ambivalence, results of earlier studies have not yet provided a clear picture as far as gender differences are concerned. Therefore, no specific assumptions with regard to gender of parents and adolescents were formulated. However, in the study by Kins et al. (2012), results differed with regard to the impact of maternal and paternal psychological control on problems in the process of separation–individuation. Mothers seemed to be more implied in dependence issues, whereas fathers were more influential regarding independence issues. Thus, mothers and fathers might be involved in particular and specific aspects of development. Also, in a study by Michels, Albert, and Ferring (2011), different themes seemed to be prevalent regarding ambivalences of adult children toward their fathers compared with mothers. Therefore, we deemed it important to include both mothers and fathers in the present study.

METHODS

Participants

The total sample comprised 233 adolescents and emerging adults between 14 and 25 years of age ($M = 19.03$; $SD = 2.68$); 64.8% were female. The majority (82.5%) of respondents were of Luxembourgish nationality, 7.5% were German, and 5.7% Portuguese. All participants were enrolled in the Luxembourgish educational system, either attending high school (60.9%) or university (39.1%; 54.9% of them studied psychology, 14.3% German philology, 11.0% educational sciences). All participants were fluent in German. They provided data on the relationships with 232 mothers and 222 fathers. Mothers' ages ranged between 35 and 61 ($M = 48.09$; $SD = 4.85$), fathers' between 37 and 70 years ($M = 50.70$; $SD = 5.72$). In all, 83.2% of the mothers (88.3% of fathers) were married to the respondent's father (respectively, mother), 7.8% of mothers (6.8% of fathers) were remarried, and 7.8% of mothers (4.1% of fathers) were divorced. Most respondents lived in the same household as their parents (86.2% with mother, 76.6% with father) and to have daily contact with them (88.4% regarding mothers, 77.8% regarding fathers).

Measures

Participants filled out a self-report questionnaire in German comprising several scales relevant for this study. Psychological ambivalence was measured both directly and indirectly. With respect to the direct measurement of ambivalence, we used the shortened version of a newly developed instrument (Michels et al., 2011) describing conflicting motives, emotions, and behaviors in everyday life situations with six items (e.g., "On the one hand I have the feeling that my mother/father is proud of me, but on the other hand she/he always wants to change me"). Items were rated on a 5-point Likert scale from 1 (*does not apply at all*) to 5 (*fully applies*).

With regard to the indirect measurement of ambivalence, we used the well-known Griffin formula to build a continuous indirect ambivalence measure. This measure was based on the assessment of 26 statements about adolescents' positive and negative emotions in the relationships to mothers and fathers on a Likert-scale from 1 (*never*) to 5 (*always*) (Ferring et al., 2009; Michels et al., 2011). Two dimensions resulted from principal axis factoring (with Varimax rotation), namely, affection/closeness (e.g., "deep affection," "secure") containing seven items and reaching satisfying reliabilities as well as dislike (e.g., "choked," "angry") containing 16 items. The two dimensions of positive and negative emotions were then introduced in the formula of indirect ambivalence = (positive + negative)/2 – |positive–negative| + 1.5 to obtain the indirect measure of ambivalence. Values ranged between 0.50 and 4.92 ($M = 2.61$, $SD = 0.95$) for relations with mothers and between 0.71 and 4.88 ($M = 2.69$, $SD = 0.87$) with regard to relations with fathers.

Perceived parental behavior was measured with a shortened version of the "Zurich Brief Questionnaire for the Assessment of Parental Behaviour" (Reitzle, Winkler-Metzke, & Steinhausen, 2001) with three dimensions: "warmth and support" with three items (e.g., "My mother/father comforts me when I am in trouble"), "behavioral control" with four items (e.g., "My mother/father gives me clear rules and regulations how I should behave"), and "psychological control" with three items (e.g., "My mother/father regards me as ungrateful when I don't obey"). Items were rated on a 5-point Likert scale from 1 (*does not apply at all*) to 5 (*fully applies*). Table 6.1 gives an overview of the psychometric properties of the instruments in the present sample.

TABLE 6.1 Descriptive Statistics and Psychometric Properties of the Study Variables

	M	*SD*	*k*	α
Maternal Relationships				
Ambivalence (direct measure)[a]	2.37	0.83	6	.81
Affection/closeness	3.47	0.84	7	.89
Dislike	1.99	0.61	16	.90
"Warmth and support"	4.04	0.88	3	.84
"Behavioural control"	2.61	1.09	4	.76
"Psychological control"	2.26	0.93	3	.77
Paternal Relationships				
Ambivalence (direct measure)[a]	2.30	0.80	6	.69
Affection/closeness	3.14	0.79	7	.86
Dislike	2.00	0.61	16	.90
"Warmth and support"	3.56	0.97	3	.79
"Behavioural control"	2.67	0.93	4	.73
"Psychological control"	2.17	0.96	3	.71

[a] One item was dropped from the original version due to low item-total correlation.
Note: k = number of items. All items were rated on a 5-point Likert scale.

RESULTS

Preliminary Analyses of Age and Gender Differences in Perceived Parenting and Ambivalence

First, we examined whether perceived parenting dimensions and experienced ambivalence toward parents vary with age and inspected the specific correlations that resulted here for reports on mothers and fathers. Differences due to adolescents' gender were tested via *t* tests.

Both maternal and paternal warmth and support were unrelated to age, whereas behavioral control and, to a lesser extent, psychological control of both parents decreased with participants' age. No relation between age of participants and experienced ambivalence toward both parents was found when applying the direct or the indirect measure (see Table 6.2).

With regard to gender differences on the main variables, girls reported significantly higher support by both mothers and fathers, whereas boys reported higher psychological control by mothers. Also, boys rated ambivalence (direct measure) toward their mothers higher than girls (see Table 6.3).

We further checked for differences on the main variables with regard to the living arrangements of participants and their parents, namely, living in

TABLE 6.2 Correlations of Participant's Age With Parenting Dimensions and Ambivalence Toward Mother and Father

Age of Participant	Warmth and Support	Behavioral Control	Psychological Control	Ambivalence: Direct Measure	Ambivalence: Indirect Measure
Maternal relationships ($n = 232$)	.04	−.57**	−.20**	−.05	−.04
Paternal relationships ($n = 222$)	.08	−.47**	−.17*	−.08	−.08

* $p < .05$; ** $p < .01$

TABLE 6.3 Mean Differences on Main Variables With Regard to Gender

	Adolescents					
	Male		Female			
	M	*SD*	*M*	*SD*	*t*	*df*
Maternal Relationships						
Ambivalence (direct measure)	2.49	0.84	2.25	0.82	2.03*	229
Ambivalence (indirect measure)	2.72	0.91	2.55	0.97	1.36	231
"Warmth and support"	3.89	0.84	4.23	0.85	4.70**	230
"Behavioural control"	2.99	0.98	2.89	0.93	0.76	230
"Psychological control"	2.48	0.99	2.14	0.88	2.66**	230
Paternal Relationships						
Ambivalence (direct measure)	2.35	0.83	2.26	0.78	0.81	220
Ambivalence (indirect measure)	2.82	0.94	2.62	0.83	1.56	149
"Warmth and support"	3.29	0.85	3.72	1.00	3.17**	218
"Behavioral control"	2.61	0.93	2.70	0.93	0.64	218
"Psychological control"	2.28	0.95	2.10	0.97	1.29	218

* $p < .05$; ** $p < .01$

the same household or living apart. A subsample of only 32 adolescents did not live in the same household as their mothers. This group differed significantly from those living with their mothers only with regard to behavioral control, which was perceived as lower.

A number of adolescents ($n = 52$) did not live in the same household as their fathers. These adolescents experienced significantly less ambivalence (direct measure) toward fathers compared with those living with their fathers, and they reported to perceive fewer behavioral and psychological

TABLE 6.4 Mean Differences on Main Variables With Regard to Living in the Same Household (or Not) With a Parent

	Household					
	Same		Different			
	M	*SD*	*M*	*SD*	*t*	*df*
Maternal Relationships						
Ambivalence (direct measure)	2.38	0.80	2.07	1.00	1.94^{+}	228
Ambivalence (indirect measure)	2.64	0.91	2.45	1.14	0.90	38
"Warmth and support"	4.03	0.83	4.07	1.20	0.20	36
"Behavioral control"	3.02	0.92	2.38	0.97	3.63**	229
"Psychological control"	2.31	0.90	2.00	1.07	1.73^{+}	229
Paternal Relationships						
Ambivalence (direct measure)	2.36	0.79	2.07	0.80	2.28*	219
Ambivalence (indirect measure)	2.73	0.87	2.57	0.89	1.16	220
"Warmth and support"	3.48	0.94	3.83	1.05	2.28	217
"Behavioral control"	2.81	0.92	2.25	0.80	3.92**	217
"Psychological control"	2.28	0.96	1.83	0.90	2.95**	217

$^{+}$ $p < .10$; $^{*}p < .05$; $^{**}p < .01$

control by their fathers, whereas—interestingly—perceived paternal support was rated as slightly higher (see Table 6.4).

Parenting and Ambivalence

To test for predictive power of each parenting dimension with regard to ambivalence toward parents, regression analyses were carried out separately for maternal and paternal relationships, first with regard to the direct ambivalence measure and second with respect to the indirect ambivalence measure as criterion (see Tables 6.5, 6.6, and 6.7). To test for participants' age and gender as moderators for the links between parenting and ambivalence, the main effects of age, gender, and parenting dimension as well as the two- and three-way interactions between them were included block wise in the regression term (Cohen, Cohen, West, & Aiken, 2003). Continuous variables were standardized before the regression terms were built.

Perceived maternal "warmth and support" (see Table 6.5) was negatively associated with experienced ambivalence (direct measure), and this effect was further moderated by an interaction among age, gender, and maternal parenting [final model: $(7, 222) = 6.21$, $p < .01$; $R^2 = .16$]. To test for the direction of effects, we carried out separate regression analyses for boys and girls. For girls, maternal support was—independently of age—related

TABLE 6.5 Linear Regression Predicting Ambivalence Toward Mothers and Fathers by Parental Warmth and Support, Respondents' Age and Gender, and Two- and Three-Way Interactions

	Maternal Relationships ($n = 232$)				Paternal Relationships ($n = 222$)			
	Ambivalence				Ambivalence			
	Direct Measure		Indirect Measure		Direct Measure		Indirect Measure	
Predictors	*B*	*SE B*	*B*	*SE B*	*B*	*SE B*	*B*	*SE B*
Step 1 R^2 change	$.12^{**}$		$.15^{**}$		$.10^{**}$		$.13^{**}$	
Respondent age (1)	–0.04	0.06	–.02	0.06	–.06	0.07	–.04	0.06
Respondent gender (2)	–.06	0.14	.05	0.14	.01	0.14	–.06	0.14
Warmth and support (3)	$–.34^{**}$	0.07	$–.39^{**}$	0.06	$–.31^{**}$	0.07	$–.35^{**}$	0.06
Step 2 R^2 change	.01		.00		.01		$–.04^{*}$	
Interaction (1) × (2)	–.11	0.14	–.06	0.14	.14	0.14	–.17	0.13
Interaction (1) × (3)	–.06	0.06	–.03	0.06	–.06	0.07	$–.11^{+}$	0.06
Interaction (2) × (3)	.04	0.15	-.04	0.15	.17	0.15	$.40^{**}$	0.14
Step 3 R^2 change	$.03^{**}$		$.01^{+}$		.00		.00	
Interaction (1) × (2) × (3)	$.39^{**}$	0.13	0.23^{+}	0.13	.05	0.15	–.15	0.15

Note: All variables are *z*-standardized.
$^{+}p < .10$; $^{*}p < .05$; $^{**}p < .01$

negatively with experienced ambivalence ($B_{\text{maternal support}} = -.38^{**}$, $SE\ B = 0.09$), whereas for boys, an interaction between age and maternal support was found ($B_{\text{age} \times \text{maternal support}} = -.33^{**}$, $SE\ B = 0.11$). Three regression lines for the regression of boys' ambivalence toward mothers on maternal support were plotted with respect to comparably low (one SD below the mean), medium (at the mean), and high (one SD above the mean) age of respondent (see Cohen et al., 2003; see Figure 6.1a). This post hoc analysis showed that maternal support was a stronger negative predictor of ambivalence toward mothers for older compared with younger boys (simple slopes at low, medium, and high age were $b_{\text{low}} = -.12$, n.s.; $b_{\text{medium}} = -.44$, $p < .01$; $b_{\text{high}} = -.77$, $p < .01$). Regarding the indirect measure of ambivalence toward mothers, perceived maternal "warmth and support" was a negative predictor independently of age and gender [final model: (7, 224) = 6.10, $p < .01$; $R^2 = .16$].

In addition, perceived paternal "warmth and support" (see Table 6.5) emerged as a negative predictor of ambivalence when measured directly and independent of age and gender [final model: $F(7, 212) = 3.82$, $p < .01$; $R^2 = .11$]. The same association was found with regard to the indirect ambivalence measure, but here an interaction between gender and paternal support was found [final model: $F(7, 212) = 3.82$, $p < .01$; $R^2 = .11$]. Separate regression analyses for boys and girls (see Figure 6.1b) showed that the negative association between paternal support and ambivalence (indirect measure) was stronger for boys ($B = -.61$, $p < .01$, $SE\ B = .13$) compared with girls ($B = -.24$, $p < .01$, $SE\ B = 0.07$).

Perceived maternal "behavioral control" predicted experienced ambivalence (direct measure), and a significant interaction between behavioral control and respondents' age further moderated this effect (see Table 6.6) [final model: $F(7, 222) = 5.56$, $p < .01$; $R^2 = .15$]. Three regression lines for the regression of ambivalence toward mothers on maternal behavioral control were plotted with respect to comparably low (one *SD* below the mean), medium (at the mean), and high (one *SD* above the mean) age of respondent (see Cohen et al., 2003; see Figure 6.1c). This post hoc analysis showed that maternal behavioral control was a stronger predictor of ambivalence toward mothers for older compared with younger participants (simple slopes at low, medium, and high age were $b_{\text{low}} = .17$, $p < .10$; $b_{\text{medium}} = .40$, $p < .01$; $b_{\text{high}} = .63$, $p < .01$).

A similar result was found regarding maternal behavioral control predicting the indirect ambivalence measure, which was again moderated by adolescents' age [final model: $F(7, 224) = 2.47$, $p < .05$; $R^2 = .07$]. In line with the results for the direct ambivalence measure, the post hoc plotting showed that maternal behavioral control was a stronger predictor of ambivalence toward mothers (indirect measure) for older compared with younger participants (simple slopes at low, medium, and high age were $b_{\text{low}} = .11$, n.s.; $b_{\text{medium}} = .27$, $p < .01$; $b_{\text{high}} = .44$, $p < .01$) (see Figure 6.1d).

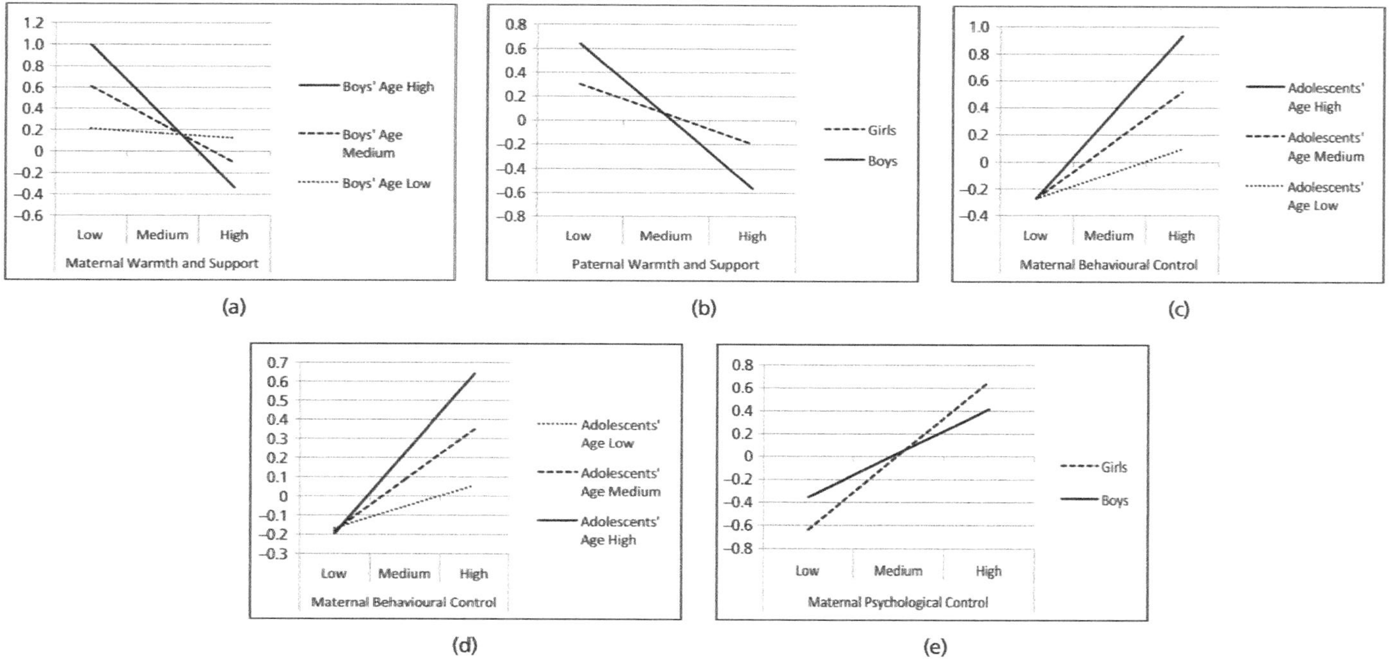

Figure 6.1 (a) Boys' Age as a Moderator of the Relation between Maternal Warmth/Support and Ambivalence toward Mothers (direct measure); (b) Adolescents' Gender as a Moderator of the Relation between Paternal Warmth/Support and Ambivalence toward Fathers (indirect measure); (c) Adolescents' Age as a Moderator of the Relation between Maternal Behavioural Control and Ambivalence toward Mothers (direct measure); (d) Adolescents' Age as a Moderator of the Relation between Maternal Behavioural Control and Ambivalence toward Mothers (indirect measure); (e) Adolescents' Gender as a Moderator of the Relation between Maternal Psychological Control and Ambivalence toward Mothers (indirect measure)

TABLE 6.6 Linear Regression Predicting Ambivalence Toward Mothers and Fathers by Parental Behavioral Control, Respondents' Age and Gender, and Two- and Three-Way Interactions

	Maternal Relationships (n = 232)				Paternal Relationships (n = 222)			
	Ambivalence				Ambivalence			
	Direct Measure		Indirect Measure		Direct Measure		Indirect Measure	
Predictors	*B*	*SE B*	*B*	*SE B*	*B*	*SE B*	*B*	*SE B*
Step 1 R^2 change	.11**		.05**		.10**		.04*	
Respondent age (1)	.18*	0.08	.12	0.08	.09	0.07	.04	0.08
Respondent gender (2)	–.29*	0.13	–.20	0.14	–.19	0.14	–.25+	0.14
Behavioral control (3)	.37**	0.08	0.25**	0.08	.35**	0.07	.20*	0.08
Step 2 R^2 change	.04*		.02		.00		.01	
Interaction (1) × (2)	–.07	0.16	.07	0.16	.14	0.16	–.12	0.16
Interaction (1) × (3)	.22**	0.07	.15*	0.07	–.01	0.08	–.10	0.08
Interaction (2) × (3)	–.18	0.16	–0.01	0.16	.02	0.16	.06	0.16
Step 3 R^2 change	.00		.00		.00		.00	
Interaction (1) × (2) × (3)	.01	0.14	.08	0.15	.03	0.16	–.04	0.16

Note: All variables are *z*-standardized.
+ $p < .10$; * $p < .05$; ** $p < .01$

TABLE 6.7 Linear Regression Predicting Ambivalence Toward Mothers and Fathers by Parental Psychological Control, Respondents' Age and Gender, and Two- and Three-Way Interactions

	Maternal Relationships (n = 232)				Paternal Relationships (n = 222)			
	Ambivalence				Ambivalence			
	Direct Measure		Indirect Measure		Direct Measure		Indirect Measure	
Predictors	***B***	***SE B***	***B***	***SE B***	***B***	***SE B***	***B***	***SE B***
Step 1 R^2 change	.47**		.30**		.33**		.25**	
Respondent age (1)	.09	0.05	.08	0.06	.02	0.06	.02	0.06
Respondent gender (2)	–.06	0.10	–.02	0.12	–.03	0.12	–.14	0.12
Psychological control (3)	.70**	0.05	.56**	0.06	.58**	0.06	.49**	0.06
Step 2 R^2 change	.01		.02		.02		.01	
Interaction (1) × (2)	–.09	0.10	.04	0.12	.17	0.12	–.16	0.13
Interaction (1) × (3)	.06	0.05	.01	0.06	–.08	0.06	–.01	0.06
Interaction (2) × (3)	.06	0.10	.26*	0.12	–.07	0.12	–.15	0.13
Step 3 R^2 change	.00		.00		.00		.00	
Interaction (1) × (2) × (3)	–.12	0.11	–.06	0.12	–.05	0.13	.05	0.14

Note: All variables are *z*-standardized.
$^{+}$ $p < .10$; $^{*}p < .05$; $^{**}p < .01$

Paternal "behavioral control" was a positive predictor of both the direct and indirect measures of ambivalence toward fathers independently of age and gender [final models: $F(7, 212) = 3.61$, $p < .01$; $R^2 = .11$; and $F(7, 212) = 1.90$, $p < .10$; $R^2 = .06$].

The strongest predictive model was found regarding perceived maternal "psychological control" (see Table 6.7), which was positively related to experienced ambivalence toward the mother (direct measure); no age or gender differences were found [final model: $F(7, 222) = 29.82$, $p < .01$; $R^2 = .48$]. When ambivalence was measured indirectly, an interaction between maternal psychological control and gender was found [final model: $F(7, 224) = 14.78$, $p < .01$; $R^2 = .32$]. Separate regression analyses for girls and boys (see Figure 6.1e) showed that psychological control was a slightly stronger predictor of ambivalence toward mothers (indirect measure) for girls compared with boys ($B = .66$, $SE\ B = .08$, $p < .01$ vs. $B = .41$, $SE\ B = .10$, $p < .01$).

Also paternal "psychological control" was a strong predictor of ambivalence toward fathers (direct and indirect measure) regardless of age and gender [final models: $F(7, 212) = 16.31$, $p < .01$; $R^2 = .35$; and $F(7, 212) = 10.63$, $p < .01$; $R^2 = .26$].[1]

DISCUSSION

The present study adds a developmental psychological perspective to the current discussion on intergenerational ambivalence by drawing on experiences of ambivalence in earlier stages of the child–parent relation—adolescence and emerging adulthood. Such a perspective has been missing because so far studies on intergenerational ambivalence have generally concentrated on older participants. Also, earlier studies have mostly focussed on structural antecedents for the occurrence of ambivalences (e.g., Van Gaalen et al., 2010), whereas the underlying psychological processes and mechanisms that might lead to the formation of specific relationship patterns and might be involved in the development of ambivalences remained unclear.

This study is the first to consider the link between perceived parental behavior and the experience of ambivalence toward parents in adolescence and emerging adulthood. As expected, parental warmth and support were related to lower levels of psychological ambivalence toward mothers and fathers in all age groups. Thus, the present study provides further evidence for the importance of parental support and warmth over the whole process of individuation (Buhl, 2008; Rohner, 2004). This is underlined by the finding that—in contrast to the two control dimensions—"perceived warmth and support" from both parents does not decrease with age of adolescents and emerging adults. Interestingly, gender was a moderator of the links between support and ambivalence. In fact, it seems that for boys, the importance of perceived warmth and support from their mothers as a factor that reduces their ambivalent feelings increases with age. Further, with regard to paternal relations, warmth and support seemed to be more important in reducing ambivalence toward fathers for boys than for girls. This finding is all the more remarkable when one considers that girls report about more support from both mothers and fathers—they may generally perceive a relatively higher level of support, whereas for boys—especially for older ones—it may make more of a significant difference whether their parents are experienced as supportive or not.

Parental behavioral control further predicted ambivalence toward both parents and independently of adolescents' gender. However, regarding maternal relations, this link was stronger for older compared with younger participants—when measured both directly and indirectly. This finding is in line with earlier studies that suppose an increase of adolescents' autonomy needs and striving for more power in the relations toward their parents during the process of individuation. As Buhl (2008) reports, with growing age, power between adolescents and their parents generally becomes more equilibrated. If parents do not allow for a renegotiation of their power relations, then this might be a source for ambivalence. Interestingly, the moderator effect of age was only found with regard to mothers. We might speculate that mothers' (compared with fathers') use of behavioral control might be more accepted by younger adolescents—and thus implying lower feelings of ambivalence—because mothers are often the primary caregivers for their children. The renegotiation of relationships in mid- and later adolescence may thus be especially important with regard to relations with mothers. This would be in line with studies that suggest specific roles of mothers and fathers in raising offspring.

Finally, both parents' psychological control was positively related to the experience of intergenerational ambivalence. With regard to maternal relations, this link was stronger for girls than for boys. Thus, we might presume that girls are more sensitive with regard to implicit messages in their relations to their mothers because mother–daughter relations have also been described as the most intimate (e.g., Youniss & Smollar, 1985).

In summary, different kinds of parental control seem to foster experiences of ambivalence under certain conditions that hinder the balancing of autonomy and relatedness: either by a strict, age-inadequate parenting that does not allow for a renegotiation of the relationship—as might be the case with high levels of behavioral control, especially at older ages—or by psychologically controlling parenting that threatens relatedness when autonomy is strived for, independently of adolescents' age. In this case, the two fundamental needs in the individuation process might appear as incompatible—one is only obtainable at the expense of the other—and this might be a typical condition for the experience of ambivalent feelings and ambivalent behavioral tendencies.

Finally, it should be mentioned that a comparison between participants who were living in the same household with their parents or in another household provided some indication for the importance of structural factors in the formation of ambivalences in child–parent relations. The availability of "exit options" (e.g., Van Gaalen et al., 2010) might reduce the experience of ambivalences, although this effect was larger with respect to fathers and only marginal with respect to mothers.

Limitations of the Present Study

Because our data stemmed from only one source—adolescents and emerging adults—one could argue that results might be blurred by the subjective perception of the study participants. Certainly, it would be interesting to compare the offsprings' reports with those of their parents. However, it has often been shown that reports of adolescents and parents with regard to their relationships might differ widely. Because we were particularly interested in the experience of ambivalences from the perspective of adolescents, it seemed reasonable to concentrate on the perceptions of adolescents. To minimize measurement effects, we included both direct and indirect measures of ambivalence. Both measures provided consistent results, thus granting validity to the present results.

CONCLUSIONS

The results show that ambivalences do not occur in a vacuum but within the family context, which is characterized by specific aspects of relationship coregulation (see also Albert et al., 2011; Albert & Barros Coimbra, 2017; Ferring, 2017). During transitional phases, it seems important how transformations in child–parent relations are tackled within the family, in particular how parental behavior is perceived by their offspring in terms of support provision, autonomy granting, and control. Some general effects were found with regard to the link between parenting dimensions and the experience of ambivalence—when measured both directly and indirectly. Further, the results also point to specific effects depending on gender of parents and adolescents as well as age of adolescents. The present study has shown that ambivalence might serve as a valid and fruitful concept for the study of child–parent relations in adolescence and emerging adulthood. In a lifespan perspective, future studies should also examine the long-term effects that earlier dynamics in child–parent relations may have for ambivalences during later transitions in adult child–parent relations. It would be desirable to examine how these relationships evolve over time in a longitudinal design because ambivalent relations might also become harmonious or conflict-laden later on depending on how relationship negotiation tasks are resolved (Ferring et al., 2009).

ACKNOWLEDGMENTS

We would like to thank Annick Arendt, BA, and Lynn Reis, BA, for their valuable work in collecting the data of this study. An earlier version was presented at the 3. Werkstattgespräch *Ambivalenz*, September 19–21, 2012, in Görlitz, Germany. We thank the *Interdisziplinärer Arbeitskreis Ambivalenz* [Interdisciplinary Work Group on Ambivalence] for their helpful comments. This work is part of the project "Intergenerational Relations in Luxembourg: Solidarity, Ambivalence, Conflict?" and was supported by a grant from the Fonds National de la Recherche (FNR) Luxembourg to the second author [FNR/06/02/11].

NOTE

1. Similar results were obtained when including only those adolescents/emerging adults who lived with their respective parent ($n = 200$ regarding maternal relations, $n = 170$ regarding paternal relations).

REFERENCES

Albert, I., & Barros Coimbra, S. (2017). Family cultures in the context of migration and ageing. *Integrative Psychological and Behavioral Science, 55*, 205–222.

Albert, I., & Steinhoff, A. (2016). Intergenerationale Ambivalenz in Eltern-Kind-Beziehungen im Jugend- und jungen Erwachsenenalter [Intergenerational ambivalence in parent-child relations]. *Zeitschrift für Soziologie der Erziehung und Sozialisation, 36*(2), 178–194.

Albert, I., Trommsdorff, G., & Sabatier, C. (2011). Patterns of relationship regulation: German and French adolescents' perceptions with regard to their mothers. *Family Science, 2*(1), 58–67.

Allen, J. P., McElhaney, K. B., Land, D. J., Kuperminc, G. P., Moore, C. W., O'Beirne-Kelly, H., et al. (2003). A secure base in *adolescence*: Markers of attachment security in the mother-adolescent relationship. *Child Development, 74*, 292–307.

Arim, R. G., Marshall, S. K., & Shapka, J. D. (2010). A domain-specific approach to adolescent reporting of parental control. *Journal of Adolescence, 33*, 355–366.

Barber, B. K., Olsen, J. E., & Shagle, S. C. (1994). Associations between parental psychological and behavioral control and youth internalized and externalized behaviors. *Child Development, 65,* 1120–1136.

Barber, B. K., Stolz, H. E., & Olson, J. A. (2005). Parental support, psychological control, and behavioral control: Assessing relevance across time, culture, and method. *Monographs of the Society for Research in Child Development, 70*(4), 1–137.

Baumrind, D. (1971). Current patterns of parental authority. *Developmental Psychology, 4,* 1–103.

Bengtson, V. L., & Roberts, R. E. (1991). Intergenerational solidarity in aging families: An example of formal theory construction. *Journal of Marriage and the Family, 53,* 856–870.

Buhl, H. M. (2008). Development of a model describing individuated adult parent-child relationships. *International Journal of Behavioral Development, 32*(5), 381–389.

Cohen, J., Cohen, P., West, S. G., & Aiken, L. S. (2003). *Applied multiple regression/correlation analysis for the behavioral sciences* (3rd ed.). Mahwah, NJ: Erlbaum.

Dotti Sani, G., & Treas, J. (2016) Educational gradients in parents' child-care time across countries, 1965–2012. *Journal of Marriage and Family, 78,* 1083–1096.

Ferring, D. (2017). The family in us: Family history, family identity and self-reproductive adaptive behavior. *Integrative Psychological and Behavioral Science, 51,* 195–204.

Ferring, D., Michels, T., Boll, T., & Filipp, S. H. (2009). Emotional relationship quality of adult children with ageing parents: on solidarity, conflict and ambivalence. *European Journal of Ageing, 6*(4), 253–265.

Fingerman, K. L., Pitzer, L., Lefkowitz, E. S., Birditt, K. S., & Mroczek, D. (2008). Ambivalent relationship qualities between adults and their parents: Implications for the well-being of both parties. *The Journals of Gerontology Series B: Psychological Sciences and Social Sciences, 63*(6), 362–371.

Fuligni, A. J., & Eccles, J. S. (1993). Perceived parent-child relationships and early adolescents' orientation toward peers. *Developmental Psychology, 29*(4), 622–632.

Furman, W., & Buhrmester, D. (1992). Age and sex differences in perceptions of networks of personal relationships. *Child Development, 63,* 103–115.

Grolnick, W. S., Gurland, S. T., DeCourcey, W., & Jacob, K. (2002). Antecedents and consequences of mothers' autonomy support: An experimental investigation. *Developmental Psychology, 38,* 143–155.

Grotevant, H. D., & Cooper, C. R. (1985). Patterns of interaction in family relationships and the development of identity exploration in adolescence. *Child Development, 56,* 415–428.

Kagitcibasi, C. (2005). Autonomy and relatedness in cultural context: Implications for self and family. *Journal of Cross-Cultural Psychology, 36,* 403–422.

Kakihara, F., & Tilton-Weaver, L. C. (2009). Adolescents' perceptions and interpretations of parental control: Differentiated by domain and type of control. *Child Development, 80,* 1722–1738.

Khaleque, A., & Rohner, R. P. (2002). Perceived parental acceptance-rejection and psychological adjustment: A meta-analysis of cross-cultural and intracultural studies. *Journal of Marriage and Family, 64,* 54–64.

King, V. (2010). Adoleszenz und Ablösung im Generationenverhältnis. *Diskurs Kindheits- und Jugendforschung, 1*, 9–20.

Kins, E., Soenens, B., & Beyers, W. (2012). Parental psychological control and dysfunctional separation–individuation: A tale of two different dynamics. *Journal of Adolescence, 35*, 1099–1109.

Kruse, J., & Walper, S. (2008). Types of individuation in relation to parents: Predictors and outcomes. *International Journal of Behavioral Development, 32*, 390–400.

Lamb, M. E., & Tamis-Lemonda, C. S. (2004). The role of the father: An introduction. In M. E. Lamb (Ed.), *The role of the father in child development* (pp. 1–31). Hoboken, NJ: Wiley.

Lüscher, K., & Hoff, A. (2013). Intergenerational ambivalence: Beyond solidarity and conflict. In I. Albert & D. Ferring (Eds.), *Intergenerational relations in society and family: European perspectives* (pp 39–63). Bristol: Policy Press.

Lüscher, K., Hoff, A., Klimczuk, A., Lamura, G., Renzi, M., de Salles Oliveira, P., Sánchez, M., . . . Canatan, A. (2017). *Generations, intergenerational relationships, generational policy: A multilingual compendium* [White paper]. Universität Konstanz. Retrieved from http://www.generationen-compendium.de/downloads/Kompendium_12sprachig_05-04-2017.pdf

Lüscher, K., Liegle, L., Lange, A., Hoff, A., Stoffel, M., Viry, G., & Widmer, E. (2010). *Generations, intergenerational relationships, generational policy: A trilingual compendium.* Bern: Swiss Academy of Humanities and Social Sciences.

Michels, T., Albert, I., & Ferring, D. (2011). Psychologische Ambivalenz in Eltern-Kind Beziehungen: Entwicklung und teststatistische Überprüfung eines Instrumentes zur direkten Konstruktabbildung [Psychological ambivalence in parent-child relations: On the development and the psychometric evaluation of a questionnaire for direct assessment]. *Diagnostica, 57*, 39–51.

Mikulincer, M., Shaver, P. R., Bar-On, N., & Ein-Dor, T. (2010). The pushes and pulls of close relationships: Attachment insecurities and relational ambivalence. *Journal of Personality and Social Psychology, 98*, 450–468.

Noack, P., & Buhl, H. (2005). Relations with parents and friends during adolescence and early adulthood. *Marriage & Family Review, 36*, 31–51.

Pillemer, K., Suitor, J. J., Mock, S. E., Sabir, M., Pardo, T. B., & Sechrist, J. (2007). Capturing the complexity of intergenerational relations: Exploring ambivalence within later life families. *Journal of Social Issues, 63*(4), 775–791.

Reitzle, M., Winkler-Metzke, C., & Steinhausen, H.-C. (2001). Eltern und Kinder: Der Zürcher Kurzfragebogen zum Erziehungsverhalten [Parents and children: The Zurich short questionnaire for parenting behaviour]. *Diagnostica, 47*, 196–207.

Rohner, R. P. (2004). The parental "acceptance-rejection syndrome": Universal correlates of perceived rejection. *The American Psychologist, 59*, 830–840.

Seiffge-Krenke, I. (2009). Leaving-home patterns in emerging adults. *European Psychologist, 14*(3), 238–248.

Shemmings, D. (2006) Using adult attachment theory to differentiate adult children's internal working models of later life filial relationships. *Journal of Aging Studies, 20(2)*, 177–191.

Silverstein, M., Parrott, T. M., & Bengtson, V. L. (1995). Factors that predispose middle-aged sons and daughters to provide social support to older parents. *Journal of Marriage and the Family, 57*, 465–475.

Smetana, J. G. (1988). Adolescents' and parents conceptions of parental authority. *Child Development, 59*, 321–335.

Smetana, J. G., Campione-Barr, N., & Metzger, A. (2006). Adolescent development in interpersonal and societal contexts. *Annual Review of Psychology, 57*, 255–284.

Steinberg, L., & Silverberg, S. B. (1986). The vicissitudes of autonomy in early adolescence. *Child Development, 57*, 841–851.

Trommsdorff, G. (2006). Parent-child relations over the life-span: A cross-cultural perspective. In K. H. Rubin & O. B. Chung (Eds.), *Parenting beliefs, behaviors, and parent-child relations: A cross-cultural perspective* (pp. 143–183). New York, NY: Psychology Press.

Van Gaalen, R., Dykstra, P. A., & Komter, A. E. (2010). Where is the exit? Intergenerational ambivalence and relationship quality in high contact ties. *Journal of Aging Studies, 24*, 105–114.

Youniss, J., & Smollar, J. (1985). *Adolescent relations with mothers, fathers, and friends.* Chicago: University of Chicago Press.

CHAPTER 7

DYNAMIC RELATIONS BETWEEN PERCEIVED PARENTAL RESPONSIVENESS, EXPERIENCES OF AMBIVALENCE, AND SELF-ESTEEEM DEVELOPMENT IN ADOLESCENCE

Annekatrin Steinhoff and Marlis Buchmann
University of Zurich

The concept of ambivalences refers to conflicting thoughts, feelings, and behavioral tendencies experienced in a relationship, which in turn inform a subject's sense of self (cf. Lüscher, 2012). One of the major sources of ambivalences in intergenerational relationships is the tension between longing for independence and still desiring close reliance to another person (Lüscher & Pillemer, 1998). Mid-adolescence seems particularly prone to ambivalences in family ties (cf. Michels, Albert, & Ferring, 2011). It is

Trans-Generational Family Relations, pages 121–140

probably the first time in life that the tension between the aims to become autonomous and stay intimately affiliated calls for the fundamental restructuring of the parent–child relationship. Interestingly enough, recent findings of a longitudinal study by Kiecolt, Blieszner, and Savla (2011) show that even parents experience rather high levels of ambivalences in the relationship with mid-adolescent children and decreasing levels when the children get older. Because adolescence is marked by major psychological and self-concept development, a corresponding consideration of the offspring's perspective is overdue.

For a long time, research on ambivalences in intergenerational relationships has targeted the linkages between experiences of ambivalence and psychological functioning, primarily examining ambivalences in family ties between adult children and their (aging) parents. The evidence gathered from these studies shows that higher levels of ambivalences are typically associated with lower levels of self-esteem (Lendon, Silverstein, & Giarrusso, 2014). Other studies almost consistently highlight negative correlations between the experience of ambivalences and components of psychological well-being (e.g., Kiecolt et al., 2011; cf. also Bengtson, Giarrusso, Mabry, & Silverstein, 2002). Surprisingly enough, research on ambivalences in intergenerational relationships has widely neglected the adolescent years, even though self-esteem is a key component of adolescent development, typically increasing with age from mid-adolescence onward (for reviews, see Huang, 2010; Orth & Robins, 2014).

Notwithstanding the negative association between ambivalence and self-esteem evidenced empirically, theoretical reasoning maintains that outcomes of ambivalences depend on the ways in which ambivalences are acknowledged and handled (Lüscher & Heuft, 2007). This underscores the significance of social interactional contexts of experiences of ambivalences. Yet little is known to date about the antecedents of differences in the levels and trajectories of ambivalences in adolescence and their outcomes. Moreover, because most empirical studies of ambivalences are based on cross-sectional data, the longitudinal interrelations between adolescent ambivalences and self-esteem development are virtually unexplored.

The aim of this chapter is to partially fill these gaps, first by taking a process-oriented view on ambivalences in adolescence. Second, we complement the parent-focused perspective (see Kiecolt et al., 2011) by investigating the intra-individual trajectory of the offspring's experiences of ambivalences in the parent–child relationship between mid- and late adolescence. Third, we aim to clarify how adolescent experiences of ambivalences relate to perceived parental responsiveness and self-esteem development across time. Our investigation is based on panel data of a representative sample of adolescents in the German- and French-speaking parts of Switzerland. The individuals were surveyed at ages 15, 18, and 21 years in 2006, 2009, and

2012, respectively. We will examine our questions using latent growth curve and latent change modeling techniques.

THEORETICAL CONSIDERATIONS AND CURRENT STATE OF RESEARCH

The theoretical framework first presents arguments for declining trajectories of ambivalence experiences between mid- and late adolescence. It then provides a rationale for why responsive parenting may be beneficial for low and decreasing levels of ambivalence in adolescence. Finally, the way in which the resolution of ambivalences is intertwined with the adolescent's self-esteem development is argued. Although the focus is on ambivalences as an outcome of parenting characteristics and an antecedent of self-esteem, we will also argue that the interrelations among these concepts may to some extent be reciprocal, paying attention to the temporal order of effects.

TRAJECTORIES OF AMBIVALENCES BETWEEN MID- AND LATE-ADOLESCENCE

The perception of social interactions as constraining one's action freedom heightens the likelihood of experiencing ambivalences (cf. Connidis & McMullin, 2002). Close family ties are generally characterized by relatively high levels of obligation, rendering parent–child relationships somewhat susceptible to ambivalences (e.g., Fingerman, Hay, & Birditt, 2004). This holds true particularly for adolescence. Also, mid-adolescence is associated with substantial personal development and the intensifying desire for autonomy, resenting the given limits mainly set by parents. Offspring increasingly dissociate from the role of the dependent child and aim to assume the role of self-reliant partners in the parent–child relationship. This requires the renegotiation of the adolescent's status in the family. However, as long as adolescents' action capacities are not yet fully developed and parents hesitate to grant their offspring increasing autonomy, the renegotiation often brings about conflict-ridden situations of social interaction (e.g., Smetana, 2011). Mid-adolescence therefore seems particularly prone to ambivalences experienced in the relationship with parents.

It is a prominent and intriguing assumption that ambivalences may for their part enhance the dynamic maintenance of social relationships (cf. Lüscher et al., 2014). In this vein, ambivalences are conceptualized "both as chances and burdens" for subjects, implying a perceptible "task of structuring relationships" (Lüscher, 2002, p. 587) and, at times, of restructuring them. This alludes to a "catalyst" function of ambivalences, triggering adolescent creativity in renegotiating social roles in the family and thus engendering successive change in relationship structures. This assumption is in line with the well-known fact that relationship representations in subjects are rooted in real experiences and inform further actions (e.g., Sroufe & Fleeson, 1986). Indeed, a longitudinal study by Hogerbrugge and Komter (2012), based on a sample of 18- to 79-year-olds, evidences that ambivalences are less stable over time than other relationship characteristics (e.g., levels of solidarity). A similar finding was reported by Kiecolt and colleagues (2011), documenting that ambivalences experienced by parents decline between offspring's mid- and late adolescent years. The pattern of intra-individual decline of ambivalences suggests that having mixed feelings in a close relationship is typically associated with discomfort, and therefore prompts subjects to struggle to get rid of their ambivalences (Bengtson et al., 2002; Hogerbrugge & Komter, 2012). Given that experiences of ambivalences are basically rooted in relationship structures, the decreasing levels of ambivalences further imply that changing relationship structures typically succeed.

Against this background, high levels of ambivalences in mid-adolescence are likely to be followed by their successive resolution. Expanding legal opportunities for self-reliance, increasing parental acceptance of offspring's independence, and the rise of action capacities may also ease the reconciliation of the simultaneous desires for autonomy and attachment when adolescents grow older. Although personal development continues well beyond mid-adolescence, and major status transitions are pending in late adolescence (e.g., Arnett, 2007), we expect that the prevalence of ambivalences experienced in the family is rather high in mid-adolescence and subsequently declines until the brink of adulthood is reached.

PARENTING CHARACTERISTICS AS ANTECEDENTS OF AMBIVALENCES IN ADOLESCENCE

Looking closely at interindividual differences in the emergence and persistence of ambivalences in adolescence, we draw on the assumption that some family environments allow for faster restructuring of the parent–child relationship than others. When offspring strive for autonomy and independence in mid-adolescence, parents face the challenge of providing them with a sense of self-reliance while remaining a "safe haven" to turn to. Warm and supportive parent–child relationships in particular facilitate constructive negotiation of diverse points of view and open dialogue about role attributions (cf. Smetana, 2010). Considerate parental response to the child's increasing aim at self-reliance is also likely to entail an adequate quantity of options for offspring's initiative to contribute to the relationship. Such options would support a subjective sense of agency in the adolescent and countervail their feelings of restrictedness. Sensing agency (or control) is closely associated with self-esteem and psychological well-being (e.g., Heckhausen, Wrosch, & Fleeson, 2001; Judge, Erez, Bono, & Thoresen, 2002; Ross & Broh, 2000). Against this background, the assumption that responsive parenting (showing warmth, approving adolescents' individuality, and supporting their autonomy) (Baumrind, 2005) lowers the likelihood of the offspring feeling restricted is underscored by empirical evidence suggesting that supportive parent–child relationships enhance adolescent development of self-esteem (Galambos, Barker, & Krahn, 2006). High levels of parental responsiveness seem to foster harmonization of the adolescent's rising aim at autonomy with the upkeep of affectionate bonding. Such high levels are therefore expected to facilitate faster restructuring of the relationship, and thus to antecede decreasing levels of ambivalences after mid-adolescence.

Changes in the bonds between adolescents and their parents typically pertain to characteristics of the relationship's surface structure, such as the amount of shared activities, whereas deep structural characteristics (see Hartup & Stevens, 1997), such as emotional connectedness perceived, tend to remain stable (cf. Collins & Laursen, 2000). Although relationship restructuring may be accompanied by temporal feelings of detachment, parents and children typically establish a new basis for feeling close in the longer run. Failing to renegotiate the foundations of the relationship, however, heightens the risk of the partners' alienation (Laursen & Collins, 2004). Against this background, our argument that persistent experience of ambivalences is a reflection of ineffective restructuring of the parent–child relationship leads to the expectation that lower rates of decline of ambivalences after mid-adolescence lead to lower levels of the adolescents' perception of their parents being responsive to their concerns.

COTRAJECTORIES OF AMBIVALENCES AND SELF-ESTEEM

Adolescence is generally associated with increasing action capacities and opportunities to realize self-reliance. In addition to the family context, adolescents get more and more involved in nonfamilial social environments (e.g., school, friendships), where they gain a sense of responsibility for themselves. Relationships within these contexts often provide adolescents with support, which adds to the emotional backing perceived in the family (e.g., Bokhorst, Sumter, & Westenberg, 2010). This support and the increasing sense of achievement are reflected in the prevalent rise of self-esteem observed after mid-adolescence (for reviews, see Huang, 2010; Orth & Robins, 2014).

The presumed co-occurrence of ambivalences and growth of self-esteem during adolescence may seem astonishing at first sight as ambivalences represent confusion about the self in relationships unlikely to strengthen a clear self-concept. This is the reason that previous research linked ambivalences to a negative sense of self and emotional distress. However, the previous argument that the successive resolution of ambivalences in adolescence may be indicative of a successful restructuring of the parent–child relationship leads to the assumption that this process is likely to enhance the adolescent's sense of self-realization, and therefore the level of self-esteem. Bringing together these lines of argument, we assume that higher levels of ambivalences in mid-adolescence may be temporarily associated with lower self-esteem but do not necessarily impair further self-esteem development. Rather, we expect that the resolution of ambivalences between mid- and late-adolescence is associated with a subject's growth of self-esteem. Looking closely at the temporal order of effects, we expect that not being able to abolish ambivalences after their anticipated peak in mid-adolescence entails successive detriment to the achieved level of self-esteem, owing to a persistent sense of lacking agency potential.

In contrast, our assumption that the abolishment of ambivalences results from successful renegotiation of relationship structures as evaluated from the adolescent perspective alludes to the significance of the adolescent's own contribution to these changes. Positive appraisal of own action potential generally encourages a subject's goal engagement and thus facilitates achievement (cf. Ross & Broh, 2000). Although empirical evidence suggests that self-esteem may not discretely affect adolescent attainment, it is an implication of influential domain-specific components of the adolescent self-concept (cf. Marsh & O'Mara, 2008). Therefore, we assume that self-esteem predicts individual chances to engage effectively in the restructuring of the parent–child relationship. More precisely, we expect that higher levels of self-esteem antecede sharper decline of ambivalences after mid-adolescence, whereas slower increase of self-esteem during adolescence is expected to result in higher levels of ambivalences in late adolescence.

DATA AND METHODS

The data set and measures used in the empirical analyses are presented. We then address missing data mechanisms and describe the statistical methods employed.

Sample

The analyses are based on data of the adolescent cohort ($N = 1{,}258$) of the Swiss longitudinal survey of children and youth COCON (http://www.cocon.uzh.ch), a representative sample of adolescents growing up in the German- (74%) and French-speaking (26%) parts of Switzerland. The sample was drawn from 131 communities (broken down by community type and size). The participants were surveyed at ages 15 (t_1), 18 (t_2), and 21 (t_3) in 2006, 2009, and 2012, respectively. The response rate at t_2 was 76% and 65% at t_3; 54% of the respondents are girls, 80% of the respondents are of Swiss nationality, 18% are of other European nationalities, and 2% are of non-European nationality. To control for underrepresentation of certain community types and nationalities, the analyses presented in the following text were replicated using a weighted sample. Because weighting did not alter the interpretation of the results, unweighted results will be reported.

Measures

All measures are based on adolescents' self-reports because we are most interested in the linkages between internal relationship representations and subjective conceptions of the self. Across survey waves, the vast majority of respondents declared that their mother was their primary caregiver (88% at t_1, 91% at t_2, and 92% at t_3), and almost all respondents (95%) referred to the same person as their primary caregiver at t_1, t_2, and t_3. Ambivalences experienced in the parent–child relationship are measured using a direct assessment of the adolescents' conflicting attitudes toward their primary caregiver and toward their relationship with that caregiver.[1] On 6-point scales, they reported the frequency of feeling "torn" about their primary caregiver (1 = *never* to 6 = *always*) and agreed with the statement, "Although I have a good relationship with [primary caregiver], it is sometimes restrictive" (1 = *totally disagree* to 6 = *totally agree*). These items addressing "awareness of ambivalences" were introduced by Lüscher et al. (2000), Lüscher, Pajung-Bilger, Lettke, and Boehmer (2000), and Pillemer and Suitor (2002), who studied mothers' ambivalences toward their adult children. In our sample, the two items are positively correlated at $r = .22$, $p = .000$ (t_1); $r = .27$, $p = .000$ (t_2); and $r = .29$, $p = .000$ (t_3). We thus specified them as indicators of a joint latent factor representing "awareness of ambivalences" at ages 15, 18, and 21. In several confirmatory factor analyses computed to test for longitudinal measurement invariance among the three time points and in the final models of latent change (see below), the standardized factor loadings were highly significant and consistently exceeded the value of .40.

Self-esteem was measured at ages 15, 18, and 21 years using four items of Rosenberg's (1965) self-esteem scale. The respondents assessed their level of agreement with statements such as, "All in all, I am satisfied with myself," on a 6-point scale ranging from 1 (*total disagreement*) to 6 (*total agreement*). High values represent high levels of self-esteem. Cronbach's alpha for the four items is satisfactory (.71 at t_1, .74 at t_2, and .77 at t_3).

Perceived parental responsiveness is assessed at ages 15, 18, and 21 years using four items taken from the Supportive Parenting Scale (Simons, Lorenz, Conger, & Wu, 1992). The respondents rated the frequency of occasions indicating supportiveness and affectionateness of their primary caregiver (e.g., "How often does [primary caregiver] show you that he/she really trusts you?"; "How often does [primary caregiver] talk to you about what is going on in your life?"). Assessments were made on a 6-point scale ranging from 1 = *never* to 6 = *always*. High values represent high levels of parental responsiveness. Cronbach's alpha for the four items is adequate at .73 (t_1), .79 (t_2), and .80 (t_3).

Missing Data

For less than 1% of the respondents, data regarding parental responsiveness, ambivalences, and self-esteem were missing due to nonresponse during an interview. Due to sample attrition, the amount of missing data ranged between 24% and 27% at t_2 and between 35% and 36% at t_3. To identify potential selectivity of attrition, we compared the groups of respondents and nonrespondents at t_3 with regard to gender, socioeconomic status, and mean scores on ambivalences, self-esteem, and parental responsiveness (scale level) assessed at t_1. Based on the International Socio-Economic Index (Ganzeboom, de Graaf, & Treimann, 1992), nonrespondents have lower levels of socioeconomic status than respondents ($t(1249) = -3.98$, Cohen's $d = -.24$, $p = .000$). This effect is rather small (cf. Cohen, 1988). As to the other variables, the groups of responders and nonresponders do not differ significantly, which suggests that "missingness" is not based on selective attrition mechanisms originated in these variables (see Allison, 2002). We account for missing data using the full maximum likelihood estimation implemented in Mplus (V7) when running the latent variable models described next.

Analytical Procedure

Second-order latent curve and latent change models (see e.g., Geiser, 2013) are used to identify intra-individual change for ambivalences, parental responsiveness, and self-esteem and to investigate their dynamic interrelations across time. This procedure allows for joint consideration of interindividual differences and intra-individual development. Using the "curve of factors" rationale in modeling change (McArdle, 1988), parental responsiveness, ambivalences, and self-esteem at t_1, t_2, and t_3 are specified as first-order latent variables. All of them are based on several manifest indicator variables described previously. In a first step, change is modeled by specifying the intercept (i.e., level at t_1) and a linear slope (i.e., rate of change within individuals across the three time points) as second-order latent growth factors for each of the first-order latent constructs. We analyze codevelopment of the constructs by estimating correlations between their intercepts and slopes. In a second step, we explore the temporal order of effects (cf. also Zuffianò, Colasante, Buchmann, & Malti, in press). Several models will be specified, where level and latent rate of change of one variable (e.g., ambivalences) between t_1 and t_2 are related to concurrent and subsequent change of another variable (e.g., parental responsiveness) between t_2 and t_3. All possible variable pairs will be considered.

To evaluate the adequateness of the various latent variable models, we refer to a set of fit indices (see e.g., T. Little, 2013; Weiber & Mühlhaus, 2010). When the χ^2 test is used as a reference, adequate model fit is indicated by a p value representing nonsignificance. This test, however, is known to be overly sensitive with large sample sizes. We therefore also use the Comparative Fit Index (CFI: adequate fit indicated by values >.90), the Root Mean Squared Error of Approximation (RMSEA: adequate fit indicated by values <.08), and the Standardized Root Mean square Residual (SRMR: adequate fit indicated by values <.08).

In preparation of the second-order latent variable models, we tested for strong factorial invariance of the first-order latent constructs at the three different time points. Confirmatory factor analyses were conducted to compare more and less restricted models using the ΔCFI < –.01 guideline proposed by Cheung and Rensvold (2002; see also T. Little, 2013). The results support the assumption of strong longitudinal measurement invariance (scalar invariance) for the latent constructs of ambivalences and self-esteem. With regard to parental responsiveness, partial scalar invariance was identified. Because scalar invariance holds for the majority of indicators, a sufficient level of invariance is still available to substantively interpret the second-order latent growth factors specified in the second-order models (cf. T. Little, 2013).

RESULTS

For ambivalences, parental responsiveness, and self-esteem, Table 7.1 shows the means and variances of the latent growth factors. All models fit the data well (ambivalences: χ^2 (5) = 7.42, p = .191, CFI = .99, RMSEA = .02, SRMR = .02; self-esteem: χ^2 (52) = 164.15, p = .000, CFI = .97, RMSEA = .04, SRMR = .05; parental responsiveness: χ^2 (51) = 144.82, p = .000, CFI = .98, RMSEA = .04, SRMR = .06). The mean slope of ambivalences is negative, which means a general decline occurs between mid- and late-adolescence. In contrast, self-esteem development is characterized by a positive slope.

TABLE 7.1 Mean and Variance of Intercept and Slope for the Latent Variables (t_1 to t_3)

	Intercept		Slope	
Variable	**Mean**	**Variance**	**Mean**	**Variance**
Parental responsiveness	5.81*	.39*	–.01	.09*
Ambivalences	3.37*	.37**	–.44*	.13***
Self-esteem	4.25*	.86*	.29*	.19*

* $p < .05$; ** $p < .01$; *** $p < .001$

Perceived parental responsiveness is, on average, stable (i.e., the mean of the slope is not significantly different from zero).

All latent constructs show considerable (nonzero) variance with regard to both intercept and slope. Therefore, we investigated how individual differences in ambivalence trajectories relate to parental responsiveness and self-esteem development. To investigate the correlation of the three trajectories, we specified a model where the intercepts and slopes of the three latent constructs were estimated simultaneously. The results are displayed in Figure 7.1. The model fit is adequate (χ^2 (384) = 793.61, p = .000, CFI = .95, RMSEA = .03, SRMR = .05).

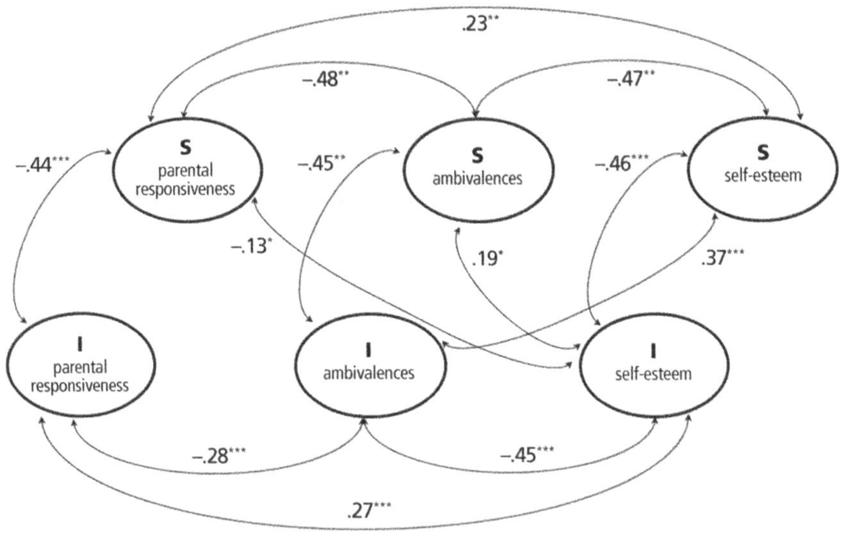

Figure 7.1 Co-trajectories of parental responsiveness, ambivalences, and self-esteem: Correlations between intercepts (I) and slopes (S).

Note: Only significant correlations are displayed.
*** $p < .001$; ** $p < .01$; * $p < .05$

The negative associations between intercept and slope of the same construct may be an indication of floor and ceiling effects (e.g., starting off with a high level of self-esteem sets a certain limit to the possible rate of further increase). More important with regard to our hypotheses is the finding of considerable correlations among the latent growth factors of the different constructs. Intercepts and slopes of parental responsiveness and self-esteem are positively correlated (i.e., they show parallel change across time). In contrast, intercept and slope of ambivalences are negatively correlated with those of the other two constructs (i.e., they show opposing trends across time). A sharper increase of parental responsiveness and self-esteem is associated with a sharper decrease of ambivalences.

We further investigated the directions of effects between initial levels and rates of change in short time intervals. Figure 7.2 is a simplified illustration of the general model. For each pair of first-order latent variables, both versions of the model were estimated. Controlling for all possible autoregressive paths, the initial level and slope (t_1 to t_2) of one variable were specified as predictors of concurrent and successive rate of change of another variable.

A summary of the results is provided in Table 7.2. It is limited to the effects of main interest, referring to the hypotheses formulated in the theory section.[2] In the different models, levels and rates of change of parental responsiveness and ambivalences (1.A and 1.B), ambivalences and self-esteem (2.A and 2.B), and, for the sake of completeness, parental responsiveness and self-esteem (3.A and 3.B) are related to each other. According to the fit indices reported in the table, all models fit the data well.

The results of model 1.A suggest that lower intercepts of parental responsiveness at age 15 are followed by relatively slow decline of ambivalences.

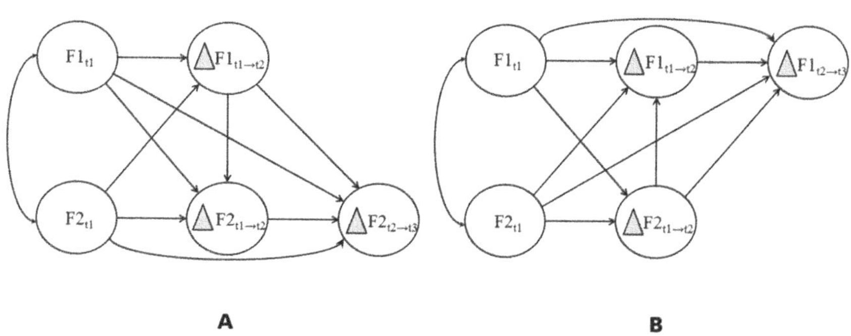

Figure 7.2 Two versions of the general model of dynamic effects between latent variable pairs.

Note: F1/F2 refers to a specific first order latent factor (i.e., parental responsiveness, ambivalences, or self-esteem) at a certain time point (t_1, t_2, or t_3); a triangle (delta) in a circle refers to latent change between two time-points.

TABLE 7.2 Results of the Models Relating Latent Change Between t_1 and t_2 in One Domain to Concurrent and Subsequent Latent Change in Another Domain

Model	Effect	Std. Coeff.	*p*	Model Fit
1.A	$A_{t1} \rightarrow \Delta PR_{t1\rightarrow t2}$	.06	.395	
	$PR_{t1} \rightarrow \Delta A_{t1\rightarrow t2}$	−.19	.001	
	$PR_{t1} \rightarrow \Delta A_{t2\rightarrow t3}$	−.03	.608	
	$\Delta PR_{t1\rightarrow t2} \rightarrow \Delta A_{t1\rightarrow t2}$	−.33	.000	$\chi^2(66) = 147.19$, $p = .000$
	$\Delta PR_{t1\rightarrow t2} \rightarrow \Delta A_{t2\rightarrow t3}$	−.05	.517	CFI = .97; RMSEA = .03; SRMR = .04
1.B	$PR_{t1} \rightarrow \Delta A_{t1\rightarrow t2}$	−.10	.088	
	$A_{t1} \rightarrow \Delta PR_{t1\rightarrow t2}$	−.10	.136	
	$A_{t1} \rightarrow \Delta PR_{t2\rightarrow t3}$	−.13	.028	
	$\Delta A_{t1\rightarrow t2} \rightarrow \Delta PR_{t1\rightarrow t2}$	−.34	.000	$\chi^2(93) = 226.93$, $p = .000$
	$\Delta A_{t1\rightarrow t2} \rightarrow \Delta PR_{t2\rightarrow t3}$	−.07	.304	CFI = .97, RMSEA = .03,; SRMR = .05
2.A	$A_{t1} \rightarrow \Delta SE_{t1\rightarrow t2}$	.10	.086	
	$SE_{t1} \rightarrow \Delta A_{t1\rightarrow t2}$	−.10	.163	
	$SE_{t1} \rightarrow \Delta A_{t2\rightarrow t3}$	−.16	.020	
	$\Delta SE_{t1\rightarrow t2} \rightarrow \Delta A_{t1\rightarrow t2}$	−.37	.000	$\chi^2(67) = 111.21$, $p = .001$
	$\Delta SE_{t1\rightarrow t2} \rightarrow \Delta A_{t2\rightarrow t3}$	−.16	.072	CFI = .99, RMSEA = .02, SRMR = .03
2.B	$SE_{t1} \rightarrow \Delta A_{t1\rightarrow t2}$	.09	.222	
	$A_{t1} \rightarrow \Delta SE_{t1\rightarrow t2}$	−.03	.677	
	$A_{t1} \rightarrow \Delta SE_{t2\rightarrow t3}$	−.00	.990	
	$\Delta A_{t1\rightarrow t2} \rightarrow \Delta SE_{t1\rightarrow t2}$	−.32	.000	$\chi^2(94) = 177.79$, $p = .000$
	$\Delta A_{t1\rightarrow t2} \rightarrow \Delta SE_{t2\rightarrow t3}$	.09	.258	CFI = .98, RMSEA = .03, SRMR = .04
3.A	$PR_{t1} \rightarrow \Delta SE_{t1\rightarrow t2}$	.07	.063	
	$SE_{t1} \rightarrow \Delta PR_{t1\rightarrow t2}$	.04	.372	
	$SE_{t1} \rightarrow \Delta PR_{t2\rightarrow t3}$	.05	.346	
	$\Delta SE_{t1\rightarrow t2} \rightarrow \Delta PR_{t1\rightarrow t2}$	.18	.001	$\chi^2(161) = 338.31$, $p = .000$
	$\Delta SE_{t1\rightarrow t2} \rightarrow \Delta PR_{t2\rightarrow t3}$	.04	.459	CFI = .97, RMSEA = .03, SRMR = .05
3.B	$SE_{t1} \rightarrow \Delta PR_{t1\rightarrow t2}$	−.06	.156	
	$PR_{t1} \rightarrow \Delta SE_{t1\rightarrow t2}$	.11	.003	
	$PR_{t1} \rightarrow \Delta SE_{t2\rightarrow t3}$	.06	.200	
	$\Delta PR_{t1\rightarrow t2} \rightarrow \Delta SE_{t1\rightarrow t2}$	.14	.001	$\chi^2(161) = 330.87$, $p = .000$
	$\Delta PR_{t1\rightarrow t2} \rightarrow \Delta SE_{t2\rightarrow t3}$	.03	.540	CFI = .98, RMSEA = .03, SRMR = .05

Note: Summary of results is limited to the effects of main interest referring to our hypotheses. Significant coefficients are in highlighted cells.
PR, parental responsiveness; A, ambivalences; SE, self-esteem.

Beyond that, the rate of change of parental responsiveness between ages 15 and 18 years affects concurrent change of ambivalences. The negative sign of the coefficient implies that a sharper increase of parental responsiveness results in lower levels of ambivalences. According to the results of model 1.B, the intercept of ambivalences negatively affects the slope of parental responsiveness in late adolescence. Further, a sharper decrease of ambivalences between ages 15 and 18 years is associated with less decrease of parental responsiveness.

According to the results of models 2.A and 2.B, ambivalences are also dynamically interrelated with self-esteem. The results of model 2.A suggest that positive self-esteem development typically averts the experience of ambivalences. A sharper increase of self-esteem between ages 15 and 18 years is associated with sharper decrease of ambivalences. Moreover, higher initial levels of self-esteem are followed by a sharper decline of ambivalences between ages 18 and 21 years. In line with that, the results of model 2.B suggest that a sharper decrease of ambivalences between mid- and late adolescence is associated with concurrently increasing levels of self-esteem. In other words, a slower decrease of ambivalences is followed by lower levels of self-esteem. It is specifically noteworthy that self-esteem development is not predicted by the initial level of ambivalences but rather by their rate of change.

Finally, the results of model 3.A suggest that a sharper increase of self-esteem between ages 15 and 18 years is associated with sharper increase of parental responsiveness. In contrast, the results of model 3.B indicate that self-esteem development by age 18 is positively affected by the initial level and slope of parental responsiveness between mid- and late adolescence. Apparently relationship quality as well as change of relationship quality has an impact on the subjects' attitudes toward the self, others, and the relationship.

DISCUSSION

The study presented here advances existing knowledge about the antecedents and outcomes of ambivalences in adolescence by taking a longitudinal perspective on developmental trajectories and their social and individual contexts. Longitudinal designs are rare in family research addressing ambivalences, but they are much needed to thoroughly understand the phenomenon (cf. Lendon et al., 2014). The longitudinal design enables us to clarify whether mid-adolescence is specifically prone to ambivalences in the parent–child relationship. Moreover, our findings confirm the assumption that perceived parental responsiveness, trajectories of ambivalences experienced, and self-esteem development are interrelated dynamically.

The Intra-Individual Trajectory of Ambivalences in Adolescence

The findings confirm our hypothesis that ambivalences are rather prevalent in mid-adolescence but then decline. Because ambivalences are particularly likely to emerge when contexts of social interaction set appreciable limits to the subjective sense of agency potential (Connidis & McMullin, 2002), mid-adolescents are more susceptible to feelings of restrictedness in the parent–child relationship than subjects who are about to reach adult age. Mid-adolescents show lower action capacities and their parents approve less the child's autonomy. Interestingly, the general decline of offspring's experiences of ambivalences between mid- and late adolescence is also in line with Kiecolt, Blieszner, and Savla's (2011) longitudinal study showing that parents have more ambivalent feelings toward younger adolescents than toward older ones. Despite the differences in measurement (direct vs. indirect) between our study and that by Kiecolt et al., and given the different perspectives taken into account (i.e., the adolescent's perspective in our study and the parents' perspective in the Kiecolt et al. study), we may draw the joint conclusion that parent–child relationships are generally marked by a peak and subsequent decrease of all relationship partners' susceptibility to ambivalences between the offspring's mid- and late adolescent years.

Experiences of Ambivalence, Relationship Dynamics, and the Development of Self-Esteem

In line with previous research (Collins & Laursen, 2000), we found indication of considerable stability of the quality of emotional bonds between offspring and parents during adolescence. However, the data revealed inter-individual variation and a negative relation between perceived parental responsiveness and experiences of ambivalence. Higher levels and a more rapid increase of parental responsiveness are associated with lower levels and a faster decline of ambivalences. This finding supports our hypothesis that considerate parenting fosters proactive handling of ambivalences and, accordingly, their abolishment. The analysis of the temporal order of effects underpins this finding. Supporting our hypothesis of reciprocal effects, we also found an indication of impairment of the emotional bond with parents due to a slow decrease of ambivalences after mid-adolescence. We may conclude that ambivalences are associated with (temporal) feelings of detachment, which severely impair closeness of partners when they fail or take long to restructure their relationship. Because we did not hypothesize the unique negative effect of the level of ambivalences in mid-adolescence on the rate of change of perceived parental responsiveness between ages 18 and 21 years, we forego speculating on possible interpretations at this point.

The significant negative mean slope of ambivalences indicates that most families successfully manage the restructuring of the parent–child relationship. As argued before, the general decline of ambivalences thereby evidences a human aim for control, urging subjects to abolish their mixed feelings once they have emerged (cf. Hogerbrugge & Komter, 2012). This interpretation is supported by the opposing trends of ambivalences and self-esteem. Growth of self-esteem, which was introduced as an implication of the subject's increasing sense of agency, is apparently closely linked to the experience of managing resolution of ambivalences. The finding of general increase of self-esteem between mid- and late adolescence is in line with previous evidence of normative self-esteem trajectories (for reviews, see Huang, 2010; Orth & Robins, 2014). Likewise, the concurrent negative association of self-esteem and ambivalences is consistent with previous findings for other age groups (Lendon et al., 2014) but adds to them a process-oriented view.

Our argument that individual outcomes of ambivalent feelings are not determined by the experience of ambivalences per se but rather by an ongoing sense of not being able to resolve them is also supported. The findings derived from analyzing the dynamic interplay between the variables suggest that the rate of change of ambivalences is more decisive than the intercept in explaining differences in the subjects' self-esteem. Ambivalences seem to become detrimental to self-esteem when subjects do not sense progress in resolving their mixed feelings but perceive them as a regular state of confusion. We may conclude that experiencing ambivalences in the family is rather normal in mid-adolescence, but struggling successfully for their resolution is a developmental task to be accomplished by late adolescence. Time, in terms of the individual life span, is thus a crucial dimension to be considered in future research investigating individual differences in the outcomes of ambivalences. This notion is underpinned by the observed effects of ambivalences on self-esteem development but also by the apparent impact of ongoing ambivalences on perceived closeness with parents discussed before.

In line with our expectations, the results of the analyses of the temporal order of effects eventually suggest that the linkages between ambivalences and self-esteem are also to some extent reciprocal. In line with the assumption that self-esteem is a reflection of a subject's sense of agency potential, high self-esteem apparently predicts proactive handling of ambivalent feelings and implies the facility to abolish them. In contrast, adolescents with low self-esteem experience rather higher levels of ambivalences later on. It is important to note that, although our results are suggestive, they eventually do not allow for causal inference. For this purpose, future research needs to directly compare competing models of directed effects.

LIMITATIONS AND SUGGESTIONS FOR FUTURE RESEARCH

Although the present investigation provides comprehensive insights into the contexts of adolescent experiences of ambivalences, the selection of variables included has its limitations. Besides ambivalences, parental responsiveness was the only aspect of the parent–child relationship considered. However, dynamics in the parent–child relationship stemming from ambivalences were assumed to pertain to other aspects as well, such as the offspring's options to exercise autonomy. Further longitudinal research is needed to confirm our assumption that the abolishment of ambivalences in the child is a reflection of a restructuring of social roles in the family. In a similar vein, the findings must be seen in view of the fact that all information used here was based on adolescents' self-reports. Using additional information provided by the parent may further add to the findings and their interpretations.

The literature maintains that the concept of ambivalences relates to the significance of norms and values in social interaction. Future research on individual trajectories of ambivalences and their outcomes may provide new insights by using sample stratifications based on general indicators of unequal constraints and opportunities to handle ambivalences (cf. Connidis & McMullin, 2002) and combining this with our focus on the significance of considerate and affectionate bonding. One of the most important parameters to be considered more carefully is probably gender. It is well known that role allocations, subjective preferences, and perceptions of relationship characteristics tend to vary with gender, already in adolescence (Maccoby, 1995). Taking up the argument that gender is closely linked to conceptions of "normal" life courses, success, and failure, empirical research has also shown gender-specific dependency of self-esteem development on life course trajectories, such as educational tracks (Bayard, Staffelbach, Fischer, & Buchmann, 2014). Although controlling for gender in the process-oriented models we conducted did not change the interpretation of the results, gender turned out to be a significant additional predictor of some of the latent variables. Therefore, a next step could be to compute separate models for male and female respondents to see whether they evidence differential correlations between the variables of the study.

Finally, we would like to comment on the measurement of ambivalences used in this chapter. Our investigation was based on a direct assessment using two indicator variables developed and validated in previous studies (see in particular Pillemer & Suitor, 2002). The analysis of their shared latent structure supported the rationale to specify them as indicators of a joint factor labeled the "awareness of ambivalences." Because the two variables are significantly correlated but the size of their correlation is rather moderate, the underlying latent structure seems to represent a rather broad domain (cf. Little, Lindenberger, & Nesselroade, 1999). Both indicators refer to ambivalences in the parent–child relationship, with a special focus on ambivalences toward the primary caregiver as a person (first item) and toward the relationship as such (second item). Exploratory analyses conducted subsequent to the main investigation revealed that, at all points of time, the number of respondents reporting ambivalences toward the relationship (item scorings equal or above 3) was considerably larger than the number of respondents who scored 3 or higher on the person-related item. Similarly, Pillemer and Suitor (2002) found that the proportion of mothers who acknowledged that they had mixed feelings toward their child was smaller than the proportion of those who perceived their relationship with the child as intimate but also restrictive. Having mixed feelings toward a close person seems to be a special facet of ambivalences in the parent–child relationship, which is less prevalent than feeling ambivalent toward the relationship as such and may be perceived as more severe. It is also possible that, for reasons of social desirability, subjects feel more inhibited from admitting ambivalence toward a close person than toward a relationship. This, however, underpins the assumption that experiencing ambivalence toward different targets is associated with different degrees of uneasiness. Although the two items can reasonably be combined to represent an overall level of ambivalences, their differential focus thus deserves due consideration in future studies of the antecedents and outcomes of ambivalences in intergenerational relationships.

Despite the limitations mentioned, the results presented in this chapter advance our understanding of the antecedents and outcomes of ambivalences in adolescence. Future research may gain from an application of the longitudinal, process-oriented view to other periods of life and from investigating these processes with due consideration of different contexts of social interaction framing the subjects' daily routine.

NOTES

1. While indirect measures of ambivalences represent the concurrence of positive and negative emotions toward a person/relationship, which the target subject is not necessarily aware of, direct measures are a reflection of the subject's conscious acknowledgment of having mixed feelings (Lüscher & Lettke, 2004; Lendon, Silverstein, & Giarrusso, 2014).
2. All other paths depicted in Figure 7.2 were controlled for. Moreover, although the results displayed are unconditioned, all models were also estimated controlling for gender and socioeconomic status. This did not result in a substantial downgrade of the regression coefficients or significance levels.

REFERENCES

Allison, P. D. (2002). *Missing data.* Thousand Oaks, CA: SAGE.

Arnett, J. J. (2007). Socialization in emerging adulthood: From the family to the wider world, from socialization to self-socialization. In J. E. Grusec & P. D. Hastings (Eds.), *Handbook of socialization* (pp. 208–231). New York, NY: Guilford Press.

Baumrind, D. (2005). Patterns of parental authority and adolescent autonomy. *New Directions for Child and Adolescent Development, 108,* 61–69.

Bayard, S., Staffelbach, M., Fischer, P., & Buchmann, M. (2014). Upper-secondary educational trajectories and young men's and women's self-esteem development in Switzerland. In A. C. Keller, R. Samuel, M. M. Bergmann, & N. K. Semmer (Eds.), *Psychological, educational, and sociological perspectives on success and well-being in career development* (pp. 19–44). Dodrecht: Springer.

Bengtson, V., Giarrusso, R., Mabry, J. B., & Silverstein, M. (2002). Solidarity, conflict, and ambivalence: Complementary or competing perspectives on intergenerational relationships? *Journal of Marriage and Family, 64,* 568–576.

Bokhorst, C. L., Sumter, S. R., & Westenberg, P. M. (2010). Social support from parents, friends, classmates, and teachers in children and adolescents aged 9 to 18 years: Who is perceived as most supportive? *Social Development, 19*(2), 417–426.

Cheung, G. W., & Rensvold, R. B. (2002). Evaluating goodness-of-fit indexes for testing measurement invariance. *Stuctural Equation Modeling, 9*(2), 233–255.

Cohen, J. (1988). *Statistical power analysis for the behavioral sciences* (2nd ed.). New York, NY: Psychology Press, Taylor & Francis Group.

Collins, W. A., & Laursen, B. (2000). Adolescent relationships: The art of fugue. In C. Hendrick & S. S. Hendrick (Eds.), *Close relationships: A sourcebook* (pp. 59–70). Thousand Oaks, London, & New Delhi: SAGE.

Connidis, I. A., & McMullin, J. A. (2002). Sociological ambivalence and family ties: A critical perspective. *Journal of Marriage and Family, 64,* 558–567.

Fingerman, K. L., Hay, E. L., & Birditt, K. S. (2004). The best of ties, the worst of ties: Close, problematic, and ambivalent social relationships. *Journal of Marriage and Family, 66,* 792–808.

Galambos, N. L., Barker, E. T., & Krahn, H. J. (2006). Depression, self-esteem, and anger in emerging adulthood: Seven-year trajectories. *Developmental Psychology, 42*(2), 350–365.

Ganzeboom, H. B. G., de Graaf, P. M., & Treimann, D. J. (1992). A Standard International Socio-Economic Index of Occupational Status. *Social Science Research, 21*(1), 1–56.

Geiser, C. (2013). *Data analysis with MPlus.* New York, NY: Guilford Press.

Hartup, W. W., & Stevens, N. (1997). Friendships and adaption in the life course. *Psychological Bulletin, 121*(3), 355–370.

Heckhausen, J., Wrosch, C., & Fleeson, W. (2001). Developmental regulation before and after a developmental deadline: The sample case of "biological clock" for childbearing. *Psychology and Aging, 16*(3), 400–413.

Hogerbrugge, M. J., & Komter, A. E. (2012). Solidarity and ambivalence: Comparing two perspectives on intergenerational relations using longitudinal panel data. *The Journals of Gerontology. Series B: Psychological Sciences and Social Sciences, 67*(3), 372–383.

Huang, C. (2010). Mean-level change in self-esteem from childhood through adulthood: Meta-analysis of longitudinal studies. *Review of General Psychology, 14*(3), 251–260.

Judge, T. A., Erez, A., Bono, J. E., & Thoresen, C. J. (2002). Are measures of self-esteem, neuroticism, locus of control, and generalized self-efficacy indicators of a common core construct? *Journal of Personality and Social Psychology, 83*(3), 693–710.

Kiecolt, K. J., Blieszner, R., & Savla, J. (2011). Long-term influences of intergenerational ambivalence on midlife parents' psychological well-being. *Journal of Marriage and Family, 73*(2), 369–382.

Laursen, B., & Collins, W. A. (2004). Parent-child communication during adolescence. In A. G. Vangelisti (Ed.), *Handbook of family communication* (pp. 333–348). Mahwah, NJ & London, England: Erlbaum.

Lendon, J. P., Silverstein, M., & Giarrusso, R. (2014). Ambivalence in older parent-adult child relationships: Mixed feelings, mixed measures. *Journal of Marriage and Family, 76*(2), 272–284.

Little, D., Lindenberger, U., & Nesselroade, J. R. (1999). On selecting indicators for multivariate measurement and modeling with latent variables: When "good" indicators are bad and "bad" indicators are good. *Psychological Methods, 4*(2), 192–211.

Little, T. D. (2013). *Longitudinal structural equation modeling.* New York & London, England: Guilford Press.

Lüscher, K., Hoff, A., Lamura, G., Renzi, M., Sánchez, M., Viry, G., & Widmer, E. (2014). *Generations, intergenerational relationships, generational policy.* Retrieved from http://www.kurtluescher.de/downloads/Comp_2014_14.05.14.pdf

Lüscher, K. (2002). Intergenerational ambivalence: Further steps in theory and research. *Journal of Marriage and Family, 64,* 585–593.

Lüscher, K. (2012). Menschen als "homines ambivalentes" [Humans as "homines ambivalentes"]. In D. Korczak (Ed.), *Ambivalenzerfahrungen* (pp. 11–32). Kroening: Asanger.

Lüscher, K., & Heuft, G. (2007). Ambivalenz-Belastung-Trauma. *Psyche, 61,* 218–231.

Lüscher, K., & Lettke, F. (2004). Intergenerational ambivalence: Methods, measures, and results of the Konstanz Study. In K. Pillemer & K. Lüscher (Eds.), *Intergenerational ambivalences: New perspectives on parent-child relations in later life* (pp. 153–179). New York, NY: Elsevier.

Lüscher, K., Pajung-Bilger, B., Lettke, F., & Boehmer, S. (2000). *Generationenambivalenzen operationalisieren: Konzeptuelle, methodische und forschungspraktische Grundlagen* [Operationalizing intergenerational ambivalences: Conceptional, methodical, and research related practical foundations] (Arbeitspapier 34.1). Universitaet Konstanz: Forschungsschwerpunkt „Gesellschaft und Familie."

Lüscher, K., Pajung-Bilger, B., Lettke, F., Boehmer, S., Rasner, A., & Pillemer, K. (2000). *Generationenambivalenzen operationalisieren: Instrumente* [Operationalizing intergenerational ambivalences: Instruments] (Arbeitspapier 34.4). Universitaet Konstanz: Forschungsschwerpunkt „Gesellschaft und Familie."

Lüscher, K., & Pillemer, K. (1998). Intergenerational ambivalence. A new approach to the study of parent-child relations in later life. *Journal of Marriage and Family, 60,* 413–425.

Maccoby, E. E. (1995). The two sexes and their social systems. In P. Moen, G. H. Elder, Jr., & K. Lüscher (Eds.), *Examining lives in context: Perspectives on the ecology of human development* (pp. 347–364). Washington, DC: American Psychological Association.

Marsh, H. W., & O'Mara, A. (2008). Reciprocal effects between academic self-concept, self-esteem, achievement, and attainment over seven adolescent years: Unidimensional and multidimensional perspectives of self-concept. *Personality and Social Psychology Bulletin, 34*(4), 542–552.

McArdle, J. J. (1988). Dynamic but structural equation modeling of repeated measures data. In R. B. Cattell & J. Nesselroade (Eds.), *Handbook of multivariate experimental psychology* (2nd ed., pp. 561–614). New York, NY: Plenum.

Michels, T., Albert, I., & Ferring, D. (2011). Emotional relations with grandparents and received support: The adolescent view. *Journal of Intergenerational Relationships, 9*(3), 264–280.

Orth, U., & Robins, R. W. (2014). The development of self-esteem. *Current Directions in Psychological Science, 23*(5), 381–387. Pillemer, K., & Suitor, J. J. (2002). Explaining mothers' ambivalence toward their adult children. *Journal of Marriage and Family, 64,* 602–613.

Rosenberg, M. (1965). *Society and the adolescent self-image.* Princeton, NJ: Princeton University Press.

Ross, C. E., & Broh, B. A. (2000). The roles of self-esteem and the sense of personal control in the academic achievement process. *Sociology of Education, 73*(4), 270–284.

Simons, R. L., Lorenz, F. O., Conger, R. D., & Wu, C.-I. (1992). Support from spouse as mediator and moderator of the disruptive influence of economic strain. *Child Development, 63*(5), 1282–1301.

Smetana, J. (2010). The role of trust in adolescent–parent relationships: To trust you is to tell you. In K. J. Rotenberg (Ed.), *Interpersonal trust during childhood and adolescence* (pp. 223–246). Cambridge, England: Cambridge University Press.

Smetana, J. (2011). *Adolescents, families, and social development: How teens construct their worlds.* Chichester, West Sussex: Wiley-Blackwell.

Sroufe, A., & Fleeson, J. (1986). Attachment and the construction of relationships. In W. W. Hartup & Z. Rubin (Eds.), *Relationships and development* (pp. 51–71). Hillsdale, NJ: Erlbaum.

Weiber, R., & Mühlhaus, D. (2010). *Strukturgleichungsmodellierung. Eine anwendungsorientierte Einfuehrung in die Kausalanalyse mit Hilfe von AMOS, SmartPLS und SPSS* [Structural equation modeling. An application-oriented introduction to causal analysis with the help of AMOS, SmartPLS, and SPSS]. Berlin & Heidelberg, Germany: Springer.

Zuffianô, A., Colasante, T., Buchmann, M., & Malti, T. (in press). The codevelopment of symapthy and overt aggression from middle childhood to early adolescence. *Developmental Psychology.*

CHAPTER 8

EMOTIONAL AMBIVALENCE IN ADULT CHILDREN OF CARE-DEPENDENT OLDER PARENTS

Heuristic Impulses From Cognitive-Motivational Emotion Theories

Thomas Boll
University of Luxembourg

This chapter focuses on the psychological ambivalence in adult children facing their older parent's dependency on care, who may or may not provide care to them. More specifically, I focus on emotional ambivalence as the copresence of the children's negative and positive emotions toward various aspects of this specific situation. Co-occurring, opposite-valenced emotions (e.g., fear and hope or happiness and pity) related to the parent produce the emotional ambivalence toward the parent. Similarly, the copresence of self-related happiness and unhappiness, fear and hope, and moral pride and guilt constitutes likely emotional ambivalence toward oneself (adult

Trans-Generational Family Relations, pages 141–175

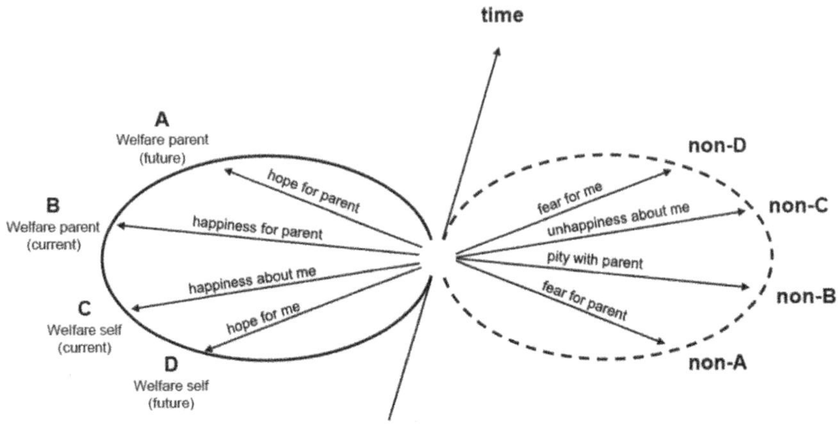

Figure 8.1 Field of ambivalent emotions of adult children related to the welfare of elderly parent and oneself (selected examples).

child) as the actual or potential caregiver. Figure 8.1 provides an initial illustration. Each of the opposite-directed vectors represents a phenomenon of emotional ambivalence.[1]

There are several reasons that emotional ambivalence in this context deserves more attention and why research in this field could profit from a solid emotion-theoretical foundation.

ENRICHED PICTURE OF EMOTIONAL LIFE AND DEEPER UNDERSTANDING

Looking at emotional ambivalence (beyond univalent emotions) can provide a richer picture of the emotional situation of adult children in care relationships. Past research has almost exclusively focused on emotional burden, that is, on the combinations of several negative emotions of family caregivers (e.g., Lin & Wu, 2014; Novak & Guest, 1989) but not on emotional gain (i.e., the combinations of several positive emotions of family caregivers) (cf. Boll & Ferring, 2013). Furthermore, little attention has been paid to the copresence of negative and positive emotions, that is, to emotional ambivalence. However, some recent studies have begun to recognize the emotional complexity of family caregivers. A few recent studies have focused on the emotions of mostly spousal (not adult children) caregivers of older people with dementia. Based on qualitative interviews, Shim, Barroso, and Davis (2012) have found, beyond two groups of family caregivers with predominantly positive and predominantly negative emotions, an additional group of caregivers with ambivalent emotions such as grief, sadness, frustration, or guilt feelings, on the one hand, and satisfaction, joy, and pride, on the other hand. Ambivalent emotions of, again, spousal caregivers have also been found in relation to a specific care-related event, namely, the elderly family member's transition to a nursing home (e.g., Kong, 2008). Losada, Pillemer, Márquez-González, Romero-Moreno, and Gallego-Alberto (2016) have developed a brief global measure of ambivalent feelings in dementia family caregivers (mostly spouses and adult children), namely, the Caregiving Ambivalence Scale (CAS). This scale is comprised of six items that each directly assesses the simultaneous experience of divergent feelings toward the care recipient or oneself as caregiver or other relatives not providing sufficient support on 4-point rating scales. Data analyses revealed that the CAS has a unidimensional structure and a good internal consistency so that a single sum score is computed to represent caregiving ambivalence; such a CAS score significantly predicts caregivers' depressive and anxious symptomatology. However, the aforementioned lines of research were not guided by emotion-theoretical approaches, which could have allowed the generation of more specific hypotheses on the kinds, causes, and consequences of such emotional ambivalence. Additional research based on emotion-theoretical approaches should help us to close these gaps and find new options for managing emotional ambivalence in adult children of care-dependent parents.

EMOTIONAL AMBIVALENCE AND CARE-RELATED DECISIONS

More theoretical insight into emotional ambivalence related to elder care should also help us to better understand how and why caring children have difficulty in making care-related decisions. For instance, the experience of the ambivalent emotions of fear and hope about the welfare of the parent and/or fear and hope about one's own welfare may hinder an adult child's decision with respect to whether caregiving should be taken over or continued, whether informal or professional support should be used, and whether the transition of a care-dependent elderly parent to a nursing home should be initiated.

In the following, emotional ambivalence toward the care situation will be analyzed from the perspective of cognitive-motivational theories of emotion. Given that emotions are essentially directed toward objects, the major facets of the care situation as possible objects of positive and negative emotions are described. This is followed by a presentation of a cognitive-motivational view on how emotional ambivalence toward the care situation arises. This kind of analysis is further illustrated for emotional ambivalence about a major care-related event, namely, the transition of an elderly parent to a nursing home. In conclusion, the benefits of a refined measurement, description, understanding, and management of emotional ambivalence in adult children of care-dependent older parents are discussed.

CARE DEPENDENCY AND CAREGIVING AS A MULTIFACETED SITUATION

According to a cognitive-motivational approach (see next section), the kind and intensity of an adult child's emotions in response to the care situation depend strongly on how the individual mentally represents that situation in his or her beliefs and desires. An individual's mental representations will depend, to some extent, on the objective situation at hand and on an individual's possibilities and tendencies for mentally representing it. Describing the objective state of affairs faced by an individual is generally a useful heuristic step that allows researchers to generate hypotheses about (a) the specific emotion types (e.g., fear, happiness, hope, guilt, pride) that may arise, and (b) the concrete aspects to which the emotions may refer in a complex situation (Boll, 1998). In the present case, it is thus helpful to look closely at the various facets of the care situation. As will become evident later, it is likely that this complex situation can give rise to a broad spectrum of emotions directed at different facets of that situation. These facets include multiple problems of the older parent, multiple caregiving tasks of the adult child, and several gains and losses for the older parent and caring child.

Facet 1: Multiple Problems of Older Parents

The multiple problems of an older parent emerge for the most part in or as a result of a disablement process, which leads to the parent's dependency on outside care. This process includes several linked steps (see Figure 8.2). It usually begins with certain age-related diseases such as neurodegenerative disorders, stroke, musculoskeletal disorders, cardiovascular diseases, diabetes, cancer, and disorders of the senses (Verbrugge & Jette, 1994). Most of these illnesses are chronic and tend to worsen, so the demand for care will probably increase with time. Age-related diseases may lead to impairments in specific body systems, which in turn lead to functional limitations that may be physical (e.g., reduced ability to ambulate, reach, or climb stairs) or mental (e.g., increasing difficulty to recognize objects or produce intelligible speech) or both. These limitations may lead, in turn, to difficulties in performing activities of daily living (ADLs), including basic activities of daily living (BADL; e.g., washing oneself, eating, using the toilet), instrumental activities of daily living (IADL; e.g., homemaking, handling

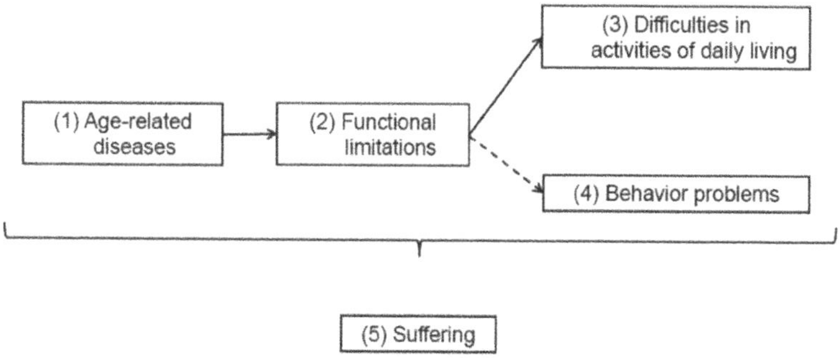

Figure 8.2 Major problems of older parents needing care.

financial and administrative issues), and activities enabling life enrichment, personal growth, or positive development such as cultural activities, hobbies, excursions, playing, and media usage (e.g., Albert, Bear-Lehman, & Burkhardt, 2009; Verbrugge & Jette, 1994; Wilms, Baltes, & Kanowski, 1998). Particularly older people with dementia often become unable to entertain normal social interactions and relationships with their caregivers. Thus, family caregivers who are no longer recognized by their relative with dementia are losing contact with their relative in a personal sense despite his or her continued bodily presence (e.g., Holley & Mast, 2009; Meuser & Marwit, 2001; Noyes et al., 2010). A further aspect associated with older people with dementia are problematic behaviors linked with disturbances of memory and thinking, emotional disturbances (e.g., depression), and general disturbing behaviors (e.g., Roth et al., 2003). A final aspect for consideration is the suffering of older parents, which can be emotional, physical, or existential/ spiritual (e.g., Schulz & Monin, in press).

Facet 2: Multiple Caregiving Tasks for Adult Children

These problems faced by older parents give rise to a multitude of caregiving tasks for adult children, as illustrated in Figure 8.3 (e.g., Wilkins, Bruce, & Sirey, 2009; Zank, Schacke, & Leipold, 2006). Among them are skilled nursing (e.g., wound care, medication management), training of mental and physical functions, in-home care management (e.g., supervising home care aids), and out-of-home management such as advocacy in negotiating with institutions and representatives of the healthcare system. Other tasks comprise help with activities of daily living, including life-enriching activities and the alleviation of their older relatives' suffering (e.g., Albert, 2004; Gaugler, Kane, & Kane, 2002; Levine, Reinhard, Feinberg, Albert, & Hart, 2003–2004; Schulz & Monin, 2017).

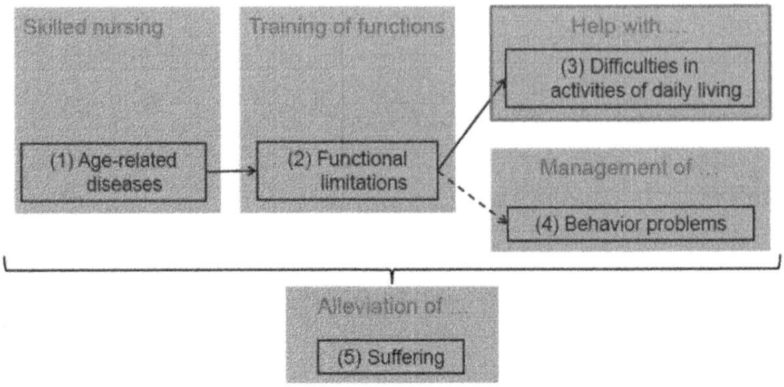

Figure 8.3 Multiple caregiving tasks for adult children arising from the various problems of a care-dependent older parent.

Facet 3: Multiple Care-Related Gains and Losses for Older Parents

If the quality of care provided by an adult child is good and coincides with some favorable conditions on the part of the care recipient, the older parent's health, psycho-physical functioning, and ability to execute various ADLs may improve or be kept from worsening (or, at least, the deterioration rate may be slowed down). The same applies to the older parent's problem behavior and suffering. Thus, admission to a nursing home may be avoided or at least postponed so that the older parent can continue to remain in his or her familiar environment. An adult child who notices such positive consequences may respond with various positive emotions (e.g., happiness, hope, moral pride). However, when the care quality is bad and/or the relevant conditions on the part of the care recipient are not that favorable, the situation may become increasingly worse: further deterioration of health, loss of mental and physical functions, loss of autonomy, more suffering, and loss of dignity, respect, and freedom. An adult child who is aware of these negative trends may thus respond with various negative emotions toward the parent (e.g., pity, fear) and oneself (e.g., unhappiness, fear, guilt).

Facet 4: Multiple Care-Related Gains and Losses for Adult Children

Providing care to their older parents can be rather strenuous and time and energy consuming for adult children, particularly if the parents are severely disabled. Such care provision likely has a negative impact on other life domains of the caregivers: family and job life, financial situation, leisure time, as well as the opportunity for contact with people beyond one's family (e.g., Aneshensel, Pearlin, Mullan, Zarit, & Whitlatch, 1995; Fast, 2015; Pearlin, Mullan, Semple, & Skaff, 1990). Extensive family care provision for older parents is usually not compatible with a full-time job. In fact, family caregivers often reduce their working time by taking a part-time job or even terminating work (e.g., Black et al., 2010; Covinsky et al., 2001). For adult children who continue working, providing support may interfere with their job performance (e.g., Barling, MacEwen, Kelloway, & Higginbottom, 1994; Dallinger, 1996; Kim, Ingersoll-Dayton, & Kwak, 2011). Moreover, reduced employment usually results in financial losses, not just during their active working time but also, depending on pension schemes, after retirement. Family care for older relatives may also interfere with adult children's responsibilities for their own families. Finally, stress in the relationships with other family members may arise (e.g., Scharlach, Li, & Dalvi, 2006; Semple, 1992). Arguments may result from disagreements on the status of the care recipient, on adequate care, as well as on the recognition expected but not received for caregiving. Family care may also involve costs for care products or the remodeling of the house (e.g., Black et al., 2010). Family care may also interfere with leisure time activities. Even if caregivers have free time, they might be kept from relaxing by anticipated guilt feelings about engaging in leisure time activities while their older relative is suffering (Losada, Márquez-González, Peñacoba, & Romero-Moreno, 2010). Family care may also interfere with maintaining social relationships with other persons outside the family.

Providing care for their older parents can also lead to several gains for adult children (e.g., Carbonneau, Caron, & Desrosiers, 2010; Kramer, 1997; Lloyd, Patterson, & Muers, 2016; Roth, Fredman, & Haley, 2015): gratitude and recognition from the care recipient and others within and outside the family, acquisition of new skills (caregiving, general social competencies), and personal growth. In addition, care provision may also result in an improved relationship between the elderly parent and his or her adult children: companionship, increased closeness, feeling loved by the care receiver, and mutual affection within the dyad due to caregiving. Moreover, care provision may also improve the relationships between adult children as caregivers and other family members: increased cohesion and cooperation among family members (e.g., adult child and siblings, spouse of the care-dependent parent) with respect to caregiving. Finally, caring for an older parent may lead to the experience of increased meaning in adult children's lives by fulfilling an important duty, adopting the caregiver role as a new goal in life, and being in line with religious or ethical principles (e.g., charity, honoring one's parents, gratefulness for what one has received).

The detailed description of the situation of adult children facing their care-dependent older parents will already evoke some initial ideas on which positive and negative emotions may arise in the children. However, the reference to cognitive-motivational theories of emotions will allow for a deeper understanding of how various positive and negative emotions toward the care situation may emerge from subjective appraisals of the various facets of that situation. It will also help us to understand how ambivalent emotions toward certain facets of the care situation may be evoked.

COGNITIVE-MOTIVATIONAL VIEW ON EMOTIONAL AMBIVALENCE TOWARD CARE DEPENDENCY AND CAREGIVING

Cognitive-motivational theories deal with several interrelated research questions regarding human emotions that are recognized and labeled in ordinary languages (e.g., hope, fear, happiness, guilt, pride, etc.). More specifically, these theories are concerned with what defines certain states of persons as emotions, what distinguishes one type of emotion from another, and how emotions arise from subjective appraisals of given situations. Moreover, they consider systematically an essential feature of specific emotions, namely, that they are directed toward objects (e.g., hope for..., fear of..., happy about..., proud of...). In particular, they conceive emotions as "intentional states," that is, as mental states that have a content that can be described by a proposition (that p; e.g., Green, 1992; Searle, 1983). Against this background, adequate ascriptions of emotions should specify at least three aspects: (a) the person experiencing the emotion (e.g., oneself or someone else), (b) the specific type of emotion (e.g., hope, fear, happiness, pride, shame), and (c) the propositional content of the emotion (in general: that p; e.g., fear that the parent's self-care abilities decline). As will become evident, these and other tenets of cognitive-motivational approaches make them particularly suited for differentiated and fruitful analyses of multiple emotions toward complex situations in general (Boll, 1999) and ambivalent emotions of adult children facing the care dependency of an older parent in particular.

Basic Assumptions of Cognitive-Motivational Theories of Emotions

Cognitive-motivational theories of emotions assume that emotions do not arise immediately in response to an objective situation (e.g., care situation or some specific part thereof) but are mediated by subjective appraisals of that situation. Such an approach can provide better explanations of several emotion-related facts than other emotion-theoretical views (e.g., Reisenzein & Horstmann, 2006; Roseman & Smith, 2001): (a) the subtle differentiation of specific emotions in humans (tracing back to the human capacity to make differentiated appraisals of situations), (b) the inter- and intraindividual differences in emotional response to the same situation (explained by different appraisals of that situation by different individuals or by the same individual at different times), and (c) the evocation of emotions by information from different channels, namely, seeing, hearing, reasoning, and receiving news from others (explanation: only the content of appraisals is decisive and not the channels through which these contents have emerged). As can be seen next, these explanatory advantages will also help to better understand adult children's positive and negative emotions (and thus emotional ambivalence) toward certain facets of their parent's care situation.

"Cognitive-motivational theories" (or "belief-desire theories of emotions" as they are sometimes called) were initially proposed by philosophers (e.g., Green, 1992; Searle, 1983) and more recently have been further elaborated on by psychologists (e.g., Reisenzein, 2009, 2015). The common assumption is that emotions about a certain state of affairs ("emotion that p") result from the combination of two different kinds of mental states, namely, beliefs (cognitive states) and desires (motivational states) about that same state of affairs ("that p"). More specifically, such emotions are conceived of as reactions emerging from perceived actual or potential fulfillment or frustration of desires.

The content of a desire (in general: "that p"; in particular: e.g., that the elderly parent should experience a good quality of life) specifies the conditions that fulfill or frustrate this desire. It is fulfilled when the condition "that p" is satisfied (e.g., the older parent has a good quality of life), and it is frustrated when the condition "that p" is not satisfied (e.g., if the older parent has a bad quality of life). Crucial for the emergence of emotions is how the individual (e.g., the adult child) perceives the given situation (e.g., care dependency of the older parent and its various facets). In other words, whether an emotion emerges, and if it does, whether it will be positive and/or negative depends on the beliefs of the individual about the given situation.

The perceived fulfillment of such desires is assumed to lead to positive emotions (e.g., happiness, hope), and the perceived frustration of such desires is assumed to result in negative emotions (e.g., unhappiness, fear). If a person certainly believes that the desired state of affairs obtains (vs. not obtains), then happiness versus unhappiness will result; if a person is uncertain about whether the desired state of affairs may emerge hope should result and if a person is uncertain about whether an undesired state may obtain, then fear should emerge (see Reisenzein, 2009). Table 8.1 presents the major assumptions on the generation of two types of positive and negative emotions

TABLE 8.1 Preconditions of Basic Emotion Types as Postulated by a Cognitive-Motivational Theory of Emotion

Emotion Types	Structural Analyses		Care-Related Specifications (Examples)	
	Desire	Belief	Desire	Belief
Happiness (p)	p	Certain (p)	I want to stay healthy despite the care load	I *am* healthy despite the care load
Unhappiness (p)	Not p	Certain (p)	I do not want to be sick due to the care load	I *am* sick due to the care load
Hope (p)	p	Uncertain (p)	I want to stay healthy despite the care load	I *may* stay healthy despite the care load
Fear (p)	Not p	Uncertain (p)	I do not want to become sick due to the care load	I *may* become sick due to care load

Note: "p" symbolizes the propositional content of emotions, beliefs, and desires, that is, the state of affairs to which these mental states refer.

and further illustrates this for the corresponding emotions experienced by an adult child in the context of care for older parents (see next section).

The cognitive-motivational theory of emotions has been further elaborated to clarify the preconditions of more differentiated types of emotions of positive and negative valence (e.g., Reisenzein, 2009, 2015). This is done, to a large extent, by specifying beliefs and desires with more complex contents. Particularly relevant for application to the care dependency and care provision situation is the idea that the beliefs and desires (and thus the more complex emotions) refer to one's own well-being as well as the well-being of other persons. So happiness for another person and gloating can be analyzed as a specific kind of happiness and envy and pity as a specific kind of unhappiness based on the fulfillment or frustration of desires for the well-being or ill-being of another person (e.g., of one's elderly parent). Furthermore, emotions such as guilt feelings and indignation or moral pride and moral elevation are analyzed with reference to desires that either oneself and/or other persons should comply with certain moral norms that can be perceived as either fulfilled or frustrated depending on the person's related beliefs (Reisenzein, 2015; see also Ben-Ze'ev, 1990, 2001; Brandtstädter, 2001, 2015; Montada, 1993; Ortony, Clore, & Collins, 1988, for several types of specific emotions in general; see Boll & Ferring, 2013, regarding emotions of family caregivers).

Multiple Desires and Beliefs of Adult Children of Care-Dependent Parents

Using the preceding cognitive-motivational framework for analyses of adult children's emotions toward the care situation requires further

Figure 8.4 Multiple desires of adult children of care-dependent parents.

specifications of the contents of major desires and beliefs relevant in this context. The focus in this section is on desires for the well-being of the persons involved in or affected by the care situation: the older parent, oneself (as adult child), and one's (i.e., adult child's) spouse and/or children. Moreover, desires for good relationships with these persons will be considered as well as a desire to follow moral norms demanding care provision for one's parents (see Figure 8.4). Arguments for taking these desires into account and additional specifications of their content will be presented later. A central assumption is that multiple desires can coexist simultaneously in an adult child facing the care dependency of a parent, and this will help to analyze the emergence of ambivalent emotions in this context.

One's Own Welfare

Adult children providing care for their elderly parents can be reasonably ascribed desires for their own welfare, which may include several domains often considered in life satisfaction research: material well-being, health, productivity, intimacy (personal relationships), and emotional well-being (e.g., Cummins, 1996). These domains can be further concretized for the care context to include specific desires such as to stay healthy despite the stress of caring, receive support from other relatives or professionals, continue one's occupational career, have sufficient leisure time, and acquire new competencies and personality traits.

Oneself: Follow Moral Norms

Elaborated models of specific emotions (e.g., Montada, 1993; Ortony et al., 1988; Reisenzein, 2015) consider, as an important category, the emotions on self-committed norm violations (e.g., guilt feelings) and norm fulfillment (e.g., moral satisfaction, moral pride). In the context of elder care, an important kind of norms is the norm of mercy, which is applicable to anyone in need and is, of course, applicable to one's care-dependent parents in particular. Another relevant category is the norm of reciprocity, which dictates individuals to support those persons from whom one has received support in the past, and this is instantiated by one's parents (e.g., Ikkink, Tilburg, & Knipscheer, 1999; Merrill, 1997; see also Silverstein, Conroy, Wang, Giarrusso, & Bengtson, 2002). Finally, specific norms of filial responsibility should also be relevant because these norms demand the provision of care specifically to one's parents if they need it (e.g., Blieszner & Hamon, 1992; Cantor & Hirshorn, 1989; Ikkink et al., 1999).

Welfare of One's Spouse and/or Children

Adult children also desire the welfare of their family of procreation, that is, their chosen spouse and/or their children. Elaborated emotion models (e.g., Ortony et al., 1988; Reisenzein, 2015) include, as one important class of emotions, the so-called "fortunes-of-others emotions" with "happy-for emotions" (e.g., happy for the other, hope for the other) and "sorry-for emotions" (e.g., compassion, pity, fear for the other) as major subclasses. These emotions presuppose desires for the welfare of other persons, which may be perceived as actually or possibly fulfilled ("happy for emotions") versus frustrated ("sorry for emotions"). These relevant desires can be easily frustrated given that multiple care tasks of adult children reduce time and energy needed to promote the welfare of their spouse and/or children.

Good Relationships With One's Spouse and/or Children

Adult children may also desire a good relationship with these family members. A desire for good relationships with their spouse may include desires for intimacy (e.g., time for each other, open communication, affection), agreement (e.g., in goals, interests, common activities), independence (maintaining one's individuality, having and allowing for freedom), and sexuality (Hassebrauck & Fehr, 2002). A desire for a good relationship to one's children may include similar desires with the exception of a desire for sexuality.

Welfare of One's Parent

Several research areas support the relevance of desires for the welfare of others in general and the welfare of one's parents in particular. A first area is devoted to empathetic concern and altruistic motivation in response to any other person perceived to be in a situation of need (Bateson, 2011). Empathetic concern and altruistic motivation can become relevant with respect to one's parents, when they can no longer care for themselves sufficiently.

A second research domain refers to "communal relationships," which, in contrast to exchange or exploitive relationships, are characterized by an intrinsic motivation to respond to the needs of closely related persons and to feel responsible for their welfare (e.g., Mills, Clark, Ford, & Johnson, 2004). This motivation can arise in specific communal relationships such as the ones between adult children and their care-dependent parents. A third research domain refers to family members' motivation to provide care for their relatives. Here, feelings of love and affection toward one's parents have been identified as an important motivating factor for the support of one's parents (cf. Merrill, 1997; Silverstein, Parrott, & Bengston, 1995; Roberts, Wise, & DuBenske, 2009).

The global desire for the "welfare of one's parent" can give rise to more specific care-related desires: the desire that the parent's diseases are cured, that the deterioration of health is stopped or slowed down, that the mental and physical functioning as well as the autonomy is maintained or improved, and that the care-dependent parent can remain in his or her preferred living environment (cf. Kaldjian, Curtis, Shinkunas, & Cannon, 2009; Kaldjian, Shinkunas, Bern-Klug, & Schultz, 2010).

Good Relationships With One's Elderly Parent

Adult children may also desire a good relationship with their elderly parents. What can compose this desire? It seems reasonable to assume that these desires have similar contents like the ones already mentioned for adult children's relationships with their spouses and their adult children: desires for intimacy, agreement in various fields, and independence.

Univalent Emotions Toward the Care Situation

The cognitive-motivational approach leads one to assume that major emotions of adult children about the parental care situation result from care-related desires of adult children if, in a comparison process, these desires are perceived as fulfilled or frustrated depending on their beliefs about the care situation (see Figure 8.5). If the care-related desires are perceived as being in fact or potentially fulfilled, then positive emotions are expected to result (e.g., happiness, hope, pride). If the care-related desires are perceived as being in fact or potentially frustrated, then negative emotions should emerge (e.g., unhappiness, pity, fear, anger, guilt feelings). This explanatory scheme is applicable to many positive and negative emotions, basic and more complex ones, and those regarding certain and uncertain aspects of the care situation involving oneself and the elderly parent.

Three examples will further illustrate the emergence of adult children's care-related emotions. First, if an adult child has a desire for the welfare of

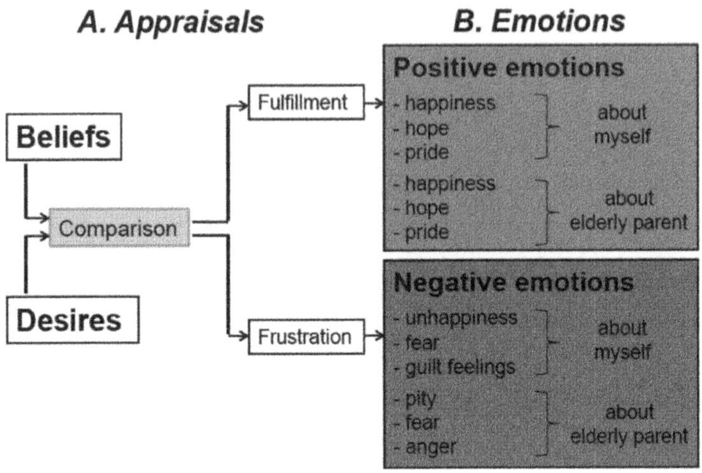

Figure 8.5 Cognitive-motivational view on the emergence of adult children's care-related emotions.

one's parent (or some of its related subdesires, e.g., that one's parent should not suffer) but comes to certainly believe that the parent is in fact suffering, then the relevant desire is perceived as frustrated, and pity with the elderly parent should arise. If, in contrast, the adult child certainly believes that the parent is not suffering, then happiness for the older parent is expected to result. Second, if an adult child has a specific desire for one's own welfare, for instance, a desire for sufficient leisure time, and comes to certainly believe that this is really the case despite care duties, then the relevant desire is perceived as fulfilled, and happiness about one's own situation should result. If, however, the adult child certainly believes that he or she no longer has sufficient leisure time due to care duties, then the perceived frustration of the relevant desire should result in unhappiness about his or her situation. Third, if an adult child desires to comply with the moral norm that one should care for the welfare of one's parents and certainly believes that he or she has done so really well even without the help of others, then moral satisfaction or even moral pride should emerge from the perceived fulfillment of that desire. If, in contrast, the belief arises that sufficient care has not been provided even though this would have been possible, feelings of guilt about oneself should emerge from the perceived violation of the relevant desire.

Ambivalent Emotions Toward the Care Situation

The emergence of adult children's ambivalent emotions toward the care situation involving the older parent is now analyzed by an extended application of the theoretical tools presented earlier.

Emotional Ambivalence Arising From the Same Care-Related Desire: Fulfilled in Some Respects and Frustrated in Others

A first kind of ambivalence is assumed to originate from one particular desire of an adult child in combination with two different beliefs. Depending on these beliefs, the adult child may perceive that desire as fulfilled in some respects and frustrated in others. This idea is further illustrated by the following two examples (see also Table 8.2).

An adult child who has a certain care-related desire (e.g., for the welfare of the parent) may have a first belief (e.g., "My care for my older parent allows the parent to stay at home"), implying that the desire is perceived as fulfilled in this respect, which in turn should evoke positive emotions (e.g., happy for the parent). The adult child may have a second belief (e.g., "My care for my older parent can't stop the health decline of my parent"), implying that the desire is perceived as frustrated in another respect, which should result in negative emotions (e.g., pity with the parent). In other words, both positive and negative emotions related to the same object (one's care provision) may co-occur, which creates emotional ambivalence toward one's caregiving for the elderly parent.

Let us consider another desire, namely, the desire for one's own welfare. The adult child may have a first belief (e.g., "My care for my older parent increases my competencies"), implying that the aforementioned desire is perceived as fulfilled in that respect, which should result in positive emotions (e.g., happy about my situation). The adult child may have a second belief ("My care for my older parent is detrimental to my career"), which implies that the desire is perceived as frustrated in that respect, resulting in negative emotions (e.g., unhappy about my situation). Again, the co-occurrence of positive and negative emotions toward the same object (my care provision) creates an additional emotional ambivalence toward my caregiving for the parent.

In a similar manner, the other care-related desires reported in Table 8.2 (first column) can be considered, and the pairs of corresponding beliefs can be identified (second column), where one belief implies a perceived fulfillment and the other belief implies a perceived frustration of the relevant desires (third column). This, in turn, is assumed to lead to a copresence of emotions (fourth column) of both positive and negative valence (fifth column) toward the same object and, thus, to further emotional ambivalence (sixth column).

Emotional Ambivalence Arising From Different Care-Related Desires: One Fulfilled, Another Frustrated

A second kind of ambivalence is assumed to emerge if an adult child has several different care-related desires (e.g., desire for the welfare of one's parent, desire for one's own welfare) and, given certain beliefs, one desire is perceived as fulfilled, whereas another one is perceived as frustrated. This, in turn, should result in the copresence of both positive and negative

TABLE 8.2 Adult Children's Ambivalent Emotions About Their Care Provision for Their Older Parent: Emergence From Perceived Fulfillment and Frustration of Different Care-Related Desires

Care-Related Desires	Care-Related Beliefs	Belief-Desire Comparison	Care-Related Emotions (Examples)	Valence of Emotions	Emotional Ambivalence[a]
	My care for my older parent…				
(1) Welfare of one's elderly parent	…allows parent to stay at home	Fulfillment	Happy for parent, hope for parent	+	
	…can't stop parent's health decline	Frustration	Pity with parent, fear for parent	–	
(2) Good relationships with elderly parent	…increases closeness to parent	Fulfillment	Happy about good relations, hope for good relations	+	
	…increases conflict with parent	Frustration	Unhappy about bad relations, fear of bad relations	–	
(3) Self: follow moral norms	…is an act of mercy	Fulfillment	Moral satisfaction, moral pride	+	
	…is less than what I should do	Frustration	Guilt, moral shame	–	
(4) My welfare (as adult child)	…increases my competencies	Fulfillment	Happy about my situation, hope for me	+	
	…is detrimental to my career (etc.)	Frustration	Unhappy about my situation, fear for me	–	
(5) Welfare of my spouse and/or children	…saves my children's grandparent	Fulfillment	Happy for my children, hope for my children	+	
	…impairs caring for my children	Frustration	Pity with my children, fear for my children	–	
(6) Good relationships with my spouse and/or children	…increases closeness to my spouse	Fulfillment	Happy about good relations, hope for good relations	+	
	…increases conflict with my spouse	Frustration	Unhappy about bad relations, fear of bad relations	–	

[a] Small arrows indicate emotional ambivalence based on perceived fulfillment or frustration of the same care-related desire. Large arrows indicate emotional ambivalence based on perceived fulfillment or frustration of different care-related desires (indicated by two examples).

emotions about providing care that is in care-related emotional ambivalence, which is further illustrated in the following.

To simplify matters, the only type of emotional ambivalence considered here involves pairs of two different care-related desires. A first pair could be, for example, the desire for the welfare of one's parent and the desire for one's own welfare. One aspect of the care situation—from the child's perspective ("My care for my older parent allows the parent to stay at home")—can then be perceived as fulfilling one's desire for the welfare of one's parent, thus leading to positive emotions (e.g., happy for parent). Yet another aspect ("My care for the parent is detrimental to my career") can be perceived as frustrating the desire for one's own welfare, thus leading to negative emotions (e.g., unhappy about my situation). Hence, both positive and negative emotions in response to the child´s care provision should co-occur, which creates an emotional ambivalence toward that object.

Let us examine a second pair of care-related desires: the desire for good relationships with one's elderly parent and the desire for good relationships with one's spouse and/or children (see Table 8.2). Here, two additional aspects of the care situation—from the child's perspective ("My care for my older parent increases my feelings of closeness to him or her"; "My care for my older parent increases the number of conflicts with my spouse")—can be perceived by the child as fulfilling the desire for good relationships with the parent, which should lead to positive emotions (e.g., happy about good relationship with the parent), and as frustrating the desire for good relations with other family members, which should lead to negative emotions (e.g., unhappy about bad relationship with the spouse). Again, positive and negative emotions co-occur and create another type of emotional ambivalence in response to caregiving for one's parent.

Interim Conclusion and Invitation to Join in Further Analyses

The present section has theoretically examined the emergence of adult children's ambivalent emotions toward the care situation involving their elderly parent. Two different pathways have been considered: (a) emotional ambivalence arising from the same care-related desire that is perceived as fulfilled in some respects and frustrated in others; and (b) emotional ambivalence arising from different care-related desires, where one desire is perceived as fulfilled and the other as frustrated depending on the adult child's beliefs. Rather straightforward examples were used to illustrate these two pathways. Looking at Table 8.2, one easily imagine more complex cases in which multiple types of emotional ambivalence arise from multiple care-related desires in combination with multiple care-related beliefs.

Considering Table 8.2, the reader is invited to follow the other paths to uncover additional types of emotional ambivalence. In addition, starting from the care-related desires mentioned in Table 8.2 (first column), the reader is invited to find further care-related beliefs that could also result in perceived frustration and fulfillment of the desire(s), thus generating additional types of emotional ambivalence in adult children in the context of elder care.

FURTHER SPECIFICATIONS: ADULT CHILDREN'S EMOTIONAL AMBIVALENCE ABOUT OLDER PARENT'S TRANSITION INTO A NURSING HOME

The theoretical tools presented earlier are now further applied to analyze emotional ambivalence about a major care transition: the permanent move to a nursing home. A concise description of what this transition implies will help to better understand the corresponding beliefs and desires that could arise in adult children and, thus, the ambivalent emotions that can be expected.

Elderly Parent's Move to a Nursing Home: A Complex Life Transition

The move to a nursing home often emerges as an option when the older parent's health and functional condition further decline so that care demands exceed the motivation, competencies, or power of adult children and their supporters to provide adequate care (cf. Gaugler, Yu, Krichbaum, & Wyman, 2009; Luppa, Luck, Weyerer, König, Brähler, & Riedel-Heller, 2010). In such cases, the transition to a nursing home may appear as a solution that, in comparison with continuing private home care, better serves the welfare of the elderly parent and/or adult child.

Nursing homes offer accommodation, meals, and skilled nursing care 24 hours a day, 7 days a week for their elderly, highly care-dependent residents. In developed countries, these homes are part of the health and social care system and, as such, are subject to legal regulations for registration, ensuring quality standards of care, and as a precondition for receiving public funding (Howe, Jones, & Tilse, 2013). Nursing homes are economic enterprises and are therefore also subject to economic principles: They provide their services in exchange for certain fees usually paid by the residents or their relatives and, depending on the country, partially (re)financed by benefits from long-term-care insurances or public welfare systems. The entry into a nursing home is associated with many changes in the lives of both the elderly parent and the adult child.

Changes for the Older Parent

These far-reaching changes involve everything, that is, the physical, social, emotional, and activity-related living conditions of the parent. On the one hand, the familiar place of living (e.g., own home) is left behind, which generally occurs in tandem with a geographical separation from the spouse, children, friends, and neighbors and with a separation from the former household, including at least some of its biographically important objects. These changes may also result in giving up certain activities that had been closely related to the familiar places, loved objects, and continuous presence of closely related persons. On the other hand, the elderly parent enters a new place of living and comes into contact with new interaction partners (e.g., other residents, relatives, nursing home staff), becomes involved in new activities (e.g., having meals together, home parties with other residents, various creative activities), and has access to full-time professional care.

These changes, however, may evoke strong reactions in an older parent, which could be positive or negative depending on the details of the transition and how they are subjectively appraised. The negative reactions may include the parent's unpleasant emotions toward the nursing home entry (e.g., feeling unhappy, lonely, homesick), stressful behaviors (e.g., accusations against the child), and problems with integrating well into the nursing home environment. Such reactions, in turn, can have an impact on the adult child, who may have initiated the transition or at least witnessed it: Strong empathetic emotions toward the fate of the older parent may emerge.

Changes for the Adult Child

The transition of the elderly parent may lead to positive or negative changes for the adult child, too. Some of these changes may be intentional or at least welcomed by the child, such as the reduction of some care responsibilities, in particular the difficult and/or burdensome ones (e.g., bodily care, care at night), and a respite from the negative impacts of caregiving on other life domains (e.g., job, own family, leisure time, health). Other changes may be mere side effects of the transition, and their valence may vary across persons. For instance, after the parent enters a skilled nursing facility, the adult child is now geographically more remote from the parent, thus making it more difficult to visit, be informed about, and control the living conditions and quality of care.

However, new burdens may also emerge for the adult child in connection with the planning and realization of the parent's transition. The move into a nursing home usually requires preparatory actions that may be stressful. One of the first actions is to make the principal decision that the parent should make this move. This decision may be made with more or less participation of the parent in question and/or other family members, and it may involve conflict-laden family interactions. Next, an adult child usually has to invest time and energy in gathering information about suitable homes, selecting the best one, and organizing and performing the actual move, including the liquidation of the parent's former household. After the transition, new tensions may arise from conflictive interactions of the adult child with the nursing home staff, for instance, about adequate care provision for the elderly parent. Finally, an adult child may be financially strained by having to bear at least some of the costs for the parent's nursing home stay if the parent is unable to cover these costs and the reimbursement regulations in a given country require a financial contribution of an adult child to the institutional care provision for their parent. Even if the elderly parent is able to pay the high nursing home costs, this expenditure can have negative financial consequences for an adult child: The assets of the parent will shrink, thus lowering the child's future inheritance.

Ambivalent Emotions Toward an Older Parent's Nursing Home Transition

According to the cognitive-motivational approach, the occurrence of both positive and negative emotions of an adult child toward the parental move to a nursing home depends on how this event is appraised by the child. This can be considered from at least two different temporal perspectives. Before the move, an adult child can anticipate the transition, and when the move is completed, the adult child may reflect on it. Illustrating the two temporal perspectives, Figure 8.6 also demonstrates that the mental representations of the elderly parent and adult child do not necessarily converge.

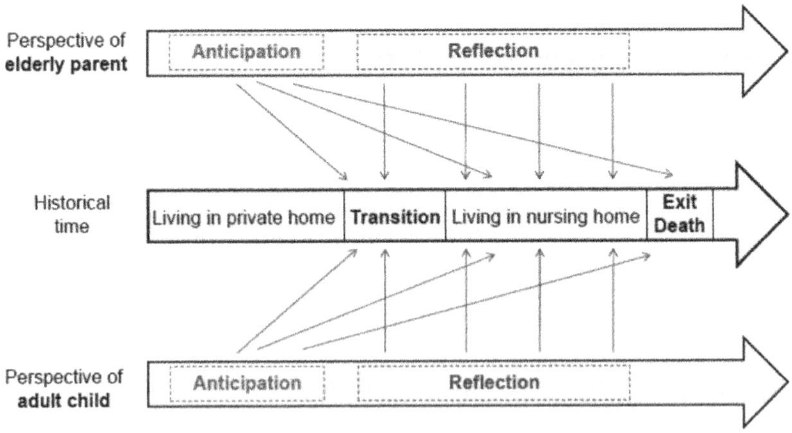

Figure 8.6 Transition into a nursing home: Two temporal perspectives for the mental representations by elderly parent and adult child.

In the following, the emergence of an adult child's ambivalent emotions will be described in more detail, focusing primarily on those arising from anticipating the nursing home transition and reflecting on the elderly parent now living in the nursing home (see Table 8.3).

Emotional Ambivalence From Anticipating the Parent's Nursing Home Transition

Anticipating this event may evoke several types of emotional ambivalence in the adult child depending on the specific combinations of his or her care-related desires and beliefs. Two of the six care-related desires (1, 3) mentioned in Table 8.3 will now be considered as a starting point from which, each in combination with two different beliefs, ambivalent emotions may emerge (see small arrows in Table 8.3, last column).

An adult child who desires the welfare of the parent may have opposing beliefs about the effect that a nursing home transition may have on the parent. On the one hand, it could be viewed as potentially improving the life quality of the parent in some respects because the parent is expected to be cared for by highly qualified nursing staff. In this case, hope for the parent should arise in the child. On the other hand, the child may assume that the transition will decrease the life quality of the parent in other respects because the parent will lose a familiar place of living and regular contact with loved persons and objects. Such beliefs should evoke the child's fear for the parent. Thus, hope–fear ambivalence (about the fate of the parent) may arise when the child thinks about the possible nursing home transition of the parent.

The adult child may also desire his or her own welfare but may have diverging beliefs about the effects of the parent's nursing home transition on one's personal welfare. On the one side, the child may believe that the transition will increase his or her own life quality by reducing the strains of caring and the negative impact of caregiving on other personal life domains (e.g., family, job, leisure time, health). This could evoke hope for oneself. On the other side, the child may also believe that a nursing home stay is expensive and that these costs could worsen his or her financial situation. Hence, fear for oneself could arise in the child. Thus, another hope-fear ambivalence (about one's own situation) may arise when the child anticipates the elderly parent's possible move into the nursing home.

Finally a different kind of emotional ambivalence is considered, which can arise from at least two different care-related desires (e.g., desire for good relationships with the elderly parent and desire for good relationships with one's spouse and/or children) if, given certain beliefs, the one desire is perceived as possibly fulfilled and the other as possibly frustrated. This could happen, for instance, if the adult child believes that the nursing home entry will lessen his or her feelings of closeness to the parent (with fear of a bad relationship with one's parent as a consequence) and that

TABLE 8.3 Adult Children's Ambivalent Emotions About the Nursing Home Transition of the Elderly Parent: Emergence From Perceived Fulfillment and Frustration of Different Care-Related Desires

Care-Related Desires	Care-Related Beliefs	Belief-Desire Comparison	Care-Related Emotions[a] (Examples)	Valence of Emotions	Emotional Ambivalence[b]
	Nursing home transition of my older parent…				
(1) Welfare of one's elderly parent	…increases life quality of my parent	Fulfillment	A: hope for parent; R: happy for parent	+	
	…decreases life quality of my parent	Frustration	A: fear for parent; R: pity for parent	–	
(2) Good relationships with elderly parent	…increases my closeness to parent	Fulfillment	A: hope for good relations; R: happy about good relations	+	
	…decreases my closeness to parent	Frustration	A: fear of bad relations; R: unhappy about bad relations	–	
(3) My welfare (as adult child)	…increases my life quality	Fulfillment	A: hope for me; R: happy about my situation	+	
	…worsens my financial situation	Frustration	A: fear for me; R: unhappy about my situation	–	
(4) Oneself: follow moral norms	…promoting it fulfills my promise to ensure best care quality	Fulfillment	A: anticipated moral satisfaction; R: moral satisfaction	+	
	…promoting it breaks my promise to not put parent in nursing home	Frustration	A: anticipated guilt; R: guilt	–	
(5) Welfare of my spouse and/or children	…allows me to care for my children	Fulfillment	A: hope for my children; R: happy about children's fate	+	
	…hinders caring for my children	Frustration	A: fear for my children; R: pity with children	–	
(6) Good relationships with my spouse and/or children	…increases closeness to my spouse	Fulfillment	A: hope for good relations; R: happy about good relations	+	
	…increases conflict with my spouse	Frustration	A: fear of bad relations; R: unhappy about bad relations	–	

[a] A, anticipation of nursing home transition; R, reflecting on present nursing home stay.

[b] Small arrows indicate emotional ambivalence based on perceived fulfillment or frustration of the same care-related desire. Large arrows indicate emotional ambivalence based on perceived fulfillment or frustration of different care-related desires (indicated by two examples).

this transition possibly increases feelings of closeness to one's spouse and/or children (with hope for a good relationship with one's spouse and/or children) as illustrated by the upper large arrow in Table 8.3 (last column).

Emotional Ambivalence Arising From Reflecting on the Parent's Current Nursing Home Stay

When the elderly parent's permanent move into a nursing home is completed, a new situation has emerged for both the parent and adult child. Again, the child may experience several types of emotional ambivalence depending on how he or she appraises this situation (see Table 8.3).

A child who desires the welfare of the parent may have opposing beliefs about the effects of the nursing home on the parent's welfare. For instance, the transition can be seen as having improved the life quality of one's parent in some areas because he or she is now cared for by highly qualified nursing staff around the clock, if necessary. Thus, happiness for the parent may arise in the adult child. In contrast, the child may believe that the transition has decreased the life quality of one's parent in other areas, given that the parent now feels lonely, homesick, and unhappy due to the loss of familiar places, persons, objects, and activities. These beliefs should make the adult child feel pity for the parent. The combination of both emotions creates a happy for–pity for ambivalence in response to reflecting on how the elderly parent now permanently lives in a nursing home.

The child may also desire to follow moral norms, and corresponding beliefs about whether one has actually done so may lead to additional types of emotional ambivalence. Think of an adult child who strongly adheres to the moral norm that one should fulfill the promises made to one's parent. A first promise could be to ensure the best care in case the parent can no longer care for him or herself. If the child believes that initiating a nursing home transition is a way of fulfilling that promise (because the parent now really needs professional care), then the child should experience moral satisfaction or even moral pride. The child may have made another promise, namely, never to allow (let alone initiate) the parent's permanent move into a nursing home. If the child has acted on the contrary, then he or she may respond with guilt feelings. Thus, when the child believes he or she kept one promise but broke another, this should evoke moral satisfaction–guilt ambivalence toward the nursing home stay of the parent.

Further types of emotional ambivalence about the elderly parent now living in a nursing home may arise from the copresence of different care-related desires such as desires for good relationships with one's parent and for good relationships with one's spouse and/or child. A child may then believe that the parent's nursing home transition has (a) lessened his or her feelings of closeness to the elderly parent, thus eliciting unhappiness about bad relationship with parent; and (b) increased the closeness to one's spouse, thus evoking happiness about good relationship with one's spouse (see lower large arrow in Table 8.3). These two emotions constitute unhappiness–happiness ambivalence about one's family relationships in response to reflecting on the parent now living in the nursing home.

As has become evident, the adult child may experience multiple types of emotional ambivalence with respect to the parent's transition into a nursing home. The reader is invited to contemplate further kinds of ambivalence in this context while referring to Table 8.3 as a source of inspiration.

BENEFITS FOR RESEARCH AND PRACTICE IN THE FIELD OF ELDER CARE

The preceding analyses moved beyond the older idea of care-related emotional ambivalence as the copresence of a negative emotion complex (emotional burden) and a positive emotion complex (emotional gain) toward the overall care situation (cf. Shim et al., 2012). In contrast, different types of specific emotions within the classes of positive emotions (e.g., happiness, hope, moral pride) and negative emotions (e.g., unhappiness, fear, guilt) were considered separately, and it was assumed that single emotions from the positive and negative classes (at least one from each) can co-occur and thus form specific types of emotional ambivalence (e.g., fear–hope, happiness–unhappiness, moral pride–guilt). The multifaceted situation faced by adult children of care-dependent parents provides the substance for several types of emotional ambivalence: for different combinations of positive and negative emotions toward a variety of objects related to the care dependency of the elderly parent, one's care provision for him or her, and the consequences of caregiving for oneself, the parent, and other family members such as one's spouse and/or children (see Table 8.2). Taken together, a rather differentiated picture of the types of possible emotional ambivalence of caring adult children has emerged. This has implications for a refined measurement and description as well as a deeper understanding and management of emotional ambivalence in the context of elder care.

Refined Conceptualization, Measurement, and Description of Emotional Ambivalence

Extending the Analysis to Additional Care-Related Transitions and Decisions

The present conceptual approach can be extended to additional major care transitions beyond the move into a nursing home: the adult child's initial taking over of the caregiver role, mobilization of further informal caregivers (other family members, friends, neighbors), and engagement of mobile home services as professional care providers. Moreover, attention can also be paid to emotional ambivalence regarding minor care decisions such as taking time off from family caregiving on a particular evening or on a weekend or during the holidays. When such analyses have been completed, emotional ambivalence related to major transitions or minor decisions could be compared for similarities and differences.

From Conceptualization to Measurement

The implications for the measurement of emotional ambivalence go far beyond a recently presented unidimensional measure of global ambivalent feelings of caregivers (CAS). This measure, composed of six items each, directly assesses the simultaneous experience of divergent feelings toward the caregiving situation on 4-point rating scales, which scores are combined into a single sum score representing caregiving ambivalence (Losada et al., 2016). In contrast, the present refined conceptualization of emotional ambivalence in adult children of care-dependent parents considers a broader spectrum of emotions directed at different facets of that situation, thus providing a good basis for a more differentiated and refined measurement. The instruments to be constructed could range from those with a rather specific focus such as emotional ambivalence toward minor care decisions (e.g., taking temporary time off from caring) or toward major care transitions (e.g., taking over caregiver role, mobilizing informal carers, engaging professional home care). Other measures could have a broader focus on emotional ambivalence toward main facets of the care situation (e.g., care dependency of elderly parent, one's care provision, consequences for elderly parent and oneself) and even toward the overall adult child–elderly parent care relationship.

All these measures can be constructed as indirect measures of emotional ambivalence in the following way. First, multiple positive and negative emotions are assessed with an object-specific emotion checklist. Second, separate scores for positive and negative emotions regarding the given object are determined. Third, continuous ambivalence scores are computed by combining scores of positive (P) and negative (N) emotions according to the Griffin formula (Thompson, Zanna, & Griffin, 1995):

$$\text{Ambivalence} = \left[(P+N)/2-|P-N|\right]+c.$$

The resulting variables allow for a description of emotional ambivalence in adult child caregivers, and the ambivalence scores can be further related to potential predictor and outcome variables. Nevertheless, a limitation must be noted. What do low continuous ambivalence scores mean psychologically? A closer inspection of the Griffin formula shows that low ambivalence scores can result from three different constellations: (a) low levels of both positive and negative emotions, (b) a high level of positive and a low level of negative emotions, and (c) a low level of positive and a high level of negative emotions. However, these three constellations are psychologically different: The first constellation reflects a generally low emotional responsiveness toward the care situation, whereas the second and third constellations reflect high emotional responsiveness (of either positive or negative valence) toward that situation. Fortunately, the ambiguity of low continuous ambivalence scores can be disentangled by a person-centered approach.

Person-Centered Description: Emotion-Based Typology of Adult Children of Care-Dependent Parents

This methodological approach also requires a separate assessment of positive and negative emotions toward the same object. These assessments can then be used as grouping variables to derive clusters of adult children characterized by different profiles of positive and negative care-related emotions (see Ferring, Michels, Boll, & Filipp, 2009, for a more general, analogous application to the adult child–elderly parent relationship). The four-fold scheme in Figure 8.7 depicts a likely result. Particular attention should be paid, of course, to the "ambivalent" adult children (high positive and high negative emotions), but they are just one group among others. How large is this ambivalent group in comparison with the other three? What are the similarities and differences between them and the three nonambivalent groups (composed of indifferent, dominant-positive, and dominant-negative adult children, respectively)? One of the three nonambivalent types has been frequently neglected but deserves more attention: the indifferent adult children.

Looking at such different groups of adult children allows us to question how and why such different types of emotional responding to the care situation emerge. The cognitive-motivational approach can trace this to the issue that different adult children may have different combinations of desires and beliefs (perceived fulfillment, perceived frustration) toward the

		Positive Emotions	
		Low	*High*
Negative Emotions	*Low*	Indifferent	Dominant positive
	High	Dominant negative	Ambivalent

Figure 8.7 A four-fold scheme of emotion profiles of adult children of care-dependent parents.

care situation. Regarding the "indifferent" adult children, this points in two directions. First, these children may have weak desires regarding (the fate of) their parents and their own situation; second, the adult children perceive only small degrees of fulfillment or frustration of their desires. The reader may generate corresponding cognitive-motivational explanations for the three remaining types of emotional profiles of adult children of care-dependent parents.

Improved Understanding and Management of Emotional Ambivalence

Understanding the Genesis of Emotional Ambivalence

The cognitive-motivational view conceptualizes emotional ambivalence as arising from simultaneously perceived fulfillment and frustration of an adult child's desires. An initial understanding of emotional ambivalence in a concrete case thus requires the identification of the desires of an adult child toward the various facets of the care situation. Moreover, it is necessary to identify the corresponding beliefs of the adult child so that one or more desires can be simultaneously perceived as fulfilled in some respects and as frustrated in others. Let us consider a simple case of emotional ambivalence related to a parent's upcoming transition into a nursing home. Hope–fear ambivalence about the parent's fate may arise from just one desire (e.g., for the welfare of the parent) in combination with two beliefs of which one (e.g., the transition may increase the parent's life quality in some areas) leads to perceived fulfillment and the other (e.g., the transition may decrease the parent's life quality in other areas) to perceived frustration of that desire. From here, one can strive for an extended understanding of the desires and beliefs involved. Questions that arise when searching to uncover the genesis of the identified desires include: What could lead to a strong desire for the welfare of one's parent and what could weaken it? To explain the weakening of this desire, one may think of some past abuse or mistreatment or the experience of an unjust treatment in comparison to siblings (e.g., Boll, Ferring, & Filipp, 2005). When looking for the genesis of the identified beliefs, on the one hand, an adult child may believe that highly qualified care personnel will be available around the clock, leading to the conclusion that this may ensure the welfare of the parent (beliefs that may be generated by marketing campaigns of nursing homes). On the other hand, the adult child may anticipate elder abuse and negligence in nursing homes, leading to the conclusion that the nursing home transition could also decrease the older parent's life quality (beliefs that may be generated by mass media reports).

As becomes evident, extensive efforts are required to systematically elucidate the genesis of the aforementioned desires and beliefs from which the different types of emotional ambivalence emerge. To perform this in detail for the examples above (Table 8.3) or similar ones and for emotional ambivalence about the care provision for one's parent (Table 8.2) is of course beyond the scope of this chapter. At the moment, it should suffice for researchers to recognize and appreciate the heuristic potential of the cognitive-motivational view for systematically generating such new research questions on the genesis of emotional ambivalence and for opening up new pathways to answer them.

Management of Emotional Ambivalence

Emotional ambivalence is not always problematic, but it can be, for instance, in connection with care-related decision making. Think of an adult child with strong hope–guilt ambivalence toward a possible nursing home admission of the parent. Such dissonant experiences may be unpleasant and prevent the adult child from making a decision. The cognitive-motivational view suggests two major starting points for managing such ambivalence. On the one hand are the care-related desires. For instance, an adult child may have an extremely strong desire to follow certain moral norms forbidding him or her from initiating the nursing home transition of a parent. On the other hand, the child may have an extremely strong desire for one's own welfare, which could be fulfilled by the nursing home admission of the parent. A first strategy for managing emotional ambivalence could aim at changing the content and/or (relative) strength of the desires involved (e.g., downgrading moral norms, changing the norm content) so that the nursing home admission and its implications can be less easily perceived as frustration (or fulfillment) of important desires. The second starting point for managing emotional ambivalence may focus on the adult child's beliefs, which underlie a perceived frustration or fulfillment of care-related desires. For instance, the perceived violation of moral norms through the nursing home admission may be based on false beliefs about how the elderly parent will live in a nursing home, with an overemphasis of negative and underestimation of positive nursing home experiences. In addition, the adult child may also have unrealistic beliefs about what the nursing home transition of the parent could contribute to his or her own welfare, with an exaggeration of the positive aspects (e.g., no further care by oneself is required) and suppression of the negative ones (e.g., conflicts with the nursing home staff). Thus, a second strategy for managing emotional ambivalence would be to change the relevant nursing home-related beliefs in such a way that the perceived frustration and fulfillment of the care-related desires of the adult child will diminish. Similar considerations can be made for further emotional ambivalence involving other types of emotions referring to other objects.

CONCLUSIONS

Cognitive-motivational theories of emotion allow fine-grained conceptual analyses of emotional ambivalence in adult children of care-dependent older parents. This opens new options for differentiated measurement as well as the description of emotional ambivalence in variable- and person-centered approaches. A person-centered approach can aim at the identification of different types of caring adult children characterized by different profiles of emotional ambivalence. The present analyses also allow for an extended understanding of the genesis of emotional ambivalence by focusing on processes that lead to simultaneously perceived fulfillment and frustration of important desires of caring children. All this can be done with respect to the major facets of the overall care situation as well as with respect to major care transitions in the course of the caregiving relationships and the minor care-related decisions in daily caregiving. A deeper understanding of the genesis of emotional ambivalence along the paths described has implications for the development of management strategies for emotional ambivalence, which use the care-related desires and beliefs (and their underlying conditions) as starting points.

However, one note of caution seems in order. Ambivalent emotions of adult children of care-dependent parents should not be regarded as phenomena that are always dysfunctional for an adult child and should thus be dissolved. The present cognitive-motivational framework also allows us to generate specific hypotheses about positive functions of emotional ambivalence for the experiencing individuals and their relationship partners. Let us examine an adult child's ambivalence that involves happiness for the parent because the care provision by the adult child allows the parent to remain in his or her familiar environment and unhappiness about one's own situation because care provision by the child is detrimental to his or her own career. Experiencing this kind of ambivalence may lead the adult child to reflect on why he or she experiences it and may so draw his or her attention to the underlying desires for the welfare of one's elderly parent (which is fulfilled) and for the welfare of oneself (which is frustrated). This combination of desires may motivate the adult child to search for alternative ways of caring for the parent that allow him or her to attain the welfare of the elderly parent as well as his or her own welfare. Concrete options for achieving this could be to mobilize other family members (e.g., siblings, grandchildren) to join in caregiving and/or engage mobile care services. Both options can reduce the adult child's care load and its negative impact on his or her own welfare without sacrificing the parent's welfare. Similar considerations apply to another kind of emotional ambivalence experienced by adult children: happiness for one's parent (as explained in the preceding example) and unhappiness for one's own children because an adult child's caring for his or her parent may interfere with caring for his or her children. This ambivalence may also motivate an adult child to search for alternative ways of providing care so that the desires for the welfare of one's older parent and one's children can both be fulfilled. Again the mobilization of support by other family members and/or engagement of mobile home care services could serve this purpose. Further reflection reveals that simultaneous fulfillment of an adult child's desires for the welfare of oneself and for the welfare of others can have positive intrapsychic functions for the caring child (e.g., by reducing tensions within him or her) and positive interpersonal functions by helping to reconcile the actual interests of the adult child and his or her relationship partners.

The present analyses of emotional ambivalence focused on adult children of care-dependent parents but can of course extend to emotional ambivalence experienced by elderly parents who receive care from their adult children (e.g., happiness about being cared for, unhappiness about burdening one's children). This can be done in separate studies using two different kinds of individuals as units of analysis, study 1 with adult children of care-dependent parents as subjects and study 2 with care-dependent parents of adult children as subjects. Of course a more complex type of study is conceivable, too, which includes real dyads composed of an adult child and his or her care-dependent parent as the unit of analysis. This would make it possible to compare the emotional ambivalence experiences of the two dyad members and determine the convergence versus divergence of emotional ambivalence within such dyads.

The present analysis can be taken as a model that is applicable in other contexts, too. The readers are cordially invited to use the heuristic impulses from cognitive-motivational emotion theories in their own analyses of emotional ambivalence in other caregiving relationships (e.g., parents caring for younger children) or more generally in other inter- or intragenerational family or even extrafamilial relationships. The results on emotional ambivalence in various kinds of relationships could then be compared to reveal structural similarities and relationship-specific differences, and this can lead to both generalized and relationship-specific knowledge about emotional ambivalence. Both kinds of knowledge can be starting points for further questions to be answered by future research endeavors.

NOTE

1. I thank Jaan Valsiner who drew my attention to this kind of illustration, which is similar to one of his own illustrations (Valsiner, 2006, Figure 4).

ACKNOWLEDGMENTS

I thank Lisa Trierweiler for her helpful support in preparing the English manuscript.

REFERENCES

Albert, S. M. (2004). Beyond ADL-IADL: Recognizing the full scope of family caregiving. In C. Levine (Ed.), *Family caregivers on the job: Moving beyond ADLs and IADLs* (pp. 99–127). New York, NY: United Hospital Fund.

Albert, S. M., Bear-Lehman, J., & Burkhardt, A. (2009). Lifestyle-adjusted function: Variation beyond BADL and IADL competencies. *The Gerontologist, 49*(6), 767–777.

Aneshensel, C. S., Pearlin, L. I., Mullan, J. T., Zarit, S. H., & Whitlatch, C. J. (1995). *Profiles in caregiving: The unexpected career.* San Diego, CA: Academic Press.

Barling, J., MacEwen, K. E., Kelloway, E., & Higginbottom, S. F. (1994). Predictors and outcomes of elder-care-based interrole conflict. *Psychology and Aging, 9*(3), 391–397.

Bateson, C. D. (2011). *Altruism in humans.* Oxford, England: Oxford University Press.

Ben-Ze'ev, A. (1990). Describing the emotions: A review of "The Cognitive Structure of Emotions" by Ortony, Clore & Collins. *Philosophical Psychology, 3*, 305–317.

Ben-Ze'ev, A. (2001). *The subtlety of emotions.* Cambridge, MA: MIT Press.

Black, S. E., Gauthier, S., Dalziel, W., Keren, R., Correia, J., Hew, H., & Binder, C. (2010). Canadian Alzheimer's disease caregiver survey: Baby-boomer caregivers and burden of care. *International Journal of Geriatric Psychiatry, 25*(8), 807–813.

Blieszner, R., & Hamon, R. (1992). Filial responsibility: Attitudes, motivators, and behaviors. In J. Dwyer & R. Coward (Eds.), *Gender, families, and elder care* (pp. 105–119). Newbury Park, CA: SAGE.

Boll, T. (1998). Intentionalitätstheoretische Forschungsstrategie für moralische Emotionen [Intentionality theory based research strategy on moral emotions]. In B. Reichle & M. Schmitt (Eds.), *Verantwortung, Gerechtigkeit und Moral. Zum psychologischen Verständnis ethischer Aspekte im menschlichen Verhalten* [Responsibility, justice, and morality. Psychological perspectives of ethical aspects of human behavior] (pp. 173–187). Weinheim: Juventa.

Boll, T. (1999). *Emotionen aus intentionalitätstheoretischer Sicht: Implikationen für psychologische Forschungsprogramme* [Emotions from an intentionality theory based point of view: Implications for psychological research programs]. *Trierer Psychologische Berichte, 26*(4).

Boll, T., & Ferring, D. (2013). Family caregiving for older people from a life-span developmental point of view. In I. Albert & D. Ferring (Eds.), *Intergenerational relations: European perspectives in family and society* (pp. 223–240). Bristol, England: Policy Press.

Boll, T., Ferring D., & Filipp, S.-H. (2005). Effects of parental differential treatment on relationship quality with siblings and parents: Justice evaluations as mediators. *Social Justice Research, 18,* 155–182.

Brandtstädter, J. (2001). *Entwicklung–Intentionalität–Handeln* [Development–intentionality–action]. Stuttgart: Kohlhammer.

Brandtstädter, J. (2015). *Positive Entwicklung: Zur Psychologie gelingender Lebensführung* (2. Auflage) [Positive development: On the psychology of a successful life management (2nd ed.)]. Heidelberg: Springer Spektrum.

Cantor, M., & Hirshorn, B. (1989). Intergenerational transfers within the family context: Motivating factors and their implications for caregiving. *Women and Health, 14,* 39–51.

Carbonneau, H., Caron, C., & Desrosiers, J. (2010). Development of a conceptual framework of positive aspects of caregiving in dementia. *Dementia: The International Journal of Social Research and Practice, 9,* 327–353.

Covinsky, K. E., Eng, C., Lui, L.-Y., Sands, L. P., Sehgal, A. R., Walter, L. C., & Yaffe, K. (2001). Reduced employment in caregivers of frail elders: Impact of ethnicity, patient clinical characteristics, and caregiver characteristics. *Journals of Gerontology: Series A: Biological Sciences and Medical Sciences, 56A,* 707–713.

Cummins, R. A. (1996). The domains of life satisfaction: An attempt to order chaos. *Social Indicators Research, 38*(3), 303–328.

Dallinger, U. (1996). Pflege und Beruf–ein neuer Vereinbarungskonflikt in der späten Familienphase. Ein Literatur-und Forschungsüberblick [Nursing and occupation—A new compatibility conflict in the late family phase. A literature and research review]. *Zeitschrift für Familienforschung, 8*(2), 6–42.

Fast, J. 2015. *Caregiving for older adults with disabilities: Present costs, future challenges.* IRPP Study 58. Montreal: Institute for Research on Public Policy.

Ferring, D., Michels, T., Boll, T., & Filipp, S.-H. (2009). Emotional relationship quality of adult children with ageing parents: On solidarity, conflict, and ambivalence. *European Journal of Aging, 6,* 253–265.

Gaugler, J. E., Kane, R. L., & Kane, R. A. (2002). Family care for older adults with disabilities: Toward more targeted and interpretable research. *The International Journal of Aging & Human Development, 54*(3), 205–231.

Gaugler, J. E., Yu, F., Krichbaum, K., & Wyman, J. F. (2009). Predictors of nursing home admission for persons with dementia. *Medical Care, 47*(2), 191–198.

Green, O. H. (1992). *The emotions: A philosophical theory.* Dordrecht: Kluwer.

Hassebrauck, M., & Fehr, B. (2002). Dimensions of relationship quality. *Personal Relationships, 9,* 253–270.

Holley, C. K., & Mast, B. T. (2009). The impact of anticipatory grief on caregiver burden in dementia caregivers. *The Gerontologist, 49*(3), 388–396.

Howe, A. L., Jones, A. E., & Tilse, C. (2013). What's in a name? Similarities and differences in international terms and meanings for older peoples' housing with services. *Ageing & Society, 33*(4), 547–578.

Ikkink, K., Tilburg, T. V., & Knipscheer, K. (1999). Perceived instrumental support exchanges in relationships between elderly parents and their adult children: Normative and structural explanations. *Journal of Marriage and the Family, 61,* 831–844.

Kaldjian, L. C., Curtis, A. E., Shinkunas, L. A., & Cannon, K. T. (2009). Goals of care toward the end of life: A structured literature review. *American Journal of Hospice & Palliative Medicine, 25*(6), 501–511.

Kaldjian, L. C., Shinkunas, L. A., Bern-Klug, M., & Schultz, S. K. (2010). Dementia, goals of care, and personhood: A study of surrogate decision makers' beliefs and values. *American Journal of Hospice & Palliative Medicine, 27*(6), 387–397.

Kim, J., Ingersoll-Dayton, B., & Kwak, M. (2011). Balancing eldercare and employment: The role of work interruptions and supportive employers. *Journal of Applied Gerontology, 32*(3), 347–369.

Kong, E. H. (2008). Family caregivers of older people in nursing homes. *Asian Nursing Research, 2*(4), 195–207.

Kramer, B. J. (1997). Gain in the caregiving experience: Where are we? What next? *The Gerontologist, 37*(2), 218–232.

Levine, C., Reinhard, S. C., Feinberg, L. F., Albert, S., & Hart, A. (2003–2004). Family caregivers on the job: Moving beyond ADLs and IADLs. *Generations, 27*(4), 17–23.

Lin, L. N., & Wu, S.-C. (2014). Measurement structure of the caregiver burden scale: Findings from a national community survey in Taiwan. *Geriatrics & Gerontology International, 14,* 176–184.

Lloyd, J., Patterson, T., & Muers, J. (2016). The positive aspects of caregiving in dementia: A critical review of the qualitative literature. *Dementia, 15*(6), 1534–1561.

Losada, A., Márquez-González, M., Peñacoba, C., & Romero-Moreno, R. (2010) Development and validation of the Caregiver Guilt Questionnaire. *International Psychogeriatrics, 22,* 650–660.

Losada, A., Pillemer, K., Márquez-González, M., Romero-Moreno, R., & Gallego-Alberto, L. (2017). Measuring ambivalent feelings in dementia family caregivers: The Caregiving Ambivalence Scale. *Gerontologist, 57*(3), e37–e46.

Luppa, M., Luck, T., Weyerer, S., König, H.-H., Brähler, E., & Riedel-Heller, S. G. (2010). Prediction of institutionalization in the elderly: A systematic review. *Age and Ageing, 39,* 31–38.

Merrill, D. (1997). *Caring for elderly parents: Juggling work, family, and caregiving in middle and working class families.* Westport, CT: Auburn House/Greenwood.

Meuser, T. M., & Marwit, S. J. (2001). A comprehensive, stage-sensitive model of grief in dementia caregiving. *The Gerontologist, 41*(5), 658–670.

Mills, J., Clark, M. S., Ford, T. E., & Johnson, M. (2004). Measurement of communal strength. *Personal Relationships, 11*(2), 213–230.

Montada, L. (1993). Understanding oughts by assessing moral reasoning or moral emotions. In G. G. Noam & T. E. Wren (Eds.), *The moral self* (pp. 292–309). Cambridge, MA: MIT-Press.

Novak, M., & Guest, C. (1989). Application of a multidimensional caregiver burden inventory. *The Gerontologist, 29*(6), 798–803.

Noyes, B. B., Hill, R. D., Hicken, B. L., Luptak, M., Rupper, R., Dailey, N. K., & Bair, B. D. (2010). The role of grief in dementia caregiving. *American Journal of Alzheimer's Disease and Other Dementias, 25*(1), 9–17.

Ortony, A., Clore, G. L., & Collins, A. (1988). *The cognitive structure of emotions.* Cambridge, England: Cambridge University Press.

Pearlin, L. I., Mullan, J. T., Semple, S. J., & Skaff, M. M. (1990). Caregiving and the stress process: An overview of concepts and their measures. *The Gerontologist, 30*(5), 583–594.

Reisenzein, R. (2009). Emotions as metarepresentational states of mind: Naturalizing the belief–desire theory of emotion. *Cognitive Systems Research, 10,* 6–20.

Reisenzein, R. (2015). Social emotions from the perspective of the computational belief-desire theory of emotion. In A. Herzig & E. Lorini (Eds.), *Cognitive foundations of group attitudes and social interaction* (pp. 153–176). Berlin: Springer.

Reisenzein, R., & Horstmann, G. (2006). Emotion [Emotion]. In H. Spada (Hrsg.), *Lehrbuch der allgemeinen Psychologie* [Textbook of General Psychology] (S. 435–500). Bern: Huber.

Roberts, L. J., Wise, M., & DuBenske, L. L. (2009). Compassionate family caregiving in the light and shadow of death. In B. Fehr, S. Sprecher, & L. G. Underwood (Eds.), *The science of compassionate love: Theory, research, and applications* (pp. 311–344). Malden, MA: Wiley-Blackwell.

Roseman, I., & Smith, C. A. (2001). Appraisal theory: Overview, assumptions, varieties, controversies. In K. R. Scherer, A. Schorr, & T. Johnstone (Eds.), *Appraisal processes in emotion: Theories, methods, research* (pp. 3–19). Oxford: University Press.

Roth, D. L., Burgio, L. D., Gitlin, L. N., Gallagher-Thompson, D., Coon, D. W., Belle, S. H., & Burns, R. (2003). Psychometric analysis of the Revised Memory and Behavior Problems Checklist: Factor structure of occurrence and reaction ratings. *Psychology and Aging, 18*(4), 906–915.

Roth, D. L., Fredman, L., & Haley, W. E. (2015). Informal caregiving and its impact on health: A reappraisal from population-based studies. *The Gerontologist, 55*(2), 309–319.

Scharlach, A., Li, W., & Dalvi, T. B. (2006). Family conflict as a mediator of caregiver strain. *Family Relations, 55*(5), 625–635.

Schulz, R., & Monin, J. (in press). Suffering and compassion in older adult caregiving relationship. In T. Boll, D. Ferring, & J. Valsiner (Eds.), *Cultures of care in aging.* Charlotte, NC: Information Age.

Searle, J. R. (1983). *Intentionality: An essay in the philosophy of mind.* Cambridge, England: Cambridge University Press.

Semple, S. J. (1992). Conflict in Alzheimer's caregiving families: Its dimensions and consequences. *The Gerontologist, 32*(5), 648–655.

Shim, B., Barroso, J., & Davis, L. L. (2012). A comparative qualitative analysis of stories of spousal caregivers of people with dementia: Negative, ambivalent, and positive experiences. *International Journal of Nursing Studies, 49*(2), 220–229.

Silverstein, M., Conroy, S. J., Wang, H., Giarrusso, R., & Bengtson, V. L. (2002). Reciprocity in parent-child relations over the adult life course. *Journal of Gerontology: Social Sciences, 57B,* S2–S13.

Silverstein, M., Parrott, T., & Bengston, V. (1995). Factors that predispose middle-aged sons and daughters to provide social support to older parents. *Journal of Marriage and the Family, 57,* 465–475.

Thompson, M. M., Zanna, M. P., & Griffin, D. W. (1995). Let's not be indifferent about (attitudinal) ambivalence. In R. E. Petty & J. A. Krosnick (Eds.),

Attitude strength: Antecedents and consequences (Vol. 4, pp. 361–386). Hillsdale, NJ: Erlbaum.

Valsiner, J. (2006). Ambivalence under scrutiny: Returning to the future. *Estudios de Psicología, 27*(1), 117–130.

Verbrugge, L. M., & Jette, A. M. (1994). The disablement process. *Social Science & Medicine, 38*(1), 1–14.

Wilkins, V. M., Bruce, M. L., & Sirey, J. A. (2009). Caregiving tasks and training interest of family caregivers of medically ill homebound older adults. *Journal of Aging and Health, 21*(3), 528–542.

Wilms, H.-U., Baltes, M. M., & Kanowski, S. (1998). Demenzerkrankungen und Alltagskompetenz: Effekte auch jenseits von ADL und IADL [Dementia and competence in activities of daily living: Effects beyond ADL and IADL]. *Zeitschrift für Gerontologie und Geriatrie, 31*(4), 263–270.

Zank, S., Schacke, C., & Leipold, B. (2006). Berliner Inventar zur Angehörigenbelastung—Demenz (BIZA-D) [Berlin Inventory of Caregivers' Burden—Dementia]. *Zeitschrift für Klinische Psychologie und Psychotherapie, 35*(4), 296–305.

PART III

EXPERIENCING AMBIVALENCE: FOCUS ON PHENOMENA

CHAPTER 9

AMBIVALENCE WHEN FAMILY VALUES CHANGE

Development of New Values in the Perspective of Sociocultural Global "Advancement"

Maliina Lyberth
Aalborg University

The tradition to study social representations is an approach that is meant to understand common collective values, social practices, norms, and beliefs of a society or community. It gives the material and social worlds meaning and order, which makes sense for the community members. The beginnings of the Social Representation Theory can be traced back to the work by Emile Durkheim in the 1890s. In the hands of Serge Moscovici (1973), the focus on collective representations has been turned into Social Representation Theory (SRT) and later on expanded to further areas (Duveen, 2001; Gaskell & Lopes, 2015). The goal of this chapter is to consider examples of ambivalence that take place between two generations, when traditionally shared family values are pressured to change over a relatively

Trans-Generational Family Relations, pages 179–195

short period of time, using examples from my native country (Greenland). With globalization especially, sociocultural changes affect people and their offspring's views on values.

Examples from qualitative interviews will make it more clear when discussing Tina (the mother) and Emma (the daughter) and their different status of values. They were both born and raised in Greenland and should have both witnessed fast and rapid changes of their society in two different currencies of time. The interest in different family values and the ambivalence that might exist is interesting to research because of the ongoing change of culture and, therefore, the constant change in social representations. The aim of this chapter is to first look at whether there are ambivalences, to then understand what these ambivalences are, and to discuss how those ambivalences might affect a family culture, with the help from the interviews. This research is limited and cannot reflect on all Greenlandic families in general. However, to understand the interviews and their cultural background, I will construct a generic image of Greenlanders close to my understanding as well as my own experiences as a Greenlander.

SOCIAL ORDER AND SOCIAL REPRESENTATION

Social representations can be seen as an ongoing structural social order (Sammut, Andreouli, Gaskell, & Valsiner, 2015). A generic example—and yet close to my experiences as a Greenlander—is that of a Greenlandic structural family order that might have been and maybe still is apparent:

1. The head of the family is the father. He provides food for the family by going hunting for seals with his boat at 5 o'clock in the early morning, if the weather allows it, because hunting seal is usually most successful during this time. The father needs to know about the weather every day and might listen more intently to the radio when the news about the weather is being told. Every day during dinner time, he listens to the radio because he needs to know whether he should wake up early the next day. This is a common Greenlandic hunter social practice example of a social representation. However, not to be misguided, social practices such as officers, academics, nurses, clerks, and so on, which can be seen in any western society, are also in the Greenlandic labor market.
2. Social representations are seen as organizers of different dynamics of the social world. Hunters' values might be to have a good wife who cooks good food and takes good care of his children, besides doing well at her office clerk job. These social representations of social practices and values change into different forms as

time moves on, but in some way they will always be referred back to the cultural form from which they develop (Duveen, 2007). The hunter might understand that what he was taught about hunting by his father is not necessarily what he is going to teach his son because there are many more possibilities of social practices than "just" hunting.

VALUES DEFINE THE APPRECIATIONS AND NEEDS

Values are at the root of social representations and considerably a fundamental part of any individual (regardless of whether the individual decides to acknowledge them). Like social representations, values emerge from while also establishing cultural practices (Branco, Palmieri, & Pinto, 2012). There can be different kinds of values, such as social values, cultural values, community values, family values, and so on. All of these values are group sized value builders, which means they involve one individual as well as other individuals and their environment and social content (Branco et al., 2012). What motivates an individual comes from values.

Going back to my fictional example, the hunter's son's values might not be as strong headed toward becoming a hunter bur rather leaning more toward having his own clothing store because this other social practice could give him something closer to his own values in the constantly changing society. His father, the hunter, and his need for hunting can be embedded by his love for nature and being in the midst of total quiet. When he grew up, his values were developed to match what he liked to do, but also with opportunities there were for him and what he became capable of doing and competent to do, when slowly leaning toward which social practice he sought to do.

As mentioned before, social representations change over time (Sammut et al., 2015). Values are a great part of social representations, and some evidence suggests that values are more likely to change through the generations when located in families that can economically contain such diversity. In theory, families with more financial troubles have more difficulties when changes happen from one generation to the next (Inglehart, 2008). From 1970 to 2006, Inglehart researched this topic and suggested that value priorities were changing between two given generations, which he thought was linked to existential conditions. The first generation grew up feeling survival to be precarious, whereas the coherent second generation could take survival for granted (Inglehart, 2008). Thus, the research revealed two distinctive value holders: materialists and self-expression holders. The materialists, the larger group, grew up during World War II, a completely different society than what it became, when the second generation, the self-expression holders, grew up (Inglehart, 2008). When cultures change over time, values change as well and vice versa. Other studies suggest something similar when talking about social class. These studies showed that middle-class families were more likely to value autonomy for their children, whereas working-class families were more likely to expect their children to follow the rules of their parents or other adults (Tudge et al., 2012). Again, it is important to note that this occurs only for some cultures, most likely Western societies.

EVERYDAY LIFE DOMAINS

What I mean by everyday life domains in the context of interview data is an inclusion of words such as activities, social practices, family culture, and so on. The Domains in the spheres of partnership, family, food, early development activities, and other aspects of values are included for some Greenlandic families.

Introducing the Interviews

Two main interviews from the same family constellation will be used in this chapter. The mother (Tina) has a husband and 6 children, whereas the other interview is with her oldest daughter (Emma) who is 29 years old, who also has a daughter who is 6 years old (Lily). Both of these women were born and raised in Sisimiut, a larger town in Greenland, and they both moved to Denmark with their families a couple of years ago. Their names as well as town names have been changed for privacy. The interviews were semi-structured, which gave more space for them to lead their interview to what they thought was important to discuss. Questions do not directly focus on the aspect of values but rather aspects of social representations in general, such as who was most important for them in their family and how they were raised growing up. This knowledge of their childhood is especially interesting given what might come up as social practices and general family activities. Because the mother and daughter are members of the same family, we have an opportunity to get a glimpse into some of the generational gaps between them and what value differences exist. The ambivalence of these women will therefore not be directly given but can be hinted through their words.

Family as an Institution

Food often relates to love and care, or of pure survival. Like in the old Inuit ways, hunting for food was a way to survive (Sørensen, 2007). Nowadays, in urban Greenland, we still find families and kinship important practically when it comes to organizing their daily life socially, economically, and culturally (Tròndheim, 2010), but getting food for survival is not crucial anymore now that the government takes care of those in need. The interview I had with the mother (Tina) had much to say about her childhood (1960s–1970s). She was raised by her parents and grew up in a big family with 12 siblings:

> **M:** So, do you have any memories about what hunting and fishing were like when you were a child? Was it important at that time?
>
> T: It was very important, ehm, all year around I would work, so when I had my vacation I would once again become aware, become aware that every year when summer came and when school was ending, that we were about to hunt for reindeer. My dad would fish and hunt, and we would hang the fish and dry them, salt them and just deal with the fish in general. So around the vacation time our freezer would get filled with Greenlandic food—fish and reindeer. We do that during all of our vacation time, and when school was about to start we would sail back home to our town. We've made a summer vacation house near the place where we fish, or my dad did. So every year, my parents, or until my dad couldn't anymore, every year from the end of May or start of June until the end of August, we would do this. Then after summer we would come back home and start working at the factory again. But the freezer would be filled as much as possible. How the year turned out would determine how much we would have for our freezer. And when my dad was off [from work] he would also go hunting for either *Appat* [Uria Aalga bird], fish, or something. We would always have a filled freezer, all year around.
>
> It was very nice, we were very lucky. I miss it now. [both of us laughing] We would never suffer from food at all.

Suffering from food seems to be far from what Tina and her family worried about when she was growing up, because their hunt for food and fishing gave them free resources. This hunter–gatherer sociocultural scenario is quite different from how her daughter Emma grew up:

> **M:** [. . .] So the final question: do you remember how important it was to hunt and fish when you grew up?

> **E:** We did not have a boat, so I have no experience of catching fish, and the thing about boats, I always get seasick. I throw up, even in a small boat. [both laughing] . . .

Not having a boat most likely determines whether you are even able to go hunting and fishing, unless you have close kinship who can take you hunting and fishing. Although both the mother and daughter did not show or say anything about how their childhoods were different from one another with regard to fishing and hunting, this is a good start to emphasize the two different experiences they had growing up. Although no ambivalences can be shown from this short example, I find this introduction of them to be helpful later during this chapter.

Family Identity

When we talk about values, we cannot avoid talking about identity. Values, social representations in general, and identity are all interrelated in the dynamics of understanding humans in a sociocultural setting (Branco et al., 2012). Identity is often correlated and used to understand individuals, although cultural identity might be just as important. As an example, people, whether in a group or individually, leave traces behind, of "footprints" as Fuhrer would call it (Beckstead, 2012). These footprints are of intentions, desires, beliefs, and values, whether material or nonmaterial. They embed to others, going from an object to then become a subjected part of the individual, and they also "constitute [a] part of our personal cultures and guide human development" (Beckstead, 2012, p. 90).

The identity of a family is the meaning of knowing and understanding a family's conception of what it means to be and what they define as family. Social collective identities, such as families, are the construction and continuous reconstruction of history and collective culture, interplaying between the individual and group(s) that subjectively assemble an individual's feeling of belonging (Branco et al., 2012).

Nevertheless, each family member has his or her own identity and individual values. An intergenerational study in Italy indicated that adolescents were more individualistic than their mothers and that the mothers were more individualistic than their mothers (the grandmothers) (Barni, Rosnati, & Ranieri, 2013). This finding shows that however one might be guided through life from one's family, varieties of values are seen within families.

Many young Greenlandics go to Denmark to study[1] because for many of them the education they want is not possible to achieve in Greenland. Living that far from home keeps them from the continuously reconstruction of their common collective family culture, so they must establish a new culture for the family by somehow staying closely connected to each other (by Skype or other social media).

When an individual goes to study in a foreign country for years, he or she connects to a new context that is different from his or her own culture. The student participates in new social activities and relationships, and therefore embeds in new values. These values are always crucial in defining general human behavior and the individual's relationships, as well as maintaining and regulating a cohesive stability over these (Bahadur & Dhawan, 2008). By maintaining new adapted values, one must also release some older values, which then leads to differentiating from one's family.

Tina (Emma's mother) had different childhood experiences than her daughter:

> **T:** [...] When we were growing up, every single Saturday we would all help each other with cleaning the house, eh, the toilet, the bathroom, we would clean everything. Every single Saturday. We didn't miss one!
> M: Right.
> T: That's how we grew up. Our parents would tell us what to do, they would tell us to clean the house every Saturday. And that was a good thing for us. It wasn't all that bad, of course there was a *bridge* during our teenage years when some days seemed more lazy than others, but thinking back to it, ehm, I think it was a positive future-oriented learning activity.

Family activities for Tina meant working together with her siblings, whether it was salting fish, cleaning the house, or going hunting with others just to help out.

> **M:** So do you remember a specific time when you [as in all of her family] went hunting or fishing? Do you have a specific memory that comes to mind?
> **T:** I used to go hunting, but I didn't catch any. [both of us laughing]
> **M:** That's what you remember? [both laughing]
> **T:** Yes. But where we used to hunt, males would mostly do the hunting, while we as females would take care of the fishnets and stuff like that.
> [...]
> So, we would row and get the fish from the fishnet and then split the fish, salt it, and then put it over a fume, which we also would make as much of, so we could have it all year

around. We would salt the fish and put it in a . . . [gesturing with her hands a bigger square] barrel?

M: Yes.

T: We would fill it up in a barrel.

[. . .]

T: Eh, I'm afraid of rifles. [both of us laughing] Even holding it makes me scared. [both of us laughing] But I also used to go with those who hunted so I could help carry what they hunted.

Tina linked this specific memory of carrying the weight of what was hunted with her childhood activities of taking care of the fishnets and so on, therefore it is easy to presume that this memory took place during her young adulthood.[2] Tina's daughter's memories of hunting and fishing include the following:

M: [. . .] Otherwise I would have asked if there was a particular moment in your life that you remember, about hunting or fishing?

E: Oh, there is. It was when, I do not know how old I was? 7–8 years. Down on, what's it called? The fish dealer. There are those who. . . . We could be many children there and play with a small fishing lace and a small string and then try and catch something. But it was mostly jellyfish [we caught] I think.

M: Yes . . . you remember stuff like that? You liked it [that kind of play]?

E: Yes.

M: And there were many [children] who did it?

E: Yes, it's probably because there was not much else you could do.

Emma's childhood experiences, in comparison with her mothers, again shows a lack of hunting and fishing with her family. For Emma, fishing meant being near the fish dealer, which was near the water and "play" fishing with other children. Her other childhood activities seemed unproductive as well, but child fun:

E: What do we do there? Everything! Playing with marbles, hide and seek, play tag. Trying not to run around the blocks because we were so . . . loud.

M: [laughing] Right.

E: There were certain people, who lived there, who we knew were gonna be mad at us. So we knew best to avoid one staircase line.
M: [laughing] Right. Good times, huh?
E: Yes. [smiling]

Tina's family activities as a child look like an organization where everyone had to help keep the machine going. Going to school, working at the factory, and working all summer long to have food for the freezer also seemed for Tina to be positive experiences for her, which she also explained:

> T: [...] That was a learning period when we were growing up... as human beings we are all different, and what we learn are different from one another, so other people might have interpreted it as something bad... when we discussed it with other kids, ehm, some would kind of make it sound like we were being mistreated. But we would be grateful and *I* learned from it.

Tina mentioned before that there was a bridge during her teen years, where some days seemed lazier than others, but she is still grateful for the learning experience. She hopes that she has provided the same value of having a clean home to her children:

> **T:** [...] And of course, we as parents did our job by teaching our kids to help each other out. We lived together, and because of that we all helped each other out. Which is why I think it's okay I take some time off, if I as an example cook, and my kids then after that take care of the rest, without any hesitation. They know it's their duty, they grew up that way. [...]
>
> **T:** [...] Some day they will have to decide what kind of home they want for themselves. Will it be messy, or will it be clean? That's up to them. But of course we are not trying to make them uncomfortable with it. We are trying to have a home with as less a mess as possible, so they will feel the same about not wanting a messy home in their future. That's why I think it's good to prepare them for when they will be alone. When they start living by themselves I'm sure not going to come by their home and start cleaning. [both of us laugh] They know that. They are raised like that. They don't always have a clean room, but we tell them our thoughts about that sometimes.

Although Tina hopes her children will have the same value of having a clean home, it seems like this activity was not as decisive as when she was growing up. Growing up, she and her family would not miss one single Saturday of cleaning the house. It was not a chore but more of a routine family activity, whereas her own children simply get her and her husband's thoughts about their messy rooms. Admittedly, she provided her own family with different duties, such as splitting the chores of who cooks and who cleans up afterward. She later explains why cleaning up after dinner also does not seem to be as heavy as a duty as it has been before. She divides this chore into her older kids' experience versus her younger kids, whom some still live with her and her husband:

> **T:** Or even the dish washer. [...] There is a difference [between her older and younger kids]. I also had the pattern of making them do the dish after dinner. Every time. And now, now that we have the dishwasher... how do I explain? It feels like the energy of doing the dishes has become low.

"My Family Is Important, But..."

Different societies based on class value differently when it comes to independence and interdependence, or, in other words, individualism and collectivism (Branco, 2004). One might suggest that larger families that profit from each other practically might value interdependence rather than independence, which makes sense, given the context of what is culture-practical.

Tina's family members were dependent on each other, especially her father. He sounds like an important member because he could build the summer vacation house and because he hunted for food (most likely with his sons). Both her parents were workers, and Tina and her siblings made sure their parents ate for lunch by cooking for them. Throughout the interview, I did not get the feeling that anyone in her family values independence in general. However, she did mention having a close little sister, which might allow for a small opening of individualism within a collectivism:

> **T:** Of course my siblings are very important to me. But I'm mostly close to my little sister. We are two years apart. And maybe also the next in line, before me, who is my big brother, but he is a man, but of course I treat him as my brother. But I'm more connected to my little sister. And we are next to each other in the line, so of course we can talk about everything between heaven and earth.

Tina's daughter Emma comes from a big family too, with five siblings, if we think about her sociocultural setting. She also mentioned her siblings as the most important ones in her family:

> **E:** Ehm. I don't know. My parents and siblings. They are my first priority. Our children. We do not have as close a contact with my aunts and such. [...] We are not that close. Or we do not talk daily. [...] Maybe more like on Christmas and birthdays.

When she says *our* children, she is referring to the fact that her younger sibling also has children. Emma's parents and siblings are important to her, but she is also aware of her own bubble of family that she has (her daughter and herself):

> **M:** But if you were to choose someone who, who's most important to you? Is it this whole family?
> **E:** Yes, yes. My daughter, of course.
> **M:** Right.
> **E:** She is. When I make decisions, then it is Lily I think about.

Family size in the context of this Greenlandic family has decreased to fewer members through the generations, which might give way to attaching to one's close family members more deeply than if there were more people in one's family. Theoretically, it seems like a child increases in value now that a family does not need to have 13 children but are okay with just one.

Greenlandic Inuit way back used to live jointly as families (Sørensen, 2007), and the application of this can still be found back in the 1950s and 1960s (Trònheim, 2010, not surprisingly for some families to this day maybe even). Nuclear families are now much more common in urban Greenlandic families, although the appreciation of and respect for one's larger family members (such as grandparents, aunts, uncles, etc.) are still strong cohesive attachments for many families, at least in smaller Greenlandic towns (Trònheim, 2010).

An individual is a recipient of former values transmitted through others (siblings, family, society, etc.), but the individual is also involved in the interpretation and reproduction of these, which makes this "organization" an ongoing process (Tudge et al., 2012). Arguably, Tina and Emma have both gone through a collectivistic culture to a more individualistic society, just at different generations and standards. Both generations are going through this ongoing change of society, which allows one to better create and form a nuclear family, hence individualism. Emma comes close to this subject:

> **E:** Also even though it may not be, eh, a good decision according to my parents. Then it's Lilly.
> [...] Ehm, when the family is gathered, I need, I need the structure. Ehm, the child's needs come first.
> How to say this...? If there is a family celebration as an example. There [at the celebration], I told my parents that we were going early because Lily had to go to the kindergarten the next day. And maybe 10 years ago that they would [Emma's parents] have said that she does not have to go to kindergarten, because she is with the family now. They, they can sometimes have the opinion that family should come first. And then I say that Lily's development comes first.

Emma is the recipient of former values, where it would be fine and notably a better fit socioculturally for Emma and Lily to stay at the party than go home early because Lily has to go to kindergarten the next day. However, Emma is living under a different sociocultural condition than her mother, and she is now interpreting those values (cf. "[...] even though it may not be, eh, a good decision according to my parents") she was taught and reproducing them into the involved culture in which she now lives. "They can sometimes have the opinion that family should come first. And then I say that Lily's development comes first." This quote proves that Tina has a more extended and culture-collective family than her daughter Emma, who seems to think more individually, quoting that her daughter, *her* family, *comes first.*

Emma's quote about this subject might not appear ambivalent in any way, and she is aware that her mother's way of raising children and her own way of raising her child is different. Nevertheless, it suggests possible ambivalence, although it was not mentioned directly.

AMBIVALENCE THROUGH FORMS OF SOCIAL REPRESENTATIONS

Going From a Collective to an Individualistic Society

We did not discuss whether actually ambivalence(s) led to occurring changes at either an individual or a sociocultural level. Tina and Emma's differences about what is okay in a social setting are a good example of that. Tensions of shared values that either belong or not, no matter in which context they are displayed, will not find homogeneity of those values. Values change. At some given time, parents will have allowed some of the values prevailing from their sociocultural group and then have to interpret them into their own given sociocultural context and to their children as well.

Those children will then also at some given time go through the same, hence Emma.

Emma was aware of a fundamental relationship with her parents about how to raise her child, and how that has led to arguments:

> **E:** That the structure I would like her to have.
> **M:** Mmm. You can see that you have other positions on how two raise a child.
> **E:** Yes! We have fought about that.

Values are first and foremost understandable in a given context—culturally, socially, and so on—as much as considering their everyday activities and individual characteristics (Tudge et al., 2012). By Emma saying that she wants her daughter Lily to have a structure, she is creating space, at least from her parent's way of raising a child. However, a more alluring act is her connecting this to how they have fought about the subject. From this small perspective, we are witnessing this ambivalence between two generations about the difference of a core value: how to raise a child. This can also be led back to the discussion of interdependence and independence (Tudge et al., 2012). We can tilt more to the fact that Tina was raised in a sphere of interdependence, where her parents probably were expecting her and her siblings to "follow" the family rules of where "everyone had to help out." This is not to conclude that her upbringing was absolutely nonautonomous because she mentioned working at a factory and so on. However, in comparison with Emma, Tina is from a more culture-collective family. Because Emma wants a different upbringing for her daughter, and society in general has become more individualistic, we can softly assume that Emma wants more individualism for her own little family.

Cultural practice has gone from a collective level, where everyone in the family helped each other out, to a more individualistic fundamental level, which has created more isolation and ignited more frustrated views on social relations because there's now competition in everyday life activities (Branco et al., 2012). Durkheim himself saw tension and confusion as being possible parts of the modernization of societies because these societies would go from being simple and socially solid to becoming more individualistic and complex. The adaptation of new norms can create an imbalance between current and previous norms, providing his concepts of exclusion and inclusion, which are deeply connected to modernized complex societies (Alexander & Smith, 2005). We cannot blame Tina and Emma for fighting about how to raise Emma's child when tensions are almost expected, going from a society of some norms to modern ones. We are not saying that Emma comes from a complex modern society but rather is living under conditions of a more rapidly changing global world.

Going From Joint to Nuclear Families

Family as a function determines the development of individuals, with sources of emotional bonding, nurturing, and socialization (Bahadur & Dhawan, 2008). Socialization depends on the given sociocultural context in which one is embedded. What we now see in urban societies is a combination of traditional and modern values, which create new identities and can affect individual members of a family (Bahadur & Dhawan, 2008).

Nuclear families are a newer phenomenon for Greenlandic families. If Tina's parents and her husband's parents hadn't died young, then would either of them have lived together with them and their 13 children? Maybe or most probably they would have been very close to them, as joint families usually are. If we do the math, with joint families and interdependence, plus the fact that working-class families[3] most likely expect their children to follow the rules of their parents' pathways (Tudge et al., 2012), such as values, this matches well for Tina's parents' way of how they raised her and their 12 other offspring. This is also based on the sociocultural context in which they were embedded.

Tina now lives with her family in a changed sociocultural context because of a time-changed generation, although also because they moved from Greenland to Denmark a few years ago. This changed context she is now living under, different from the one in which she grew up, is sometimes visible through the interview, as when she was talking about her other daughter:

> **T:** But she is 18 now, ehm, and she doesn't ask for things like, "Can I cook today?" [...] She doesn't do that. But her little brother does that. Eh, of course we [her husband and her] see the mistakes that we have made [laughing]. But we make sure to talk about the mistakes we have done [about parenting] even while the kids are listening to us.

We cannot know for sure whether Tina's parents questioned *their* parenting when Tina grew up. However, if they valued interdependence for their children, they would probably expect for their children to follow their rules and provide more autonomy throughout her and her siblings' childhood. Tina, according to the current sociocultural context, seems to have raised more independence in her own children, taking from what she quoted earlier: "Someday they will have to decide what kind of home they want for themselves. Will it be messy, or will it be clean? That's up to them."

Even Emma expressed her childhood as being more independent:

> **E:** So the thing about dad determining any of our decisions, it, I didn't care much for it. And I think I expressed that a lot of times in my teens.

Given Tina's early experiences of what was valued in her family context, she will be bias or "printed" of the footsteps from which she was taught (Beckstead, 2012). Her childhood and adulthood were objectively, by her environment, attached to the intentions of what it then meant to have a good human development, which at a given time subjectively established her own identity (Beckstead, 2012). These environmental affections from the early years of life easily influence one's development, but they get slower and slower when one's growth starts to detain (Lachman, 1983). The challenges that then come are to "allow" new values to correlate anew with already established values. Given how Tina was raised and for her to have valued raising her own children in a more independent way, it seems she has been affected by the environment, and probably in later socialization of her life (Lachman, 1983). The theory of late socialization is based on assumptions and results of core values not to be changed, when socialization of modernity is happening. However, late socialization can easily change periphery values (Lachman, 1983) because they are not as skin deep as core values.

Ambivalence as a Rule Rather Than an Exception

Wanting one's family and loved ones to accept and understand what is socially appreciated in their common society is comprehensible. The bigger goal for this chapter was to find what those appreciated shared values were and how they differed from one generation to another, rather than pinpoint some of the challenges, conflicts, or ambivalence. Going through the interviews theme by theme and discovering what looked conflicting, with the help of theories of social representations, to some extent illuminated what some of these ambivalences were. We acknowledge that not everything is visible through two short interviews. However, the examples provided a look inside some more or less important aspects of how shared values decrease over time to become anew with values that are featuring along with the current time of one's culture. Emma's seasickness is especially a funny coincidence, given that she grew up with her family not having a boat and did not hunt and fish like her mother did during her childhood. We do not know whether Tina also has seasickness, this is a common experience for Greenlandic people in general, or other variables could have been a factor in this small observation, but it is a playful way to make changes of smaller dynamics from social representations visible.

The examples of Tina and Emma give insight to the indication of values being less shared in their family and in their context of a changing society. However, this is not less relevant to some other parts of the world. Changing societies are detectable through various tools. Globalization as defined earlier is about gathering aspects of cultures and integrating them internationally. The challenges that are implemented in this process are beneficial to observe, if not only to discuss the pros and cons about certain issues that can advance one's perspective. Ambivalence about changing aspects of one's culture is essential.

NOTES

1. In 2006, for example, 89 Greenlandic students started further educating themselves in Denmark. In 2009, the number rose to 117, and in 2012, this number became 125. Other possible educational tracks, such as upper secondary or vocational school, were not included in these numbers. http://www.stat.gl/default.asp?lang=en
2. It is a heavy job to carry any animals through long fells and bumpy nature. I am highly assuming this happened during or after her teenage years, when her body was capable of doing this heavy job.
3. This is not confirming Tina's parents as a working-class family because Westernized imported definitions are difficult to interpret into Greenlandic examples at their time, but this is merely a sense of reaching closer to this definition.

REFERENCES

Alexander, J. C., & Smith, P. (2005). *The Cambridge companion to Durkheim.* Cambridge, England: Cambridge University Press.

Bahadur, A., & Dhawan, N. (2008). Social value of parents and children in joint and nuclear families. *Journal of the Indian Academy of Applied Psychology, 34*(Special Issue), 74–80.

Barni, D., Rosnati, R., & Ranieri, S. (2013). Value transmission between parents and their adolescent children: The process and its outcomes. A psycho-social perspective. In I. Albert & D. Ferring (Eds.), *Intergenerational relations in society and family: European perspectives* (pp. 101–117). Bristol, England: Policy Press.

Beckstead, Z. (2012). Values internalization on the move: The revivification of faith along the pilgrims path. In A. U. Branco & J. Valsiner (Eds.), *Cultural psychology of human values* (pp. 87–111). Charlotte, NC: Information Age.

Branco, A. U., Pessina, L., Flores, A., & Salomão, S. (2004). A sociocultural constructivist approach to metacommunication in child development. In A. U. Branco & J. Valsiner (Eds.), *Communication and metacommunication in human development* (pp. 3–31). Greenwich, CT: Information Age.

Branco, A. U., Palmieri, M., & Pinto, R. G. (2012). Cultural practices and value constructions: The development of competition and individualism within societies. In A. U. Branco & J. Valsiner (eds.), *Cultural psychology of human values* (pp. 31–62). Charlotte, NC: Information Age.

Duveen, G. (2001). Social representations. In C. Fraser, B. Burchell, D. Hay & G. Duveen (Eds.), *Introducing social psychology* (pp. 268–287). Cambridge, England: Polity.

Duveen, G. (2007). Culture and social representations. In J. Valsiner & A. Rosa (Eds.), *The Cambridge handbook of sociocultural psychology* (pp. 543–559). New York, NY: Cambridge University Press.

Gaskell, G., & Lopes, C. A. (2015). Social representations and societal psychology. In G. Sammut, E. Andreouli, G. Gaskell, & J. Valsiner (Eds.), *The Cambridge handbook of social representations* (pp. 29–42). Cambridge, England: Cambridge University Press.

Inglehart, R. F. (2008). Changing values among western publics from 1970 to 2006. *West European Politics, 31*(1–2), 130–146.

Lachman, R. (1983). Modernity change of core and periphery values of factory workers. *Human Relations, 36*, 563–580.

Lopes, X., & Gaskell, G. (2015). Social representation and societal psychology. In G. Sammut, E. Andreouli, G. Gaskell, & J. Valsiner et al (Eds.), *The Cambridge handbook of social representations* (pp. 29–42). Cambridge, England: Cambridge University Press.

Manning, W. D., Longmore, M. A., & Giordano, P. C. (2007). The changing institution of marriage: Adolescents' expectations to cohabit and to marry. *Journal of Marriage and Family, 69*(3), 559–575.

Sammut, G., Andreouli, E., Gaskell, G., & Valsiner, J. (Eds.). (2015). *The Cambridge handbook of social representations.* Cambridge, England: Cambridge University Press.

Sørensen, A. K. (2007). *Denmark-Greenland in the twentieth century.* Kopenhagen: Museum Tusculanum Press.

Tróndheim, G. (2010). Kinship in Greenland: Emotions of relatedness. *Acta Borealia: A Nordic Journal of Circumpolar Societies, 27*(2), 208–220.

Tudge, J. R. H., Piccini, C. A., Lopez, R. S., Sperb, T. M., Dansokho, S. C., & Freitas, L. B. L. (2012). The cultural ecology of human value. In A. U. Branco & J. Valsiner (Eds.), *Cultural psychology of human values* (pp. 63–83). Charlotte, NC: Information Age.

CHAPTER 10

TRANSGENERATIONAL AMBIVALENCE IN THE TIME TO COME

How Meanings Regulate Being Pregnant and Facing Miscarriage

Vívian Volkmer Pontes and Lívia Mathias Simão
University of São Paulo

The main goal of this chapter is to propose and discuss the extension of the psychological notion of ambivalence in the experience of women in transition to motherhood who suffer spontaneous abortions. Here we argue that transgenerational ambivalence reaches a myriad of tensional situations that emerge in the I–Other–World relationship (Simão, 2010). Such tensions provide, simultaneously, reconstructions of those same I–Other–World relationships in the scope of temporality (Simão, 2015).

To achieve this goal, we depart from the theoretical elaborations of Abbey (2006) on ambivalence—understood as a constant tension between what is ("the world as it is") and what could be the next moment, which

Trans-Generational Family Relations, pages 197–215

motivates the construction of meaning. Understood as such, ambivalence sets itself in a triadic structure that encompasses three different aspects: (a) the world as it is now, (b) what could be of the world now, and (c) the world as it is in the "new" now.

Our proposal of extension of the notion of ambivalence to the context of the experience of women in transition to motherhood who suffer spontaneous abortions will be illustrated through Juliana's1 reproductive trajectory to motherhood, which was recurrently interrupted by the occurrence of spontaneous abortions.

TRANSITION TO MOTHERHOOD: INTERGENERATIONAL AMBIVALENCES

Motherhood is an event that implies diverse changes in the familiar life cycle, instituting discontinuities in the feminine social identity and responsibilities. The existence of such discontinuities can be understood as comprising two main events: (a) the changes of context and social role that must be fulfilled, which generally follow changes in a determined field of the person's life; and (b) the changes in the meaning of self, which result from the different ways a woman starts to perceive herself due to the new treatment she receives in relation with others because of the new status she assumes: that of being a mother (Cole, 1999). The discontinuity in the meaning of self occurs concomitantly to a process of gradual adaptation to the new condition, by means of which personal and collective practices and fields of meaning prepare the individual under transformation for what is to come. In this sense, culture can be understood as a symbolic field constraining action (Boesch, 1991).

Part of this action field is constituted by myth stories (Boesch, 1991), in this case family stories about pregnancy, birth, and child upbringing, which constrain (Valsiner, 1997, 1998) "things as they are," "things as they should be," and "how they could be" in the everyday experience of a woman that discovers herself pregnant. As Simão (2003) highlighted years ago,

> Constraint captures the dimension of the possible, which emerges from the field of the indeterminate. The notion of constraint touches upon the philosophical issue of the inescapable concomitancy of determinism and free will in human action in general, and in human symbolic action in particular. As such, the concept allows—and even demands—a focus on the permanent tension between the *possible (now)* and the *not possible (now or not yet)*, between *what can be* and *what exceeds* meaning in current human experience. (p. 450)

Therefore, considering the family stories about pregnancy, birth, and child upbringing as a manner of constraining the experience of the woman who discovers herself pregnant means taking her experience under the perspective of the concomitance between what she imagines and wishes about her new roles and what will be possible and soon desirable by the constraints of her family relations, among others.

In this sense, the mythical family stories can constrain the pregnant woman's personal elaborations in the direction of reorganizing her experience, given the new occurrence. This reorganization implies a personal dialogue in the scope of temporality (Pontes & Bastos, 2015; Simão, 2015), articulating personal experiences relative to the past (what is valued by the family based on the group's previous experiences, what the now pregnant woman previously valued), present (what it means to the family group that woman being pregnant, and what it means to herself), and future (what the family group projects for the future of this woman that is now pregnant, and what she projects for herself).

To illustrate, we may refer to the common practice in Brazil of advising, orienting, and warning women about their present condition of pregnancy, as well as making previsions about future events surrounding birth and the postpartum period. By means of polyphonic dialogues, generally promoted by women of the older generation, a varied range of considerations is propagated to channel the development of the youngest. Thus, in some families, for example, the following utterances are usually addressed to pregnant women: "When the baby is born you'll know what to do, it's the maternal instinct," "As soon as you see your newborn child, you will experience unconditional love," or even "Enjoy sleeping during your pregnancy because when the baby is born you will never again sleep as you did before." Intrafamiliar communication, therefore, characterizes itself as strategic and oriented toward the future (Valsiner, 2012). Nevertheless, it is important to highlight that what could be in the next moment is marked by uncertainties in relation to the factual proximity between what "should be" and what "in fact is," between the "aimed value" and the "real value," in Boesch's terms (1991).

In this way, when a woman becomes pregnant, a process of reconstructing personal meaning given the new condition takes place and gradually transforms itself throughout time. This reconstruction of meaning is inherently marked by ambivalences because it is not solely oriented to "the world as it is" but follows in the direction of what is not preestablished, what comes next, and the possible and expected outcome of this new condition; in this case, the birth of a child. This event will transform the woman who is developing as well as the dynamics of the family.

Pregnancy and birth of a new family member demand reorganization and transformation in family relations and interactions, as well as reformulations in family roles and rules of functioning (Minuchin, 1985). Such circumstances promote a movement that encompasses all the generational systems throughout time by means of which the generations must simultaneously accommodate to the transitions in the circle of life, mutually influencing each other during this process (Carter & McGoldrick, 1995). In this way, ambivalences may arise not only in the interior of the self of a woman, but also in the interior of the family system to which this woman belongs.

In this sense, the transition to motherhood produces intergenerational ambivalences touching I–Other–World relationship. However, can we understand generational ambivalences as personal events that take place as reconstructive tensions in the I-Culture-Other temporality? If so, does this understanding contribute to research and professional practice? Aiming to discuss these and other related issues, we will present the case of Juliana,2 whose trajectory to motherhood is marked by successive spontaneous abortions.

AMBIVALENT EXPERIENCE IN TRANSITIONS ALONG THE COURSE OF LIFE: THE CASE OF JULIANA

Juliana is a Brazilian gynecologist who was age 36 at the time she was interviewed. Her reproductive history is marked by three pregnancies and three spontaneous abortions, which happened during a period that lasted over a little more than one year. She indicates that she "has always wished to be a mother," that "every woman must have children," and that not having them means "being alone in life." The prospect of a lonely future, in case she didn't become a mother, was constructed through the dialogues and stories narrated and lived by other women in her family, one generation above her: "I was raised with this idea, women must have children. Without children, one is alone, one has no motivation." Thus, having a child would give her "peace of heart" and be the "end of solitude,, and through children "there would be no more emptiness." Nevertheless, despite the intense desire for maternity she reported, professional goals made her delay this project, which was considered a "normal" stage, personally and socially expected in the life of any woman:

> In truth, I have always wished to be a mother, always, always, always. But, well, I always postponed it, also because of my profession, you know, first I wanted to graduate, after graduating I wanted to specialize, then I wanted financial stability, I think women today, most will postpone it, really.
>
> To me, being a mother was something normal, everybody.... What is the normal sequel in a person's life? Getting a diploma, getting married, having children. It's the basics, it's normal. So being a mother was, at that time, normal for me, I had graduated, married, all that was lacking was what, a child, I was just waiting, as I said, for things to settle down, for better financial stability, but in my mind I was going to be a mother, and would live a normal life just like everybody else. Which in fact didn't happen.

However, the network of meanings surrounding the sign and desire for maternity reveals itself to be a bit more complex. After all, Juliana has a conflictive relation with her current partner: being without a child was a central issue in this conflict. This is because her partner has children from previous relations. To Juliana, the fact that another woman has "given" him a child guarantees advantages to this woman in terms of her social value to this man and their close social network. Therefore, the only solution seen by Juliana is to have a child with this man to then acquire some symbolic value for herself, her partner, and other significant social relations.

Because Juliana could only envision the future with the existence of a child—this being a possible solution for her marital problems—she decided to get pregnant. She had three pregnancies followed by three spontaneous abortions.

The news of her first pregnancy was received with great happiness by Juliana and her family:

> When I found out I was pregnant, it was happiness, for me and my family, my mother always wanted to have grandchildren.... In my family, we have always been raised to be able to give birth, generate, raise a family, preferably a large one, with three, four children, and so when I found myself pregnant it was very satisfying, a great joy, I was going to make my dream and my family's dream come true.

Some weeks later, however, she had a small amount of bleeding, which led her to search for medical assistance. During the ultrasound exam, the doctor verified the fetal age was incompatible with its size, confirming the diagnosis of spontaneous abortion. The experience of the abortion did not raise concern for Juliana, who, as a gynecologist, considered it a normal event, which may happen in a first gestation: "First I thought: 'Oh, it's normal, it's just one abortion, everybody has it, especially if you take pills for a very long time, the egg cells get kind of old.'"

About one month after the abortion, Juliana got pregnant again, but she only discovered it after a new miscarriage. The second abortion provoked a certain emotional disturbance ("I was shocked"), which she tried to minimize by constructing the idea that these lost embryos could be malformed. She performed a series of medical exams to identify a possible cause for the occurrence of the abortions. Once no organic factor could be identified as a possible cause for the gestational losses, an emotional cause was brought up, related especially to conflicts with her partner.

The third gestation brought up ambiguous feelings of "happiness" and "fear." The feeling of fear was related to the memories of the previous losses (past) and to the expectation that a new loss could come to happen (future): "I was already afraid; since I had already had two previous abortions, I was already afraid, this was already a completely, well, apprehensive pregnancy, you know, I was completely apprehensive." Juliana reports that for the first time, she could hear the heartbeats of the baby through the ultrasound exam, which made her think this pregnancy could be successful.

However, another mark, physical and symbolical at the same time, would put an end to her hopes. In the eighth week of pregnancy, she had a slight amount of bleeding: "This is a very cruel memory... a deep anguish." When she sought medical assistance and performed the ultrasound exam, she received the diagnosis of fetal death. Because the miscarriage was retained within her body, she had to go through a procedure called an intrauterine manual aspiration (AMIU). The experience of hospitalization consists of a painful memory, not only due to the medical procedure she underwent but because she was admitted to the maternity ward. She reports a contrast between her pregnancy loss and the birth of other babies, whose rooms had symbolical elements on the door representing the birth of children:

> That was the worst part, the worst part of all of this abortion, of these losses, it was this internship, the frustration of being there is already very big, of having lost the third child and they put you in a, in the maternity ward, I stayed in the maternity ward, *all the children being born and only mine dying*...

The experience of the third loss raised, in this way, a "total despair." After all, as a doctor, she knew she was dealing with a recurrent miscarriage, which made evident the uncertainty in relation to her reproductive future: "The third, a situation of despair, was the worst one, because then it was really confirmed that it was a recurrent miscarriage."

In the days following this loss, Juliana reports having felt very sad, a feeling of "emptiness," "uselessness," and "anguish": "The feeling is that I will never feel joy again.... I was fragile, I slept with pills, I felt like a walking-dead." The inevitable question that persisted in her mind was, "Why me?" In search for an answer that could explain the experiences of loss in the past and minimize the uncertainties in the future, she searched for specialists in recurrent miscarriage, giving rise to an ample investigation. Despite the obstacles experienced along her trajectory, Juliana's expectation continued in the direction of maternity:

> I hope to get pregnant. [laughter] I hope to be a mother, it was all I *still* want [emphasis]. Then, when I imagine the possibility of getting pregnant, I remember the pain, the despair I went through in this last abortion and that I don't want ever again in my life, then, I feel afraid, the fear comes, the trauma I had from that Portuguese [hospital], from that maternity ward, but beyond, in spite of all this, not beyond, but in spite of the fear, of the trauma I had, I still want it.

DYNAMICS FOR AMBIVALENCE MANAGEMENT IN THE SCOPE OF THE SELF

We can understand the early interruptions in the gestations as a rupture with the expected (Zittoun, 2003) through the occurrence of spontaneous abortions, which are lived by Juliana as disquieting experiences (Simão, 2003, 2007, 2016), generating ambivalence (Abbey, 2006) in her I-World relations, in which the Others are included. While the ambivalence is generated by a disquieting experience of rupture with the expected, it produces new disquieting feelings that Juliana incessantly strives to integrate in her preexistent symbolic structure, in her biography.

In this way, she constructs meanings for the possible causes of abortion at the same time she persists in her attempts at having a child (having her own mother as an emotional-affective support), resorting to diverse types of investigations and medical treatments. Having a child—a goal in her life trajectory, influenced by family myths, cultural mores, and personal values—may, therefore, be understood as the conquest of a symbolic object with an important integrative function for the consistency of her identity and biography. It does, after all, allow the mediation, offer continuity and consistency between her personal and familiar past, present, and future.

The meanings reconstructed during her reproductive trajectory constituted strategies, not necessarily conscious, to produce cohesion in a complex self (Abbey & Falmagne, 2008) in the face of the symbolic rupture of successive spontaneous abortions, lived as disquieting experiences that produce ambivalence in the I-World (Others) relations.

Reconstructing meanings given disquieting experiences demands reconstructing distinctions "between what something is, as it seems to us, and what it should be in our thought, wish and desire" (Simão, 2010, p. 161). In other words, it demands reconstructions in the scope of what is perceived as real, of what is intentioned and desired to be real, and in the relationship between these.

Returning to Juliana's reproductive trajectory, we notice that the experience of the first gestational loss gained meaning through the medical perspective, through the knowledge she possessed, as a gynecologist, about the relatively frequent occurrence of spontaneous abortions in a first pregnancy. Thus, despite the rupture experienced in relation to what was expected to occur, the meaning of "normality" associated with this event minimized its emotional impact on the scope of the self—creating continuity amid the rupture.

The occurrence of a second gestational loss, however, seemed to have caused a more significant emotional impact, amplifying the degree of ambivalence that was experienced. In this situation, two unexpected events happened simultaneously: the news of the pregnancy by means of its spontaneous interruption. Once more, Juliana strived to build meaning for the event of the loss by means of her medical knowledge. This way, she attributed the spontaneous abortion to the possibility of a fetal malformation. That is, she tried to codify the disruptive event in a repairing sign[3] (Pontes, 2013, 2015), of the point type (Valsiner, 2012), which led her to a restricted selection of the field of reality.

However, because this constituted only a possibility about which it was impossible to be sure of—once Juliana did not perform, for example, the fetal karyotype exam to determine a supposed malformation—the repairing sign that was built could not reduce significantly the level of ambivalence. Therefore, other repairing signs had to be co-constructed in the dialogue with her gynecologist, such as the possibility of an emotional cause—due to the conflicts existing with her partner. In this second moment, the abortion experience was thus codified under the descriptive category of the field type ("emotional cause") (Valsiner, 2012), which in a certain way managed to minimize the level of ambivalence—for having configured itself as an orientation toward a goal. In other words, to avoid a new spontaneous abortion, Juliana needs to minimize her interpersonal conflicts with her partner.

The third abortion, however, configured itself as an episode marked by a high level of ambivalence. Its occurrence shook the fragile network of meaning previously constructed, provoking significant repercussions to the sense of self. This happened as the third gestational loss framed the abortions in the diagnosis of recurrent miscarriage, demanding the resignification of the previous losses. The meanings previously attributed were thus deconstructed, lost consistency, and the uncertainties in relation to a reproductive future were largely amplified. This happened because Juliana, as a doctor, knew that with this diagnosis, the probability of a new spontaneous abortion was greater, and identifying its causes was also more difficult. Many questions emerged reflecting these uncertainties: "Will I be able to have children?" and "What if I don't have any children?" The doubts were made even stronger by the feeling of the flow of time perceived in her own body, through the biological limitation established for her reproductive capability. That is, Juliana built the idea that she did not have much time left to have her own child because she was already 36 years old. The amplification of the tension between Juliana's perception of her wish, which also reflected, in its turn, the wish of her family and sociocultural expectations, and the barrier to its realization brought by the occurrence of the successive spontaneous abortions made itself present. Understood as barriers to the goal of maternity, the spontaneous abortions require Juliana to make cognitive-affective regulations and take a specific action to overcome these obstacles. They are disquieting situations that shake the level of coherence in her I-World relations and defy her to go beyond. The diagnosis of recurrent miscarriage, however, seems to set a frontier, which may require specific adaptations in the form and direction of action taken by Juliana in striving for maternity because it can mean an unsurmountable obstacle for the personally, familiarly, and culturally valued goal of becoming a mother. Such a diagnosis raises subjective inquiries surrounding the viability of mothering a biological child. All these meanings had an impact in the affective field, producing sadness in looking to the past and fear in trying to foresee the future.

In choosing to become a mother and get pregnant and despite her choice to go through successive spontaneous abortions, Juliana experiences her action potential—that is, the measure of felt confidence involved in reaching for her own personal standards in any situation (Boesch, 1991)—by contributing to the structuring of her psychological world. The action potential constitutes at the same time subjective and contextual evaluations, through which Juliana describes the perception she constructed about herself in relation with the world. Such a subjective evaluation reveals a reduced possibility of controlling the course of her own life in the direction of her wish, which in turn brings important implications to her own identity. This is because certain understandings and/or identities taken as certain, such as the personal and social experiences of becoming a mother, but also the notion of control over your own life ("I like having everything under control") and the capacity to obtain what you wish for ("I've always got everything I wished for"), were seriously threatened. That is, Juliana reports being someone used to planning and controlling all the aspects of her life, and when that was not possible—due to the involuntary abortions—structuring aspects of her identity were put at risk. The experience of involuntary nonmaternity, in this way, threatened some of the meanings she attributed to herself while also threatening to undermine the symbolic position she believed she had in relation with her significant others.

Having this in mind, Juliana strives incessantly to optimize her action potential, that is, her capacity to organize, to give meaning to her own experience, "which implies dealing with challenges to reach goals that mean, above all, personal and cultural values" (Simão, 2010, p. 163). In acting, Juliana is moved by feelings related to the goals of her actions.

The I-mother position is highly valued by Juliana, and there are many personal-collective reasons for that. First, becoming a mother consists of a symbolic-cultural value that is an object to a transgenerational mediation and transmission by her family, by means of significant other's symbolic actions as well as by the family stories and myths commonly narrated in conversations. Thus, Juliana describes, for example, the life trajectory of aunts who had no children and currently live what she describes as a life without purpose, "without motivation," in opposition to the life trajectory of her own mother, whose meaning is articulated to the life of her children. In this way, the other's action (family members of previous generations) represents cultural patterns and values and offers the subject models of action, "models which are, in the end, cultural offers and limits for the formation of the subject's identity" (Simão, 2010, p. 153). Moreover, these symbolic actions find themselves articulated to certain stories and myths related to the valorization of maternity frequently narrated in family conversations: "I was raised with this idea: a woman must have children. Without children she is alone, she has no motivation. The mother, on the other hand, lives around her children." It is fitting to highlight that these "familiar texts are cultural-collective ideologies that orient the sculpting of people's realities of social interaction, which develop along their whole course of life. As such, these texts operate as promoter signs, giving crushing affective value to the concrete limits imposed by family" (Valsiner, 2012, p. 147).

In this sense, the symbolic actions and family myths constrain some modes of action, offering models for Juliana's action: On the one side, they exclude not having children from the field of future possibilities because they relate it to a negative affective field, such as that of solitude. On the other side, they promote becoming a mother once they attribute a highly positive affective value to maternity. In effect, they evoke the construction of a cultural field of action through which "culture offers and constrains possibilities for the formation of individual subjectivity" (Simão, 2010, p. 154). This means that these social suggestions set themselves as a vehicle for regulating Juliana's personal life. She self-evaluates herself from the standpoint of these family and cultural patterns and values, which reflects on her identity.

It is worth mentioning, however, that Juliana's narrative reveals personal cognitive-affective elaborations of family and cultural suggestions, that is, this version of the family myths is resignified by her own personal experiences, indicating "the momentary and contextualized visions . . . about the I-World (Other) relationship" (Simão, 2010, p. 158). In this sense, the construction of meanings between maternity and nonmaternity can be analyzed throughout the reproductive trajectory—departing from the presupposition that all meaning construction involves signs of dual nature—which is situated in the nucleus A and its interdependent immediate context non-A (Cabell & Valsiner, 2011). That is, we depart from the central notion of the human potential of thinking in terms of polarities, oppositions, and antinomies (Marková, 2003; Simão, 2010). Hence, in the development of her reproductive trajectory, oriented by the affective experience of pregnancy and spontaneous abortions—and influenced by significant social others—Juliana constructed new signs, related to the "nonmaternity" counterpart, such as suffering, pain, failure, inferiority, and solitude. Other signs were created and articulated concomitantly, related to the other counterpart, that is, "maternity," which was progressively valued, idealized, and, consequently, aspired by Juliana. Thus, for example, having a child began meaning the opposite of solitude, that is, "ending the emptiness," which in turn associated itself with the hypergeneralized sign (Valsiner, 2012) of "happiness."

Another reason for Juliana choosing to follow in the direction of maternity consisted of the fact that her partner already had children with other women but not with her. According to her, the partner desired another child, and she desired to "give him one." This situation raised in her a sense of urgency to have a child and, consequently, to recover her symbolic value not only to her partner but to all her immediate social network, such as family and friends: "I wanted to prove to society that I had a child with him."

The experience of spontaneous gestational losses and the diagnosis of recurrent miscarriage brought, in this way, significant implications to her identity, temporarily modifying the structure of the dialogical self through the orientation of signs. Juliana began to feel "different" from other women considered "normal"—that is, women who don't face difficulties to have their own children. She therefore felt excluded from the female universe—that has maternity as one of its most significant expressions—besides "incomplete" and "nonfulfilled": "You feel yourself different. You can't... you feel you are *the* different person, *the* excluded" (emphasis given by the interviewed). Because of this, Juliana made efforts to belong to a determined social unity, classified by her as that of the "normal" women, that is to say, the fertile women, those who have children. Thus, the deeply sought for participation in this social unity is a personal ideation, sustained by concrete social interactions between people: "I would like to be like everybody else."

The "incapability of being a mother" is then considered as a "disappointment" to herself and her family. Additionally, this experience destabilizes the personal belief of control over one's own life, leading to the emergence of a feeling of "failure" and loss of control. In this sense, the future and potential I-mother position is threatened by the experience of spontaneous abortions, as well as the I-woman position. Such disquieting and disruptive events demand processes of self-repositioning and solicit new acquisitions, understandings, and personal redefinitions (Zittoun, 2004). Transformations in the personal meanings surrounding maternity are, therefore, performed in the flux of time; they acquire value and go beyond the mere fulfillment of the gender role or social expectations:

> I began to give more value, because... we only value the things we lose, most people are like that, so,... I thought being a mother was a normal thing, but today I think it's the best thing in the world. Since I can't, then... I started valuing it much more, so much that if I can be one, I will value it more than other people, because to me, it came, it will come, with more difficulty.

CREATIVE SYNTHESIS FOR THE SELF-REGULATION AND REORGANIZATION OF THE SELF

To reestablish a sense of continuity in the self, Juliana directed all her efforts to obtain a successful pregnancy. After all, she believed that becoming a mother would allow her to recover central aspects of her identity, such as having control over her own life, satisfy the social demands that were implicit in the family texts, and recover her symbolic value toward significant social others. To help her in this purpose, she had the support of her family—especially her mother, who encouraged her to persist in the attempt of having a child and had a constitutive role in the attempts of optimization and evaluations made by Juliana of her own action potential:

> My mother is the one who participates the most, you know. My mother is very, very desperate, because when the child suffers, the mother suffers too, isn't it? So she keeps trying: "No, there's nothing wrong, you're going to get pregnant and if you don't it's because it's God's will," those things everybody says.... But she thinks I have to try... treatment.... She thinks what I just said here, that if I get pregnant I must try everything. She thinks I'll still get pregnant....

The social support network constituted, in this way, a fundamental symbolic resource for the self-regulation and organization of the self after the experience of the disruptive events:

> "Good Lord," if it wasn't for that, no one goes through that alone, actually, to me, what truly kept me like this, trying, trying to take things forward, was precisely the support from my mother, you know.... No one goes through that alone, there has to be, there has to come some sort of support.

The search for medical specialists constituted, in turn, another important resource for Juliana in her attempt to minimize the high level of ambivalence and appease the uncertainties facing her reproductive future. She reports that what she wanted most was to be able to identify a responsible factor for the losses that could be subjected to treatment so she could get pregnant again without the overpowering fear of a new loss. In this way, undergoing the most varied medical exams had the function of giving her answers, reducing the uncertainty and tensions a future pregnancy could raise:

> As you investigate, you will try to find a cause to treat to then have a child. In my mind I wanted to know why, first to be sure, everybody who has something, wants to know the reason for this something, so I wanted to find out, if I can't have a child, why can't I, first of all that. In second place, I wanted to find out why so I could treat it, you can't treat something without knowing what it is.

In doing the many exams solicited by the medical specialists, she did not obtain definitive answers but only identified some factors that could be related to the losses she experienced: "But it is all like this, a possibility, we are not sure." In the search for certainties, Juliana resorted to other specialists and performed other exams. However, the uncertainties came back in the divergences between the specialist's discourses about the causes and possible treatments for the recurrent miscarriage. Again, the level of ambivalence was intensified. With the purpose of minimizing this effect to then plan a new pregnancy, she resorted to the strategy of bricolage meanings, putting together the myriad treatment possibilities suggested by the specialists, aiming to cover all the possible causes of spontaneous abortions and, in this way, avoiding a new loss. Juliana's efforts to construct some certainty in relation to her reproductive future and reduce the ambivalence in the present moment are thus made visible:

> I will continue to investigate. Now, if I get pregnant again, he (medical specialist A.) doesn't want me to get pregnant again, nor does Dr. M. (medical specialist B.), neither of them allowed it yet, but I think that if I get pregnant again I will use heparin, aspirin, everything there is to try. . . . If no one knows? One doctor says one thing, the other says another, so, I don't know. . . .

Besides this, because one of the main causes of the abortions could be emotional, due to conflicts with her partner, Juliana began a psychotherapeutic process. In this way, through her actions and thoughts, Juliana strived to regain control over her life, acting as an active agent, appropriating herself, resisting, transforming, and modulating the different social discourses and symbolic resources available (Abbey & Falmagne, 2008), persisting in the direction of maternity.

Juliana became pregnant again, some months after the interview. Despite the previous planning in submitting herself to all the possible medical treatments—to avoid the repetition of spontaneous abortions—the pregnancy was only noted after the period considered critical in medicine for the occurrence of spontaneous abortions. For this fact, Juliana built the meaning of "divine providence." In other words, she believes "God" granted her with not knowing about the pregnancy, a condition in which there was no tension between "certainty" and "uncertainty." Therefore, ambivalence did not emerge. During the pregnancy, she tried to constrain the affective field related to the process of becoming a mother: "You have no idea what happiness is." So, instead of trying some medical treatment, she just continued the psychological follow-up she had been doing since her last miscarriage. And the forth gestation resulted in a baby at term: "All my life I have desired this. 37 years waiting for this, my dream comes true. . . . Today I feel like I made it".

FINAL CONSIDERATIONS

The case presented illustrates how a personal-cultural life-course pathway such as pregnancy, birth of a child, or occurrence of a spontaneous abortion can lead to the emergence or intensification of intergenerational ambivalences that take place as reconstructive tensions in the I-Culture-Other temporality. This is because events such as these can generate a myriad of tensional situations in the personal and collective symbolic world. Tension emerges from the difficulty in establishing a momentarily coherent and plausible organization between and within the two dimensions of subjective experience: the collective and the personal (Simão, 2016).

In the illustrative case presented in this chapter, not only was the occurrence of a spontaneous abortion felt as a disquieting experience but, above all, its repetition over time, which resulted in the diagnosis of spontaneous recurrent miscarriage. This diagnosis was perceived and felt by Juliana as a disruptive event in the I–Other–World relationship because it broke significant personal-cultural expectations related to her future life project, that is, that of becoming a mother.

This way, in the disquieting experience lived in the rupture caused by the recurrent abortions, Juliana strives incessantly to find an organization that is coherent to her experiences in the world by means of intra- and intersubjective interactive and symbolic dynamics (Simão, 2016) by the use of semiotic strategies of dynamic self-repairing and by the construction of repairing signs (Pontes, 2013). In this sense, it is possible to affirm that the amplification of the tension between what is and what could or should be, due to a critical event of rupture (Zittoun, 2003) experienced as disquieting (Simão, 2003, 2010, 2016) and generating ambivalence (Abbey, 2006), beaconed the construction of new meanings that, once created in the present, integrated the elements of the past experience in relation to the future that cannot be fully determined in the present (Abbey & Valsiner, 2004).

More than this, the construction of a new plausible articulation to reorganize her experiences demands new symbolic actions that, directed at others, promote transformative processes in the I–Other–Worlds relationship. Additionally, in case such articulations become significant in the relation between personal and collective culture (Boesch, 1992; Simão, 2016; Valsiner, 2012), they can become a part of the system of group semiotic regulation that touches culture as a system (Valsiner, 2012).

Because family is a social group formed of members of different ages, which are related among themselves by some degree of kinship and common life (Valsiner, 2012), a constant movement of adjustment to internal and/or external demands makes itself present. This movement is marked by dialogues, tensions, conflicts, and negotiations among its members, oriented toward the tacit goal of intergenerational continuity in the family group. In the roles assumed for the maintenance of the temporal unity and continuity of the family, each member and the whole family group transform themselves in a dynamic way, given the mutually interdependent condition of its members, linked to the same articulated social network.

In this sense, intrafamiliar communication reveals itself to be fundamental for the maintenance of the unity and continuity of the family groups, especially in the critical and ambivalent moments involving transitions in the course of life, because it constrains some forms of action, orienting the sculpture of the realities of social interaction of the family members, who are developing throughout their whole life trajectory (Valsiner, 2012).

Nevertheless, the interactive dialogue that takes place in the interior of the family characterizes itself by sharing, reciprocity, and mutual recognition, as well as tensions, differences, negotiations, disputes, and conflicts. "Intersubjectivity involves not 'only mutuality and reciprocity, but, above all, dialogical asymmetry and tension'" (Simão, 2010, p. 117; see also Marková, 2003).

Therefore, while family conversations guarantee reconstructive continuity in traditions, values, experiences, patterns of behavior, myths, and rituals of a specific family culture, in which the canonical voices of social narratives can also be heard, and offer and set the scripts that structure the family narratives (Grandesso, 2006), tensions and ambivalences emerge from this communicative dynamics.

Another aspect that can be highlighted is that the intrafamiliar communicative dynamics, which is marked by reciprocity and mutuality as well as tensions and I-Other asymmetries, implies distinct spatial-temporal, personal, and transgenerational relations. Each family member lives and has already lived distinct inter- and intrasubjective experiences due to their particular position in a group-symbolic action field that changes throughout their personal and collective life times. The meanings of these experiences express themselves, in their turn, in the dialogue between family members from different generations in the form of mythical stories and norms of conduct. These mythical stories and norms of conduct also speak of relatively well-established expressions in the family group, which supply in part its identity. Many of them focus temporality, understood as personal experience in time, relative to the passing of the years, periods of life, future, permanency, and transcendence, themes that, overall, are part of human concerns.

We may once more resume the previously analyzed illustrative case to highlight the existing tension between Juliana's subjective experience of time (intrasubjective) and that of significant social others (intersubjective). Influenced by family myths in which cultural values echo (attributing a positive value to maternity—i.e., children give meaning to life—and a negative value to the absence of children, related to solitude and depression); by the experience of spontaneous abortions (that reinforce the power of the family myth because they are perceived and felt by Juliana as unexpected, difficult, and painful events); and by her marital situation, characterized by conflicts due to the partner's children with other women, we can affirm that Juliana possesses a sense of urgency to get pregnant. This sense of urgency is emphasized by the perspective of the biological time of medical knowledge that indicates 35 as a border age for the greater or lesser probability of getting pregnant. This last aspect, related to the age for becoming a mother, reflects tensions between generations because the sociocultural demand to invest in one's own professional carrier was not prominent in the lives of the previous generations of women from Juliana's family. She chooses to postpone maternity to invest in her formation and professional carrier—a choice that may be linked to the occurrence of spontaneous abortions and nonmaternity as a potential future. Besides this and in the opposite direction of the sense of urgency to get pregnant, there is the voice of the other (her mother) alerts her about the necessity of waiting for God's time to concretize maternity. This time has no relation to medical statistics, but to faith, patience, and perseverance, revealing distinct temporal experiences between the generations.

Therefore, the spontaneous abortions were felt and perceived by Juliana as events of intergenerational discontinuities, discontinuities in the I–Other–World relationship. The third abortion in particular establishes a tensional relationship between the past and the time to come, inviting Juliana to think about its effects. After all, its occurrence frames Juliana's story, in the medical point of view, in the diagnosis of recurrent abortion—a condition that makes maternity an ever more distant reality. In this sense, the abortion is an event that sets itself in the present and demands from Juliana unequivocal rational and emotional participation. Such an event is perceived as interrupting the continuity between past memories (family myths about maternity) and future desires and expectations. The co-constructed meaning reveals the difficult future consequences related to the possibility of not having children.

Distinct but interdependent temporalities that lead to the emergence of tensions and ambivalences in their turn lead to the mutual transformation of the whole family system. After all, the different generations possess an interconnected existence by means of their intersubjective relations. In this scene, disquieting feelings may arise and lead to intra- and intersubjective reorganizations.

In short, we have attempted to understand the temporal dimension in the I–Other–World relationship by means of analyzing an illustrative case, focusing on the relationships between ruptures (Zittoun), disquieting experiences (Simão), and ambivalences (Abbey) in the reorganization of the I–Other–World relationship that can transform the self.

Lastly, we may yet highlight that understanding intergenerational ambivalences as personal-cultural events that take place as reconstructive tensions in the I-Culture-Other temporality brings interesting theoretical-methodological implications to research and professional practice in psychology. This is because the focus on the personal-collective phenomenon of intergenerational ambivalence, based on the personal-cultural experience of a significant event, such as the transition to motherhood, the birth of a child, or the involuntary interruption of a pregnancy, opens the possibility of the analysis and comprehension of certain dynamic and complex processes in human lives.

By means of the subjective narrative construction of a life experience by the person who experienced it, and who addresses this narrative to the other of the researcher, we may interpretatively reconstruct an articulation of her experiences in the dynamic I–Other–World relationship in culture. This interpretative work began with the dialogical confrontation of the theoretical perspective here adopted and the dimensions selected by the participant in the research (Juliana) as those possible and relevant to be narrated to the researcher (the first author), generating the emergence of aspects of the illustrative case that are relevant for the understanding of the human experience involving the generation of generations.

NOTES

1. For ethical reasons, "Juliana" is a fictitious name given to one of the participants in the research developed by the first author.
2. The case of Juliana was extracted from the data of the corpus that was analyzed in the first author's doctoral thesis: Pontes, V. V. (2013). *Building continuity in face of successive ruptures: semiotic strategies of dynamic self-repairing.* Doctoral thesis, Institute of Psychology, Federal University of Bahia, Salvador, Brazil.
3. According to Pontes (2013, 2015), the repairing signs are created by the self in situations of existential rupture. They have the power to restore the connection between the fragments of the interrupted trajectory by propitiating some articulation between them, recovering some sense of continuity. Thus, the repairing signs promote the construction of meaning for the present moment, the reconstruction of meanings attributed to past experiences (previous losses), and a new orientation to the acceptable range of meaning construction directed toward the future, connecting them, recasting them in a new, always singular—and, in a certain way, unified and coherent—narrative about oneself, one's own life and "destiny."

REFERENCES

Abbey, E. (2006). Triadic frames for ambivalent experience. *Estudios de Psicología: Studies in Psychology, 27*(1), 33–40.

Abbey, E., & Falmagne, R. J. (2008). Modes of tension work within the complex self. *Culture & Psychology, 14*(1), 95–113.

Abbey, E., & Valsiner, J. (2004). Emergence of meanings through ambivalence. *FQS: Forum QualitativeSozialforschung, 6*(1), Art. 23. Available at http://www.qualitative-research.net/fqs-texte/1-05/05-1-23-e.htm.

Boesch, E. (1991). *Symbolic action theory and cultural psychology.* Berlin, New York, NY: Springer.

Boesch, E. E. (1992). Culture–individual–culture: The cycle of knowledge. In M. von Cranach, W. Doise, & P. Mugny (Eds.), *Social representations and the social bases of knowledge* (Swiss Monographs in Psychology, Vol. I, pp. 89–95). Lewiston, NY: Hogrefe & Huber.

Cabell, K. R., & Valsiner, J. (2011). Affective-hypergeneralization: Learning from psychoanalysis. In S. Salvatore & T. Zittoun (Eds.), *Cultural psychology and psychoanalysis: Pathways to synthesis* (pp. 87–113). Charlotte, NC: Information Age Publishers.

Carter, B., & McGoldrick, M. (1995). *As mudanças no ciclo de vida familiar: uma estrutura para a terapia familiar* (2nd ed.). Porto Alegre: Artmed.

Cole, M. (1999).Culture in development. In M. H. Bornstein & M. E. Lamb (Ed.), *Developmental psychology: An advanced textbook* (pp. 73–123). Mahwah, NJ: Erlbaum.

Grandesso, M. A. (2006). Famílias e narrativas: histórias, histórias e mais histórias. In C. M. Oliveira (Ed.), *Família e....* São Paulo: Casa do psicólogo.

Marková, I. (2003). *Dialogicality and social representations: The dynamics of mind.* Cambridge, England: Cambridge University Press.

Minuchin, P. (1985). Families and individual development: Provocations from the field of family therapy. *Child Development, 56*(2), 289–302.

Pontes, V. V. (2013). *Construindo continuidade frente a sucessivas rupturas: estratégias semióticas de reparação dinâmica do self.* Unpublished PhD dissertation, Instituto de Psicologia, Universidade Federal da Bahia, Salvador, Brasil.

Pontes, V. V. (2015). The experience of recurrent gestational losses: semiotic strategies of dynamic self-repair after sequential ruptures. In K. Cabell, J. Valsiner, P. Marsico, & C. Cornejo (Eds.), *Annals of cultural psychology* (pp. 177–196). Charlotte, NC: Information Age.

Pontes, V. V., & Bastos, A. C. S. (2015). Unaccomplished trajectories: Shadows from the past in the present and future. In L. M. Simão, D. S. Guimarães, & J. Valsiner (Eds.), *Temporality: Culture in the flow of human experience, advances in cultural psychology.* Charlotte, NC: Information Age.

Simão, L. M. (2003). Beside rupture-disquiet: Beyond the other-alterity. *Culture & Psychology, 9*(4), 449–459.

Simão, L. M. (2007). We researchers: Unquiet people disquieting others. A commentary on Duarte & Gonçalves' "Negotiating motherhood: A dialogical approach." *International Journal for Dialogical Science, 2*(1), 277–285.

Simão, L. M. (2010). *Ensaios dialógicos: compartilhamento e diferença nas relações eu-outro* [Dialogic essays: Sharing and diffrence in I-other relationships]. São Paulo: Editora Hucitec.

Simão, L. M. (2015). The temporality of tradition: Some horizons for the semiotic-cultural constructivism in psychology. In L. M. Simão, D. S. Guimarães, &

J. Valsiner (Eds.), *Temporality: Culture in the flow of human experience, advances in cultural psychology*. Charlotte, NC: Information Age.

Simão, L. M. (2016). Culture as a moving border. *Integrative Psychological and Behavioral Sciences, 50,* 14–28.

Valsiner, J. (1997). *Culture and the development of children's action: A theory of human development* (2nd ed.). New York, NY: Wiley.

Valsiner, J. (1998). *The guided mind: A sociogenetic approach to personality*. Cambridge, MA: Harvard University Press.

Valsiner, J. (2012). *Fundamentos da Psicologia Cultural: mundos da mente, mundos da vida* (A. C. Bastos, Trans.). Porto Alegre: Artmed.

Zittoun, T. (2003). The hidden work of symbolic resources in emotions. *Culture & Psychology, 9*(3), 313–329.

Zittoun, T. (2004). Symbolic competencies for developmental transitions: The case of the choice of first names. *Culture & Psychology, 10,* 131–161.

CHAPTER 11

SAUDADE

A Unique Feeling Within the Lusitanian Soul

Stephanie Barros and Gaby Marinho Ribeiro
University of Luxembourg

Saudade—um mavioso nome que tão meigo soas nos lusitanos lábios [a melodious name that sounds so sweet on Lusitanian's lips]—that is how Garrett (1858) describes this feeling in his poem, *Camões*, a complex but omnipresent emotion in Lusitanian cultures. It is indeed a worldwide well-known word by persons originating from Lusitanian (e.g., Western Iberian, Brazilian, Cape-Verdean cultures) as well as from non-Lusitanian cultures.

The concept of *saudade*, its nature, and its components have largely been discussed as a crucial concept by Portuguese poets, writers, philosophers, and linguistics as well as by the general public (Lourenço, 1978; Vasconcelos, 1914). Nevertheless, little research has been done from a psychological perspective. Therefore, the aim of the present study will be to analyze the different emotional components of the phenomenon of saudade. The important features linked to the concept from Portuguese individuals' point of view, living in Luxembourg, will specifically be investigated from

Trans-Generational Family Relations, pages 217–245

a phenomenological standpoint. Another goal will be to compare different sociopolitical generations with migrant background (i.e., immigrants who migrated to the host country vs. those who were born in the host country from immigrant parents, i.e., Luso-descendants) to observe whether their conceptualization of the notion of saudade is notably different from one another.

HISTORICAL AND CULTURAL BACKGROUND

Saudade, Its Definitions and Dimensions

The etymology of saudade seems to be quite controversial (Silveira, 2010); in fact, two poles may be distinguished. Some authors argue that the word saudade has an Arab origin—*saudah*—involving the influence of *saudar* (greeting) and *saude* (health, salvation in an archaic meaning) (Castro, 1980; Tobias, 1997). The second pole includes authors who believe in a Latin origin (*solitate*) of the word saudade (Costa, 2014; Vasconcelos, 1914) yielding the Portuguese word *solidão*, meaning loneliness (Farrell, 2006).

In her book *In Portugal*, Bell (1912) describes saudade as being a perpetual desire and passion felt for something or someone that might not even physically exist in the present with a temporal dimension as one keeps a look toward past and future. Here, saudade is not entirely conceived as a lack of satisfaction or an intensely felt sadness but more as a feeling near to nostalgia without being just nostalgia. As for the *Grande Dicionário da Língua Portuguesa*, it states that saudade is "Lembrança triste e suave de pessoas ou coisas distantes ou extintas, acompanhada do desejo de as tornar a possuir ou ver presentes; pesar pela ausência de alguém que nos é querido"[1] (Figueiredo, 1996, p. 2297). For its part, the *Dicionário da Língua Portuguesa* describes it as a "melancolia causada pela lembrança de um bem de que se está privado; mágoa que se sente pela ausência ou desaparecimento de pessoas, coisas, estados ou ações; pesar; nostalgia"[2] (Almeida Costa & Sampaio e Melo, 1999, p. 1479). This feeling of saudade is often accompanied by a repressed awareness that the object of longing will probably never come back or be returned.

These diverse definitions embody many important and salient components of the word saudade common to several definitions and prove the emotional scope of the concept. First of all, it includes the notion of *solitude*, which probably is a reference to the Latin origin of the term (i.e., solitate). *Saudade* as a matter of fact usually induces a feeling of loneliness felt by the loss of a person, place, or situation. Another important dimension is the ambivalence (Bulat-Silva, 2012). In his work, Kaplan (1972) assumes that ambivalence requires "a situation in which an individual has the opportunity to simultaneously indicate both a favourable and an unfavourable attitude toward a given stimulus object" (p. 362). Ambivalence characterizes an indefinable balance between negative emotions, on the one hand, and positive emotions, on the other hand, toward a same object (Brown, 1965). The ambivalent character is conferred to saudade insofar that this emotion often induces opposed feelings, bringing several different emotions altogether, one being torn in between them: negative feelings, such as sadness or anxiety, for missing someone or something lost while rekindling positive feelings, such as happiness or joy, for having had the opportunity to experience those feelings even if they are now lost (Braz, 2006; Brazette, 1989). In general, one aspect does not come along without the other: "It is a delightful pain of the absence, a feeling of smooth melancholia, especially savoured by the one who misses someone or something [...] a delectable pain" (Costa, 2014, p. 90), "tormento puro, doce e magoado" (pure, sweet and painful torment) (Camões quoted in Roquete & Fonseca, 1974, p. 439) or even "it's when we learn to love melancholy as much as we love happiness, because both of them make us feel alive" (Magalhães, 1995, p. 113, quoted from Leal, 2000). Farrell (2006) also talks about saudade as being a typically positive feeling without, however, being able to neglect a certain feeling of affliction related to it. This ambivalent dimension is omnipresent while describing and feeling saudade, incorporating a good example of dialectical synthesis where opposites—delight and pain—become united in a new quality—a delightful pain—not only generally accepted but most striven for. Brazette (1989) analysed, for example, the ambivalent dimension of the concept of saudade by carrying out a review of the Portuguese literature and concluded that it was an emotion possibly giving rise to a pathological behavior characterized by depressive symptoms. Nevertheless, the author highlights that the felt desire distances saudade from the state of depression. Furthermore, one should not forget the notion of temporality: "saudade is a cultural construct that defines Portuguese identity in the context of multiple layers of space and (past) time" (Feldman-Bianco, 1992, p. 145) or "unlike simple nostalgia, saudade has resonance in the past, present, and future" (Vieira, 2007, p. 127). Saudade is in fact linked to the memory of feelings, experiences, places, or events that entailed pleasure and well-being in the past but are as from now distant in terms of time and space. However, these memories trigger in the present a tender emptiness because of the felt absence of someone or something missing that should actually be present. The feeling of saudade becomes in this context a tool to cope with loss and to preserve in the present and future what was lost in the past (Braz, 2006). One may also foresee a potential future feeling of saudade while still being in the presence of a person, place, or situation but already fearing the absence of that beloved person, place, or situation, referring in this respect to the future dimension of the concept (e.g., *Eu vou ter saudades tuas* [I will have saudades of you]).

In view of these elements, the main difference between saudade and other specified emotions (e.g., nostalgia, melancholia, etc.) is the incorporation of all these rather negatively connoted dimensions as well as simultaneously a positive valence explaining the highly ambivalent aspect of this emotion (Braz, 2006).

Saudade and the Portuguese Culture

Many authors argue that saudade is a uniquely Portuguese feeling by debating about the untranslatability of this feeling as well as the fact that it appears not to have a real equivalent in other languages (Costa, 2014; Leal & Féblot-Augustins, 1999; Vieira, 2007). In 1606, Dom Duarte Nunes Leão already upheld the position that saudade, as a feeling, would never possibly be properly translatable even by multiplying words and expressions to do so (Braz, 2006). Furthermore, according to Costa (2014), saudade is a feeling that can only be felt and expressed by Lusitanian populations because only the Portuguese language has a word to express it. For instance, in English, the word is usually translated as "longing," "yearning," "missing," "homesickness," or even "nostalgia." The German language uses the word *Sehnsucht* without ever capturing the wholeness and entirety of the concept such as it is understood in the Lusitanian culture. This wholeness of saudade is possible and based on the primacy of affect, whereas the German *Sehnsucht,* for instance, might be seen as subordinating the effect to the cognitive fact of longing. In fact, the translation of this concept is not evident due to its embodiment of several feelings within a specific cultural construction (Braz, 2006). According to Costa (2014), saudade is not only solitude neither nostalgia nor pain nor smoothness but is an amalgam of all those feelings melted together. Furthermore, as stated in the *Pequeno Dicionário da língua portuguesa,* "saudade is the most characteristic feeling of the Portuguese soul" (Figueiredo, 1981, p. 1249), revealing the special and unique status the word has within Lusitanian, and especially within the Portuguese culture. It is indeed not only a felt emotion but is entirely part of the Portuguese national identity (Feldman-Bianco, 1992). Leal and Féblot-Augustins (1999) went further in their research by emphasizing the role of saudade as one of the main characteristics of the Portuguese "national soul" and national identity (Braz, 2006). Nascimento and Menandro (2005), for their part, investigated the relationship between saudade and the social memory, where saudade appeared to function not only as an individual memory but also as a social common memory. The consistency among the various memories belonging to individuals and diverse groups that "remember" as well as the maintenance of an integrated picture of this specific emotion are, according to the authors, proof of its function as a social common "shared" memory. In 2012, Bulat-Silva was interested in the cultural significance of the concept of saudade and highlighted the importance of the concept in the Portuguese culture that was not to be seen as a simple marginal feeling.

Moreover, an important step in the history of saudade was the so-called "saudosismo movement." The latter was a nationalist movement, a poetical and philosophical doctrine based on saudade initiated by Teixeira de Pascoaes in the beginning of the 20th century, only two years after the fall of the Portuguese monarchy. Back then with this movement, he transformed the word saudade into a key concept used at that time to describe the spiritual intricacies of Portugueseness (Almeida Costa & Sampaio e Melo, 1999; Leal, 2000).

However, this does not imply that solely Portuguese and in general Lusitanian cultures are able to feel and live this particular emotion. One may in fact consider that, despite the untranslatable character attributed to the word, the meaning and emotion related to it can still be experienced by non-Lusitanian individuals sensible to this particular emotion (Bulat-Silva, 2012; Vasconcelos, 1914). Interestingly, Leal (2000) analyzed, for example, the relationship between saudade and the national feeling of Portuguese population in the context of ethnic psychology and came to the conclusion that saudade was not a symbol of Portugueseness anymore among the majority of Portuguese generations back then. Nevertheless, none can deny the existence of a specific Portuguese word for this feeling with a particular and special importance for the Lusitanian culture (Krause, 2012; Lamas, 2003; Silveira, 2010).

Saudade has a special and unique status for Portuguese people as being part of the Portuguese national identity. Saudade is, for example, likewise strongly related to a specific Portuguese music style, Fado, similarly associated to the Portuguese identity. In fact, many authors agree on the key component of Fado being saudade, the mournful tunes of Fado expressing indeed the bittersweetness and painful nostalgia of saudade. It is unequivocally a particular Portuguese urban folk song style originating from the Latin word "fatum," which literally means "fate" and is referred to as the Portuguese blues (Shepherd, 2011). This unique type of music was born in the poor districts of Lisbon during the 19th century and was mainly sung in the so-called "houses of Fado" or brothels where blind beggar-musicians and prostitutes poured out their troubles in songs (Bulat-Silva, 2012). Yet with time it also became appreciated by intellectuals, artists, and middle-class members (Shepherd, 2011). Especially with the internationally well-known Portuguese Queen of Fado, Amália Rodrigues, Fado gained a new fresh and international look being nowadays accessible to the wide audience. Other older and younger generations of "Fadistas," as singers of Fado are called, endeavored to make Fado known throughout the world, such as Cesária Évora, Dulce Pontes, Madredeus, Mariza, or even Ana Moura. In November 2011, UNESCO even officially recognized Fado as the World's Intangible Cultural Heritage (Lopes, 2011; UNESCO, 2011).

One may assume that the entire historical and cultural process has turned the word saudade into a key symbol of Portuguese alleged "national soul" (Leal & Féblot-Augustins, 1999) and that it has become entirely part of the social collective memory of Portugal (Feldman-Bianco, 1992).

Saudade and Emigration

Migration is a phenomenon as old as humankind, people having always moved from one place to another for many different reasons. The Portuguese populations are no exception, be it during the great Portuguese oversea explorations and colonizations going back to the 15th century (Dunlevy & Hutchinson, 1999; Feldman-Bianco, 1992) or as labor forces from the 20th century on to countries of Northern Europe such as Luxembourg, Belgium, Germany, France or the Netherlands (Baganha, 1998; Phalet & Swyngedouw, 2003; Van Oudenhoven, 2006). Some Portuguese also fled the country's dictatorship under Salazar (i.e., push factor), that lasted from 1926 until the 25th of April 1974, putting an end to it with the so-called "Revolução dos Cravos" *(the revolution of the carnations)* (Dunlevy & Hutchinson, 1999). By the early 1990s, however, Portugal manifested new emigration characteristics, such as an increase in the proportion of females, rising skill levels, or the dominance of temporary emigration to other European Union member states (Baganha, 1994).

Regarding the concept of saudade as such, it is believed to originate from the epoch of the great Portuguese discoveries in the 15th and 16th centuries (Feldman-Bianco, 1992). During Portugal's Golden Age, its sailors and seamen departed on journeys to the unknown without certainty of a future return, leaving their families in the agony of absence and longing for their return. Thereby, as stated by Feldman-Bianco (1992), it might be assumed that since then "saudade has been associated with the Portuguese unending wanderlust" (p. 145). Nevertheless, not only did families feel saudade of those sailing to the unknown but the navigators themselves also felt a rush of saudade toward their beloved ones as well as their homeland they had to leave behind all at once.

Hence, from a historical point of view, a strong bond between saudade and emigration becomes evident due to the long separations from relatives and homeland (Bulat-Silva, 2012), which explains its importance as the *saudade da terra* (saudade of homeland) appearing in several definitions of the word. Many authors agree, in fact, on emigration being an important concept in Portuguese culture (see e.g., Feldman-Bianco, 1992) as does the "myth of return" to the homeland. The decision to emigrate has always been consistently taken with consideration of eventually returning one day to Portugal. So, at the beginning, mainly men migrated while women waited for their return. Emigration was, as mentioned, originally supposed to be only a temporary way to increase life quality and build up capital to one day return to their homeland with pride and an increased quality of life. However, many men never returned, and in the 1970s, a new characteristic of Portuguese emigration became family reunification. The latter was facilitated by the nearness of the host countries (in the case of European countries), additionally to the simplified and multiplied opportunities of finding employment as a woman. Still, the utopic desire to return and the saudade felt for the homeland seemed not to be forgotten by Portuguese immigrants (Baganha, 1998). In this context, the Portuguese philosopher Coimbra (1986) defined saudade as the "memory of the homeland with desire of return" (p. 183).

Saudade somehow, through time and sociocultural contexts, turned into a general tool for migrants to cope and deal with issues related to dislocation and distance to home and family (Hannerz, 1993). For instance, in her first novel called *Saudade*, Vaz (1994) narrates her personal experience as an Azorean immigrant in California using saudade as an instrument to face and handle challenges related to the migration experience. Another example is the 1991 documentary *Saudade* by Feldman-Bianco (1992) built on interviews of seven Portuguese immigrants in the United States. The latter illustrates accurately how immigrants make use of the strong ties to their families and friends left in Portugal as well as to the country to endure potential problems related to emigration.

Saudade and Portuguese Immigration in Luxembourg

The last Statec population census revealed that in January 2015, about 258,700 migrants out of 563,000 inhabitants were living in the Grand-Duchy of Luxembourg. These numbers correspond to almost half of the global Luxembourgish population (43%). Among these migrant minorities, Portuguese immigrants are the most represented, with a total of 92,100 Portuguese citizens (i.e., 16% of the total population).[3] Luxembourg saw the major Portuguese immigration arrive starting from the mid-1960s with a higher proportion particularly in the 1970s and 1980s (Ministère de la fonction publique, 2010).

The proportion of young people with Portuguese nationality is significantly higher than in the general population. The majority of them are either below (30% ages 0–20 years) or of working age (60% ages 25–60 years). The number of retired Portuguese in Luxembourg is for its part quite low, with only 3,011 Portuguese immigrants being ages of 65 years or more (3.7% of the Portuguese population in Luxembourg). However, because the general Luxembourgish population is constantly graying, so is the elderly Portuguese migrant community (Statec, 2013).

METHODOLOGY

Aim of the Study and Hypothesis

As discussed previously, the concept of saudade has barely been studied from a psychological perspective. With this in mind, we considered it important to analyze the different aspects and psychological scope for Portuguese-speaking individuals with a migrant background living in Luxembourg. Indeed, we aimed to assess the dimensions and importance conferred to the word saudade by them.

The present study therefore had two main objectives. The first, more explorative, was to analyze the most salient features and definitions related to saudade from the perspective of Portuguese-speaking individuals living in Luxembourg. The second goal was to compare different subgroups, such as individuals born outside the host country versus those born in the host country from immigrant parents—the so-called Luso-descendants. The younger generation, often the first immigrants' offspring, born or grown up in the "new" country, frequently perceived as the Eldorado by their parents, have also been included in our sample to compare the different generation's perspectives and comprehension of the word saudade. We would in fact assume a difference between the selected features of Lusofone immigrant offspring, the Luso-descendants born in Luxembourg, and Lusofone immigrants in general. Furthermore, a difference between immigrants who arrived only a few years ago to Luxembourg (i.e., ≤ 0 years) and those already living in the host country for a longer period of time (i.e., >10 years) might be highlighted. In fact, because saudade can be considered a key symbol of Portuguese nationality (Leal & Féblot-Augustins, 1999), the features associated to the meaning "saudade of the homeland" could possibly be more salient for some groups (e.g., individuals born outside the host country who are geographically distant from their home country).

Moreover, we assume that there might be a divergence in the evaluation of these different groups concerning the affective valence of saudade. In fact, Lusofones, who were born in Luxembourg, the Luso-descendants, might potentially have a different conceptualization of their national identity and therefore possibly also of their understanding of saudade as the actual Portuguese immigrants born outside of the Luxembourgish boarders.

Instruments and Sample

The questionnaire was available online and took about 5 to 10 minutes to be completed. Inclusion criteria required each participant to have a Lusofone background (e.g., be born in a Lusofone country such as Portugal or Brazil or be a Luso-descendant of Portuguese parents) living in the Grand Duchy of Luxembourg, and basic knowledge of the Portuguese language and therefore be familiar with the Portuguese/Lusofone culture. Thus, the questionnaire was only available in Portuguese because the word saudade is here considered a specific word belonging to the Lusitanian culture. Moreover, we were interested in assessing how Portuguese migrants and kin assimilate, understand, define, and relate to this specific concept of saudade.

For the current study, we collected the responses of 190 participants ranging in age from 16 to 80 years ($M = 35.0$; $SD = 13.1$). Women constituted about two-thirds of our sample (66.8%). About one-third of the participants (34.2%) were born in Luxembourg, 52.6% were born in Portugal, and 13.2% were born in other countries, such as Brazil, Cape Verde, and so on.[4] Participants who were born outside Luxembourg ($n = 125$) had come to Luxembourg at an average age of 21.7 ($SD = 12.0$) and have been living there for 16.8 years on average ($SD = 14.2$).

All participants reported Portuguese to be their mother tongue except for one who indicated the Creole language as mother tongue. However, this participant reported to be born in Cape Verde and thus has knowledge of the Portuguese language.

A majority of our participants claimed to have only the Portuguese nationality (78.8%), 5.3% reported to be only Brazilian, whereas 12.1% reported to have only the Luxembourgish nationality. Just one presented himself as a Cape Verdean. The remaining participants reported having double nationalities, mostly oscillating between the Luxembourgish and Portuguese nationalities. Regarding the filling procedure, participants had to first answer several general demographic questions regarding age, nationality, and professional activity to control for these variables.

The second part of the questionnaire was about features that participants connected to the word saudade. We used a list of 67 words, developed in a study conducted in Portugal with young Portuguese native students by Neto and Mullet (2014).[5] For our study, participants were thus presented with the mentioned final 67 features out of which they had to choose five traits that were, from their point of view, the most related to the word saudade.

In the next step, we followed a similar procedure as used by Neto and Mullet (2014) regarding the affective valence (i.e., to what degree the characteristic is either a negative or positive feature of saudade). However, we required our participants to evaluate the affective valence of just the five features they chose as the most salient in relation with saudade (6-point

Likert scale ranging from –3 = *extremely negative feature* to +3 = *extremely positive feature of saudade*[6]).

With regard to the third and final part of the questionnaire, participants had to read ten different sentences defining each aspect of the concept saudade we were interested in further analyzing. The presented sentences were selected by the investigators of the current study.[7] Participants were asked to select only one definition out of the ten that according to their personal opinion was the most representative and closest to what they define as being saudade. The sentences represented different components of the word analyzed in the present study: (a) ambivalence (e.g., "A pure, sweet, and painful torment"), (b) temporal dimension (e.g., "Saudade is to love a past that hasn't yet passed. It's to refuse the present that hurts us. It's not to see the future that invites us"), (c) migrant context of the word (e.g., "Saudade is our soul telling us where to go back"), and (d) cognitive and affective components (e.g., "Feeling of sadness at someone's death or the loss of something to which one was affectionately very connected to," "Saudade is the memory of the heart"). It seemed necessary to understand and evaluate which one of these various components, often attributed to the concept of saudade (Bulat-Silva, 1992; Neto & Mullet, 2014; Vieira, 2007), was the most chosen by laypeople. In other words, what dimension inspires the most substantial majority of individuals familiar with the concept?

RESULTS

Most Salient Features of Saudade

Participants were asked to select 5 features (out of a list of 67 features) considered to be the most related to their personal concept of saudade. The most selected characteristics for the word saudade by our sample were: *missing someone* (58.1%), *memories* (47.1%), *nostalgia* (35.1%), *distance* (33%), *missing something* (28.7%), and *family* (27.9%). For the purposes of the present study, only the five most chosen characteristics will be considered and analyzed (cf. Table 11.1 for other features).

The feature *missing someone* was selected by more than half of our total sample (57.4%),[8] which can therefore be considered as a representative trait of saudade. Participants who chose this feature were on average age 35.2 years (SD = 13.2; range: 16–73). Furthermore, more than half of these participants were born in Portugal (56%), more than one-third (33%) was already born in Luxembourg, and the rest of them (11%) being born in other countries (i.e., Brazil, Cape Verde, etc.), reflecting the general sample distribution as well as the distribution within the Luxembourgish society (Statec, 2013). Migrants were ages 21.9 (SD = 11.0) years on average

TABLE 11.1 Features Related to *Saudade*

	Participants		Affective Valence	
	N	%	(*M*)	*SD*
1. Missing someone (*sentir falta de alguém*)	109	57.4	4.38	2.19
2. Memories (*recordações*)	99	52.1	5.65	1.45
3. Nostalgia (nostalgia)	65	34.2	4.72	1.49
4. Distance (*distância*)	63	33.2	4.20	2.13
5. Missing something (*sentir falta de algo*)	54	28.4	4.59	1.76
6. Family (*família*)	53	27.9	5.88	1.80
7. Wanting to go back in time (*vontade de voltar atrás no tempo*)	38	20.0	4.17	1.81
8. Sense of constriction in the heart (*aperto no coração*)	31	16.3	3.58	1.86
9. Sadness (*tristeza*)	28	14.7	3.31	2.21
10. Feeling (*sentimento*)	28	14.7	4.69	1.85
11. Wanting to be close (*vontade de estar perto*)	27	14.2	5.26	1.53
12. Native land (*terra natal*)	24	12.6	5.45	1.56
13. Love (*amor*)	22	11.6	6.05	1.62
14. Melancholy (*melancolia*)	18	9.5	3.50	1.79
15. Absence (*ausência*)	17	8.9	3.12	1.90
16. People deceased (*pessoas falecidas*)	17	8.9	3.13	2.19
17. Crying (*chorar*)	13	6.8	4.00	2.34
18. Feeling empty (*sensação de vazio*)	13	6.8	3.83	2.29
19. Fado (*fado*)	13	6.8	5.77	0.93
20. Thinking (*pensar*)	12	6.3	5.09	1.51
21. Feeling emotional (*a saudade deixa-nos emotivos*)	12	6.3	4.75	1.66
22. Pain (*dor*)	11	5.8	3.18	2.14
23. Joy (*alegria*)	11	5.8	5.90	0.99
24. Feeling incomplete (*sensação de incompleto*)	11	5.8	4.64	1.86
25. Desire (*desejo*)	11	5.8	4.50	1.96
26. Holidays (*férias*)	10	5.3	6.30	1.06
27. Motherland (*pátria*)	9	4.7	5.63	1.19
28. Sensation of loss (*sensação de perda*)	8	4.2	2.67	1.03
29. Past (*passado*)	8	4.2	5.13	0.99
30. Liking (*gostar*)	8	4.2	6.00	1.07
31. Well-being (*bem-estar*)	8	4.2	6.13	0.99
32. Loneliness (*solidão*)	7	3.7	3.00	2.45
33. Associating small things (*associar pequenas coisas*)	6	3.2	4.83	1.33

(*continued*)

TABLE 11.1 Features Related to *Saudade* (continued)

	Participants		Affective Valence	
	N	%	(*M*)	*SD*
34. Separation (*separação*)	6	3.2	2.00	0.63
35. Friendship (*amizade*)	6	3.2	6.50	0.84
36. Affection (*afecto*)	6	3.2	5.50	1.38
37. Anxiety (*ansiedade*)	5	2.6	4.25	1.71
38. Butterflies in stomach (*aperto no estómago*)	5	2.6	4.00	2.00
39. A new meeting (*reencontro*)	5	2.6	5.80	1.10
40. Hope (*esperança*)	5	2.6	6.50	0.58
41. Lack (*carência*)	5	2.6	3.60	1.67
42. Happiness (*felicidade*)	4	2.1	6.33	1.16
43. Home (*casa*)	4	2.1	4.00	2.45
44. Dreaming (*sonhar*)	4	2.1	6.33	0.58
45. Calling often (*telefonar muitas vezes*)	3	1.6	5.00	1.73
46. Sighing (*suspirar*)	2	1.1	4.50	0.71
47. Anguish (*angústia*)	2	1.1	3.00	1.41
48. Kindness (*carinho*)	2	1.1	6.50	0.71
49. Time stop (*paragem no tempo*)	2	1.1	5.50	2.12
50. Impotence (*impotência*)	2	1.1	5.00	1.41
51. Eating the favorite dish (*comer o prato preferido*)	2	1.1	5.00	1.41
52. Depression (*depressão*)	2	1.1	2.50	0.71
53. Commotion (*comoção*)	2	1.1	5.50	2.12
54. Distrust (*desconfiança*)	1	0.5	2.00	/
55. Unhappiness (*infelicidade*)	1	0.5	1.00	/
56. Worrying (*preocupação*)	1	0.5	4.00	/
57. Boy/girlfriend (*namorado/a*)	1	0.5	6.00	/
58. Suffocation (*sufoco*)	1	0.5	4.00	/
59. Fear (*medo*)	1	0.5	7.00	/
60. Dancing (*dançar*)	1	0.5	6.00	/
61. Despair (*desespero*)	/	/	/	/
62. Nervousness (*nervosismo*)	/	/	/	/
63. Lack of concentration (*falta de concentração*)	/	/	/	/
64. Insomnia (*insónias*)	/	/	/	/
65. Aministies (*aministias*)	/	/	/	/
66. Revolt (*revolta*)	/	/	/	/
67. Unsafeness (*insegurança*)	/	/	/	/

Source: Neto & Mullet, 2014

when arriving to Luxembourg and have since then been living there for 16.8 (*SD* = 14.7) years.

Regarding the valence of the feature *missing someone*, almost one-third of the participants who had chosen it evaluated it as an extremely positive characteristic of saudade (26.6%). Around 11% indicated that it has a very positive valence, whereas at the opposite end 13.8% considered it to be a very negative characteristic of saudade, and 11.9% considered it an extremely negative characteristic; 15.6% believed in the neutral character of this feature related to saudade (see Appendix 11.2 for all the reported valences). Thus, the subjective perception of the attributed valence appears quite balanced among the sample who selected this characteristic.

Participants who selected the feature *memories* as one of the most illustrative of saudade (52.1%) had a mean age of 36.3 years (*SD* = 13.8; range: 16–80). Those not born in Luxembourg arrived there with an average age of 21.8 years (*SD* = 13.1) and have taken official residence there for 18.6 years (*SD* = 14.0). Of those born in Luxembourg, 34.3% chose this specific feature. Participants born in Portugal constituted a majority (53.5%), the remaining being born in other countries (12.1%). Most of these participants rated its valence extremely high. In fact, most immigrants identified it either as an extremely positive (36.4%) or as a very positive feature of saudade (22.2%), whereas only 2% considered it as an extremely negative and 4% as a very negative trait of saudade. Moreover, around 18% opted for the neutral valence of this characteristic of saudade.

Participants who considered the feature *nostalgia* as one of the five most representative of saudade (34.2%) were on average 35.5 years old (*SD* = 12.5; range: 16–67). Of those born in Luxembourg, 33.8% chose this feature, 52.3% were born in Portugal, and the rest (13.8%) was born in other countries. Furthermore, participants born in a different country than their host country arrived to Luxembourg on average with 22.1 years (*SD* = 14.1) and have been living there for an average of 17.1 years (*SD* = 14.5); 23.1% deemed the feature to be very positive and 12.3% as extremely positive, whereas only 1.6% of them evaluated it as an extremely negative characteristic of saudade. Interestingly, *nostalgia* was the feature most identified as neutral (by 35.4%).

The feature *distance* was selected by 33.2% of our total sample. They were on average 33.6 years old (*SD* = 14.4; range: 18–80) by the time of the data collection. Participants born in Luxembourg were estimated to be on the order of 28.6%, more than half was born in Portugal (52.4%), and the rest originated from another country (19%). Those born in a different country than Luxembourg were on average 22.6 years old (*SD* = 13.9) when arriving to Luxembourg and have since then been official residents of Luxembourg for an average of 14.8 (*SD* = 12.9) years.

With regard to the affective valence of the feature, almost 50% believed in the positive valence of the word as a feature of saudade (extremely positive characteristic: 19%; very positive: 14.3%; positive: 12.7%). Still, more than 40% perceived *distance* as a negative characteristic (extremely negative characteristic: 14.3%; very negative: 11.1%; negative: 14.3%). Yet 9.5% saw its affective valence as neutral.

The feature *missing something* was selected by 28.4% of the participants. The mean age was 35.8 years (SD = 13.5; range: 17–80), and half of them were born in Portugal (50.0%). On average, migrants came with the age of 24.6 years (SD = 11.1) to the host country and have spent since then 15.9 (SD = 14.6) years in Luxembourg.

This feature was considered to be a strongly positive characteristic of saudade by almost half of the total sample that selected it (extremely positive: 16.7%; very positive: 20.4%). Only 3.7% considered it as an extremely negative and 5.6% as a very negative characteristic of saudade. Still 22.2% considered it to be a rather negative feature. In general, when having a closer look at Appendix 11.2 and the results regarding valence evaluations, it can be observed that features were more often evaluated positively than negatively.

Gender differences (of the global sample) regarding the choice of the features were almost not significant. Both genders seemed to agree quite well on the salient features of saudade. Only the feature *distance* showed a significant difference, women having chosen it more often than men [X^2 (1, N = 188) = 12.54, p = .00]. Although not significant, the feature *nostalgia* showed a tendency as men are indeed more inclined to choose this feature compared with women (see Table 11.2 and Appendix 11.4).

Differences in the Evaluation of Valence of the Features

After having chosen the five features most associated with the concept of saudade, participants had to rate their affective valence. The following text will focus on the analysis of whether participants distinguished themselves in the evaluation of the valence according to age, gender, and time spent in the host country, Luxembourg.

Differences in the Evaluation of Valence According to Age

One-way analysis of variance (ANOVA) between subjects was conducted to observe whether participants differed in the evaluation of the features' valences according to their respective age. To that purpose, participants were divided into three different age groups. The first group, which we will name the emerging adults (EAs), encompasses participants ages 18 to 29. The second group, designated as the middle age group (MA), comprises

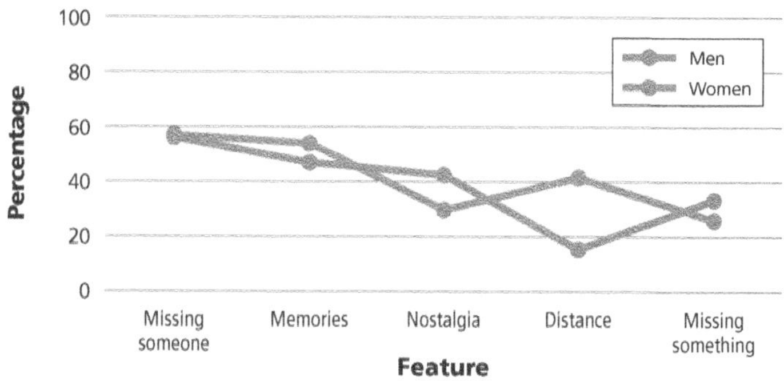

Figure 11.1 Features chosen according to gender of the whole sample.

TABLE 11.2 Features Chosen According to Gender		
Missing someone	$X^2(1, N = 188) = .00$	$p > .05$
Memories	$X^2(1, N = 188) = .68$	$p > .05$
Nostalgia	$X^2(1, N = 188) = 3.29$	$p = .07$
Distance	$\mathbf{X^2(1, N = 188) = 12.54}$	$\mathbf{p = .00}$
Missing something	$X^2(1, N = 188) = 1.20$	$p > .05$

persons ages 30 to 49. The third and last group is composed of persons more than 50 years (50+).

The evaluation of the valence showed some effects regarding valence assessment. Interestingly, the groups presenting significant mean differences were the groups of the EAs and the 50+. As a matter of fact, post hoc Tukey test showed that young and old generations have a different evaluation regarding the valence of some features related to saudade. The features *memories* [$F(2, 90) = 3.59$, $p = .03$], *distance* [$F(2, 57) = 5.18$, $p = .01$], and *missing someone* [$F(2, 48) = 3.75$, $p = .03$] presented significant differences between the two mentioned groups, with the 50+ group always judging the features as more important than the EA group (cf. Appendix 11.3).

Differences in the Evaluation of Valence According to Gender

The *t*-tests for independent samples were conducted to compare participants according to their gender. Men and women did not differ with regard to their evaluation of the valences of the five most chosen features of saudade. In fact both evaluated the valence in similar ways. Only the feature *missing something* presented a tendency [$t(49) = -1.88$, $p = .06$], although not significantly. Men ($M = 5.2$; $SD = 1.7$) tended to evaluate the valence of this feature higher than women ($M = 4.2$; $SD = 1.8$), meaning that for women this feature was indeed actually quite negative (see Appendix 11.4).

Differences in the Evaluation of Valence According to the Years Spent in Luxembourg

Participants were divided into three different groups regarding the years spent in Luxembourg. The aim was to assess whether individuals with a Portuguese background might differ as to the selection of the most representative features of saudade considering their years spent in the host country versus those already born there.

The first group consists of individuals who recently arrived to Luxembourg (i.e., <10 years in Lux; $n = 60$). The second group comprises people who have been living in Luxembourg for a longer period of time (i.e., >10 years in Lux; $n = 66$), and the last group is composed of participants already born in Luxembourg, the Luso-descendants ($n = 64$ people).

One-way ANOVAs showed no significant differences among the three categories. Only the *distance* feature highlighted an interesting difference between two groups [$F(2, 57) = 3.33$, $p = .04$]. As a matter of fact, Portuguese immigrant residents in Luxembourg for more than 10 years appear to evaluate the valence of the word *distance* (related to saudade) significantly higher than do individuals already born in Luxembourg. Interestingly, according to mean values, those born in Luxembourg evaluate the feature *distance* more negatively than do immigrants living there for more than 10 years. The immigrants present in Luxembourg fewer than 10 years, despite choosing that feature way more often (see Appendix 11.5) than the other two groups, interestingly didn't differ from either of them in terms of valence evaluation.

DEFINITION OF SAUDADE

Out of the ten presented definitions to describe saudade, the most chosen one by our total sample was saudade é a memória do coração (Saudade is the memory of the heart), with 17.9%. This definition was selected by immigrants and their offspring with an average age of 36.5 years ($SD = 13.96$), of which 64.7% were females and 35.3 males reflecting thus the general demography of our sample. Almost half of the participants were born in Portugal (47.1%), more than one-third was already born in Luxembourg (35.3%), and the others (17.6%) were born in other countries. On average, these Lusofone immigrants have been living in Luxembourg for 19.1 years ($SD = 14.2$) and arrived there with an average age of 22.6 ($SD = 11.9$) years. Analysis showed no significant differences neither for gender [$X^2(1, N = 190) = .09$, $p = .77$], age categories [$X^2(2, N = 190) = 2.33$, $p = .31$], or years spent in Luxembourg [$X^2(2, N = 190) = 1.34$, $p = .50$].

The second most chosen definition was *recordação [de alguém ou] alguma coisa que foi agradável mas que está distante no tempo ou no espaço* (memory [of someone or] something that was pleasant but is from now on distant in space and time). This definition was selected by 15.8% of the participants ages on average 35.83 years (SD = 11.7), of which 70% were women. Those born outside the Luxembourgish boarders were on average age 26.4 years (SD = 13.3) when arriving to Luxembourg and have since then been living there for an average of 12.14 years (SD = 12.1). Again, analysis revealed no significant differences for gender [$X^2(1, N = 190) = .16, p = .69$], age categories [$X^2(2, N = 190) = .84, p = .66$], or years spent in Luxembourg [$X^2(2, N = 190) = .46, p = .80$].

CONCLUSION AND FUTURE PERSPECTIVES

The present study delivers a first understanding of how individuals with a Portuguese/Lusofone migrant background relate to the concept of saudade. The different selected features as being the most representative of saudade illustrate the complexity of the concept as a whole. In fact, the selection of these diverse characteristics highlights the multifaceted aspects and dimensions that saudade makes resonate in each Lusofone individual.

General Interpretation

Interestingly, the five most selected terms to describe saudade were similar for our sample comprised of individuals with a Lusofone background, be it for those born in Luxembourg (i.e., the Luso-descendants) or those born in Lusofone countries (i.e., Portugal, Brazil, Mozambique, etc.). Likewise they were similar to the sample described in the study led by Neto and Mullet (2014) comprised of Portuguese young natives living in Portugal. Therefore, saudade seems to have a dimension of collective meaning common to Lusofone individuals regardless, among others, of the country of birth. A social common memory around the concept of saudade, as described by Nascimento and Menandro (2005), seems to emerge out of our results among the individuals with a Lusofone migrant history, be it a common memory from the migrants or transmitted by parents to their children.

Because the immigrants are indeed far from their country of origin, we expected features related to the home country (e.g., *native land, home,* or *separation*) to be selected among the most important features of saudade from the Portuguese immigrants' perspective. However, in the present study, this assumption was not proven right. As a matter of fact, features related to emotional states (e.g., *nostalgia, memories*) as well as to a feeling of absence and unavailability (e.g., *missing someone/something, distance*) were chosen more often. Therefore, the chosen words can be seen as strongly related to the general situation of migrants, habitually more or less far away from their larger family. Indeed, features such as *missing someone* (57%) and *distance* (33%) of the total sample might be reflections of the immigrant context. In fact, because Portuguese immigrants in Luxembourg are known to maintain strong ties with their families left behind in their country of origin (Fleury, 2010), the physical as well as the emotional distance from their respective families might be in this specific context a salient feature in relation to their comprehension of the word saudade. In the context of migration, these features may also be related to the beloved ones, immigrants left behind besides their country of origin, be it for the living or the dead to whom they are not able to pay their respects anymore as often as they probably would like to. The features *memories* and *nostalgia* might as well refer to the memories of the country of origin and the time spent there, memories recalled with a certain nostalgia as time passes by.

Moreover, in contradiction to our initial hypothesis, individuals with a Portuguese background did not seem to differ in their conception of the notion of saudade. No significant differences emerged between the considered age groups or the groups according to their length of residence in the host country. Concerning gender, a common shared stereotype is to consider women generally as more emotional and sensitive compared with men (Fabes & Martin, 1991), although no significant differences emerged regarding gender. As a matter of fact, women did not relate more or more strongly to the concept of saudade than did men. The conceptualization of saudade is thus independent of the different considered factors (i.e., age, gender, and years spent in the host country). This corroborates the fact that the concept of saudade is indeed strongly anchored in the personal and collective meaning of Portuguese as well as in all the Luso-speaking cultures (e.g., Brazilian or Cap Verdean cultures). It truly seems to be a culturally shared construct (Fehr, 2005, quoted by Neto, 2014). The studied sample comprised Portuguese immigrants who left their country of origin for a more or less lengthy period and their offspring, the "second generation" or Luso-descendants, often already born in the host country and with usually less strong ties to their parents' culture of origin as they grow up between two cultures. The concept of saudade can therefore be assumed to be a social and cultural common memory (Nascimento & Menandro, 2005), a strong transmitted heritage through generations regardless of country of birth, gender, or age, a construct deeply anchored in the transmitted culture.

Furthermore, regarding the ambivalence of saudade, the results indicate a simultaneous involvement of both pleasure and pain, such as described by the definition of Lüscher et al (2010). As a matter of fact, the top five features seem at first reading to have quite negative connotations. Nevertheless, they interestingly were primarily conceptualized as positive. In fact, it depicts the opposite of what most of the definitions and translations of saudade usually bring to light, where the negative characteristics are often put in the foreground.

As a matter of fact, our participants seem to perceive the concept in a more positive way, as described by Bulat-Silva (2012), "English nostalgia lacks the positive connotations that all the afflictive emotions have in the Portuguese culture" (p. 208), and by Magalhães (1995), "It's when we learn to love melancholy as much as we love happiness, because both of them make us feel alive" (pp. 113, 114, quoted from Leal, 2000). This quite singular way to define saudade using words with a rather negative scope and opposite emotions accentuates the ambivalent and unconventional aspect of the concept. By examining the Appendix 11.2 with the valence values, it can indeed be observed that the different features were generally seen as rather positive even though no real consensus was established highlighting the deep subjective and ambivalent character of the concept saudade.

DIFFERENCE IN VALENCE ACCORDING TO YEARS SPENT IN LUXEMBOURG

If we have a closer look at the specific features picked out by the selected subgroups according to the years spent in the host country, namely, individuals born in Luxembourg, immigrants living in Luxembourg for more than 10 years and immigrants living in Luxembourg for fewer than 10 years, several observations can be made. In general, the three groups did not differ in the selection of the five most typical features of saudade. Hence, the ranking scheme of the five most representative features of saudade remains quite similar throughout the three groups (see Appendix 11.5). Interestingly, the group comprising the Luso-descendants, children of immigrants already born in the host country, followed a slightly different path. Indeed, Appendix 11.5 shows that "second-generation children" reported the feature *missing something* as being more important to them than the feature *family* or *distance*, which was inversed for the other two groups. Even if the feature *family* was not integrated in our general analysis, we can observe that it was actually more important than *missing something* for Portuguese immigrants regardless of the years spent in the host country, which might be related to the family these immigrants left behind in their country of origin, most often parents and siblings.

Furthermore, the group with immigrants having spent fewer years in Luxembourg (<10 years in Lux) selected the feature *distância* as the third most important feature, whereas it was only ranked fourth for the two other groups. This finding reflects indeed the distance (emotional, geographical, and distance in time) they still feel toward their country of origin and their family left behind.

It is interesting to highlight that many participants from the subgroup comprising immigrants not born in Luxembourg but living there for more than ten years selected *memories* particularly more often than the two other groups. It may be assumed that memories of their former lives and countries of birth become particularly salient for this subgroup because of the largest period of time spent in a country that is indeed not their native land and all it may symbolize for them.

Definition

Regarding the definition participants had to choose to describe best the word saudade from their personal point of view, results are quite scattered without real consensus. As a matter of fact, participants related to the Lusofone culture of our present sample did not agree on a specific definition of saudade. Although a larger group (17.9%) chose a definition containing both an affective and a cognitive element (i.e., *saudade é a memória do coração*). However, each definition was chosen at least once, demonstrating the divergence of opinions regarding the definition of the word saudade (see Appendix 11.6). It may indeed be seen as a word related to diverse aspects as mentioned in the several presented definitions: For example, for some it relates more to the emotional and cognitive dimension and for others more to the distance in time and space. The diverging opinions regarding the different presented definitions of saudade and the fact that there seems to be an absence of a general consensus among the Lusofone cultures regarding a specific and clear definition of the word illustrates once again the diversity and complexity of the concept. The fact that Portuguese individuals do not agree on one final definition of the word highlights even more the ambivalent dimension of the word but also the ambivalent feeling individuals feel toward the word saudade. Indeed, they did not seem capable of putting the word into one unique and specific predefined box without considering other aspects of it. A Portuguese immigrant lady wrote down her own definition as a comment to highlight the fact that it was difficult for her to choose only one definition for the word. This participant interestingly regroups all the dimensions of the concept saudade, consistent also with the previous analyzed features chosen by the participants as being the most relevant for saudade:

> Portuguese female participant: Saudade é um estado de espírito nostálgico, provocado pela distância e (ou) pela separação de seres Amados, (família, filhos, amigos), é a pátria, o lugar onde se nasceu e viveu. Só sente saudade quem tem boas recordações na vida! Portanto saudade quer dizer Amor, Recordação e Distancia que se transformam em Nostalgia sempre no sentido positivo.[9]

Limitations and Future Research

As Apresjan and Apresjan (2000) argue, "language contains the experience of millennia of psychological and cultural introspection, and its data are every bit as reliable as those provided by experimental research" (p. 7).

Therefore, the conceptualization of a unique concept within a certain language can be the key to better understand the underlying consensus of a population. Saudade, a concept with a long tradition (De Noronha, 2009), could be especially helpful in comprehending the social consensus of the different Portuguese populations around the world. Further studies, such as for example to compare the migrant's conceptualization of saudade with the native Portuguese who are still living in Portugal, would likewise be a means to a better understanding of the concept. Besides, it would be interesting to further study the conceptualization of the concept among other Luso-immigrant communities living in different countries, such as, for example, Switzerland or even France, where Portuguese immigrant communities are also quite widespread. In this sense, qualitative data might provide supplementary information about immigrants' understanding of saudade to identify further underlying dimensions of the concept by giving meaning to migrant histories potentially related to saudade.

Going one step further in the investigation of saudade would be to examine whether other cultural groups might relate to this specific concept. Can this unique feeling be felt by other cultures, such as argued by Bulat-Silva (2012) or Vasconcelos (1914), or does it indeed specifically and only extend to the Lusofone mind and soul (Costa, 2014)?

Related to the immigrant dimension, it would be interesting to take a further look into the expression *ter saudades da pátria* (to have saudades of the home land) to analyze which elements of the home country are the ones that are most important for immigrants when they feel saudade*s* for their *pátria* (home land). Our study already indicates that features such as *distance* and *missing someone* (or even the feature *family*) seem to be important concepts for Portuguese migrants' understanding of saudade. Nevertheless, whether this is related to their migration situation or whether the term *distance* refers to their home country, family, or friends, to the Portuguese language, or to another element still remains an unanswered question. Furthermore, we ignore what members of the family and what characteristics the term *family* might be related to. Analyzing different proverbs related to saudade could therefore help to highlight different pertinent aspects of it, such as, for example, the well-known Portuguese proverb *matar saudades* (killing saudades) as a method to deal with the ambivalence of the felt feelings caused by saudade. Saudade might indeed be the synthetic solution that becomes a prevailing lingering feeling, unifying ambivalence into a whole that keeps it and is indulged to deal with the overwhelming emotions and feelings caused by saudade. Yet sometimes this may be an obstacle, where "killing saudade" becomes crucial. Saudade can then be a catalyst for daily acceptance of the complexity of living.

Another interesting path to follow would be the similarities between generations and the underlying processes regarding the definitions as well as the features conferred to the concept saudade. In fact, because a common memory seems to exist, regardless of age, gender, and country of birth, a certain value and cultural transmission related to that concept might be further investigated. Is it indeed a rather family (e.g., an intrafamily, across-generation, in-depth study) or societal cultural transmission, or should it be seen more as an intertwined global transmission?

NOTES

1. Translation made by the first author: a sad and sweet memory of persons or things distant or inexistent, accompanied by the desire to have them back or see them again; regret at the absence of someone we hold dear.
2. Translation made by the first author: melancholy caused by the memory of something we are being deprived of now; a wound felt because of the absence or disappearance of someone, something, state, or actions; sorrow; nostalgia.
3. Retrieved from http://www.statistiques.public.lu/stat/TableViewer/tableView.aspx?ReportId=384&IF_Language=fra&MainTheme=2&FldrName=1
4. We also included immigrants born in other Portuguese-speaking countries, such as Brazil or Cape Verde, because the aim of the study was mainly to understand the conception of the word saudade in general from Portuguese-speaking immigrants and their kin living in Luxembourg.
5. This list was obtained by asking participants to indicate all the features and characteristics that came to their mind while thinking about saudade. After categorizing the obtained features, a final list of 67 features was identified by the authors and their collaborators, the list we used in our current study.
6. In SPSS, the valences were coded as followed: $-3 = 1$; $-2 = 2$; $-1 = 3$; $0 = 4$; $+1 = 5$; $+2 = 6$; $+3 = 7$. Mean values less than 4 define a rather negative global evaluation, mean values more than 4 refer to positive global evaluation of the features, and 4 is the neutral threshold.
7. Sentences were selected out of different Portuguese sayings, expressions, poems, songs, literature, and so on that represented the different aspects of the word saudade. Prior to the study, these various sentences were presented to a pilot sample to get their impressions and select the ten most salient sentences with consideration to specific dimensions the sentences related to (see Appendix 11.1).
8. The percentages indicated in this section always refer to the percentages related to the individuals who chose the respective features and not to the whole sample.
9. Translation made by the author: Saudade is a nostalgic state of mind provoked by distance and/or separation from beloved ones (family, children, friends), it is the homeland, the place where one was born and lived. Only those with good memories in life can feel saudade. Thus, saudade means love, memories, and distance that become nostalgia but always in a positive sense.

APPENDIX 11.1 Definitions for the Word *Saudade*

Definition in Portuguese	Translation	Source	Component
Sentimento de tristeza pela morte de alguém ou perda de alguma coisa a que afetivamente se estava muito ligado.	Feeling of sadness at someone's death or the loss of something to which one was affectionately connected to.	Dicionário da língua Portuguesa contemporânea, Academia das Ciências de Lisboa, 2001	Cognitive
Um tormento puro, doce e magoado.	A pure, sweet, and painful torment.	Luís Vaz de Camões (Portuguese poet), Canções e elegias, 1595	Ambivalent
Saudade é amar um passado que ainda não passou. É recusar o presente que nos magoa. É não ver o futuro que nos convida.	Saudade is to love the past that has not yet passed. It's to refuse the present that hurts us. It is not to see the future inviting us.	Quote: Pablo Neruda (Chilean poet, diplomat, and politician)	Temporal
A saudade é a memória do coração.	Saudade is the memory of the heart.	Quote: Henrique Maximiano Coelho Neto (Brazilian author & politician)	Cognitive and affective
A saudade é a nossa alma dizendo para onde ela quer voltar.	Saudade is our soul telling us where to go back.	Quote: Rubem Alves (Brazilian theologian, philosopher, educator, writer, and psychoanalyst)	Migration
Saudade é o estado da mente em que não podemos lembrar nem o momento em que começamos a sentir felicidade nem o momento em que começamos a sentir tristeza. É quando aprendemos a amar a melancolia tanto como a felicidade, porque os dois fazem-nos sentir viver.	Saudade is the state of mind in which we cannot remember neither the moment we started to feel happiness nor the moment we started to feel sadness. It is when we learn to love melancholia as much as happiness because both make us feel alive.	Portuguese singer Pedro Magalhães, in Pires P., 1995	Ambivalent
Quem parte leva saudades, quem fica saudades tem.	The one leaving takes saudades, the one staying saudades has.	Portuguese proverb/saying	Migration
Saudade é um sentimento que quando não cabe no coração, escorre pelos olhos.	Saudade is a feeling that when it does not fit into the heart, it runs through the eyes.	Quote: Bob Marley (Jamaican singer)	Affective
Recordação [de alguém ou] de alguma coisa que foi agradável mas que está distante no tempo ou no espaço.	Memory [of someone or] of something that was pleasant but is from now on distant in space and time.	Dicionário da língua Portuguesa contemporânea, Academia das Ciências de Lisboa, 2001	Temporal and space; cognitive
Amor e ausência são os pais da saudade.	Love and absence are the parents of saudade.	Francisco de Manuel Melo, in Epanáfora Amorosa, 1676	Affective

APPENDIX 11.2 Valences of the Five Most Chosen Features for *Saudade*

Feature	Extremely –		Very –		–		Neutral		+		Very +		Extremely +	
	N	%	*N*	%	*N*	%	*N*	%	*N*	%	*N*	%	*N*	%
Missing someone	13	11.9	15	13.8	10	9.2	17	15.6	6	11.0	12	11.0	29	26.6
Memories	2	2.0	/	/	4	4.0	18	18.2	**11**	**11.1**	**22**	**22.2**	**36**	**36.4**
Nostalgia	1	1.5	3	4.6	6	9.2	**23**	**35.4**	5	7.7	15	23.1	8	12.3
Distance	9	14.3	7	11.1	9	14.3	6	9.5	8	12.7	9	14.3	12	19.0
Missing something	2	3.7	3	5.6	12	22.2	9	16.7	5	9.3	11	20.4	9	16.7

APPENDIX 11.3 Valences of the Five Most Chosen Features for *Saudade* According to Age

Feature	*F* (df)	*p* value	>29		30–49		50+	
			M	*SD*	*M*	*SD*	*M*	*SD*
Missing someone	$F(2, 100) = 2.04$	.14	4.03	2.3	4.34	2.1	5.29	1.9
Memories	$\mathbf{F(2, 96) = 3.59}$	**.03**	**5.16**	**1.3**	5.77	1.6	**6.22**	**1.1**
Nostalgia	$F(2, 29.6) = 1.00$	.38	4.72	1.2	4.43	1.4	5.23	2.0
Distance	$\mathbf{F(2, 57) = 5.16}$	**.01**	**3.57**	**2.0**	4.30	2.2	**5.90**	**1.4**
Missing something	$\mathbf{F(2, 48) = 3.75}$	**.03**	**3.82**	**1.7**	4.72	1.7	**5.67**	**1.6**

APPENDIX 11.4 Valences of the Five Most Chosen Features for *Saudade* According to Gender

Feature	*F*(df)	*p* value	Women			Men		
			%*	*M*	*SD*	%**	*M*	*SD*
Missing someone	$t(101) = -0.64$	.52	57.5	4.28	2.5	57.1	4.57	2.1
Memories	$t(91) = -1.49$	.14	54.3	5.49	1.5	47.6	5.97	1.3
Nostalgia	$t(59) = -0.74$	.46	29.9	4.60	1.4	42.9	4.88	1.6
Distance	$t(58) = -1.14$	.26	**41.7**	4.06	2.2	**15.9**	4.90	1.6
Missing something	$t(49) = -1.88$	.07	26.0	4.23	1.8	20.6	5.15	1.7

* Percentage of women who chose those features out of the whole female sample.
** Percentage of men who chose those features out of the whole male sample.

APPENDIX 11.5 Valences of the Five Most Chosen Features for *Saudade* According to Years Spent in Luxembourg

Feature	*F*(df)	*p* value	Born in LU			>10 years			≤10 years		
			%	*M*	*SD*	%	*M*	*SD*	%	*M*	*SD*
Missing someone	$F(2, 98.63) = 1.28$	.28	54.7	4.00	1.9	57.6	4.83	2.3	60.0	4.28	2.3
Memories	$F(2, 90) = 0.53$	.95	51.6	5.58	1.2	57.6	5.66	1.5	46.7	5.70	1.7
Nostalgia	$F(2, 58) = 1.27$	.29	34.4	4.85	1.2	36.4	4.35	1.7	31.7	5.06	1.5
Distance	$\mathbf{F(2, 57) = 3.33}$	**.04**	**28.1**	**3.12**	**1.9**	**31.8**	**4.70**	**2.0**	**40.0**	**4.57**	**2.2**
Missing something	$F(2, 48) = 2.39$	.10	32.8	4.05	1.6	25.8	5.31	2.0	26.7	4.50	1.6
Family*	$F(2, 37.9) = 1.97$	.15	25.0	6.40	.91	27.3	6.12	1.6	31.7	5.26	2.3

* The feature *familía* was added to this table because it was ranked fifth for two out of the three groups (living in Lux >10 years and ≤10 years). However, it only arrived at the sixth place of the general ranking and was thus kept out of the general analysis.

APPENDIX 11.6 Definitions for the Concept of *Saudade*

Definition	%	*n*
A saudade é a memória do coração.	**17.9**	**34**
Recordação [de alguém ou] de alguma coisa que foi agradável mas que está distante no tempo ou no espaço.	**15.8**	**30**
Saudade é um sentimento que quando não cabe no coração, escorre pelos olhos.	11.1	21
A saudade é a nossa alma dizendo para onde ela quer voltar.	10.0	19
Quem parte leva saudades, quem fica saudades tem.	9.5	18
Saudade é o estado da mente em que não podemos lembrar nem o momento em que começamos a sentir felicidade nem o momento em que começamos a sentir tristeza. É quando aprendemos a amar a melancolia tanto como a felicidade, porque os dois fazem-nos sentir viver.	7.4	14
Amor e ausência são os pais da saudade.	7.4	14
Sentimento de tristeza pela morte de alguém ou perda de alguma coisa a que afetivamente se estava muito ligado.	5.8	11
Saudade é amar um passado que ainda não passou. É recusar o presente que nos magoa. É não ver o futuro que nos convida.	5.3	10
Um tormento puro, doce e magoado.	2.6	5

ACKNOWLEDGMENT

This research was supported by a grant from the Fonds National de la Recherche Luxembourg (C12/SC/4009630/IRMA/Albert–Intergenerational Relations in the Light of Migration and Ageing) of which the first author was the research associate.

REFERENCES

Almeida Costa, J., & Sampaio e Melo, A. (1999). *Dicionário da língua portuguesa* [Dictionary of the Portuguese language] (8th ed.). Porto, Portugal: Porto Editora.

Apresjan, J. D., & Apresjan, V. I. (2000). Metaphor in the semantic representation of Emotions. In J. Apresjan (Ed.), *Systematic Lexicography* (pp. 203–214). Oxford, England: Oxford University Press.

Baganha, M. I. B. (1994). As correntes emigratórias portuguesas no século XX e o seu impacto na economia nacional [The Portuguese migration flows in the 20th century and its impact in national economy]. *Análise Social, 128*(29), 959–980.

Baganha, M. I. (1998). Portuguese emigration after World War II. In A. C. Pinto (Ed.), *Modern Portugal* (pp. 189–205). Retrieved from http://ies.berkeley.edu/research/files/cp02/cp02-port_emigration.pdf

Bell, A. F. G. (1912). *In Portugal.* London, England: John Lane.

Braz, A. (2006). L'intraduisible en question: l'étude de la saudade [The untranslatable: the study of saudade]. *Revue des littératures de l'Union Européenne, 4*(4), 1000–1021.

Brazette, M. M. (1989). *Saudade normal e patológica* [Normal and pathological saudade]. *Análise Psicológica, 4*(7), 533–536.

Brown, R. (1965). *Social psychology.* New York, NY: The Free Press.

Bulat-Silva, Z. (2012). *Saudade:* A key Portuguese emotion. *Emotion Review, 4*(2), 203–211.

Castro, A. B. de. (1980). *Saudade, ensaio: Etimologia (árabe), significação, antologia* [*Saudade,* essay: Etymology, meaning, anthology]. Porto, Portugal: A.B. de Castro.

Coimbra, L. (1986). *O mistério* [The mistery]. In A. Botelho & A. B. Teixeira (Eds.), *Filosofia da Saudade* (pp. 161–173). Lisboa, Portugal: Imprensa Nacional–Casa da Moeda.

Costa, L. P. J. (2014). Mitos da língua: o caso da palavra saudade [Myths of the language: The case of the word saudade]. *International Studies on Law and Education, 18,* 89–92.

De Noronha, M. T. (2009). *Saudade* and memory in the ontopoiesis of life. In A.-T. Tymieniecka (Ed.), *Memory in the ontopoesis of life* (pp. 195–205). Dordrecht, the Netherlands: Springer.

Dunlevy, J. A., & Hutchinson, W. K. (1999). The impact of immigration on American import trade in the late nineteenth and early twentieth centuries. *The Journal of Economic History, 59*(4), 1043–1062.

Fabes, R. A., & Martin, C. L. (1991). Gender and age stereotypes of emotionality. *Personality and Social Psychology Bulletin, 17*(5), 532–540.

Farrell, P. (2006). Portuguese saudade and other emotions of absence and longing. In B. Peeters (Ed.), *Semantic primes and universal grammar: Empirical evidence from the Romance languages* (pp. 235–258). Amsterdam, The Netherlands: John Benjamins.

Feldman-Bianco, B. (1992). Multiple layers of time and space: The construction of class, ethnicity, and nationalism among Portuguese immigrants. *Annals of the New York Academy of Sciences, 645*(1), 145–174.

Feldman-Bianco, B. (2014). *Saudade, imigração a construção de uma nação (portuguesa) desterritorializada* [*Saudade,* immigration, the construction of a (Portuguese) deterritorialized nation]. *Revista Brasileira de Estudos de População, 9*(1), 35–49.

Figueiredo, C. (1981). *Pequeno dicionário da língua portuguesa* [Small dictionary of Portuguese language] (13th ed.). Lisboa, Portugal: Livraria Bertrand.

Figueiredo, C. de. (1996). *Grande dicionário da língua Portuguesa* [Large dictionary of the Portuguese language] (25th ed.). Lisbon, Portugal: Bertrand Editora.

Fleury, C. (2010). *Migration et solidarité intergénérationnelle: le cas des immigrants portugais du Luxembourg* [Migration and intergenerational solidarity: The case of Portuguese migrants in Luxembourg]. *Lien Social et Politiques, 64,* 95–111.

Garrett, A. (1858). *Camões.* Lisboa: Viúva Bertrand e filhos.

Hannerz, U. (1993). Cosmopolitans and locals in world culture. In M. Featherstone (Ed.), *Global Culture: Nationalism, Globalization and Modernity* (pp. 237-287). London, England: SAGE.

Kaplan, K. L. (1972). On the ambivalence-indifference problem in attitude theory and measurement: A suggested modification of the semantic differential technique. *Psychological Bulletin, 77*(5), 361–372.

Krause, J. R. (2012). Translating Rosalía de Castro's saudade into English. *Decimonónica, 9,* 69–87.

Lamas, M. P. (2003). *Reflexões sobre a saudade* [Reflections on saudade]. Lisboa, Portugal: Impressão José Fernandes.

Leal, J. (2000). The making of saudade: National identity and ethnic psychology in Portugal. In T. Dekker, J. Helsloot, & C. Wijers (Eds.), *Roots and rituals: The construction of ethnic identities* (pp. 267–287). Retrieved from http://run.unl.pt/bitstream/10362/4386/1/The%20Makin...pdf

Leal, J., & Féblot-Augustins, J. (1999). *Saudade, la construction d'un symbole: "Caractère national" et identité nationale* [*Saudade,* the construction of a symbol: National character and national identity]. *Ethnologie française, 2,* 177–189.

Lopes, P. J. (2011). Fado, UNESCO's world intangible cultural heritage. *Academic Forum, 29,* 27–32.

Lourenço, E. (1978). *O labirinto da saudade: Psicanálise mítica do destino português* [The labyrinth of saudade: Mythical psychology of the Portuguese destiny]. Lisboa, Portugal: Publicações Dom Quixote.

Ministère de la fonction publique. (2010). *Épreuve d'histoire et de culture luxembourgeoise, carriers supérieures et moyennes.* Impression: CTIE division imprimées et fournitures de bureau de lÉtat.

Nascimento. A. R. A., & Menandro, P. R. M. (2005). *Memória social e saudade: especificidades e possibilidades de articulação na análise psicossocial de recordações* [Social memory and nostalgia: Specificities and possibilities of articulation in psychosocial analysis of recollections]. *Memorandum, 8,* 5–19.

Neto, F., & Mullet, E. (2014). A prototype analysis of the Portuguese concept of saudade. *Journal of Cross-Cultural Psychology, 45*(4), 660–670.

Phalet, K., & Swyngedouw M. (2003). Measuring immigrant integration: The case of Belgium. *Migration Studies, 40,* 773–803.

Roquete, J. I., & Fonseca, J. (1974). *Dicionário dos sinónimos poético e de epítetos da língua Portuguesa.* Porto, Portugal: Lello & Irmão.

Sarkissian, M. (2000). A history of the Portuguese fado (review). *Notes, 57*(1), 160–161.

Shepherd, A. (2011). Fado and the place of longing: Loss, memory and the city. *Ethnomusicology Forum, 20*(1), 118–120.

Silveira, L. L. P. A. (2010). *Para além da origem da palavra saudade (ou antropologia de um sentimento coletivo* [Beyond the origin of the word saudade or anthropology of a collective feeling]. *Revista Litteris, 4.* Retrieved from http://revistaliter.dominiotemporario.com/doc/paraalemdaorigemdapalavrasaudade.pdf

Statec. (2013). *Recensement de la population 2011: Les portugais au Luxembourg* [*Population census 2011: Portuguese in Luxembourg*]. Retrieved from http://www.statistiques.public.lu/fr/publications/series/rp2011/2013/18-13-portugais/index.html

Tobias, J. A. (1997). *Saudade: ideia ou sentimento* [*Saudade*: Idea or feeling]. São Paulo, Brasil: AM Edições.

UNESCO. (2011). Retrieved from http://www.unesco.org/culture/ich/en/RL/fado-urban-popular-song-of-portugal-00563

Van Oudenhoven, J. P. (2006). Immigrants. In D. L. Sam & J. W. Berry (Eds.), *The Cambridge handbook of acculturation psychologie* (pp. 163–180). Cambridge, England: Cambridge University Press.

Vasconcelos, C. M. (1914). *A saudade portuguesa* [The Portuguese *saudade*]. Porto: Renascença Portuguesa (Praça da República). Retrieved from https://drive.google.com/file/d/0B739_KUAF41vMjY5MTY1NmEtMTg1ZS00MDc0LWI5NTMtYmZhMmJkMzA2YTc4/view

Vaz, K. (1994). *Saudade.* New York, NY: St. Martin's Press.

Vieira, E. (2007). *Saudades e soledad*: Fernando Pessoa and António Machado on nostalgia and loneliness. *Romance Notes, 48*, 125–133.

CHAPTER 12

DESIRED AMBIGUITIES AND DEALING WITH AMBIVALENCES IN THE CONTEXT OF SOCIAL WORK

Mogens Jensen
Aalborg University

In this chapter, I focus on ambivalence and intergenerational relations in the case of the relationship between social workers and adolescents placed in residential care because of behavioral or personal problems. The aim is to analyze the relation from the perspective of both ambivalence and ambiguity to reach a better understanding of social-pedagogical treatment as it is carried out in these institutions and to use this context to throw some light on the phenomenon of ambivalence.

PRELIMINARY ANALYSIS OF AMBIGUITY AND AMBIVALENCE IN SOCIAL WORK

Humans tend to create meaning out of their perceptions, and the more unusual they are, the greater the effort to integrate them in earlier experience and

Trans-Generational Family Relations, pages 247–262

understanding (Bruner, 1990). This doesn't mean people seek a thorough understanding in every case. Investigations of people's way of handling problems show a tendency to find sufficient understanding in a balance between time invested and the importance of the problem at hand (Lave, 1988; Rasmussen, 1986; Schön, 1983). In fact we seldom reach a total understanding but act on a kind of "loose linkage" between our comprehension and the situation.

Evolutionary seen meaning-making can be understood as establishing an understanding, which qualifies your expectations to the near future and thereby facilitates a feeling of security (Rothbaum, Weisz, & Snyder, 1982). The creation of meaning also makes it possible to influence the development of the situation and thereby for humans to be agents in their own lives. Both as agents in their lives and in the meaning making humans not only experience ambivalences, but they actively set them up (Abbey & Valsiner, 2005). The process of creating a meaning connected to a sense of security is described in attachment theory (Bowlby 1969/1997), where the child is conceptualized as needing a secure base to start from when exploring the world. To develop the skills needed for survival, curiosity can be seen as a motive for exploratory behavior and developing competences even when you are not forced to it. This addresses the character of ambiguity and ambivalence: It can be both appealing and frightening depending on personal characteristics, biographical background, current situation, and the match among these.

Ambiguity can preliminarily be characterized as related to the perceptual process when a phenomenon can be interpreted in more than one way. In itself, ambiguity can be seen as neutral, although some people may find it discomforting. The way people perceive the world around them is an active process, where they create an understanding in relation to their intentions in the situation under the constraints the specific situation leaves them, and ambiguity provokes a choice of understanding without total certainty and some find this discomforting.

Ambivalence is generally associated with negative emotional aspects of experience. It implies some kind of conflict between different interpretations, a mix of positive and negative feelings toward an interpretation, and may even result in indecision because the person cannot choose how to handle the situation, and when this experience is realized, it results in discomfort. Later in the chapter, we will return to a discussion of this negative aspect of ambivalence.

Several aspects of ambiguity and ambivalence are productive for analyzing social-pedagogical treatment. They are connected to a feeling of both security and of curiosity, which touches on one of the core dilemmas of adolescents and their development. In their childhood, they often have not had sufficient support to develop an attitude of curiosity, which again restricts their development. Ambiguity and ambivalence also play an important role in the creation of meaning and development of understanding, thereby facilitating an active engagement in forming one's own life—again a core theme for these adolescents.

THE FIELD OF SOCIAL-PEDAGOGICAL TREATMENT

The institutions are carrying out pedagogical treatment to help the adolescent find a way to handle their lives within the frames of society. The following understanding of social-pedagogical treatment is my description of a well-established tradition at least in Germany and the Nordic Countries dating back to the 19th century and Continental philosophers such as Paul Natorp (1854–1924) and Wilhelm Dilthey (1833–1911) within the hermeneutic tradition (Gustavsson, Hermansson, & Hämäläinen, 2003; Hämäläinen, 2012; Mathiesen, 1999).

The basis of social-pedagogical treatment is forming a fellowship between the adolescent and the social worker—what I term a *social-pedagogical fellowship* (Jensen, 2011, 2015). This fellowship is formed to handle a common project for the social worker and the adolescent, and this could be stated as the life of the adolescent with all the challenges his background and development up to now bring along and the impediments for realizing the the adolescent's future plans. Seeing it as a fellowship implies the development of some shared norms for interaction and expectations toward each other in the cooperation, but both parts have to accept these norms, and in each episode of interaction the fellowship is negotiated, resulting in confirmation, weakening, or strengthening. The aim is that the adolescent gradually develops socially acceptable norms and attitudes as his personal positions, and here it is important that he makes his own construction of the social norms, as described in a bidirectional model for cultural transfer (Valsiner, 2007). Another part of the aim is the development of the adolescent's competences to act and thereby take over responsibility of his own life.

The social worker and adolescent are both members of the fellowship, but they don't have the same competencies. The social worker should—because of education, age, and experience—have more advanced competencies in handling the challenges of ordinary life and foreseeing coming challenges than the adolescent. In contrast, the adolescent has better knowledge of his background and wishes for the future. When it comes to decisions on which life the adolescent wants to live in the future, he in fact has a power of veto. In the beginning, the social worker has to take great responsibility for establishing and handling the fellowship and the common project, but gradually he should hand over the responsibility for coping with the life to the adolescent.

This short description resembles normal parenthood, where the parents decide for the infant but gradually hand over the responsibility to their child according to the pace of developing competencies. A couple of important differences are evident, however. First, parents normally have opportunities for bonding beyond any deliberate choice. When an adolescent is placed in out-of-home treatment, the social worker has to establish these bonds (or a social-pedagogical fellowship, as I call it) and get the acceptance of the adolescent to their mutual cooperation. The adolescent is often skeptical toward adults, especially adults who are part of the official system, so the social worker has to appear reliable even or especially in spontaneous reactions. In addition, the adolescent often has learned to cope by acting quickly and may turn the situation into something well known as conflicts, which they are quite skilled at, so the social worker needs catch up with the adolescent. In summary, a social worker in social-pedagogical treatment has to be able to act spontaneously, taking care of the current situation and still in accordance with the plans of treatment and the common project of the social-pedagogical fellowship—a demand for planned spontaneity as I have termed it (Jensen, 2010).

In daily life, every situation can be understood and handled in several ways, and the situation is not fixed but still developing depending on the actions of the participants. Here the social worker should try to handle the situation in a way where the adolescent gets the opportunities to develop the skills he will need to handle his life by himself in the future. The adolescent should become a competent actor in his own life. Just the same, he might want the situation to develop differently to avoid confronting a demand or defeat, to achieve a short-term goal at the expense of a long-term goal, or simply because of different priorities. What a situation can be used for pedagogically depends on many different factors and can change from day to day and even from moment to moment as the situation develops.

THE ADOLESCENTS IN QUESTION

Adolescents placed in out-of-home care have had to develop a way of handling their lives as best they could in the context of their childhood. You can see their behavior as their best attempt to handle this (Fischer et al., 1997), but now these competencies either do not fit new contexts as school, are in violence with the norms in society, or are hindering their further development. When exposed to neglect, they often have had to take care by themselves, and in these environments, it is beneficial to act quickly and turn the situation into something well known as conflicts for which they have well-trained skills. They have a lot of experience in dealing with conflicts, although not always in ways we find productive. The benefit of ending up in a well-known situation is a feeling of security—you know what to expect, so the near future is not so frightening.

This leaves little room for elaborating on different understandings of situations or different possible acts, and when you talk with them, they often express a belief in one single way of interpreting—one truth. In fact these adolescents often seem to be more uncomfortable with ambiguous situations and ambivalent feelings than with conflicts, so they deliberately create conflicts instead of elaborating the ambiguous situation for possible positive developments (Carr, 2006), as in case 2 later in the text. These patterns put them in a situation where they see themselves as reacting to situations in their lives. They don't see themselves as agents who can deliberately influence and create their future.

These processes mainly go on outside conscious awareness, and to change these patterns, they will need many experiences before establishing new ways of perceiving situations. This can be facilitated by a social-pedagogical fellowship, where they are not alone, and this security can make them take the risk of trying something new. Gradually, they can then take over by themselves.

CASE 1. ROLE OF TRUST IN FELLOWSHIP

The following is quoted from an interview with a social worker where the aim of the study was to characterize social-pedagogical treatment. The social worker, Hans (all names are changed to ensure anonymity), was selected in cooperation with the head of the institution, and the criteria were to find a skilled and experienced social worker who had done a difficult but successful job with adolescents. He was asked to tell about the core of social-pedagogical treatment and was allowed to do this in his own chosen way so the interview was little structured by the interviewer. It turned out that he told several narratives of adolescents he had worked with during the years—a common way to mediate professional experience and expertise among these social workers (Jensen, 2010). The following is selected to shorten the narrative, omitting digressions. Translation and selection were done by the author. Here he tells about working with a girl, Jeanett, who was 16 years old when the narrative starts. Jeanett's parents are drug addicts, and social service is worried and decides to place her in residential care, where Hans meets her:

> So Jeanett came here.... The police had found her and put her directly into the car of the social worker from the municipality,[1] and she had then driven her to our institution...and you in fact meet a girl with her arms twisted at her back...and very angry...very resistant to what is going to happen and away from her town and context...where she in a way had been doing okay.

Together with a female social worker, Hans and Jeanett immediately drive off to stay for a week in a rented weekend cottage to initiate the pedagogical treatment. On the drive, Hans starts talking to Jeanett:

> I tell Jeanett that I can see she is weary and angry, and I can understand that... that I hope it isn't me she is angry at because I am just part of the institution and shall try to help her, and I hope we can establish something in cooperation.... I know she won't trust me at first, and it is okay if she will try me out.

The first evening, their dialogue develops:

> It doesn't take long before she starts talking with me.... She tells some stories from her context... now let's see if she is reliable.... One of the first stories is that she has participated in stealing a car and driving it through town.... "Can you drive a car?" "Yes, sure she can." I didn't know the girl, and we were in this empty weekend-cottage area, and I say let's go driving now.[2] She looks at me. Sure, she says, and we changed sides, and Jeanett went out and started the car and backed out of the driveway and then she drove a tour with me... so I thought all her stories, there is some truth in them.... I remember she said to me that evening, "You are a strange person, Hans," and I ask, "What do you mean?", and she says she had never before experienced any social worker who....
>
> Another topic: one of the first things I said to her was, "Jeanett, there is no doubt as I have been told by the social worker that at first chance you would like to run off to go back to your hometown. You think it is unfair you have been removed... and so on... so please promise me one thing so I can sleep better at night. If you want to run off, then wake me up and I will drive you to the train station, I promise you. And then you will have some hours off, and I will have to call the municipality and tell them: Jeanett ran off. There is no reason to do something stupid. Of course, I will try to convince you to stay so we can establish something together, but I won't hold you back. I will help you to the train, but you know what it means: You will be hunted again."

Hans continues to state his opinion on pedagogical treatment exemplified by the story of Jeanett:

> Another point that I think is important is—I think it is extremely important that I showed a great curiosity to learn about her network and meet them—both her mother, her father, her own friends even though many of them of course acted on the wrong side of the law, but I really wanted to meet her friends... even though the social worker from the municipality had told us not to go to her hometown. But I thought if I am going to work with Jeanett, then I have to go and see what she is telling me about.

> I think already when we returned from the weekend cottage and she started to show interest in me and started to trust me, then I said, "Let's go to your hometown." It was extremely exciting. Then I told Jeanett that I thought she should have a couple of hours on her own, and I would sit down and drink a cup of coffee and she could go around. I thought it should be tried out—could I make a deal with her or couldn't I? And she kept her part. After two hours, she came back, and we could return and talk about her town and friends.

Jeanett stayed at the place for two years, started an education, and cooperated well. When she finely moved from the institution and back to her hometown, the municipality decided that a social worker there should take over, and Hans was off the case. Within the first year, she dropped out of her education. In this case, the perception Jeanett has of Hans changes from unambiguous to ambiguous to certain and her feelings from negative to ambivalent to positive, so what enables these changes?

CASE 2

This case is based on the author's own participation in social-pedagogical treatment as a social worker. It is written several years after the work was carried out but discussed with and confirmed by colleagues from that period.

> Kris is 17 years old and comes from an institution specialized in children suffering from severe neglect and sociopathic traits. He is a merry fellow and always active, but he lacks forethought and has very low self-esteem. He participates in the craftsman work at the place rebuilding the house, but when he ends a task, he just drops the tools, and later on he cannot remember where he left them. He often gets creative ideas and tries them out without considering consequences, which sometimes creates dangerous situations. After a year at the place with almost no changes in his behavior, supervision is organized, where social workers and Kris meet once a week with the supervisor. Here they list episodes during the previous week, where Kris succeeded in doing what was agreed on (doing his duties, remembering to put things back in place after use, etc.). Kris starts by denying that there have been any episodes to report, but the social workers supply some examples. They are counted and kept for next week. Next week there are a few more positive episodes, and this continues for 5 to 6 weeks with growing success. Then Kris "breaks down," crashes all the furniture in his room, and refuses to participate. After a couple of days, Kris agrees to start again counting episodes. This cycle repeats four to five times with no changes and no progress in any direction, and the institution gives up when he turns 18 and can decide to leave if he wants (due to legislation in Denmark).

The supervisor interprets the problem as Kris becoming very anxious as soon as he starts to hope for some change for the better and realize that he maybe can do something active in his own life. This feeling is too threatening.

ANALYSIS

Case 1 is an example of ambivalent feelings and one way of handling them. Jeanett surely had negative feelings when arriving at the place, but there is nothing indicating they were ambivalent. On the contrary, it sounds as if they are clear-cut negative. Nevertheless, Hans succeeds in changing them to ambivalent feelings, which opens up the opportunity to "give him a chance" and finally establish cooperation for the next couple of years. Given the background that Jeanett had, the accompanying experiences, and the situation in which she was moved to the institution, it is only reasonable if she does not trust Hans. At this stage of the treatment, he can only be "an adult from the system who removed her from her parents and her childhood world." What is done, first of all, is to establish a close context in the summer cottage, where they have plenty of time to interact. Then Hans acts in ways that do not fit Jeanett's expectations: He admits her right to be weary and angry because of the situation she is in, and he trusts her when she tells him stories of her experiences, such as having tried to drive a car. In the last case, he "tries her out" by letting her drive the car, which is clearly illegal and therefore unexpected behavior from "an adult from the system." Apparently as a consequence, the first evening she says, "You are a strange person Hans."

From the beginning, the situation is seen as fixed and negative from Jeanett's perspective, but Hans succeeded in changing it to ambivalent, so although Jeanett presumably wants to return to her hometown and parents, she nevertheless stays because Hans "is different." Because of this ambivalence, she gives him a chance to influence her development, or you could say Jeanett finds the ambivalence so attractive that she postpones her flight.

RUPTURES

Kadianaki and Gillespie (2015) analyze how social representations (Marková, 2003; Moscovici, 2001) change in relation to self-reflection and in this outline four kinds of alterity that make it clear that the hitherto used social representation has to be changed. The point is that some kind of rupture appears and demonstrates the need to develop the social representation that more or less unnoticed has supported your way of understanding and handling your life world up until now. The four kinds of alterity are:

1. Rupture with the physical world (alterity in action), where the physical or social world does not conform to your representations.
2. Social contact (alterity in other), where other people have different understandings that do not fit your representations.
3. Movement between contexts (alterity in self), where you experience yourself differently in different contexts and become aware of these differences.
4. Semiotic dialogicality (alterity in the structure of knowledge), where dialogue with established knowledge in society reveal differences from your previous representations.

This is related to the development of self-reflection, but if we parallel to Jeanett's social representation of "adults from the system," she experiences Hans as acting differently from expected. This makes her wonder whether he is worth relying on and maybe cooperating with to achieve something in the future. It could be seen as "alterity in action," which shows alternative patterns of interaction and thereby different representations of both "adults from the system" and herself. Through the dialogue with Hans, starting in the car on their way to the summer cottage, she is confronted with understandings different from her own—"alterity in other." Beyond the first week, you can see the different context at the institution as the third kind of rupture. Here the pedagogues and other adolescents interact with her in a way where Jeanett experiences herself in new ways, which demonstrates new possibilities in her self-understanding—"alterity in self"—and this can be supported by physical facilities at the institution that enable new activities. Along the way, she might meet new perspectives on experiences in her life as understood by professionals in the municipality, and so on—rupture of the fourth kind through "alterity in the structure of knowledge." She has no doubt met ruptures of this kind before, so the crucial point is how to ensure that these ruptures are allowed to influence her understanding.

All four kinds of ruptures did in fact change the situation from a fixed understanding to an ambiguous situation. The representation of "adults from the system" as one homogenous category became changed because Hans was different, and Jeanett's self-representation had to be changed because she managed to do reasonable in school. At least in the first period, this must have been an ambivalent experience for Jeanett.

In case 2, Kris has a fixed understanding of himself and his abilities to influence his own life. In fact, he has given up learning and becoming better at doing what adults expect of him. The introduction of a simple system of counting his successful behavior becomes a rupture that enables a more ambivalent self-representation. He finds this so attractive that he starts trying to change. Hoping to become better is, however, also threatening because he can fail, and his own understanding and memory of his life tells him that he will. This threat becomes unbearable, and he withdraws from the activity of making statistics. Still he finds the ambivalent feeling of possible changes so attractive that he agrees to try again—and again.

An important point is that Hans showed a genuine interest in Jeanett and her experiences, and he even joined her visiting "her world." On several occasions later in their cooperation, he supported her in opposition to the social worker at the municipality and her teachers at school. They established what I have called a social-pedagogical fellowship, where together they handled her life, and gradually she could take over by herself. He not only acted as a more or less distanced professional, but he related to her as one person to another. In the Danish social-pedagogical tradition, this is conceptualized as a distinction between being professional, personal, or private (Hämäläinen, 2012; Jappe, 2010; Smith, 2012). You should, of course, be professional by having an overview and a long-term perspective on the development of the adolescent, but this is not enough. To make the adolescent engaged in the cooperation, you have to be personal—you have to relate to and engage with him as one person to the other and not just performing a professional role. However, you should not involve the adolescent in your private life or let your private life influence your professional work. This point is evident when talking to the adolescents, where characterizing somebody as "being pedagogical"—that is, acting in a (stereotypical) role of a professional pedagogue—is almost the worst adjective you can use.

Hans is aware that he had an interest in getting to know Jeanett's world, and during the whole interview, you get the impression that maybe this curiosity sometimes dominated his work and influenced some of his decisions—he maybe became too private. However, it is certain that this curiosity strengthened the fellowship between Jeanett and Hans, and he states that he saw it as necessary that he knew about her hometown and friends to cooperate with her. Jeanett had a knowledge and competence that he needed when working in the social-pedagogical fellowship. Later in the interview, Hans compares the situation with working at a children's home, where they have rules and regulations for acting in every situation, and he quickly finds this boring. He enjoys the work with Jeanett partly because he likes her (being personal) and partly because he ends up in several situations he would otherwise not have experienced, and he then has to find some solution to these. For Hans, the work is exciting because it puts him in situations he does not anticipate in advance, and they raise challenges for which he has to develop solutions. It is then important to balance the professional interest in constraints and situations of importance with the pedagogical treatment and not let private interests and curiosity take over.

TRUST

Zittoun (2014) describes and analyzes a process in teaching literature at the high school level where she focuses on the influence of trust on both the process and outcome of teaching. Trust is seen here "as a form of belief in the positive outcome of a commitment toward another person or another agent" (Zittoun, 2014, p. 128). She makes some useful distinctions—between relational and epistemic trust, where relational trust is a more general interpersonal trust in line with the definition mentioned. Epistemic trust concerns teaching and is divided in monologic and dialogic epistemic trust. The monologic trust is based on the relations of power, where the teacher is placed in an institution and position that leaves him with power to decide how the knowledge taught must be understood. The dialogic trust is based on a belief from the students that the teacher is able and willing to help them achieve the knowledge in question. Zittoun and colleagues make interviews and analyze classroom situations and for this purpose use an operational definition of showing trust from Lahno where "a person is showing trusting behavior or behavioral trust, if she (he) is making herself (himself) vulnerable to the actions of another person" (Zittoun, 2014, p. 136). From their observations, they describe a possible sequence in establishing and handling trust in the relationship between the teacher and students, where the teacher starts by telling how a text moved the teacher while still stressing that the students are different and must judge by themselves how the text influences them. Using this method, the teacher makes herself vulnerable to the students, and this communicates trust in them as does the emphasis that they must judge by themselves. This sequence stresses relational trust, which again facilitates a dialogical epistemic trust to be established.

In pedagogical treatment, you do not have the same element of curriculum, but you can still parallel at least part of the process. During the drive to the summer cottage in case 1, Hans appeals for establishing some kind of trust to start cooperation with Jeanett, but maybe the turning point is when he trusts her story about driving a car. He even makes himself vulnerable because he encourages her to do something illegal—driving the car in the deserted summer-cottage area. If she now or later wants to hurt him, she could mention this to the social worker at the municipality, and she would probably be moved somewhere else. This reciprocity continues because several times he does things such as visiting her hometown, which they both know he is not allowed to formally do. So she starts entrusting him to influence her future life, which can be understood as dialogically epistemic trust. To combine the concepts introduced here, he presents alterity in making himself vulnerable, which is not the way social workers normally act, and he does this in a nonthreatening way showing trust in her.

In case 2, the element of trust is different. The social workers show trust in Kris by participating and finding successful cases from the latest week, but they do not establish trust by making themselves vulnerable. Because they see the experience of success as exclusively positive, they do not see the need for extra support and trust needed by Kris because of this ambivalent feeling of emerging hope for change. He is left alone and does not have the necessary trust in himself. You could say that he needed dialogic epistemic trust—trusting that the social workers could help him manage the changing self-representation—but they did not manage to establish this trust.

Linell and Marková (2014) and Allwood (2014) point to the layered structure of trust. Beneath all interaction, we normally trust people to act in more or less predictable ways, which in itself is a level of trust, never mind whether the person is friendly or evil. Trust is not a dichotomy that is present or not but rather layered, so we should talk about what kind of trust is present. This fits well with Zittoun's (2014) different kinds of trust in teaching. In case 1, Hans is able to establish a tight and trustful social-pedagogical fellowship that even balances on the edge of becoming too private. In case 2, Kris cannot handle the ambivalent feeling of possible changes by himself, and the social workers have not established a social-pedagogical fellowship strong enough to convinnce him that they can handle these new challenges in cooperation, even though he has a clear experience that they like him. There is a general relational trust, but it is not developed to the level of a dialogical epistemic trust.

Cornejo, Tejero-Gonzalez, Sallis, & Veiga (2014) reflect on the relation between reflection and trust, where he sees reflection not as establishing trust but rather as necessary when trust ends or is limited. Then there is a need for reflection on how much you can trust the other person and in which contexts. If we analyze case 1 in relation to this, you could also say that reflection ends distrust. Jeanett had a fixed opinion on adults who are part of the system, but she experiences something with Hans, which makes her reflect: "You are a strange person Hans." This reflection is connected with the ambivalent feeling that replaces her fixed opinion. It may be more correct to state that reflection appears when alterity is experienced, and this raises the need for creating a new understanding or explanation through reflection. Reflection appears when the value or field of validity of trust and distrust is changed. Ambivalence can sometimes be seen as uncertainty about whom and what to trust in which connections and can initiate reflection to settle this topic. In the second case, even establishing a common reflection on progress is not enough to convey sufficient trust.

WHEN IS AMBIGUITY AND AMBIVALENCE ATTRACTIVE?

In the beginning of the chapter, ambiguity was connected with the perceptive-cognitive processes alone and seen as neutral. In contrast, ambivalence was defined as an experience of mixed feelings or changing reactions in similar situations, of conflict between different motives for actions or a situation of indecision. The ambivalent aspect or element is the different force experienced, which precludes handling the situation through routine actions. This is why ruptures connect to ambivalence: When ruptures in routines occur, you have to consider and decide, but if it is not possible to make a clear decision, you experience ambivalence. This need not be negatively perceived but could be an opportunity or interesting challenge. Whether it is perceived as such or as a stressor depends on the intentionality of the person and conditions such as feeling of security and surplus.

In this definition, I do not necessarily see ambivalence as negative. You could restrict the concept of ambivalence to experiences such as feeling discomfort and then use ambiguity as an overarching concept, but then ambiguity must also include emotional aspects to handle the positive experience of ambiguous perception. Then we may lack a concept of the more purely perceptive-cognitive description of empirical data being potentially perceived and interpreted in different ways only because it is not clearly specified. I prefer to keep ambiguous to this phenomenon and discard the negative association from ambivalence. Characterizing ambivalence in this way, it becomes closely connected to development and learning. In both cases, ambivalence occurs when ruptures establish a possibility for change, but several factors influence the outcome.

As mentioned in the beginning of the chapter, attachment theory describes a balance between a secure base and exploring the world (Bowlby, 1969/1997). Transferred to case 1 mentioned earlier, a balance allows Jeanett to leave her fixed conception of social workers as antagonists and be open for an ambivalent feeling of a possible new understanding of Hans being different and reliable. Of course she will maintain the old conception and see Hans as an exception, but the appearance of an exception creates the ambivalence. The challenge for Hans is to introduce this possibility in a way that simultaneously establishes enough feeling of security for Jeanett to give her the surplus to explore this new possibility. In other words, he has to introduce ambivalence in a nonthreatening way that makes her trust in the social-pedagogical fellowship. In case 2, Kris is attracted to the ambivalence and its promising possibilities, but the social workers do not manage to establish the sufficient trust, and therefore he cannot benefit from the ambivalence and withdraws.

Shifting to the perspective of Hans, the social worker in the first case, he states that he likes to meet Jeanett's friends and experience her hometown. This also puts him in several situations that imply ambivalence. In fact, one of them did turn out to be life threatening when they helped her mother get rid of a drug dealer. When he compares this job with the children's home, where he worked for a period, he prefers a job where unforeseen challenges appear; he finds routine work, where everything is arranged by rules in advance, boring. This could be interpreted as characterizing a prerequisite for social workers in this field: They need a well-developed secure base to manage the exploration of adolescents' life-world. This work implies unforeseen situations, and to be attracted by ambivalent situations is beneficial.

Ambiguity can be seen as implying a possibility for development because it enables new ways of perceiving and interpreting. For Jeanett, the opportunity for development comes through changing a fixed conceptualization to an ambiguous one: Social workers are sometimes worth trusting. This must imply ambivalence toward social workers, and ambivalence is not necessarily negative. Likewise, Hans seems to prefer challenges instead of routine, and thus seeking ambivalent situations becomes positive. Whether ambivalence is negative seems to depend on personal preferences and sufficient feeling of security. For Kris, this did not succeed. We could add that this might change in time because sometimes even social workers can be worn out by workload, private problems, organizational stress, and so on, and then they might have less surplus for challenges, and there might also be individual differences in which challenges they feel comfortable with. We cannot judge a single isolated situation because the perception and interpretation of this situation is a figure understood on the background of the personal history of the person and the rest of their life-world.

POSTSCRIPT

This chapter could have a more general interest concerning intergenerational relations. In contemporary Denmark, we have a diversity of family forms following from divorces and new marriages. Thus, adults meet a demand for forming relationships with the children of their partner whom they chose because of her or him but maybe not or despite the children, and at least the children seldom are the ones who made the choice. Both adult and child have different conditions for forming these relationships than in biological parenthood, which is somewhat similar to the contingencies in social-pedagogical treatment.

NOTES

1. In Denmark, we have two different educations in social work: one for pedagogical work in kindergarten, social institutions, psychiatry, and so on called

a pedagogue, and another for more administrative work at social offices at municipality. Both are at the bachelor level.

2. The age to get a driving license in Denmark is 18 years.

REFERENCES

Abbey, E., & Valsiner, J. (2005). Emergence of meanings through ambivalence. *Forum Qualitative Sozialforschung/Forum: Qualitative Social Research, 6*(1).

Allwood, C. M. (2014). On the issue of an appropriate culture concept for the indigenous psychologies and on the limits of philosophy. *Social Epistemology Review and Reply Collective, 3*(3), 41–48.

Bowlby, J. (1969/1997). *Attachment and loss* (vols. 1–3). London, England: Random House.

Bruner, J. (1990). *Acts of meaning.* Cambridge, MA: Harvard University Press.

Carr, A. (2006). *The handbook of child and adolescent clinical psychology* (2nd ed.). London, England: Routledge.

Cornejo, I., Tejero-Gonzalez, C. M., Sallis, J. F., & Veiga, O. L. (2014). Physical activity and cognition in adolescents: A systematic review. *Journal of Science and Medicine in Sport, 18*(5), 534–539.

Fischer, K. W., Ayoub, C., Singh, I., Noam, G., Maraganore, A., & Raya, P. (1997). Psychopathology as adaptive development along distinctive pathways. *Development and Psychopathology, 9,* 749–779.

Gustavsson, A., Hermansson, H.-E., & Hämäläinen, J. (Eds.). (2003). *Perspectives and theory in social pedagogy.* Göteborg: Daidalos.

Hämäläinen, J. (2012). Social pedagogical eyes in the midst of diverse understandings, conceptualisations and activities. *International Journal of Social Pedagogy, 1*(1), 3–16.

Jappe, E. (2010). *Håndbog for pædagogstuderende* [Guide for pedagogue-students]. Copenhagen: Frydenlund.

Jensen, M. (2010). *Det ufærdige arbejde* [The never-ending work]. Unpublished PhD dissertation, Aalborg University.

Jensen, M. (2011). Socialpædagogisk behandlingsarbejde [Social-pedagogical treatment]. *Tidsskrift for Socialpædagogik, 27,* 3–10.

Jensen, M. (2015). Catalytic models developed through social work. *Integrative Psychology and Behavioral Science, 49,* 56–72.

Kadianaki, I., & Gillespie,A. (2015). Alterity and the transformation of social representations: A sociocultural account. *Integrative Psychology and Behavioral Science, 49,* 73–88.

Lave, J. (1988). *Cognition in practice.* Cambridge, England: Cambridge University Press.

Linell, P., & Marková, I. (2014). *Dialogical approaches to trust in communication.* Charlotte, NC: Information Age.

Marková, I. (2003). *Dialogicality and social representations.* Cambridge, England: Cambridge University Press.

Mathiesen, R. (1999). *Sosialpedagogisk perspektiv* [Socialpedagogical perspective]. Norge: Sokrates AS.

Moscovici, S. (2001). *Social representations.* New York, NY: New York University Press.
Rasmussen, J. (1986). *Information processing and human-machine interaction.* New York, NY: North Holland.
Rothbaum, F., Weisz, J. R., & Snyder, S. S. (1982). Changing the world and changing the self: A two-process model of perceived control. *Journal of Personality and Social Psychology, 42*(1), 5–37.
Schön, D. (1983). *The reflective practitioner.* London, England: Temple Smith.
Smith, M. (2012). Social pedagogy from a scottish perspective. *International Journal of Social Pedagogy, 1*(1), 46–55.
Valsiner, J. (2007). *Culture in minds and societies.* New Delhi: SAGE.
Zittoun, T. (2014). Trusting for learning. In P. Linell & I. Markova (Eds.), *Dialogical approaches to trust in communication* (pp. 125–151). Charlotte, NC: Information Age.

CHAPTER 13

YOUR DUTY TOWARD MY RIGHT

Ambivalent Traps of Rights and Duties

Kevin R. Carriere
Georgetown University

A semiotic cultural psychology, a theoretical perspective applied in a multitude of chapters within this book, has at its core a perplexing problem—that of methodology (Valsiner, 2014). Cultural psychology attempts to explain the everyday meaning-making of an individual(s) through the examination of the signs and symbols constructed at a moment for a certain goal yet struggles to clarify ways to observe the theory and provide replicable developments. Although we provide theoretically rich, idiographic examinations of the individual's life course, the lack of clear methodological tools causes us to grow horizontally in knowledge, but risks us from developing our knowledge in higher order, building block-like theoretical developments.

A potential route to solve this lack of repeatability around a semiotic cultural psychology is placing our methodology around a given set of tools and activities. One proposed methodological tool has been examining the individual's use of mechanisms that manipulate and drive semiotic regulators,

Trans-Generational Family Relations, pages 263–279

catalyzers, and signs to a certain goal (Cabell, 2011; Carriere, 2013). In each moment, the individual must construct not only what is important and present in their life at that given moment. The generative process of sign creation and destruction is continuously generated toward the future by the functionality of semiotic mechanisms. These mechanisms allow individuals to make meaning through the use of regulators and catalyzers to build, speed, or slow the meaning-making process. Semiotic regulators are intramental devices that are actively used toward building a given psychological mechanism, whereas a catalyzer provides the support and conditions necessary for certain mechanisms and processes to be available. Catalysts are employed as a way to overcome the ambivalence of a situation through enabling the production of new meanings by using a given mechanism in a different, unique, or otherwise novel way.

Imagine a child faced with a large group of friends who are all taking candy from the teacher's desk when the teacher is not around. This child, who has lived his life by a variety of rules and regulations, carries with him a social norm that says, in some degree, "People like it when you follow the group." The child is faced with two choices: (a) not steal the candy and be shamed by others for not following the group's decision, or (b) steal the candy and feel ashamed for not following a secondary rule taught by his parents to not steal. The child is trapped—both ways seem to lead to poor outcomes, yet to not steal is seemingly worse—immediate punishments are present to not following the group. The regulators present (here, the social norms) may be heightened or reduced in strength by the catalysts (here, the peers surrounding the child, the hunger of the child). Once we have established a formulation of how a mechanism of the meaning of candy stealing may occur in one individual, we can move beyond simply other cookie stealers toward car thieves, money launderers, and broken hearts.

In what follows, I will take a proposed model of semiotic traps (Cabell, 2011) and examine it through the family interactions of rights and duties. I will first outline the proposed mechanism of a semiotic trap—its structure, function, and where we can see some clear extensions. Next, I will use rights and duties within the family as a unique arena in which a semiotic trap may occur. I will show how the ambivalence created by a semiotic trap (such as the guilt associated with seeing dirty dishes while the child wants to play games instead) can lead toward its eventual downfall of the trap (they aren't so dirty after all! They aren't my dishes anyway). In doing so, I will discuss examples in which overcoming such guilt requires further ambivalence (a duty-based trap) or requires reducing ambivalence (a rights-based trap). I will show that the methodological power of a mechanistically based cultural psychology does a fair job at tracking and explaining the development of family norms and issues across generations.

Semiotic Traps "If All Your Friends Jumped Off the Cliff, Would You Too?"

Of course the statement is preposterous. Who would willingly jump off a bridge because of peer pressure! Yet the necessity to ask the question (even if rhetorical) recognizes that choices are not simply decided by the individual. The parent recognizes that the child has a full range of choices available to him. He can do what his friends are doing, he could not, or he could do some other thing that is neither here nor there (tie yourself to a bungee cord prior to jumping, jump with a parachute, or jump up but not off the cliff). One may feel restricted in one's choices because of peer pressure or other symbolic meanings. This is the definition of a semiotic trap—where an individual feels strongly due to an imagined violation of a social norm, which ultimately leads him to engage in a directed action because of the restricted choices from the violation (Cabell, 2011). The child, faced with the idea that people will like him more if he does what others are doing while faced with the pressure of not wanting to do it, feels restricted on the peer pressure and engages in the undesirable action. To escape these traps, an individual must circumvent the violation with redefining the situation. A trap could be cast on oneself (suicidal thoughts) or onto others to guilt trip them into a certain action.

At this present moment, the child must make a decision between A (not steal the candy) and B (steal the candy) (see Figure 13.1). If the individual chooses to not steal the candy, the movement toward A′ falls in contrast

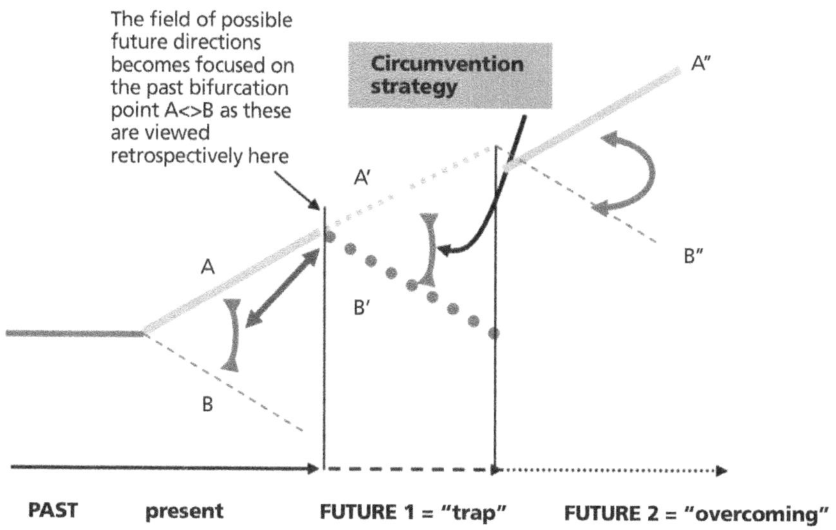

Figure 13.1 The semiotic trap.

with the generalized rule (but everyone else is stealing). This can cause conflict with the child, and the pressure may be enough to persuade the individual to reconsider B′ (I should steal the candy in the next moment) as the better decision. The reversal in this way—where B′ becomes the more highly preferred action compared to A in the past, causes an "affective capture," in which the individual feels badly because of the discrepancy (see Future 1). To escape the trap (in which B′ has taken importance over A′ and A), one must create a circumvention strategy (Josephs & Valsiner, 1998) to re-create the dominance of A″ to B″ (Future 2). If an individual fails to properly provide themselves with a relevant circumvention strategy, they may continue to B″ and continue to steal, continuing to fall to the trap of their social networks.

To summarize, a semiotic trap is a mechanism by which an individual deals with the tension of facing some kind of symbolic imperative (you should do X) and the recognition of violating this imperative (but I am not doing X, and I do not want to do it but I feel I should). In feeling trapped within this tension, the individual can only imagine a limited set of actions in which to resolve the tension—either taking part in the should or reasoning the should away (but I am different, so I should not).

One can examine semiotic traps as a type of societal structuring to move individuals toward a socially appropriate action at the border of A and B, A′ and B′, or A″ and B″. Truly, it is the ambivalence of the future borders to come—the acknowledgment of the discrepancy between A and B′—that creates, maintains, and permits the trap to occur. The discrepancy is caused by the child wanting to not steal (as he was brought up—A) but deciding to steal anyway (B′). This action must be dealt with—there is cognitive dissonance present in what the child wanted and what the child did. Hence, the child says, "But everyone else was!" in an attempt to escape this guilt—it was not that he wanted to do B′ but felt it was necessary to act B′. The agency of the action is taken away from the child, and he can try and avoid the guilt and see a future where A″ will occur (even if he continues to fail).

THE AMBIVALENCE OF SEMIOTIC TRAPS

Ambivalence is incongruence in attitudes (Priester & Petty, 2001), where uncertainty arises with acknowledgment of counteracting feelings toward the object—not necessarily opposing but with some differentiation in the strength and direction of the feelings (Abbey & Valsiner, 2005). Within traps, there is a socially demanded action that one does not wish to do (but should) and one action that one wishes to do (but feels guilty for doing). In short, semiotic traps require ambivalence to function—the ambivalence created by the A–B′ differentiation of the action taken (or the soon-to-be-taken action).

The Necessity of Ambivalence Between Meanings

However, this acknowledgment brings up an important point—ambivalence is required for the trap to exist. The ambivalence between what the meaning or action should be and what an individual accepts it to be allows for divergent accounts and understandings of the signs in play. If the individual rejects the social should be meaning from the start ("I will do A because A is the right way"), then there is no ambivalence between B and A′ because we do not allow for B to have the opportunity to emerge stronger than A′. If there is no active acknowledgment of B (perhaps I do not recognize I could even do B in this instance, I am unaware of the social norms that demand B, or I simply reject B), then there is no semiotic trap.

Who Is the Trapper?

Because the trap requires an acknowledgment from the trappee ("Yes, B is truly what society desires of me"), the trap can be ignored as well as reversed. When we examine the beggar, the beggar tries to evoke pity and remind us of our duty to take care of those less fortunate. In doing so, the beggar tries to place a trap, in which, while you may not wish to give money to another person, you feel guilty for his situation and remember your duty exists, and by not giving you are ignoring that duty. Yet some U.S. politicians are quick to disregard this group, blaming them for problems and making them feel bad for their own existence to extreme degrees (Itkowitz, 2015). Here, what started as duty to serve less fortunate quickly transitions toward a right to a homeless-free city—even at drastic consequences. In this way, the politician tries to set the trap back toward the homeless person: "You should feel guilty for being homeless, as it runs against our desire for a homeless-free society." The trap's ambivalent nature presents the risk of being flipped back to the first caster. The mother who attempts to punish the child faces the defense of, "You didn't tell me not to do that, it's your fault!"

Applications of Trapping

We have outlined two main ways in which semiotic traps are ambivalent in their existence and, with that, two places in which semiotic traps provide interesting room for exploration. First, a trap exists only if an individual is willing to engage with the trap. This provides an opportunity to examine both situations in which traps may set but also situations in which traps do not set (but were meant to). More so, it forces us to recognize that the individual must in some way be willing to be trapped, if only for a moment, by allowing the social norm to influence his decision-making process. Second, semiotic traps, by virtue of being interactive with trapper and trappee, are quick to develop and change targets. We can easily see multiple iterations of semiotic trapping within the confines a family, forced to continually negotiate ambivalent interpretations of rights and duties.

For a family, rights and duties offer a semblance of clarity—a rulebook for what an individual should and should not do. This guidance of desired action potentially traps the individual toward a certain course of action and restricts his meaning-making toward alternative actions. When an individual challenges the border of desired action and attempts to break free of the trap, he challenges the structure of the system of rights and duties within the family.

In what follows, I will apply the discussed mechanism of a semiotic trap toward rights and duties within the family. First, I will outline the general ideas of rights and duties. Next, I will argue that their existence in a family is inherently ambivalent and provides the ability for semiotic traps to emerge. Finally, I will show how introducing further ambivalences deconstructs the semiotic trap by redefining the roles of rights and duties within the family.

RIGHTS AND DUTIES

Historical

History, particularly the last century, has revealed a human transition inward in Western societies (Finkel & Moghaddam, 2005; Lasch, 1979), moving further away from group ideals and medieval notions of fealty and moved toward personal achievements and strength. In 1948, The United Nations released the Universal Declaration of Human Rights (not duties), which defined the equal and unalienable rights due to all individuals. Throughout the document, duties are only mentioned once: "Everyone has duties to the community in which alone the free and full development of his personality is possible" (Universal Declaration of Human Rights, 1948). Otherwise, the focus, even within the family, is on rights (specifically, see Articles 12, 16, 25, and 26 for family-based rights). It seems strange, in many ways, to focus so highly on rights. We raise our children to be obedient to their parents, elders, and teachers. We raise them to be dutiful to their parents (e.g., the Ten Commandments: Honor your mother and your father) and to revere the State (with memorizing the nation's song or pledge). We impress the notions of community and that we should always take care of our grandparents or parents as they get older. Yet still the Declaration of Human Rights solidified the acknowledgment of a cultural paradigm shift of rights over duties. Research has followed this trend, with a larger focus on rights than duties (Moghaddam, 2015). With protests in Ferguson, migrants from Syria, and riots in Baltimore all taking place within the same year, rights, freedoms, and responsibilities are striking at the heart of our conversations in the United States and Europe. Yet beyond the mesolevel issues is a more pressing, microlevel issue—that of the rights, responsibilities, and freedoms within the family.

Family Life

For the family life, meaning-making occurs through a continuous overlapping of intergenerational systems. It is impossible to acknowledge the meaning-making of the individual without factoring in the individuals that molded them. The parents who define the rules for the child to obey are at the same time restricted to enforce the rules they set out. The child, faced with the rules, must decide which rules to challenge and which to obey, not simply for the present moment but for the moments in the yet-to-come future. Within this negotiation of social norms, meaning is being exchanged, accepted, and defined in a constant cycle of interaction and identification of uncertainty in the family unit.

One can examine rights and duties through rules of the house—cleaning a room, staying out too late, eating all of their vegetables, providing for the family. These everyday rights and duties are key elements of development, moving the child from a world of duties slowly toward a world of rights (Moghaddam & Riley, 2005). Yet the development of the child's duties is contingent on the development of the rights—a responsibility for a car can only be given if the child has the right to drive but at the same time is dependent on a prior duty to pass the driving test. In general, it has been argued that all rights have an a priori duty, but not all duties have a priori rights (Finkel & Moghaddam, 2005). These constructs guide action by teaching and instructing an individual what one should or should not do (and could or could not do). They provide boundaries of appropriate action within a dialogue between two persons. Their border construction and maintenance is not simply the individual acting on a border of what I want to do but also the consequences for taking (or not taking) such an action based on what the other would expect or want.

Rights and Duties Are Inherently Ambivalent

The negotiation of rights and duties is an arena of ambivalence, where one strives for more rights but at the same time must be willing to take an addition of duties with regard to those rights. Rights are inherently ambiguous—I have the right to swing my fist, but it ends where the other man's face begins. My duty to pay my taxes informs me exactly how much of my paycheck I have the right to spend, and my duty to not harm others outlines how far my arm can swing. Rights are designed in such a way as to allow for unpredictability, whereas duties are designed to instill predictability (Worchel, 2005). However, that is not always the case. When the government decides that the parents's duty is to provide an education for their children, whose duty is it to enforce? Which choices do the parent, or other individuals involved have in this duty? Although it solves one ambiguity (how many of our children receive education), it creates many more (where, how long, how much).

THE TRAP OF RIGHTS AND DUTIES

The action taken at the border of social norms, from what I want to do versus what I should do, creates the conditions necessary for a semiotic trap. The semiotic trap can be used to examine the development, maintenance, and future orientations of ambivalences of rights and duties. Both rights and duties are semiotic traps in their own way. Duties are more obvious of a semiotic trap, so they will be examined first.

Duties as a Semiotic Trap

If the child should decide to cross the border into the zone of inappropriate actions (and disregard his prior duty), then he is quickly met with a new problem—that of generally "feeling bad" for his actions (see Figure 13.2). In the case of the beggar, where we must face the tension between our duty to help with our action of not providing money, emerges a duties-based trap. The duty-based trap, in its simplest form, defines an area of promoted action and tries to evoke guilty feelings when one crosses (or even considers crossing) the boundary into arenas of nonpromotion. To escape such a trap, one must employ some means to circumvent the trap. Here, an increase in the ambivalence of B′ ("It was not my duty to do X, it was yours!" or "I did not have that duty anyway, that duty does not mean to assist in that case.") provides the circumvention strategy to escape the trap.

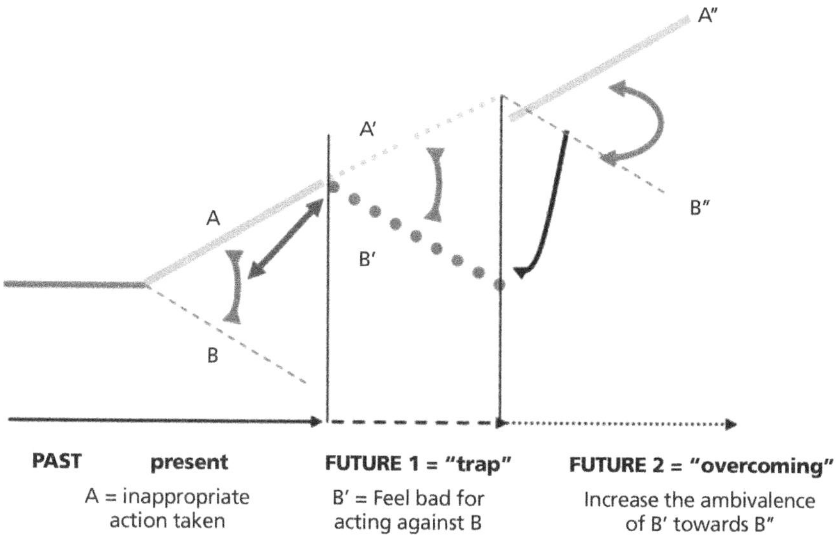

Figure 13.2 A modeled duties-based trap.

Parents have many duties, one of which is to provide for their family through bringing in income. There is opportunity for a new job, but it is unclear whether the parent would get it, and by going after the new job, although it would make him or her happier, risks losing both the current job and also not receiving the new job. Looking toward the future, the parent wants to choose A (the new job) because it would make him or her happier. Yet applying for that new job risks going against the duty to provide, and so instead the parent feels compelled toward the suboptimal B′ (not taking the job). The guilt of risking the family's finances causes tension, and the only way to rationalize out of the ambivalence of B′ (not taking the job) is to either make the decision of B′ more ambivalent (I am staying only because there are chances of promotion that I am not yet aware of) or exceedingly high level, where the parent then says, "But staying is even further risk! I must leave now." Note that decreasing the ambivalence (I stay because the duty is correct) keeps the parent in the suboptimal state.

Rights as a Semiotic Trap

Rights provide the ability to fall into a trap of limited freedom—that while being given the ability to do whatever you would like, the ambivalence on what that describes may inhibit individuals to come up with creative solutions in fear of the uncertain future of retribution. The acknowledgment of new ambivalences (you can do X up to a certain but undefined point) traps the individual through granting them undisclosed responsibilities and undefined new borders of acceptability. Instead of the tension created through the switch from A to B′ in dominance, it is instead the tension created from a not-yet-realized A′, which forces the individual to define a new border of A″ to negotiate the ambivalence provided by allowing B′.

The adolescent, who has spent his life with the knowledge of A (You cannot drive) lives with the understanding that B (You could steal the ca, and then drive) is possible but heavily downregulated. Yet at some point the child is given the right to drive (B′). Now, although B′ exists as a higher order, it is unclear at the outset how far A′ extends. How far, fast, or reckless can the child drive? What additional limitations come with B′? What duties restrict the choices toward B′ now because earlier to the adolescent was restricted so forcefully toward A? This ambivalence, created by the onset of additional duties, as well as the switch from A to B′, could cause the individual to be trapped (see Figure 13.3). If the individual is able to clarify this ambivalence by some means—restricting himself, ignoring all duties, turning the trap on another, and so on—then the trap can be overcome.

Both rights and duties function as potential catalysts for the mechanism of a semiotic trap to take place. This is because both rights and duties prescribe some semblance of a social norm, typically the attached dutyand ambivalence between what is allowed and what is desired or what is not known if allowed or not. The interaction at the border of promoted and decided actions provides the ability for a trap to be attempted. Although we can see

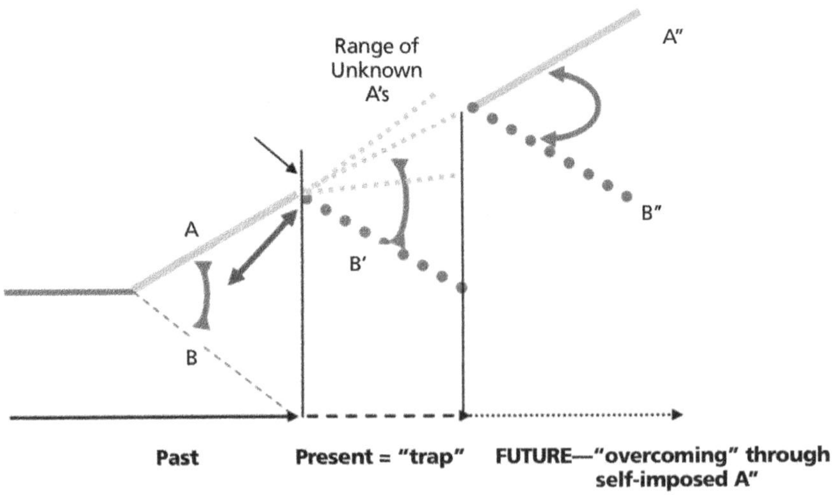

Figure 13.3 The semiotic right-based trap.

how rights and duties trap individuals into desired actions, we still have not accounted for the agency of the individual within a given trap and the agency of the trapper himself.

THE ACCEPTED TRAPS TO COME: AGENCY AND FUTURE-ORIENTEDNESS

A smaller point that should be noted in our discussion of semiotic traps is that of both agency and time. Both are important factors—agency forces us to acknowledge that to be trapped is in part an individual's choosing, whereas the future-orientedness allows us to consider the cost and benefits of a trap now, compared with a trap later.

Traps Are Done With an Individual, Not Toward an Individual

Grandparents are not always visited, children leave their dishes out, and parents punishing their child does not require that they always feel guilty or feel dutiful to provide a child his happiness. Although there are times when semiotic traps simply do not capture our affects and do not function, there are also times in which we prepare ourselves to not be trapped (a prejustification of breaking the given social norm). The soldier who goes to war is given reasons that war is justified to not feel guilty killing others and, in doing so, remains focused during battle. Yet the threat of the trap remains and can have drastic consequences with posttraumatic stress disorder, suicide, and other issues. Because semiotic traps are an everyday occurrence, it is sensible that individuals are able to predict, with an unknown amount of certainty, the likelihood of being trapped by another person. Parents can predict the reaction of their parents when discussing the educational decisions of the grandchild, and the child knows the punishment and guilt he will receive from taking more cookies. This agency of working alongside semiotic traps shows not simply something that is done to an individual (even if that individual is himself), but something that is done with an individual. Ambivalence is used within semiotic traps to both set the trap (Do I do action X?) and escape it (No, because of Y).

Traps Can Be Negotiated Based on Future Possibilities

The simple promise of future rights or duties may lead to restricted positionings. A man may limit his decision to switch jobs, feeling guilty over risking his job security because of his future responsibilities for a child he does not yet have. At the same time, the father may enter into the trap of a new job willingly in the hopes that his decision will be seen as his right to take chances and that everything will end well and provide an even better life. How the father deals with the proposed trap—by increasing ambivalence (this is truly a risk, but that is good) or decreasing it (I have a duty to provide for my family so I will not switch)—both rely on recognition of future not-yet-known outcomes.

They may be willing to endure a certain duty or ambivalent state in the present for a larger payoff in terms of rights and duties in the future. Those who protest in the face of a totalitarian state face extreme levels of ambivalence on the outcomes of their efforts, yet they protest anyway. The child who washes dishes—something he does not wish to do but feels as if he should—does so that he reaps the reward later. In each, the interaction among trapper, trappee, and ambivalence use links together to form how a trap is remembered toward future traps in the near-to-come future.

One fruitful expansion to explore semiotic traps, and all the perceived consequences from the limited choices of action, is within the notion of imagination. Tateo (2015), in a recent special issue on imagination, poses this important consideration of imagination and ambivalence:

> The imaginative process is involved as a source of comparison, suggestions, guidance but also resistance and, finally, self-regulation. The feature of the imaginative semiotic process always elaborates meaning in both linguistic and iconographic forms. In some specific moment in time, you experienced the ambivalence of experiencing ("I can do (or be) it but won't do (or be) it"; "I cannot do (or be) it but will do (or be) it"; "I cannot do and won't do it"; "I can do it and will do it"; "I cannot do it now but..."; I could do it now but..."; "I could do like (someone else) but..."; "I cannot do like (someone else) but...", etc.). (p. 158)

In many ways, we can see the imaginative qualities of a semiotic trap. The trap can occur after an action has taken place—both within duties (It was my duty to not steal, yet I stole) or rights (It was my right to drive, yet perhaps not this far away from home). Yet imagination provides the preaction conditions for traps to occur, be managed, and be circumvented prior to the action. Imagining the future to come—prior to any action—can lead to the same restricted positionings as the action taken. We also rely on imagination to trap others—by imagining the consequences of various courses of action. Further examinations of the imaginative qualities of semiotic traps—how they function, which types of unique, imaginative traps work, if a more concrete-overt trap is stronger or weaker, or how imagination allows us to avoid being trapped—by not becoming restricted in our positioning of further actions all provide new contexts and avenues of research in which the intergenerational relations can be examined.

THE BENEFITS OF A SEMIOTIC TRAP

When the semiotic trap has been discussed in the literature, it is frequently expressed as something negative—"a form of symbolic 'capture' of the other person's self in a web of shame, inferiority, or any other form of showing the trapper's superior relation to the trap" (Valsiner, 2009, pp. 29–30). But what of disgust? We use disgust to help train infants that certain things are bad or dangerous, such as touching their own feces or putting certain things into their mouths. Here, a basic form of a semiotic trap—feeling shame for a certain action—can lead to evolutionary adaptive behavior.

In another form, we frequently view traps as restricting positions, directing action toward one goal instead of another. However, there are times when a restricted amount of choice is actually beneficial and an overabundance of choices can be paralyzing (Schwartz, 2004). Throughout development, children are necessarily scaffolded and guided through decisions they would not be able to make on their own. We are guided—for better or worse—to donate to starving children, buy certain products, and support certain agendas and policies. The ambivalence between choices is mediated for us by the social structure, taking away the trap in favor of a singular route (it is not that you should do B but that you must, and there is no question).

Evidence is growing that these type of traps have become so engrained in the mind of those with less power that they are the most likely to justify the system (Jost, Pelham, Sheldon, & Sullivan, 2003). Understanding how this process of helpless justification occurs, and how it can be turned into engagement against the system, provide researchers with ways to comprehend how family relations against toxic members develops, how familial dependence saturates, and how children act out against the parents but yet remain obedient. Although commonly it is the powerful placing a trap onto the powerless (Your duty was to do the dishes –> You should feel guilty –> You will do the dishes and clean your room), that is not always the case. If a trap is highlighted and brought to light, where one can say, "Look at what they are doing! Look how they restrict our choices through guilt!" movements toward equality, or at least the conversation of how to get there, may start. This is particularly salient in the family setting, where a child continues to press the limits of a certain social norm, to varied success, and continues to challenge the rules and duties the child is forced to follow.

REVIEWING: SEMIOTIC TRAPS WITHIN RIGHTS AND DUTIES

The semiotic trap develops a boundary that demands negotiation between individuals and contexts—between what one wishes to do and what one is expected to do. This tension, which is ambivalent in both its creation and dissolution, directs the individual to act in a given way to negotiate the ambivalence around it. Many of these tensions are created based on the structure or presence of a social norm. If one attempts to circumvent this norm—by either increasing or decreasing the ambivalence on the defined state of such a norm—one may be able to escape the guilty feelings by having solved one's cognitive dissonance. Yet asking an individual to willingly examine and change his position and beliefs regarding norms proves difficult when trying to generate new norms (Castro & Batel, 2008).

Semiotic Traps Function by Constantly Negotiating Social Norms Through Ambivalence

The willingness to take on a new guidance of action is difficult without the full support of the culture to accept and help regulate the expectations of shame and guilt. The border construction and maintenance of a social norm is not simply the individual acting on a border of what I want to do but also the consequences for taking (or not taking) such an action. Social norms, and the institutions that support them, "are active 'semiotic trappers' of human beings for their particular purposes" (Valsiner, 2009, p. 31). The majority of semiotic traps are a function of not the "moral imperatives" that Cabell (2011) defines but instead social norms. Semiotic traps are placed as a second reviewer—guidance for what our culture aspires us to be while affectively punishing us for failures to adhere to the social rules. Although norms are "simultaneously boundary-setting [, the] boundary is the trigger for its overcoming—by way of transformation" (Valsiner, 2009, p. 22). Although some may argue that higher ambivalence-present systems should elicit higher norm-consistent behavior (Gelfand & Harrington, 2015), there seems to be no reason to assume that higher ambivalent systems could not also provide the sufficient conditions for new norm generation. The varied construction, use, and directions of semiotic traps all provide examination of how certain traps functioned in the past, and how their failure or success provides new information in the future. The permeability of the borders of the trap (where at times they succeed and at others we circumvent them) continue to provide an opportunity for novel interactions and meaning constructions of the social norms in play.

INTERGENERATIONAL ISSUES

What does this mean for the generations now and generations to come? How can we understand the relationships among family members? First, semiotic traps provide us with a clearer examination of the developmental trajectories of responsibilities, freedoms, and rules of a family unit. By examining how a semiotic trap functions across time, we can trace its development from an accepted trap toward a challenged trap to finally a redefined or deconstructed trap. This can move our science from a developmental psychology of individuals in relation to structure toward a developmental psychology of structure relating to individuals. It also allows for a historical view of how rights and duties are negotiated in the past and how they develop along with the family. It allows a larger focus on the development of adults as well, focusing on how their meaning-making redevelops from seeking freedoms to gaining significant responsibilities, only to possibly give them up when reaching the elderly age.

This issue is particularly salient as we reflect on the increase in the aging population. When placed in nursing homes or other assisted living situations, it may be critical to reflect on what kinds of traps we are allowing individuals to be placed within. The shift away from independence back toward dependence can cause ambivalence between the past and present (growing up, desiring freedom, gaining responsibilities, now losing personal responsibility and desiring freedom again) and can also cause ambivalence in wanting to see family but being further removed from them. Semiotic traps can be utilized by the elderly to drive their families toward directions they wish (the guilt trip of visitations), but psychologists should look toward using traps to guide our elderly population. By directing their actions toward activities in which they can find consistency and control and giving more independence, psychologists may be able to combat ambivalence about their lives through directed meaning-making.

TOWARD A MECHANISTIC CULTURAL PSYCHOLOGY

I have presented a discussion of how we can extend the notion of semiotic traps (Cabell, 2011) to see how these mechanisms are used not simply to trap an individual toward a certain goal but are used to manage and maintain social norms (such as rights and duties) and continue a cycle of development of those norms across time and generations.

A mechanism-based cultural psychology allows for a clearer understanding of psychological processes. The malleability and flexibility of a well-detailed mechanism allows for the general explanations of a semiotic psychology while also providing chances to deal with ambivalent notions that occur throughout the meaning-making process. Beyond this, mechanisms need to move from person as individual agent toward person as interacting agent, recognizing the I-Other relationship (Lyra, 2014) that is inherent within the process.

This movement toward mechanisms, mediators, and regulators can help move cultural psychology toward a science that is not only observational and theoretical but also able to be tested in experimental situations. Although certain tasks may be harder to evoke within the laboratory setting (how do you create guilt?), it would be interesting to see how individuals make decisions based on a thinking-aloud protocol (Jourdenais, Ota, Stauffer, Boyson, & Doughty, 1995) or to see how rules with regard to economic games are conceptualized by individuals. In cooperation games, the ambivalence between the lack of information and the desire for the group goal in contrast to the individual goal would be an interesting area in which cultural and even intergenerational psychologists could provide insight. Experiments that use everyday notions of rights and duties to see how an individual makes sense of and applies these conceptions would provide useful information to see how these tools are used or ignored in regulating, moderating, and catalyzing new actions and opinions.

REFERENCES

Abbey, E., & Valsiner, J. (2005). Emergence of meanings through ambivalence. *Forum Qualitative Social Research / Forum Qualitative Socialforschung, 6*(1), 1–18.

Cabell, K. R. (2011). *Captured between a rock and a hard place: A cultural psychological analysis of semiotic traps.* Unpublished master's thesis, Clark University.

Carriere, K. R. (2013). Introduction to the Special Issue: Semiotic mechanisms in everyday life. *Psychology & Society, 5*(3), 5–18.

Castro, P., & Batel, S. (2008). Social representation, change and resistance: On the difficulties of generalizing new norms. *Culture & Psychology, 14*(4), 475–497.

Finkel, N. J., & Moghaddam, F. M. (2005). *The psychology of rights and duties: Empirical contributions and normative commentaries.* Washington, DC: American Psychological Association.

Gelfand, M. J., & Harrington, J. R. (2015). The motivational force of descriptive norms: For whom and when are descriptive norms most predictive of behavior? *Journal of Cross-Cultural Psychology, 46*(10), 1273–1278.

Itkowitz, C. (2015, March 5). Rep. Don Young: Wolves would solve homelessness. Retrieved from http://www.washingtonpost.com/blogs/in-the-loop/wp/2015/03/05/rep-don-young-wolves-would-solve-homelessness/

Josephs, I. E., & Valsiner, J. (1998). How does autodialogue work? Meaning maintenance and circumvention strategies. *Social Psychology Quarterly, 61*(1), 68–83.

Jost, J. T., Pelham, B. W., Sheldon, O., & Sullivan, B. N. (2003). Social inequality and the reduction of ideological dissonance on behalf of the system: Evidence of enhanced system justification among the disadvantaged. *European Journal of Social Psychology, 33*, 13–36.

Jourdenais, R., Ota, M., Stauffer, S., Boyson, B., & Doughty, C. (1995). Does textual enhancement promote noticing? A protocol analysis. In R. W. Schmidt (Ed.), *Attention and awareness in foreign language learning* (pp. 183–216). Honolulu: Second Language Teaching & Curriculum Center, University of Hawaii at Manoa.

Lasch, C. (1979). *The culture of narcissism.* New York, NY: Norton.

Lyra, M. C. (2013). Process-product dynamics: The role of otherness in cultural cultivation. *Integrative Psychological and Behavioral Science, 48*(2), 204–210.

Moghaddam, F. M., & Riley, C. J. (2005). Toward a cultural theory of rights and duties in human development. In N. J. Finkel & F. M. Moghaddam (Eds.), *The psychology of rights and duties: Empirical contributions and normative commentaries* (pp. 75–104). Washington, DC: American Psychological Association.

Moghaddam, F. M. (2015). Editorial. *Peace and Conflict: Journal of Peace Psychology, 21*(1), 1–2.

Priester, J. R., & Petty, R. E. (2001). Extending the bases of subjective attitudinal ambivalence: Interpersonal and intrapersonal antecedents of evaluative tension. *Journal of Personality and Social Psychology, 80*(1), 19–34.

Schwartz, B. (2004). *The paradox of choice: Why more is less.* New York, NY: Ecco.

Tateo, L. (2015). Giambattista Vico and the psychological imagination. *Culture & Psychology, 21*(2), 145–161.

The Universal Declaration of Human Rights. (1948, December 10). Retrieved from http://www.un.org/en/documents/udhr/

Valsiner, J. (2009). Cultural psychology today: Innovations and oversights. *Culture & Psychology, 15*(1), 5–39.

Valsiner, J. (2014). Needed for cultural psychology: Methodology in a new key. *Culture & Psychology, 20*(1), 3–30.

Worchel, S. (2005). The rightful place of human rights: Incorporating individual, group, and cultural perspectives. In N. J. Finkel & F. M. Moghaddam (Eds.), *The psychology of rights and duties: Empirical contributions and normative commentaries* (pp. 197–220). Washington, DC: American Psychological Association.

PART IV

MEASURING AMBIVALENCE

CHAPTER 14

ATTACHMENT AMBIVALENCE

The Concept, Psychological Importance, and Measurement Issues

Katarzyna Lubiewska
Kazimierz Wielki University, Bydgoszcz

Temporal co-existence of opposite cognitions, emotions, feelings or social approach and avoidance motives is a determinant of needs fulfillment (Moss & Wilson, 2015; Nikitin & Freund, 2008), indicates ability of an individual to dialectical thinking as the mature stage of cognitive development (Basseches, 1980) and fosters social development (Nikitin & Freund, 2008), adaptation and therapeutic processes (Kelly, Wood, Shearman, Phillips & Mansell, 2012). Awareness of own ambivalence in a close relation may also indicate accurate and not defensive evaluation of the relationship as a complex system. Thus, in general, experience of ambivalence is normal and adaptive.

Nonetheless, outcomes of ambivalence seem to be also a matter of its dose. When ambivalence is high, it may overload an individual regarding information processing, emotions, and related tensions inhibiting goal-directed behavior and the basic needs fulfillment. Thus, high ambivalence may be less adaptive or even detrimental. One example refers to attachment ambivalence in which

Trans-Generational Family Relations, pages 283–307

situational threat-related activation of need for closeness is not followed by goal-directed proximity seeking but is inhibited by relational anxiety. The tension related to a conflict between a need for closeness and a high anxiety may become disadvantageous for an anxious individual and his or her relationships.

The extent to which people differ in the way they experience ambivalence in close relationships depends on individual differences in personality traits (e.g., cognitive style), relationship quality and some other factors (e.g., contextual or cultural). Nonetheless, attachment theory provides probably the most explanative answer to the question how and why some individuals are more prone than others to experience ambivalence in their close relations. It also suggests that in some domains ambivalence may be related with high individual costs inhibiting optimal adaptation. In the following sections of this chapter I will characterize ambivalence in attachment, highlight reasons for which attachment ambivalence is worth of profound studies, and describe issues which should be considered when the measurement of attachment ambivalence is planned.

ATTACHMENT

Although attachment is intuitively linked with an emotional bond between individuals in close relationships (e.g., romantic or parent-child relations), it is also studied in psychology as a more general mental representation (internal working model) of the self (as worth of love) and a model of the other (as providing security), related with attachment anxiety and avoidance in close relationships (Bartholomew & Horowitz, 1991). This mental representation is formed on the foundation of our past life experiences in close relations. Yet, it also guides our attitudes toward close others which we will engage in our close relationships in the future (Bowlby, 1973). In this perspective, attachment is detached from a particular close-other relation and is treated as generic attachment, a construct similar to (but not the same as) a personality trait (Noftle & Shaver, 2006). Both, the affectional bond and the mental model are inter-related and may be marked in varying degree by ambivalence. Individual differences in attachment arise from early experiences with the primary caregiver during the first year of life and may be in general summarized by secure and two insecure organized attachment patterns: anxious-avoidant and anxious-ambivalent (Ainsworth et al., 1978).

Ambivalence and Attachment Patterns

At the general level individual differences in attachment are delineated by the way an individual balances between two basic psychological needs for autonomy (independence) and relatedness (interdependence, connectedness) (Deci & Ryan, 2000) especially in times of stress. The strength of autonomy or relatedness needs activates interpersonal goals of proximity (to attain connectedness by approaching behavior) or distance (to attain autonomy by exploration or avoidance). Autonomy is related with autonomy of thoughts and behavior, while relatedness refers to the sense of connectedness, closeness and proximity with close other. The strength of autonomy or/and relatedness needs, and related proximity and distancing interpersonal motives, are adaptively regulated by situational and relational factors but also by individual strategies primed in human brain since early life-experiences in close relations.

From a biological perspective, attachment is one of several innate behavioral systems which is activated (in infants, children and adults) in times of stress, illness or tiredness and entails immediate motivation for (physical or symbolic) proximity seeking with an attachment figure who potentially shall serve as the source of security and support (Bowlby, 1969; Hazan & Shaver, 1987). In times when no threat is detected, another innate–exploration behavioral system–is activated and serves to satisfy autonomy needs.

Although both, proximity and autonomy seeking, are in general opposed (moderately negatively correlated) for all individuals (Hagemeyer, Neyer, Neberich & Asendorpf, 2013), insecure, compared to secure individuals are less able to balance adaptively proximity and distance within their close relationships (Dewitte & De Houwer, 2008). Secure individuals manage to balance closeness (proximity) and distancing behaviors relatively more adequately in response to adaptation demands (e.g., the strength of the threat) by using a primary attachment strategy. It means that in times of stress these individuals implicitly or explicitly seek for physical or symbolic closeness with an attachment figure. This strategy characterizes around 60% of individuals across various cultures (van IJzendoorn & Sagi-Schwartz, 2008) who can be described in terms of secure attachment. For these individuals low or moderate levels of ambivalence may be expected and indicate a balanced and adequate perception of an attachment figure and the relationship (Thompson & Holmes, 1996). A study by Nikitin and Freund (2010) indeed revealed that secure attachment predicted positively social approach motivation, negatively social avoidance motivation but also predicted interaction between both.

Managing closeness in times of stress for the rest, around 40% of individuals classified as insecure, is based on secondary attachment strategies in which the innate need for proximity seeking in times of threat is managed less adaptively. The need for closeness is inhibited (deactivated) for avoidant individuals, and boosted (hyperactivated) for anxious-ambivalent individuals (Mikulincer & Shaver, 2007). For these individuals, very low ambivalence (e.g., related with devaluation or idealization of a partner) or high ambivalence (as indicated by anxiety) may underlie attachment insecurity (Thompson & Holmes, 1996).

Highly avoidant individuals use a deactivating secondary attachment strategy. While faced with stress, they inhibit proximity seeking, reveal distancing interpersonal goals toward closeness and handle the threat by themselves (Dewitte & De Houwer, 2008). When overwhelmed by intense emotions they deactivate, repress, dissociate away from emotions and focus more (than anxious and secure individuals) on externally oriented thinking (Stevens, 2014). As the result they experience problems with recognizing and acknowledging emotions, describing feelings (Oskis, Clow, Hucklebridge, Bifulco, Jacobs & Loveday, 2013; Stevens, 2014), and are prone to relationship dissatisfaction because of their indifference regarding emotions (Birnbaum, Mikulincer, Szepsenwol & Shaver, 2014). Avoiding closeness, they become aware predominately of negative aspects of their relationships, which is not typical for anxious individuals, more sensitive to threats but also more aware of positive and negative feelings (Li & Chan, 2012). There is evidence suggesting that avoidant individuals may experience some (less than for anxious individuals) degree of ambivalence which is rather akin to indifference (no interest) than to ambivalence (MacDonald, Locke, Spielmann & Joel, 2013).

Ambivalent Attachment in Close Relations

Anxiously attached (ambivalent) individuals hold ambivalent attitudes toward attachment figures (e.g., Collins & Read, 1990; MacDonald et al., 2013; Mikulincer, Shaver, Bar-On & Ein-Dor, 2010). While faced with a threat eliciting the need for closeness, they use a hyperactivating strategy toward their emotions. Their ambivalence is reflected in simultaneously present excessive need for closeness inhibited at behavioral level by doubts about availability, responsiveness and commitment of the attachment figure. They become preoccupied by ambivalence between love-anger and wanting/approaching-distancing closeness. Related discomfort and tension are not only less optimally adaptive but may be detrimental for their health, well-being and quality of their close relationships. Their hyperactivating strategy implies a strong desire for closeness, insufficient sense of security, and lower threshold of sensitivity toward (real or over interpreted) cues threatening the relationship (Mikulincer & Shaver, 2007). As the result they are more tensed and less focused (than secure individuals) on expressing intimacy and warmth in their relationships (Campbell & Marshal, 2011).

On the emotional level, anxious individuals have deficits in controlling their response to emotions. They are more likely to let their emotions interfere with their goals and engage in impulsive behaviors (Oskis et al., 2013; Stevens, 2014). Furthermore, their behavioral tendencies are overly emotional (exaggerated) in efforts to gain the attention of an attachment figure. Yet, as compared with avoidant individuals, they are more aware of the whole range of their emotions (including ambivalence between them). They may even deliberately tend to intensify the magnitude of their positive and negative emotions and cognitions toward their partner to attain proximity and support. The pattern of interpersonal goals is also characteristic for individuals with ambivalent attachment.

Attachment behaviors are set by two interpersonal goals (motives) related with: (a) approach and (b) avoidance of closeness with an attachment figure. The contradicted, mutually inhibiting tendencies to desire closeness (as indicated also by avoidance of distance) with partner and avoiding or lack of approaching closeness, along with instability of such tendencies across studies and time seem to be core for anxious-ambivalent attachment. This conclusion seems to stem from various studies on implicit and explicit ambivalence.

First, in line with findings of studies investigating effects of ambivalence for personal attitudes (e.g., Wilson & Hodges, 1992) interpersonal goals and motivational tendencies of anxious individuals seem to be more unstable in time and fragile than for secure and avoidant individuals (e.g., Bell & Esse, 2002). For example, interpersonal goals of individuals with an ambivalent attachment pattern during everyday interactions with their partners, were found as relatively unstable in the time-lag of 15 days reports (Locke, 2008), as compared to individuals revealing other attachment types.

Lack of time-staility may influence inconsistency in conclusions from studies investigating interpersonal goals related with explicit ambivalence. Results of these studies indicate that attachment ambivalence (anxiety) is related with motivation and desire for closeness in intimate attachment relationships (Dewitte & De Houwer, 2008; Hagemeyer et al., 2013; Locke, 2008). Furthermore, ambivalent (anxious) attachment was found as an antecedent of approach social motivation (Nikitin & Freund, 2010). Yet, other studies revealed a lack of relations between ambivalence and desire for closeness (Hagemeyer et al., 2013, study 2) or insignificant effect of attachment anxiety on approaching closeness to the partner (Locke, 2008). At a more general social (not relational) level Nikitin and Freund (2010) found that preoccupied attachment (anxious) predicted separately both approach and avoidance social motivations.

Findings from studies on implicit ambivalence (unconscious motives) are even less conclusive. Dewitte and De Houwer (2008) found that anxiety of individuals was not related with Implicit Association Task (IAT) proximity-distance. This finding is at odds with other research demonstrating that anxious individuals display a strong desire for proximity also at the unconscious level (Gillath, Mikulincer, Fitzsimons, Shaver, Schachner & Barg, 2006; Mikulincer, Birnabaum, Woddis & Nachmias, 2000).

Summarizing the nature of ambivalence within attachment, three issues seem to be crucial: 1) tension (e.g., anxiety) related with inconsistencies within emotional, motivational and cognitive aspects of attitudes toward and in relation with an attachment figure; 2) instability of behavior and interpersonal goals across time and studies; and 3) emotional hyperactivation of the need for closeness. Although this description of attachment ambivalence unfolds its complex nature, its measurement in the majority of attachment studies is focused on the assessment of the level of anxiety (fear, doubts and worries about the partner's feelings and availability in self-reports) or classification of an individual into one of four attachment patterns, including anxious-ambivalent or preoccupied category (mainly in observational and interview-based methods). Even though the classification of individual attachment used in the Adult Attachment Interview (AAI) is based (among others) on the analysis of inconsistencies in the narration related with the state of mind regarding attachment-related experiences with parents in childhood, and parental idealization (lack of ambivalence), ambivalence is not assessed in its extent but in terms of its presence or absence (the AAI), or the level of anxiety which is only one of indirect indicators of ambivalence.

REASONS FOR STUDYING THE EXTENT OF AMBIVALENCE IN ATTACHMENT

The question is whether and what studies focusing on assessment of the extent of ambivalence in attachment in its complex nature may add to attachment theory above and beyond numerous research investigating varying degrees of anxiety or categorization into the anxious-ambivalent (versus other) attachment pattern. To answer this question, I analyze further results of studies carried out in two domains of research in which the effects of the extent of ambivalence are investigated in a more detailed manner. Both seem to suggest that the assessment of the extent of ambivalence in its complex nature may be beneficial for attachment theory and practice.

Reason 1: Evidence From Studies on Emotional Expression

Although there are studies indicating that ambivalent emotions may be likely to promote satisfaction and fulfillment (Moss & Wilson, 2015), the ambivalence resulting from basic need activation and its inhibition or emotional ambivalence inhibiting goal-directed activity needed to reduce tension is rather detrimental (Traschel, Ferrari & Holtforth, 2012).

Within psychological research on emotions, conflicts related with motivational tendencies are studied recently under the construct of the *ambivalence over emotional expression* proposed by King and Emmons (1990). The authors suggested, and further studies supported, the notion that inconsistency of results from studies investigating the relation between styles of emotional expression (e.g., "bottle-up" own emotions or lack of emotional expression) and cancer or coronary diseases, may be triggered by an ambivalent combination of lack of emotional expression and the desire to express emotions (not purely by expression style). Ambivalence, namely incongruence between the extent of one's desire for emotional expression and his/her behavioral expression, may arise as the effect of internal control (e.g., lack of trust toward the partner inhibiting disclosure) or external obstacles (e.g., social norms of emotional expression). Two forms of ambivalence over emotional expression were distinguished. *Inhibition* (emotional suppression) occurs when one wants to express emotions but is not able to. *Rumination* takes place when one expresses emotions later regretting it. Rumination, defined as coping style characterized by unproductive, repetitive and passive rehearsal of recent life events and internal experiences, was found to be significantly higher in anxious-ambivalent individuals (Reynolds, Searight & Ratwik, 2014).

Ambivalence, as defined in these studies, was found to be a negative predictor of psychological well-being, and a positive predictor of some physical symptomatology and depression (King & Emmons, 1990). Further studies revealed numerous outcomes of ambivalence over emotional expression, including problems in benefiting from social support (Emmons & Colby, 1995), and lower satisfaction with: marriage (Tucker, Winkelamn, Katz & Bermas, 1999), life (Chen, Cheung, Bond & Leung, 2005); or low relationship quality (Ben-Air & Lavee, 2011).

Furthermore, not only ambivalence in emotional expression but also ambivalence in one's perception of social support (during disclosure of negative events) and capitalization (during disclosure of positive events) provided by own spouse in every-day situations was found to predict cardiovascular risk (Uchino et al., 2013).

These studies indicate that ambivalence related with own desire for disclosure and inhibition of its realization may be detrimental for physical and psychological health. The similarity between ambivalence over emotional expression and hyperactivation of attachment seems to be very high. Within attachment, the desire for closeness with an attachment figure is inhibited by own fears, doubts and distrust toward an attachment figure. Thus, autonomic arousal and psychological discomfort seem to underline also every-day episodes evoking attachment ambivalence-related responses carrying health risk for anxious individuals (presumably higher than for avoidant and secure individuals). If this assumption is true, ambivalent attachment should not be defined only in terms of individual differences but also as a risk factor which might be analyzed from the perspective of disorders rather than clinical norm.

Reason 2: Evidences From Cognitive Psychology

First, in line with research on emotional ambivalence, cognitive studies indicate that inconsistencies between and within elements of an attitude are aversive for most individuals (e.g., Cialdini, Trost & Newsom, 1995; Festinger, 1957; Newby-Clark, McGregor & Zanna, 2002; van Harreveld, van der Pligt & de Liver, 2009). Studies on attitudes evidenced that the degree of attitudinal ambivalence is linked with physiological arousal, negative mood and other negative outcomes (van Harreveld, Rutjens, Schneider, Nohlen & Keskinis, 2014; van Harreveld, van der Pligt & de Liver, 2009).

As the tension (anxiety) related with ambivalence is unpleasant, people activate different strategies to cope with ambivalence. For this purpose, they use problem-focused, emotion-focused or compensatory coping strategies (van Harreveld et al., 2009; van Harreveld et al., 2014). The first is based on an increased effort to integrate contradictory attitudes, including processing information in accordance with the slight evaluative inclination the individual may have. Emotion-based coping aims to reduce the unpleasant feelings related with ambivalence without affecting the ambivalent attitude itself (e.g., by procrastinating the decision and downplaying the importance of the decision). Compensatory coping strategies may address affirmation and heightened commitment to an alternative object. For example, if ambivalence brings a threat for the self, an individual may affirm certain personal values or conspiracy theories to reduce the tension and maintain self-integrity (van Harreveld et al., 2014).

As anxious individuals experience more tension than secure or avoidant individuals, they may be also more prone to use coping strategies. It seems possible that their tendency to hyperactivate the attachment system may prime emotion- and compensatory-coping strategies as the first choice candidates engaged to deal with discomfort. This expectation is in line with the compensation hypothesis which assumes (and studies evidence) that anxious individuals whose attachment needs are not satisfied in the relation with the primary attachment figure may turn to compensatory objects being a substitute of an attachment-like figure, for example to God (Granqvist & Kirkpatrick, 2008).

Results from cognitive studies might add significantly to what we know about therapeutic interventions fostering attachment security in individuals with different unsecure attachment patterns. It seems possible that sensitivity of anxious individuals to such interventions may be higher than for individuals with avoidant attachment. Avoidant individuals experience rather indifference than ambivalence related with low (if any) ambivalence-related discomfort. Therefore, they may deny the need for any change in their perception of close relations and be resistant to both, activation of coping strategies and interventions fostering their attachment security. In contrast, anxious individuals seem to be more aware of their ambivalence marked by felt discomfort (tension). They balance between contradicting motives, feelings and cognitions unfolding unstable behavioral patterns over time. This tensed balance overly experienced by anxious individuals may make them more open (than avoidant individuals), not only to activation of coping strategies but also to external interventions fostering attachment security. These interventions might introduce problem-solving strategies and supplement emotion-based and compensatory coping strategies oftentimes activated by anxious individuals to reduce their tension caused by ambivalence.

An experimental study of McClure, Bartz and Lydon (2012) indicates that priming chronically-anxious individuals with attachment security indeed decreased their ambivalence in pro-social behavior. Assessment of the extent of individual ambivalence may therefore indicate susceptibility of an individual to therapeutic influences and mark the group of individuals who may be more likely than others to *earn security* during therapy.

ISSUES RELATED WITH ASSESSMENTS OF ATTACHMENT AMBIVALENCE

Two issues were stressed so far to support the need to go in measurement of individual differences in adult attachment beyond the categorization of individuals into an anxious-ambivalent category or the measurement of the attachment anxiety/preoccupation level (which only indirectly indicates the extent of ambivalence). First, attachment ambivalence, as defined through the incongruence between the strength of one's need for closeness and his/her satisfaction-directed behaviors, may identify the area of health risk overlooked so far in attachment studies on nonclinical samples. Then, although attachment ambivalence seems to be a risk factor, it also may be a marker of sensitivity to therapeutic attachment-based interventions which may be tailored regarding ambivalence level.

At last, three problems seem to be worth of considering when assessment of attachment ambivalence is planned. The first refers to the level of its measurement related with potential versus felt, and implicit versus explicit ambivalence. Then, the extent to which indicators of an instrument are close to attachment theory. The last issue concerns divergent validity and relates to the question about the extent to which the measure of attachment ambivalence taps the construct under scrutiny instead of other related or underlying constructs.

Despite the abundant research on individual differences in attachment, to my knowledge only few widely available studies investigated ambivalence within or related with attachment (Maio, Fincham, Regalia & Paleari, 2004; McClure et al., 2012; MacDonald et al., 2013; Mikulincer et al., 2010; Levy, Blatt & Shaver, 1998; Surjadi, Lorenz, Conger & Wickrama; 2013).

Levels of Assessment: Potential Versus Felt Ambivalence

In research on attitudes, *potential ambivalence* refers to the existence of inconsistent thoughts, emotions or motives not necessarily related with psychological discomfort. So, potential ambivalence is rather not represented at the awareness of an individual in contrast to *felt ambivalence* which is experienced by the person. According to van Harreveeld and colleagues (2009) potential ambivalence is likely to turn into felt ambivalence, indicated by arousal, when a choice between ambivalent components has to be made and/or when the outcome of such decision is uncertain. Moreover, potential ambivalence may turn into felt ambivalence more easily for some individuals than for others. Similarly, felt ambivalence may not have the same consequences for everyone. Potential moderators may address: simultaneous accessibility of inconsistent evaluations, individual differences in personality traits, or cultural factors (all discussed further in this chapter).

Beyond mechanisms underlying both types of ambivalence, the distinction between potential and felt ambivalence in cognitive and intergenerational relations studies is also referring to a more or less direct assessment of the construct (e.g., Connidis, 2015; Newby-Clark et al., 2002; Suitor, Gilligan & Pillemer, 2011). *Potential ambivalence* is measured less directly than felt ambivalence. Individuals participating in the study are asked to evaluate separately and not simultaneously positive and negative aspects of the estimated object. Having two unipolar, positive and negative, evaluations researchers implement a mathematic formula to calculate the extent of personal ambivalence over the estimated object based on the strength of positive and negative evaluation. Thompson, Zanna and Griffin (1995) propose the following equation:

$$\text{Ambivalence} = |\text{positive component} - \text{negative component}| + \text{mean (of positive and negative components)}$$

Within attachment in intimate relations this strategy was used in the Ambivalence in Relationships Survey (AIRS) scale developed by Thompson and Holmes (1996) and used also in the study of Mikulincer, Shaver, Bar-On and Ein-Dor (2010). The scale measured the cognitive representation of the partner in the intimate relationship assessing affective and motivational ambivalence. In their scale, Thompson and Holmes provided a set of attributes, traits describing partners in intimate relationships. Respondents were asked to focus on only the positive or favorable aspects of each attribute or trait of own partner (e.g., degree of partner's expressiveness), while ignoring the negative aspect, and to indicate (using the Likert response format) the extent to which each attribute was a source of cognitive (beneficial for the relationship) and affective comfort (make you feel good). Then, respondents were asked to focus only on negative or unfavorable aspects of each attribute and assess it in terms of cognitive (harmful for the relationship) and affective discomfort (make you feel bad).

A similar, although less extended measure of potential relational ambivalence was used also by Surjadi, Lorenz, Conger and Wickrama (2013) to assess the extent of adolescents' ambivalence toward parents. Respondents had to rate the frequency to which the parent makes the adolescent feel cared about and understands him/her (positive items); and the frequency of parental demands and critics (negative items). A more open assessment procedure was used in the study of Maio, Fincham, Regalia and Paleari (2004) who asked young adolescents to list their feelings and beliefs about their mother, then to evaluate each of them regarding their positivity and negativity. Finally, Levy, Blatt and Shaver (1998) asked participants to describe their mother and father. The level of ambivalence was assessed by judges who scored the description contents using several criteria, including the degree of ambivalence about the parent.

The other strategy of ambivalence assessment focuses on the psychological experience of *felt ambivalence* where ambivalence is measured directly by asking respondents about their mixed feelings and how conflicted or torn they feel between two motives, feelings or cognitive evaluations (Connidis, 2015; Suitor, Gilligan & Pillmer, 2011). It is assumed that individuals are aware of their ambivalence (Connidis, 2015). Although this measurement approach is used in adult parent-child relations (e.g., Michels, Albert & Ferring, 2011), to my knowledge, only one study assessed attachment ambivalence using this method. Braiker and Kelly (1979, following Thompson and Holmes, 1996) used five items to tap ambivalence in the relationship with partner. They asked respondents directly how confused, ambivalent or unsure they feel about the partner and relationship with him/her. Lack of such studies may be related with doubts about meta-cognitive abilities of respondents to get insight into the level of own ambivalence which may be additionally masked by tension-reducing coping strategies (defensive mechanisms). Lack of such studies may be also due to the concern about confusion of ambivalence with indifference about the partner (Thompson & Holmes, 1996).

The way between both, indirect and direct strategies of ambivalence assessment, seems to rely on simultaneous activation of positive and negative components of an attitude in the respondent's awareness. Respondents are asked to evaluate not separately but simultaneously their positive and negative evaluations, however without direct estimation of the level of their perceived conflict. Kaplan (1972, p. 362) highlights that "the measurement of ambivalence seems to require a situation in which an individual has the opportunity to simultaneously indicate both a favorable and an unfavorable attitude toward a given stimulus object." Kaplan postulated the use of a semantic differential to assess simultaneously both components, however the recent application of this strategy is based on the use of the evaluative space grid (Larsen, Norris, McGraw, Hawkley & Cacioppo, 2009). Using the grid (e.g., 10 × 10 cells), respondents are asked to indicate simultaneously their positive and negative evaluations, for example the degree of their approach (e.g., horizontal axis) and avoidance (e.g., vertical axis) motives toward an estimated object.

The problem which my team and myself found in our attempts to assess ambivalence by simultaneous activation of positive and negative aspects of attachment motives and feelings in intimate relations using the evaluative space grid, was related with the increase of the explicit irritation of respondents. In our opinion the assessment procedure might be the source of increased tension. First, the task of reporting simultaneously the level of own contradicting attachment-related motives and feelings toward own partner might force transfer of potential ambivalence into felt ambivalence. This might weaken self-defensive and emotion-based coping strategies (e.g., procrastination and deny of responsibility for the relationship) bringing to awareness and increasing the pressure for decisiveness regarding own commitment to the relationship which is marked by tension.

Levels of Assessment: Implicit Versus Explicit Ambivalence

Another perspective, widely used in psychological assessment, refers to the implicit and explicit manifestation of traits, motives and emotions. It is assumed that *implicit* traits, motives and emotions are unconscious and hidden from conscious awareness of the individual, while *explicit* traits, motives and emotions can be observed or verbally reported by the individual who is aware of them. Implicit traits are predominantly assessed using the latency of response time toward a particular stimulus, whereas explicit traits are mostly gauged by self-report measures. Both types of measures correlate rather low showing unstable patterns of correlations across studies (Hofmann, Gawronski, Gschwendner, Le & Schmitt, 2005). This problem was also widely discussed in attachment literature (overview in Mikulincer & Shaver, 2007).

At least five reasons for weak and varying relations between both measures were highlighted in a meta-analysis carried out by Hofmann and colleagues (2005). First, implicit measures are unbiased by motivational influences, while self-reports are affected by social desirability. Between-measures correlations may be high for relatively mundane topics, and low for socially sensitive topics. Another reason, which seems to be important for research on ambivalence, refers to introspective accessibility of an individual to own traits, emotions, motives, thoughts and their inconsistencies. Specifically, some traits may be beyond the reach of self-report measures. Then, implicit measures gauge processes activated automatically (spontaneous judgements). Explicit measures, in contrast, retrieve more recently acquired representations from memory (deliberate processing). Finally, method-related factors or randomness may bias low and varying correlations between explicit and implicit measures.

As a distinction between potential and felt ambivalence was also proposed in this chapter, the question arises, to what extent potential ambivalence is gauged by implicit measures of ambivalence, and felt ambivalence by explicit measures. It seems likely that both are overlapping. The relation between them may be conceptualized as related with the extent to which each measure of ambivalence scratches the surface of awareness. Indirect assessment seems to bring the issue of ambivalence closer to awareness than implicit assessment. In indirect ambivalence assessment, an individual is asked to report on both contradicted aspects in a small time-lag which increases the probability that he or she may become aware of own ambivalence. Following this line of reasoning, implicit ambivalence would be seen as less represented/gauged at the awareness level than potential ambivalence, whereas explicit ambivalence would be less extensively experienced than felt ambivalence. Taking an information processing perspective, it would also mean that the felt/explicit level of ambivalence assessment taps also implicit and potential ambivalence underlying conscious processes.

At last two studies investigating relational, or in particular, attachment ambivalence used more or less implicit measures. McClure, Bartz and Lydon (2012) assessed manifested behavior as the indicator of ambivalence. Specifically, social dilemma games were used in their study to assess relational ambivalence. The inconsistency of choices (between game strategies) and time of individual response (choice decision) made by (not acquainted) participants in a relational game were indicating the extent of ambivalence. Although attachment ambivalence was assessed by an additional self-report measure in this study, the authors revealed that anxious individuals were more inconsistent in their choices and slower in the game strategy selection.

Implicit ambivalence was also assessed in the study of Mikulincer and colleagues (2010). These authors used an approach-avoidance task developed by Chen and Bargh (1999), in which participants were presented with a set of positive and negative words related with closeness and distance from relationship partners. Participants were asked to pull the lever backward (approach) or push it forward (avoidance) when they encoded the meaning of the word. Latencies of pushes and pulls to a closeness- or distance-related word (whether positive or negative) were indicative for relational ambivalence.

PROXIMITY OF AN INSTRUMENT TO THE ATTACHMENT THEORY

Another issue important for attachment ambivalence measurement refers to the question of how close domains of ambivalence (traits of an attachment figure, behaviors or the relationship features) assessed by the instrument are linked to attachment theory. Instruments assessing explicit relational ambivalence used in studies published up to date assessed traits more or less tightly linked to attachment.

Among these, the self-report AIRS scale developed by Thompson and Holmes (1996) is probably the most closely linked to attachment. Although authors drew partner's traits and relationship attributes used in their scale, and tested with regard to ambivalence, from several sources—the interpersonal circumplex model, the Five Factor Model of personality and intimacy process dimensions—the domains assessed in the measure seem to be rather at the heart of attachment theory. For example, among the AIRS items drawn from the interpersonal circumplex model—partner's degree of independence versus dependence on the relationship, or degree of comfort with emotional closeness are also represented in attachment measures (e.g., Collins & Read, 1990). However, partner's tendency to be critical and controlling as reflected in the AIRS items seems to be rather more marginal for attachment assessment. Similarly, the AIRS items derived from the intimacy process dimensions seem also to be in general indicative for attachment and assess respondents' perception of partner's degree of responsiveness, dependability, emotional support, effectiveness in dealing with conflict in relationship. Among the AIRS items, affirmation of respondent as unique and valued, and encouragement of shared activities, are probably less core for assessment of individual differences in attachment. Finally, the group of the AIRS items which was relatively most distant from attachment theory was drawn from the Five Factor Model of personality traits. These items assessed partner's degree of expressiveness, general sociability, and partner's tendencies to be conventional and passionate.

The AIRS scale was used also in the study of Mikulincer and colleagues (2010). Authors modified the measure to target more narrowly partner's traits differentially linked with attachment. The authors assessed affective ambivalence asking about effectiveness in dealing with conflict in relationship, sociability, comfort with emotional closeness, relationship commitment, and sexual passion. Motivational ambivalence was assessed in this study based on approach and avoidance relational goals related with approach episodes (weekend trip, asking advice about career problem, sharing feelings with the partner) and avoidance episodes (having an exciting interaction with an attractive woman/man without the partner's knowledge, vacation without the partner, career-related changes without sharing them with the partner).

An even narrower domain of relational ambivalence related with attachment was investigated by MacDonald, Locke, Spielmann and Joel (2013). These authors investigated the relation between attachment dimensions and ambivalence that may arise from strong perception of important threats (e.g., rejection or negative evaluation) and rewards (e.g., closeness or intimacy) in romantic relationships. They targeted the tension caused by being simultaneously concerned about obtaining rewards and avoiding emotional threats from the partner.

Other instruments used in studies investigating relational attachment-related ambivalence seem to be less tightly related with attachment theory and focused more on respondent's mental representation of an attachment figure (parent or partner, for example as carrying, understanding, demanding or criticizing in the study of Surjadi et al., 2013). Levy, Blatt and Shaver (1998) settled the assessment of ambivalence in their study on evaluations of external judges regarding the extent of respondents' ambivalence toward parents derived from respondents' open (not necessary attachment-relevant) descriptions of each parent. Similarly, respondents in the study of Surjadi and colleagues (2013) and Maio and colleagues (2004) were asked to list their feelings and beliefs about each parent. It is worth of noting that these authors assessed attachment separately and did not aim to tap precisely attachment ambivalence using their ambivalence measure.

Finally, one study in which explicit (AIRS) and implicit measures of ambivalence were used was carried out by Mikulincer and colleagues (2010). These authors used an experimental procedure mentioned already to assess implicit relational ambivalence tightly linked with attachment theory for which motivational (felt/explicit or potential/implicit) ambivalence related with closeness and distance is focal. Participants of the experiment were presented with positive and negative words related with closeness (e.g., hug, closeness, trust versus dependence, cling, intrude) and distance (e.g., independence, privacy, free versus lonely, separated, rejected), which are markers of core domains of attachment.

Validity of the Attachment Ambivalence Construct

Two additional issues related with the construct of ambivalence have to be considered when the measurement of attachment ambivalence is planned. First, ambivalence has to be differentiated from similar constructs, especially indifference. Then, various traits related with individual differences and more external factors may moderate the extent to which ambivalence (or cognitive dissonance) is translated into felt discomfort and dealt with. These factors should be treated as sources of ambivalence which are additional to life-experiences of an individual underlying his or her anxious attachment. However, both pave the way to the final decision about the extent to which the attachment ambivalence gauged in the study should be treated as a state or more chronic trait of personality.

Ambivalence or Indifference

When individuals have to define the extent of own positive and negative evaluations, the degree of their evaluations indicates whether ambivalence or indifference underlie their attitude. According to Kaplan (1972) indifference is captured when both positive and negative evaluations of an individual are equal to zero. In contrast, when both are high, ambivalence becomes the object of the study. Even though the cut-off degree from which we define the attitude in terms of ambivalence, not indifference, may be problematic and context-dependent, the distinction should be considered for each participant in the background of felt and potential ambivalence. It seems that indifference in attachment, for example related with closeness with an attachment figure, might be related with simultaneous declaration of low levels of both contradicted dimensions within: relational goals—closeness *approach* and closeness *avoidance*; or relational needs—*need* for closeness and *aversion* of closeness. In this example attachment ambivalence would be indicated by high estimations of both contradicted dimensions of relational goals and needs within attachment-related closeness.

Furthermore, some personality traits, relational and more external factors, like culture, may moderate the extent of felt discomfort triggered by attachment-related ambivalence and engagement of coping strategies. All of these factors may moderate the level of ambivalence, however if not controlled for or carefully considered, may introduce confusion to what extent results of the study are indicative for ambivalence or stem from other sources.

Personality Traits

The importance of personality traits in ambivalence seems to be supported in the study of Thompson and Zanna (1995) who, assessing social policy attitudes, found considerable consistency (correlations) of ambivalence across unrelated domains of attitudes. There seems to be a general individual tendency to experience ambivalence. In general, personality cognitive and emotional characteristics related with ambivalence are briefly described in the next paragraphs.

Regarding cognitive traits, Thompson and Zanna (1995) evidenced that greater *need for cognition* may foster high levels of attitudinal ambivalence. Need for cognition (NFC) is related with a tendency of an individual to engage into effortful endeavor and perception of self as an effective problem-solver. High NFC individuals dislike ambiguity, thus they work through, understand and bring coherence to issues (Thompson & Zanna, 1995). As an outcome they may not suppress the ambivalence-related tension, but bring it into conscious level (felt ambivalence). Then, they may feel more internally pressured to make the decision between contradicted evaluations, increase their involvement, including problem-solving coping strategies and reduce their ambivalence and related tension.

Tolerance for ambiguity (e.g., Furnham & Ribchester, 1995) is a similar personality trait which may underlie ambivalence. Ambiguity (in)tolerance (AT) refers to the way an individual perceives and processes information about incongruent clues. Low AT individuals experience strong tension, stress, and avoid ambiguous stimuli (Furnham & Ribchester, 1995). They are unable to tolerate ambivalence, therefore they reveal a generalized tendency to: make an early selection and maintenance of one solution in ambiguous situations, premature closure, rigidity, over-confident judgements, and formulate dogmatic attitudes (Furnham & Marks, 2013; Furnham & Ribchester, 1995). Individuals with high AT may tolerate better the experience stemming from felt ambivalence and related tension.

Need for closure (redundant to a *need for structure*) is another, very similar to AT, trait which may be related with ambivalence. It is related with the extent to which an individual, faced with a decision or judgement, desires ANY answer, as compared with confusion or ambiguity. A person high in need for closure prefers order and predictability, to be decisive, and is uncomfortable with ambiguity (Neuberg, Judice & West, 1997).

Then, *personal fear of invalidity* (PFI) is a trait which may foster maintenance of one's ambivalent feelings, cognitions and emotions. It refers to the possible error and its costs related with making the wrong decision and is manifested by hesitation in making such decisions (Thompson & Zanna, 1995). High fear of invalidity may therefore evoke maintenance of a prolonged ambivalence state. Thompson and Zanna (1995) evidenced in their study that high PFI was associated with greater attitudinal ambivalence.

Another, attachment-related personality trait or ability which may overlaps with ambivalence refers to the *mentalization,* studied also as *reflective function,* (Fonagy, Steele, Steele, Moran, et al., 1991; Slade, Grienenberger, Bernbach, Levy & Locker, 2005). Reflective function refers to the capacity to mentalize and reflect on the mind of self and others (Fonagy et al., 1991). Ability to mentalize means being able to understand mental states (emotions, motives, points of view) of others and have insight into own mental states. Although mentalization in attachment research is studied mostly as the capacity of mothers which, when lacking, may underlie disorganization of the infant-mother attachment relation (e.g., Slade et al., 2005), it seems to be also important when attachment ambivalence is investigated. A similar construct studied in psychology which focuses in particular on this capacity relates to *mindfulness* (Brown & Ryan, 2003) defined as keeping one's consciousness alive to present reality. It seems plausible that reflective and mindful individuals may be more aware of their ambivalence, and the transfer of potential to felt ambivalence may be faster for them as compared to less reflective individuals regardless of their attachment style. It seems also possible that the mentalization process may result in activation of coping strategies to reduce tension (decreasing felt ambivalence) or in a long-term increase of tolerance for ambiguity (increasing felt ambivalence).

Relationship Factors

Although I treat so far attachment ambivalence as an internal state based on life-time experiences and personality factors, it has to be also highlighted that the state of ambivalence may be evoked by objective factors not related with chronic hyperactivation of the attachment system or one's cognitive style. The state of ambivalence in intimate relations may be provoked by the *quality of relationship* and the resulting perception of *relationship satisfaction.* Then, the state of ambivalence would be a marker of conflicts and negativity in a particular relationship (Gottmann, Coan, Carrere & Swanson, 1998; Thompson & Holmes, 1996).

Moreover, not only individuals but also their relationship partners differ regarding their personality and life-histories which may amplify or trigger ambivalence through lack of trust toward own partner. *Individual trust,* defined as one's capacity to assess the trustworthiness of one's potential partner, arises also from the objectively assessed risk assumed in the relationship (Sheppard & Sherman, 1998). One's perception of the own relationship in which the partner is seen as not reliable, discreet or supportive in the past would probably bias one's closure and (multifold) ambivalence in this relationship, which may be not present in other relationships which an individual maintains.

Another relationship-like factor influencing ambivalence relates to *commitment* in the relationship. It reflects the investments made in the relationship (*dedicated commitment*, related with wanting to stay in the relationship; or *constrained commitment*, related with forces that propel a person to stay) (Owen, Rhoades, Shuck, Fincham, Stanley, Markman & Knopp, 2014). Investment in the relationship encompasses not only time or resources but also sacrifices, and this differs for anxious individuals and individuals revealing other attachment patterns (Etcheverry, Le, Wu & Wei, 2013; Impett & Gordon, 2010). As the extent of involvement was found also in attitude studies to be positively related with ambivalence (Thompson & Zanna, 1995), it seems possible that high commitment may amplify felt attachment ambivalence in the relationship.

Owen and colleagues (2014) proposed that ambivalence may seem part and parcel of commitment uncertainty, and that the two are clearly linked. Yet, according to these authors commitment uncertainty is relationship specific, whereas ambivalence may take two forms. First, it can relate to the notion of commitment, which is a more trait-like feature than commitment uncertainty in a specific relationship, and relates to being ambivalent about commitment in general. Such ambivalence may cause varying investments in the relationship and relates to attachment hyper- or deactivation of the attachment system. Second, ambivalence may be similar to commitment uncertainty and may arise in a specific relationship. However, commitment uncertainty reflects how one thinks about the commitment to the particular relationship, not how ambivalent his or her commitment is (Owen et al., 2014).

Culture

Social norms determine what is normative and thus acceptable in a particular society. Cross-cultural studies revealed that societies differ regarding *core cultural ideas* (Markus & Kitayama, 1994), in which members of a particular culture are socialized and which affect the way people view themselves and the world. For example, Western cultures differ from Asian cultures in the level of ambiguity tolerance (Hofstede & Hofstede, 2005), cognitive styles (Nisbett, 2009) but also self-reported attachment (Friedman, Rholes, Simpson, Bond, Diaz-Loving & Chan, 2010; Lubiewska, van de Vijver, Mayer, Trommsdorff, & Nauck, 2016). Avoidance, anxiety or ambivalence may be differentially fostered by cultural norms.

According to the cultural fit hypothesis perceived or actual differences between an individual and the culture in which he or she is situated are related to psychological discomfort (Ward & Chang, 1997) and thus, trigger more negative outcomes. For example, Friedman and colleagues (2010) found that intimate partner's avoidance was related with more negative outcomes (like relationship dissatisfaction or a lower level of relationship investments) in Asian cultures where avoidant relational behaviors are less normative than in Western cultures. The divergence between own hyperactivating behavior in close relationships and cultural norms defining the extent to which such hyperactivation is normatively acceptable, may increase the tension of anxious individuals amplifying their level of ambivalence, including ambivalence over emotional expression. This mechanism seems to be supported in the study of Thompson and Holmes (1996). Even though these authors did not investigate cross-cultural differences, they described underlying mechanisms by providing evidence that divergence between the perceived level of partner's attribute and the ideal level of this attribute they hoped their partner would have was positively associated with relational ambivalence. Although the same effect may be weaker for culture, it is also worth of considering.

CONCLUDING REMARKS

In this chapter I aimed to highlight the importance of in-depth studies focused on attachment ambivalence for attachment theory and practice, and discuss issues important for attachment ambivalence assessment. Although, as the content of this chapter reveals, the assessment of attachment ambivalence seems to be a difficult task, the relative lack of studies and their value for health and positive psychology seems to call for more attention of attachment researchers.

Not all problems related with attachment ambivalence assessment were discussed in this chapter. For example, some factors influencing the strength of felt ambivalence were characterized, yet not directly discussed in terms of factors amplifying the extent of ambivalence. In particular, aside simultaneous activation of contradicted evaluations, one's involvement in or commitment to the relationship or personal traits and culture, other factors might be also considered. For example, personal importance of particular relationship and the extent of one's decisiveness regarding commitment to the relationship may moderate the level of ambivalence. In this vein, parent-child and intimate relations maintained in adulthood may foster ambivalence differently. The parent-child relation is usually not the core relationship in adulthood and it is also not a matter of choice, thus ambivalence in this relation may evoke less decision-related tension, engage coping strategies (e.g., procrastination) and some, but not strong, commitment to this relationship. In contrast, ambivalence and related tension in intimate relationships is the background of everyday experiences and is core for most adults. However, the commitment to the relationship is also more the matter of choice (especially in Western cultures). We can divorce partners but not own parents. Thus higher agency (potential decisiveness about commitment) and importance of the intimate relationship in adult life may generate higher ambivalence-related tension and engage coping strategies. Therefore, it is worth considering to what extent self-reported assessment of ambivalence in core relationships of a respondent is just a sample of declaration, or an experimental manipulation in itself where potential ambivalence is forced to appear in awareness overthrowing defensive coping mechanisms and increasing pressure for respondent's decisiveness (or just the decision how to respond to the survey question). Such a self-report assessment of attachment ambivalence seems not to be psychologically equivalent to self-report assessments of ambivalence related with social attitudes which are less core for the self.

REFERENCES

Ainsworth, M. D. S., Blehar, M., Waters, E., & Wall, S. (1978) *Patterns of attachment: A psychological study of the Strange Situation.* Hillsdale, NJ: Erlbaum.

Bartholomew, K., & Horowitz, L. M. (1991). Attachment styles among young adults: A test of four-category model. *Journal of Personality and Social Psychology, 2,* 226–244.

Basseches, M. A., (1980). Dialectical schemata: A framework for the empirical study of the development of dialectical thinking. *Human Development, 23,* 400–421.

Bell, D. W., & Esses, V. M. (2002). Ambivalence and response amplification: A motivational perspective. *Personality and Social Psychology Bulletin, 28,* 1143–1152.

Ben-Air, A., & Lavee, Y. (2011). Ambivalence over emotional expressiveness in intimate relationships: A shift from an individual characteristic to dyadic attribute. *American Journal of Orthopsychiatry, 81,* 277–284.

Birnbaum, G. E., Mikulincer, M., Szepsenwol, O., & Shaver, P. (2014). When sex goes wrong: A behavioral system perspective on individual differences in sexual attitudes, motives, feelings, and behaviors. *Journal of Personality and Social Psychology, 5,* 822–842.

Bowlby, J. (1969). *Attachment and loss: Volume 1: Attachment.* New York, NY: Basic Books.

Bowlby, J. (1973). *Attachment and loss: Volume 2: Separation, anxiety, and anger.* New York, NY: Basic Books.

Brown, K. W., & Ryan R. M. (2003). The benefits of being present: Mindfulness and its role in psychological well-being. *Journal of Personality and Social Psychology, 84,* 822–848.

Campbell, L., & Marshall, T. (2011). Anxious attachment and relationship processes: An interactionist perspective. *Journal of Personality, 79,* 917–947.

Chen, S. X., Cheung, F. M., Bond, M. H., & Leung, J.-P. (2005). Decomposing the construct of ambivalence over emotional expression in a Chinese cultural context. *European Journal of Personality, 19,* 185–204.

Chen, M, & Bargh, J. A. (1999). Consequences of automatic evaluation: Immediate behavioral predispositions to approach or avoid the stimulus. *Personality and Social Psychology Bulletin, 25,* 215–224.

Cialdini, R. B., Trost, M. R., & Newsom, J. T. (1995). Preference for consistency: The development of a valid measure and the discovery of surprising behavioral implications. *Journal of Personality and Social Psychology, 69,* 318–328.

Collins, N. L., & Read, J. R. (1990). Adult attachment, working models, and relationship quality in dating couples. *Journal of Personality and Social Psychology, 58*, 644–663.

Connidis, I. A. (2015). Exploring ambivalence in family ties: Progress and prospects. *Journal of Marriage and Family, 77*, 77–95.

Deci, E. L., & Ryan, R. M. (2000). The "what" and "why" of goal pursuits: Human Leeds and the self-determination of behavior. *Psychological Inquiry, 11*, 227–268.

Dewitte, M., & De Houwer, J. (2008). Proximity and distance goals in adult attachment. *European Journal of Personality, 22*, 675–694.

Emmons, R. A., & Colby, P. M. (1995). Emotional conflict and wellbeing: Relation to perceived availability, daily utilization, and observer reports of social support. *Journal of Personality and Social Psychology, 68*, 947–959.

Etcheverry, P. E., Le, B., Wu, T.-F., & Wei, M. (2013). Attachment and the investment model: Predictors of relationship commitment, maintenance, and persistence. *Personal Relationships, 20*, 546–567.

Festinger, L. (1957). *A theory of cognitive dissonance.* Evanston, IL: Row, Peterson.

Friedman, M., Rholes, W. S., Simpson, J., Bond, M. Diaz-Loving, R., & Chan C. (2010). Attachment avoidance and cultural fit hypothesis: A cross-cultural investigation. *Personal Relationships, 17*, 107–126.

Fonagy, P., Steele, M., Steele, H., Moran, G. S., & Higgitt, A. C. (1991). The capacity for understanding mental states: The reflective self in parent and child and its significance for security of attachment. *Infant Mental Health Journal, 12*(3), 201–218.

Furnham, A., & Marks, J. (2013). Tolerance of ambiguity: A review of the recent literature. *Psychology, 4*, 717–728.

Furnham, A., & Ribchester, T. (1995). Tolerance of ambiguity: A review of the concept, its measurement and applications. *Current Psychology, 14*, 179–199.

Gillath, O., Mikulincer, M., Fitzsimons, G. M., Shaver, P. R., Schachner, D. A., & Barg, J. A. (2006). Automatic activation of attachment-related goals. *Personality and Social Psychology Bulletin, 32*, 1375–1388.

Gottmann, J. M., Coan, J. A., Carrere, S., & Swanson, C. (1998). Predicting marital happiness and stability from newlywed interactions. *Journal of Marriage and the Family, 60*, 5–22.

Granqvist, P., & Kirkpatrick, L. A. (2008). Attachment and religious representations and behavior. In J. Cassidy & P. R. Shaver (Eds.), *Handbook of attachment. Theory, research, and clinical applications* (pp. 906–933). New York, NY: The Guilford Press.

Hazan, C., & Shaver, P. (1987). Romantic love conceptualized as an attachment process. *Journal of Personality and Social Psychology, 52*, 511–524.

Hagemeyer, B., Neyer, F. J., Neberich, W., & Asendorpf, J. B. (2013). The ABC of social desires: Affiliation, being alone, and closeness to partner. *European Journal of Personality, 27*, 442–457.

Hofmann, W., Gawronski, B., Gschwendner, T., Le, H., & Schmitt, M. (2005). A meta-analysis on the correlation between the Implicit Association Test and explicit self-report measures. *Personality and Social Psychology Bulletin, 31*, 1369–1385.

Hofstede, G., & Hofstede, G. J. (2005). *Kultury i organizacje* [*Cultures and organizations. Software of the mind*]. Warsaw, Poland: Polskie Wydawnictwo Ekonomiczne.

Impett, E. A., & Gordon, A. M. (2010). Why do people sacrifice to approach rewards versus to avoid costs? Insights from attachment theory. *Personal Relationships, 17*, 299–315.

Kaplan, K. J. (1972). On the ambivalence-indifference problem in attitude theory and measurement: A suggested modification of the semantic differential technique. *Psychological Review, 77*, 361–372.

Kelly, R. E., Wood, A. M., Shearman, K., Phillips, S., & Mansell, W. (2012). Encouraging acceptance of ambivalence using the expressive writing paradigm. *Psychology and Psychotherapy: Theory, Research and Practice, 85*, 220–228.

King, L. A., & Emmons, R. A. (1990). Conflict over emotional expression: Psychological and physical correlates. *Journal of Personality and Social Psychology, 58*, 864–877.

Larsen, J. T., Norris, C. J., McGraw, A. P., Hawkley, L. C., & Cacioppo, J. T. (2009). The evaluative space grid: A single-item measure of positivity and negativity. *Cognition and Emotion, 23*, 453–480.

Levy, K. N., Blatt, S. J., & Shaver, P. R. (1998). Attachment styles and parental representations. *Journal of Personality and Social Psychology, 74*, 407–419.

Li, T., & Chan, D. K.-S. (2012). How anxious and avoidant attachment affect romantic relationship quality differently: A meta-analytic review. *European Journal of Social Psychology, 42*, 406–419.

Locke, K. D. (2008). Attachment styles and interpersonal approach and avoidance goals in everyday couple interactions. *Personal Relationships, 15*, 359–374.

Lubiewska, K., van de Vijver, A. J. R., Mayer, B., Trommsdorff, G., & Nauck, B. (2016). *Adult Attachment Scale: Mean differences across 14 cultures and 3 generations.* Manuscript in preparation.

MacDonald G., Locke, K. D., Spielmann S. S., & Joel, S. (2013). Insecure attachment predicts ambivalent social threat and reward perceptions in romantic relationships. *Journal of Social and Personal Relationships, 30*, 647–661.

Maio, G. R., Fincham, F. D., Regalia, C., & Paleari, F. G. (2004). Ambivalence and attachment in family relationships. In K. Pillmer & K. Lüscher (Eds.), *Intergenerational ambivalences: New perspectives on parent–child relations in later life* (pp. 285–312). Bingley, England: Emerald.

Markus, H. R., & Kitayama, S. (1994). The cultural shaping of emotion: A conceptual framework. In S. Kitayama & H. R. Markus (Eds.), *Emotion and culture: Empirical studies of mutual influence* (pp. 339–351). Washington, DC: American Psychological Association.

McClure, M. J., Bartz, J. A., & Lydon, J. E. (2012). Uncovering and overcoming ambivalence: The role of chronic and contextually activated attachment in two-person social dilemmas. *Journal of Personality, 81*, 103–117.

Michels, T., Albert, I., & Ferring, D. (2011). Psychologische Ambivalenz in eltern-kind-baziehungen. Entwicklung und teststatistische uberprufung eines instrumentes zur directen konstruktabbildung. *Diagnostica, 57*, 39–51.

Mikulincer, M., Birnbaum, G., Woddis, & Nachmias, O. (2000). Stress and Accessibility of proximity-related thoughts: Exploring the normative and individual components of attachment theory. *Journal of Personality and Social Psychology, 78*, 509–523.

Mikulincer, M., & Shaver, P. R. (2007). *Attachment in adulthood: Structure, dynamics, and change.* New York, NY: Guilford Press.

Mikulincer, M., Shaver, P. R., Bar-On, N., & Ein-Dor, T. (2010). The pushes and pulls of close relationships: Attachment insecurities and relational ambivalence. *Journal of Personality and Social Psychology, 98*, 450–468.

Moss, S. A., & Wilson, S, G. (2015). The positive emotions that facilitate the fulfillment of needs may not be positive emotions at all: The role of ambivalence. *EXPLORE, 11*, 40–50.

Neuberg, S. L., Judice, T. N., & West, S. G. (1997). What the need for closure scale measures and what it does not: Toward differentiating among related epistemic motives. *Journal of Personality and Social Psychology, 72*, 1396–1412.

Newby-Clark, I. R., McGregor, I., & Zanna, M. P. (2002). Thinking and caring about cognitive inconsistency: When and for whom does attitudinal ambivalence feel uncomfortable? *Journal of Personality and Social Psychology, 82*, 157–166.

Nikitin, J., & Freund, A. M. (2008). The role of social approach and avoidance motives for subjective well-being and the successful transition to adulthood. *Applied Psychology, 57*, 90–111.

Nikitin, J., & Freund, A. M. (2010). When wanting and fearing go together: The effect of co-occurring social approach and avoidance motivation on behavior, affect, and cognition. *European Journal of Social Psychology, 40*, 783–804.

Nisbett, R. E. (2009). *Geografia myslenia* [*The geography of thought. How Asians and Westerners think differently . . . and why*]. Sopot: GWP.

Noftle, E. E., & Shaver, P. R. (2006). Attachment dimensions and the big five personality traits: Associations and comparative ability to predict relationship quality. *Journal of Research in Personality, 40*, 179–208.

Oskis, A., Clow, A., Hucklebridge, F., Bifulco, A., Jacobs, C., & Loveday, C. (2013). Understanding alexithymia in female adolescents: The role of attachment style. *Personality and Individual Differences, 54*, 97–102.

Owen, J., Rhoades, G., Shuck, B., Fincham, F. D., Stanley, S., Markman, H., & Knopp, K. (2014). Commitment uncertainty: A theoretical overview. *Couple and Family Psychology: Research and Practice, 3*, 207–219.

Reynolds, S., Searight, H. R., & Ratwik, S. (2014). Adult attachment styles and rumination in the context of intimate relationships. *North American Journal of Psychology, 16*, 495–506.

Sheppard, B. H., & Sherman, D. M. (1998). The grammars of trust: A model and general implications. *Academy of Management Review, 23*, 422–437.

Slade, A., Grienenberger, J., Bernbach, E., Levy, D., & Locker, A. (2005). Maternal reflective functioning, attachment, and the transmission gap: A preliminary study. *Attachment & Human Development, 7*, 283–298.

Stevens, F. L. (2014). Affect regulation styles in avoidant and anxious attachment. *Individual Differences Research, 12*, 123–130.

Suitor, J. J., Gilligan, M., & Pillemer, K. (2011). Conceptualizing and measuring intergenerational ambivalence in later life. *The Journals of Gerontology, Series B: Psychological Sciences and Social Sciences, 66*, 769–781.

Surjadi, F. F., Lorenz, F. O., Conger, R. D., & Wickrama, K. A. S. (2013). Harsh, inconsistent parental discipline and romantic relationships: Mediating process of behavioral problems and ambivalence. *Journal of Family Psychology, 27,* 762–772.

Thompson, M. M., & Holmes, J. G. (1996). Ambivalence in close relationships: Conflicted cognitions as a catalyst for change. In R. M. Sorrentino & E. T. Higgins (Eds.), *Handbook of motivation and cognition,* Vol. 3: *The interpersonal context* (pp. 497–530). New York, NY: Guilford Press.

Thompson, M. M., & Zanna, M. P. (1995). The conflicted individual: Personality-based and domain-specific antecedents of ambivalent social attitudes. *Journal of Personality, 63,* 259–288.

Thompson, M. M., Zanna, M. P., & Griffin, D. W. (1995). Let's not be indifferent about (attitudinal) ambivalence. In R. E. Petty & J. A. Krosnick (Eds.), *Attitude strength: Antecedents and consequences* (pp. 361–386). Hillsdale, NJ: Erlbaum.

Trachsel, M., Ferrari, L., & Holtforth, M. G. (2012). Resolving partnership ambivalence: A randomized controlled trial of very brief cognitive and experiential interventions with follow-up. *Canadaian Journal of Counselling and Psychotherapy, 46,* 239–258.

Tucker, J. S., Winkelman, D. K., Katz, J. N., & Bermas, B. L. (1999) Ambivalence over emotional expressiveness and psychological well-being among rheumatoid arthritis patients and their spouses. *Journal of Social Psychology, 29,* 271–290.

Uchino, B. N., Bosch, J. A., Smith, T. W., Carlisle, M., Birmingham, W., Bowen, K. S., ... O'Hartaigh, B. (2013). Relationships and cardiovascular risk: Perceived spousal ambivalence in specific relationship contexts and its links to inflammation. *Health Psychology, 32,* 1067–1075.

van IJzendoorn, M. H., & Sagi-Schwartz, A. (2008). Cross-cultural patterns of attachment. Universal and contextual dimensions. In J. Cassidy & P. R. Shaver (Eds.), *Handbook of attachment. Theory, research, and clinical applications* (pp. 880–905). New York, NY: The Guilford Press.

van Harreveld, F., Rutjens, B. T., Schneider, I. K., Nohlen, H. U., & Keskinis, K. (2014). In doubt and disorderly: Ambivalence promotes compensatory perceptions of order. *Journal of Experimental Psychology, 143,* 1666–1676.

van Harreveld, F., van der Pligt, J., & de Liver, Y. N. (2009). The agony of ambivalence and ways to resolve it: Introducing the MAID model. *Personality and Social Psychology Review, 13,* 45–61.

Ward, C., & Chang, W. C. (1997). "Cultural fit": A new perspective on personality and sojourner adjustment. *International Journal of Intercultural Relations, 21,* 525–533.

Wilson, T. D., & Hodges, S. D. (1992). Attitudes as temporary constructions. In A. Tesser & L. Martin (Eds.), *The construction of social judgement* (pp. 37–65). Hillsdale, NY: Erlbaum.

PART V

GENERAL CONCLUSIONS

CHAPTER 15

TRANSCENDING AMBIVALENCE

Overcoming the Ambiguity of Theory and Practices

Jaan Valsiner
Aalborg University

Isabelle Albert
University of Luxembourg

Emily Abbey
Ramapo College

Ambivalence[1] is a deeply ambiguous concept. Contributions to the present book, viewed all together, exemplify that verdict, as they are situated in the intellectual space among theory, phenomena, research practices, and basic assumptions about the world.

Starting from the latter—any possibility for inventing any notion of ambivalence becomes possible only if one axiomatically assumes that the

Trans-Generational Family Relations, pages 311–331

phenomena of our interest involve more than one characteristic at the same time. In the case of common sense, the saying "Every coin has two sides" illustrates the fixed unity of opposites. Although the copresence of opposites is everywhere, the same commonsense patterns of thinking work against the possibility of seeing their duality. We enforce unitary identity on complex phenomena, forgetting the comparison that makes such assertions possible. While claiming "this mountain is high," we overlook that the height of the mountain is contrasted with the low valley next to it (Bleuler, 1914). In observing social acts, we guide ourselves to follow the Boolean logic—that tolerates no coexistence—in claiming "She is either a hero or a murderer" (Figure 15.1).

There is no option for a simultaneous determination that the person performing the operation—the biblical figure of Judith depicted in the act

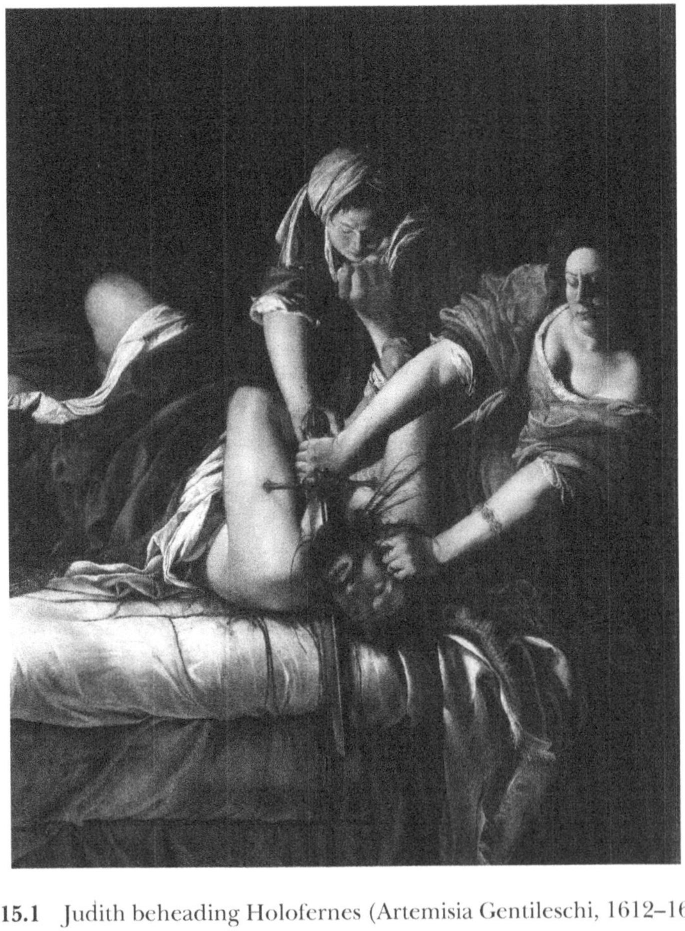

Figure 15.1 Judith beheading Holofernes (Artemisia Gentileschi, 1612–1614).

of cutting off the head of a man[2] who has been designated as a dangerous enemy—would be simultaneously both. Naturally, various narrators of the Judith and Holofernes story over the centuries would not accept both interpretations at the same time. For the purposes of propagating the patriotic duty, it is only the heroine—rather than the murderer—status that is enforced on the figure of Judith. The listener—or viewer of paintings—is required to accept the axiom of heroic duty carried out through the hands of a beautiful widow. As Kevin Carriere (Chapter 13, this volume) points out, the notions of rights and duties are "semiotic traps" that capture us through the subliminal affective bonding filled with tensions that is framed by ideologically monological superimposition of value. The duties and rights are affectively ambivalent concepts where the ambivalence is overcome in their framing.

There is no ambiguity in the act depicted in Figure 15.1—it is brutal act of killing that we can observe—although for our contemporary reader/viewer, it is an event shrouded in deep ambivalence. The moral imperatives "You should not kill!" and "Your duty is to kill the enemy" are inherent in the organization of any society—in our time or others. Their copresence only can be masked by the intentional forgetting of the other—depending on whether the time is that of peace or war.

INVISIBLE AMBIVALENCE

If we theoretically assume that our worlds consist of objects of dual nature, what about cases of no detectable ambivalence? In these cases, ambivalence needs to be posited as either hidden (masked) or reduced to minimum. Yet even in the latter case, it is presumed to exist—by observing the moon and not being able to see its reverse side, we cannot assume that our failure to see it indicates that the other side is absent. Or—if we consider that the whole observed is an illusion—the "phantom of the moon"—it would be all of its sides the existence of which we doubt.

Accepting unity of opposites in the same object is a kind of cognitive accomplishment. It is not coincidental that the notion of ambivalence was invented relatively recently (Bleuler, 1910, 1914) and in the context—psychological phenomena displayed by psychiatric patients—where cardinally different characteristics are copresent within the same person. A mother who has killed her own newborn child feels deep love for the child. Phenomena of love turn into hate, and vice versa, with remarkable ease.

Interestingly, a gap in the history of European thought in considering the unity of opposites exists. Bleuler's invention was preceded by more than a century of focus on the unity of opposites within the same whole—within the dialectical view of the world—that was developed by Solomon Maimon,

Johann Gottfried Fichte, and Georg Wilhelm Hegel at the end of the 18th century. Bleuler's goals were different. He was a practicing psychiatrist of empirical interests and the tendency to invent new terms. By inventing the notion of *Ambivalenz*, he wanted to give ontological status to the copresent phenomena (as in diagnosis of schizophrenia—another of his terminological inventions)—while the dialectical philosophy of the 19th century was obsessed with the question of conflict and the overcoming the opposites as a result of dynamic tension. One can detect intellectual discomfort of the philosophers in this focus on overcoming—the tension between mutually linked opposites was to be transformed into an abyss of no tension, even if temporarily. In contrast, Bleuler's psychiatric patients did not display the rapid capacities for overcoming the opposites by circumvention (Josephs & Valsiner, 1998) or through dialectical synthesis (Valsiner, 2012). They displayed phenomena of copresence of opposite tendencies, their "flip-flopping" (dominance reversal), and tension as they could not overcome the tension between the opposites. That became for psychiatrists the criterion of detection of their psychiatric status. Once phenomena of ambivalence were usable for diagnosis, no further use of theirs was necessary.

However, there were mental models on which to build. In European thought models that preceded the invention of *Ambivalenz*, the mathematical model of the Möbius loop[3] fits Bleuler's invention most fittingly. In that loop, the front and back sides are constantly seamlessly changing places, yet at every moment on the loop the fixed opposition of back and front are discernible. The Möbius loop is an eternal unity of linked opposites that are never in tension with one another yet dynamically take the place of one another with strict regularity.

DEVELOPMENTAL SCIENCE: NEED FOR AMBIVALENCE

Pathology is usually an extension of the normal ways of being, and these ways of being are actually those of becoming. As Abbey (2012) has pointed out, our life spaces are composed by forces that pull him or her in differing if not outright opposing directions. All over a person's life course, he or she necessarily experiences ambivalence caused by the future-oriented nature of human meaning-making. Ambivalence is a developmental necessity—axiomatically given by the need to coordinate in the present the meaningful aspects of the vanishing past and the yet-to-be-known future. This is done through signs that mediate the relation of the irreconcilable opposites—in irreversible time. In that process, signs emerge in different forms, ranging from total undifferentiation (null sign) to total determinacy ("strong sign" marking inflexibility). The functional realm of ambivalence is mediated in between these two opposites:

> The person starts to experience ambivalence on the basis of the contrast between a sign's representational and presentational sense. In this condition, the ambivalence is of a mild to moderate level, and as the person continues to overcome these tensions, new meanings emerge in a relatively erratic basis. The person concludes that one idea may be appropriate and then this sense shifts as his or her life experience shifts and new meanings are made. (Abbey, 2012, p. 993)

Ambivalence here is not a state of phenomena but a means for development. Yet human development is not left to itself—it is heavily socially guided. Such guidance creates complex forms of ambivalences in the teaching–learning processes.

LINKED AMBIVALENCES: SOCIAL WORK IN PRACTICE

Complexities of the practical uses of ambivalences are profoundly illustrated by the case examples by Mogens Jensen (Chapter 12, this volume). As part of human development, the sociopedagogical fellowship that characterizes Danish social work practices with adolescents who are diagnosed (as "troubled") involves development of both the adult and the adolescent. At the same time, the power differential between them is large. The adolescent is segregated into special holding place that is distanced from the "problematic" home environment. It depends on the ingenuity of the social worker to navigate the ambiguity of the places of "helpful segregation" with the social relation of the social worker with the "troubled adolescent." In Chapter 12, we can observe a skillful set-up of functional ambivalences in these relations—an example of anticipatory recognition in Elsa de Mattos' terms (Chapter 5, this volume). Thus, the social worker ("Hans") is explicit in his communication with "Jeanett":

> Jeanett there is no doubt as I have been told by the social worker that at first chance you would like to run off to go back to your hometown. You think it is unfair you have been removed... and so on.... So please promise me one thing *so I can sleep better at night.* If you want to run off, then *wake me up and I will drive you to the train-station, I promise you.* And then you will have some hours off *and I will have to call the municipality and tell them: Jeanett ran off.* There is no reason to do something stupid. Of course *I will try to convince you to stay so we can establish something together,* but *I won't hold you back....* I will help you to the train, but *you know what it means: you will be hunted again.* (p. 250, emphasis added)

Hans here does something courageous (from the perspective of social work practices) by building a semiotic trap (see Chapter 13, this volume) for the working relation—as it turned out, a successful one, as long as he was kept on "Jeanett's case." The success ended with the end of their joint work.

Hans charted out the existing ambivalence in both the girl's and his own life spaces. Jeanett is assumed to be tempted to run away—as well as to know it is stupid ("You will be hunted again"). Hans is clear about what kind of ambivalence Jeanett's would bring to him—not sleeping at night, eliminating what they "establish together," and having to report on her running away, should that happen. His solution—hypothetically helping her to run away while having to report on her, yet hoping she would not want to leave. These mutually linked ambivalences of the adolescent and the adult are made explicit in the context of pedagogical effort to keep the girl from executing her right to be herself (i.e., run away) while being bound by the duty of "being helped." The social worker is maintaining his right to be a compassionate human being while working under the duty of being the warden for the semi-imprisoned adolescent who is institutionally designated to "need help." He crossed the border of the professional and personal domains in the life of a social worker—a move that is risky in any profession where professionals work with fellow human beings while representing social institutions that provide their income. It thus makes sense that Jeanett was surprised about "Hans" being a "weird person." Most people acting out their professional social roles build a wall between that and their personal ways of being human. Social institutions support such segregation. Human beings live under the social suggestions of self-gating their personal lives.

Mutually linked ambivalences are not specific to interpersonal relations—they occur within the psyche of any human being. Of course any person is socially embedded within one's *Umwelt*, and at times the ways of maintaining the status quo of such ambivalences are supported by societal frames. The example of the feeling of *saudade* (Chapter 11, this volume; Silva, 2012) in the Portuguese language room gains its societal framing in the characteristic sounds of the music of *fado* and its local performances in *fado* singing clubs where ordinary people burst into the soul-penetrating expression of the totality of their momentary feelings (Nielsen, Soares, & Machado, 2009).

UNIVERSALITY OF *SAUDADE*

Saudade is a hypergeneralized and arrested vibration of feeling. It includes the feeling into the present within which four ambivalences are mutually linked due to the nonattainability of exploration of the four directions ("*Saudade* is to love a past that hasn't yet passed. It's to refuse the present that hurts us. It's not to see the future that invites us"; Chapter 11, this volume). Despite the linguistic untranslatability of the Portuguese word in precise terms, the feeling it presents is universal—longing for something that is desired but unattainable, while reflecting in bittersweet ways to that process of longing (Figure 15.2).

Figure 15.2 is an extension of William Stern's (1935) personological scheme of the link of two "infinities"—that of environment ("external infinity") and its intrapsychological corresponding part ("internal infinity"). To these are added two time perspectives from the current moment of a life course—"past infinity" and "future infinity." All the four have limited access to the exploring person: the past is vanishing in the memory, the future not preknown, the external world explorable up to the horizon, and the internal infinity limited to the semiotic devices that allow one's "soul searching." Although not accessible, the four need not be blocked—but can be. *Saudade* emerges as a hypergeneralized feeling when all four are blocked. The only way out of the blocked situation of here and now is an affective reflexive stance in which opposite feelings are felt as penetrating one another.

A person attempting to explore the outer infinity is blocked by A, turning back to the status quo. The effort to explore past is blocked by B, the future by C. What is left is inner infinity—but if that also is blocked (D), the status quo becomes either an arena for arrested action ("fear

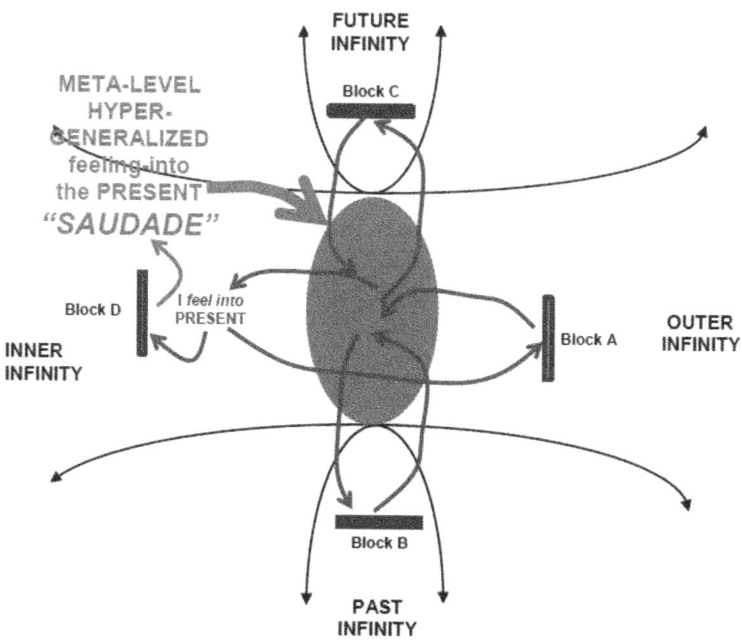

Figure 15.2 Saudade as a result of mutually linked ambivalences.

of action"; Janet, 1921, 1928) or evolves into a hypergeneralized feeling about the status quo—which is *saudade*. One feels "stuck" in the present status quo in a state that is simultaneously liked and disliked in a bitter-sweet way—preserving the totality of feeling within the extended present[4] (e.g., by *fado* singing[5]).

Of course under ordinary circumstances, not all of the four infinities are blocked for the experiencing person. Pontes and Simão (Chapter 10, this volume) provide a dramatic example of the subjective life course of Juliana, who, in her fight with impending infertility (block of outer infinity and future infinity), arrived at a new deep feeling within herself ("I wanted to prove to society that I had a child with him"), which created further blocks against external infinity (e.g., blocking adoption of a child or semen donor by another man—both pathways denying the relatedness—shared past—with her husband). It is not a child that Juliana begins to desire but his child—and precisely that possibility continues to be biologically blocked for her.

How cognitive and motivational aspects might interplay in the emergence of emotional ambivalences is outlined in a systematic analysis by Thomas Boll (Chapter 8, this volume), who makes two important distinctions. First, ambivalences can either arise from one desire that is experienced as partly fulfilled and partly frustrated by an individual or from different desires where one might be fulfilled and the other frustrated. Second, he underlines the importance of the temporal perspective, noting that ambivalences might both be oriented toward past or future (i.e., arise from anticipation but also from reflection).

AMBIVALENCE IN IDENTITY

All of these examples indicate the role of ambivalence as an inherent condition for human living. It is a condition of inherent dealing with ambiguities of living, between the person and the Umwelt, and between the past and the future. This use of the notion expands the concept far beyond its original descriptive role for what Bleuler coined it. Furthermore, after 1920s, the word has entered into common language and acquired surplus normative meaning—the unity of opposites that obscures clarity of thinking. "Being ambivalent about something (X)" is an indicator of a person's inability to decide about X or its opposite, rather than a description of a basic developmental process that include X and its opposite (non-X). The commonsense notion of ambivalence has been viewed as challenging the notion of identity (Lüscher, 2002), which is usually supposed to be a unitary notion. Speaking of somebody's identity, one is referencing an abstract prototype ("I am Australian") rather than a dialogical state ("I am Australian in deep dispute with my English ancestral roots"). The notion of identity is best elaborated within a framework of dialogical science (Hermans & Hermans-Konopka, 2010), where the axiomatic starting point is that of a relationship between opposites that exists within the same whole. In other terms, the commonsensically unitary notion of identity cannot be scientifically elaborated in unitary terms but requires a multicomponent systemic conceptualization. Identity ("this is X") is thus axiomatically analyzable in terms of a duality ("identity of X is relation between X and non-X").

Furthermore, the implicit affective meaning of ambivalence can be traced to have negative undertones.[6] This indicates interpenetration of the commonsense (evaluative) social representations into scientific terminology. In the latter, the notion of ambivalence serves as the ground for further conceptualization of dynamic processes—those of vacillation (*Vaszillieren*) and oscillation (*Oszillieren*; Lüscher, 2013) or of semiotic mediation through various kinds of dynamically changing signs on the border of past and future (Abbey, 2012; Surgan, Pefferkorn, & Abbey, 2018). Barni and Donato (Chapter 4, this volume) emphasize the interplay between opposing forces as it distinguishes a dialectical perspective from a dualistic perspective. Bleuler's original perspective was clearly that of duality but not of dialectical relationship of the ambivalent parts.

The condition for the use of the ambivalence notion in our theorizing is the unity of the general and the particular. On the meta-theoretical side, we need to posit that ambivalence exists—as unity of opposites. Yet that is not sufficient—we also need to specify concretely where it exists and what its functions are in the locations where we can find it. Merely descriptive categorization of the human psychological domain into "ambivalent" and "nonambivalent" categories does not provide for any understanding of either of the categories.

DETECTING AMBIVALENCE: LEVELS OF APPROACH

Kasearu, Raid, and Kutsar (Chapter 3, this volume) introduced a three-level organizational scheme for detecting phenomena of ambivalence. Starting from the societal (macro) level of values, norms, and societal structures, they charted out the central mesolevel role of the family in intergenerational mediation of the society and the developing person. Still the realities of ambivalence at all levels depend on their being observed at the microlevel—that of the person who reports "mixed feelings" about various aspects of living.[7] It is the person who detects ambivalence in the society and oneself and who utilizes it as a tool for further development—including efforts to overcome the ambivalence.

TRANSGENERATIONAL CHANGES AS ARENAS FOR AMBIVALENCE

It may be almost trivial to state that ambivalence is most likely detectable at the transition periods in human or societal life courses. Any social revolution is inherently a rupture of ambivalent kind—the "old" and the "new" are set into opposition in everyday life practices. Thus, Greenlandic families moving to Denmark or from rural to urban areas (Lyberth, Chapter 9, this volume) are situations where the "young" break away from the "old" traditions. Aside from change in traditions it is the values that change—and result in profound rupture with the past. The question is then how at the family level different generations can still negotiate their connectedness despite such value gaps and how to connect the past with the future? Thereby, it is clear that the transmission of values per se entails potential ambivalence—for the parents, one question might be how to reconcile the goals of raising a new generation which shares "old" values and at the same time knowing that children will need innovation and further capacities to encounter upcoming challenges in the future. Value change, on the one hand, is as essential for successful adaptation as is value transmission for intergenerational communication, on the other hand (see also Schönpflug, 2001).

The notion of continuity can be of help to reconcile these different goals. As put forth by Barni, Rosnati, and Ranieri (2013), continuity in the family may be more important than the actual value similarity. The intergenerational negotiation of such continuity might entail many instances of ambivalence—implicit and explicit—but the result of such processes could be a sense of family identity, which is more than the mere sharing of similar values. It is more of the kind of a joint conviction that "we in our family do like this," and this goes even beyond values that might be shared or not (Ferring, 2017). We can assume that ambivalence plays a crucial role here as a catalyzer that helps family members to come to terms with mutual expectations and to regulate their behavior, encountering each other's expectations even if not in line with own preferences, or deciding not to respond to the expectations of others, which both might however go along with feelings of ambivalence (see also Albert & Barros Coimbra, 2017). Here, it becomes clear that ambivalence might be a catalyzer or a result of regulation processes depending also on the point in the dialectic negotiation. In the end, it might be more important, how we deal with ambivalence—taking it as a promoter that triggers certain negotiation and developmental processes or taking it as a relationship quality and thus as a (preliminary) end state.

Kasearu, Raid, and Kutsar (Chapter 3, this volume) propose a way to link changing family behaviors and the theoretical perspective of ambivalence. Looking back to the works of Robert K. Merton—one of the first proponents of ambivalence in sociology—and following Connidis (2015), they argue that changes at societal level have an impact on the family institution, also shaping the relations between family members and increasing individual ambivalence in family behavior; the other way round, individuals—while negotiating their family relations—influence the social world surrounding them. Kasearu and colleagues therefore advocate a multilevel study of ambivalence in family studies.

CATALYTIC FRAMING OF AMBIVALENT RELATIONSHIPS

Human developmental processes are primarily catalyzed by specific conditions that enable—rather than cause—development (Cabell & Valsiner, 2013). Traditional samples-based methodological focus in psychology, based on correlational evidence, would allow for detecting the presence of such catalytic conditions. In our book, the role of parental warmth and support were found to be in correlational relation with ambivalence (Albert & Ferring, Chapter 6). Self-esteem may be another of such catalytic conditions (Steinhoff & Buchmann, Chapter 7, this volume). In that sense, a supportive family climate might help adolescents to deal with potential ambivalences that occur typically in the process of individuation when negotiating autonomy and relatedness between children and parents. Such a developmental context might foster self-esteem development, which the other way around will enable the individual to deal with ambivalences. Instead, family conditions containing a high use of parental psychological control—entailing intrusion and love withdrawal as parenting tools—might not allow for exploration of the offspring if they want to retain their relatedness to parents (i.e., offspring in this case might feel they have to decide between autonomy and relatedness, but they cannot have both) (Albert & Ferring, Chapter 6, this volume). This would probably correspond with the "captivation" mode as described by Lüscher and Hoff (2013).

This being said, the role of ambivalence as a catalyzer might be hampered in certain family constellations or also depending on personal characteristics (i.e., high ambivalence may also be less adaptive or even detrimental). In fact, in the case of attachment ambivalence, a situational threat-related activation of need for closeness might not be followed by goal-directed proximity seeking but be inhibited by relational anxiety as described by Katarzyna Lubiewska (Chapter 14, this volume). Such tension between a need for closeness and a high anxiety may have negative impacts for the individual and his or her relationships. Some individuals may be more prone to feel ambivalences in certain situations than others, and also these felt ambivalences may have different consequences depending on further factors such as differences in personality traits or their capacity to access inconsistent evaluations simultaneously.

These examples remind us once more that ambivalence is a multifaceted concept. As Eugenia Gouvedari (Chapter 2, this volume) suggests, the use of ambivalences in the plural form might be more adequate.

How do the catalytic processes work? Elsa de Mattos (Chapter 5, this volume) suggests that active self-positioning has a role in this process. As she suggests, youth transitions involve a process of self-positioning and repositioning, in which individuals seek to develop new meanings of themselves as well as of the world as they participate in increasingly diverse spheres of life presented by their social-historical context. This process brings ambivalence and tensions into the center of investigators' interests. The notion of anticipatory recognition emphasizes the agentive role of the person—the person expects something from the future, but the something needs to be recognized as coming, in the present.

Human development could be seen as a self-feeding process of dynamic tensegrity (Tateo, Chapter 1, this volume) between the organism oriented toward the future goals and its environment. Studying education and transgenerational family relationships by looking at the elements of ambivalence and tension as systemic features would then enable to account for a wider range of phenomena.

CONCLUSIONS: TRANSCENDING AMBIVALENCE TOWARD PROCESSES OF DIALECTICAL SYNTHESIS

Eugen Bleuler's beautiful terminological invention—ambivalence—has survived for a century. Yet it has its limits—lack of temporality and inflexibility of the posited relation between the opposites. These limits were not relevant for Bleuler at his time and context of psychiatric practices. Yet these obstacles become crucial if we want to consider developmental issues at all levels—of persons, family contexts in transgenerational angle, or societies as a whole. For example—sociological surveys regularly miss the social ambivalences that are crucial for sociopolitical transitions within societies (Smelser, 1998). In the case of development of human beings, the notions of temporal embeddedness (Surgan, Pfefferkorn, & Abbey, 2018) and anticipatory recognition (Mattos, Chapter 5, this volume) constitute a starting point for moving the use of the ambivalence concept from phenomena-descriptive to dialectically explanatory direction—as Barni and Donato (Chapter 4, this volume) suggest.

Calling for making research on ambivalent processes dialectical is no easy step. Let us not forget that all previous efforts—since the turn of the 18th and 19th centuries—to bring dialectical thought models into psychology's theoretical and methodological core have been episodic and have failed.[8] How could a new perspective on ambivalence bypass the conceptual traps into which science has entered repeatedly over the last two centuries?

TIME AS DURATION (*DURÉE*)

Using the temporal embeddedness of human lives as a starting point for moving research toward the dialectically explanatory direction, let us begin with a necessary axiomatic assumption that all researchers must adopt. It is the axiom of nonsameness of human life phenomena—of irreversible time. This notion is ensured by Bergson's (1913) notion of time as duration (*durée*), wherein the ego is understood to endure through each successive moment, accumulating a richer whole such that no two experiences can be alike. If one is to consider the emergence of two seemingly mundane days of life, following the "predictable" routine, it is possible to understand the idea that Bergson had in mind. Even two very "similar" events completed every day of one's life are different when approached from this axiom. Take, for instance, the act of waking from sleep and eating breakfast—something humans lucky enough to have nourishment at the ready complete regularly. On one day, sleep was restful, dreams were filled with lovers from decades past, and breakfast was toast, satisfying, yet not perfectly cooked, as toast always seems to be. On day two, sleep refused to come until the early hours of the morning and then was fitful. No dreams could be remembered. The morning was rushed due to lack of sleep and over breakfast of a roll, and thoughts drifted to how nice it would be to skip responsibilities to rest in bed for the day. These two seemingly identical experiences, waking from sleep to eat, are in fact quite unique—and so are all moments of all human lives. There is no sameness in human lives. This is because, as Bergson (1913) points out, life is not something that time happens in, as if time is merely an inert shelf holding up our existences. Our experiences, however ordinary and similar to one another, never feel exactly the same because they are lived through time. Our lives emerge much like the song falls from the fingers of the improvising Jazz musician—written by overcoming the ambivalence of the notes of the present and general tones of the future. We know what is happening at the present moment, and yet because of the nonsameness of the future, we are not sure what will come next. This nonsameness creates the context for ambivalences to emerge and become the object of our study; thus, this axiom must be the start of any empirical research program.

STUDYING EMERGENCE

Accepting the temporal embeddedness of human lives, to see what the process of one dialectical opposition transformations into another, we must understand the process of emergence. Methodologically, studying emergence can be challenging, for the researcher has to explain that which is not yet in existence on the basis of what is not yet in existence using only two pieces of information: what is known and what could be (Valsiner, 2001). As such, it is critical to maintain the time sequence of the data that are being produced, and so too, to use methods that allow the researcher to glimpse the intermediary forms. It is in these intermediary forms, rather than the "outcomes" of development" that emergence can be viewed as it occurs. Sometimes researchers confuse intermediary forms for a small time scale, but this is not always the case. Development cannot be seen by looking at outcomes sequenced in time—even if those outcomes occur over a short period of time as occurs in time series analysis. To document emergence, the researcher needs to gain access to the intermediary forms as transition occurs.

Rather, when considering how to transition ambivalence from a phenomena-descriptive to a dialectically explanatory concept, future research agendas might consider taking general guidance from the first portion of the 20th century and the tradition of *Ganzheitspsychologie* (see Diriwächter & Valsiner, 2007). The method, which in English is often referred to as the "microgentic method," involves the investigation of emergence by treating forms as merely boundary states, focusing instead on the intermediary forms. For example, instead of being interested in a series of outcomes A → B → C a microgenetic study is concerned with the progression from A–B and B–C (e.g., A → ab → B, and B → bc → C). Historically, the microgenetic method has been used to study the emergence of visual percepts (see e.g., Wohlfahrt, 1925/1932) and general meaning constructs (Werner, 1954). So, too, more recently researchers have begun to reincorporate such methods into developmental study (Abbey, 2015; Abbey & Diriwächter, 2008; Siegler, 1996).

Such an emergence and process-focused approach is a beginning response to the question posed previously. Yet it is ill advised for any researcher to take practices used by one researcher and simply apply them to another project. This too has been a problem in the modern world of psychology, seeing methodology as consisting of a personal "tool box" of ready-to-use methods (Branco & Valsiner, 1997) that are simply employed in the research at the specific moment that it is time to work with empirical data. On the contrary, methodology is better viewed as a cycle, wherein axiomatic assumptions, theory, phenomena, and method are all united with one another (Branco & Valsiner, 1997). Of critical importance for answering the earlier question, in this model, the researcher does not use reconstructed methods, but instead his or her methods are influenced by other aspects of the research cycle, most directly phenomena and theory have the most power in the system (Valsiner, 2000). On this understanding of methodology, it is not possible to specify completely an answer to the question or through history alone. Methods are emergent and come into being as researchers work through the tensions they face as they create projects. What is important to stress here, however, is that there must be coherence among all four aspects of the cycle: axiomatic assumptions (here, time as duration), theory, phenomena, and method.

INTUITION, AMBIVALENCE, AND POETRY

Outlined within Branco and Valsiner's (1997) model is that the researcher can use his or her intuition as a resource in the research process. Our intuition reflects the researcher's privileged knowledge of the research process, which can lead to valuable insights. In the present case, through 25 years of studying ambivalence, one intuition is that poetry may be the space where we get most directly to emotions and ambivalences (Lehmann, Chaudhary, Bastos, & Abbey, 2017). As such, poetry is one underused source of data available to researchers. We can see ambivalence in poetry—many kinds of ambivalence—and we can also see its transformation in time. Take, for example, the poem (untitled, author unknown):

> It is a good night for ghosts. The rabbit in the Moon is full and waiting to take souls to far shores as it crosses the sky.
>
> I dreamt a dream that I was with you tonight. I awoke and my lips were numb from saying your name.
>
> I dreamt that we were dreaming a dream together you and I and we were trapped in a house, big as memory. Countless doors.
>
> You were there. I could hear you laughing, but I only caught glimpses of you in the glass. Eventually I gave in and found myself staring at myself, reflected. Looking at myself looking back at me. Both of us trying to decipher the face that was in front of us. My eyes seeing me in mine and countless.
>
> I have retreated into twos because of you.
>
> I wonder, when you look in the mirror, who stares you down at night?
>
> But it is late, and my mind is running away with itself.
>
> Sleep well, wherever you are.
>
> It is a good night for ghosts. And between us, we have a pocketful.

In this poem, the author moves from a rather extended period of moderate ambivalence, and there we see the start-and-stop movement of meaning that is typical when ambivalence is at a moderate level. As the poem crescendos, there is a period of maximum ambivalence, and for a moment the meaning halts. A circumvention strategy is employed (Josephs & Valsiner, 1998), however, which allows the ambivalence to move from maximum back to a moderate level, and the poem concludes as it began, with erratic, start-and-stop meaning-making.

MODERATE AMBIVALENCE

This poem is about a lover, and as it begins, he is pining for his love: "I dreamt a dream that I was with you tonight. I awoke and my lips were numb from saying your name . . ." As we read on, moderate ambivalence is already visible because we learn that the author is not only yearning for his love, but it is a more delicate situation, for the woman he desires—the one of whom he dream—may not share his romantic interests as she is visible in his dream but only in small "glimpses": "You were there. I could hear you laughing, but I only caught glimpses of you in the glass." The world "glass" refers to a mirror, and mirrors become an important component of the poem, expressing concretely the lived duality of having part of ones self-caught up in someone else—as can be the case in a romance. The author expresses the moderate ambivalence of not wanting to look into that mirror, as if perhaps not wanting to acknowledge he may be the only one who is caught up in this particular love affair. Yet in the end, he cannot help himself, maybe hoping for another "glimpse' of her and "looks into the glass," so to speak. "Eventually I gave in and found myself staring at myself, reflected./ Looking at myself looking back at me./ Both of us trying to decipher the face that was in front of us." Here, the author is likely alluding to a difficult moment in life. Looking into the glass, he does not see her at all. It is a moment in a relationship where we understand perhaps only we are the ones in love. Certainly there is an expression of moderate ambivalence here and likely one that is escalating toward maximum ambivalence as that understanding sinks in deeper. Looking in the mirror and knowing who one is while simultaneously (and metaphorically) having to "decipher our face" is perhaps an experience many of us have had at some moment, and it is likely not a pleasant one.

MAXIMUM AMBIVALENCE

What comes next expresses, potentially, the lover's desperation and maximum ambivalence of realizing he may be alone in the duality of the love affair—that where one's partner's eyes should look in return, it is only his own, over and over and over again: "My eyes seeing me in mine and countless./I have retreated into twos because of you." He is saying that she, in her refusal to appear in the glass, has left only himself to stare back at himself: "I have retreated into twos because of you." What follows can be understood as a continuation of this maximum ambivalence of this position for the heart that loves so purely, perhaps moving the author to become almost curt for a moment: "I wonder, when you look in the mirror, who stares you down at night?"

RETURN TO MODERATE AMBIVALENCE

The ambivalence of this situation is maximum, but as the poem progresses, ambivalence returns to a more moderate level because the author uses a circumvention strategy (Josephs & Valsiner, 1998): "But it is late, and my mind is running away with itself." With this statement overriding the previous statements and thus lowering the level of ambivalence back to a moderate one, the poem can return to the emotional tone in which it began. The author speaks to his lover, who is still unidentified but clearly desired. He wants to say goodnight, although there is ambivalence still as he points out her whereabouts is unknown: "Sleep well, wherever you are." The last line (as the first) now makes some sense. It reads, "It is a good night for ghosts. And between us, we have a pocketful." "Ghosts" presumably refer to the selves we are when we love and cannot say for sure whether our love is returned. We drift around, half-selves, caught up into a dualistic relationship with another person. We cannot, in this understanding of love anyway, be "real" unless our lover should choose to join us.

FINAL THOUGHTS

Using a poem like this is just one example of how we might consider novel and innovative directions for research on ambivalence. For example, we might have participants write poetry about their feelings. One cannot predict the direction researchers will move in as their methodologies emerge through the tensions inherent in the research cycle. The main hope is that the study of ambivalence will move in the dialectically explanatory direction, keeping in focus the axiom of irreversible time, from which the first theoretical tensions grew and the notion of emergence through ambivalence began.

ACKNOWLEDGMENTS

The preparation of this chapter was made possible by a grant from the Fonds National de la Recherche Luxembourg (FNR, 2013–2016; Project: Intergenerational Relations in the light of Migration and Ageing [IRMA]; PI: Dr. Isabelle Albert). The first author acknowledges the support of Danske Grundforskningfond to his Niels Bohr Centre of Cultural Psychology.

NOTES

1. The term was invented in German—*Ambivalenz*—by Eugen Bleuler in 1910, linking "both" (*ambo*) and "strength" (*valentio*) in one word. It referred to the unity of fixed opposites *without modifiable relations* between them, yet with

tension due to their simultaneity. Thus, a drink (or feeling) can be "bitter" and "sweet" at the same time ("bittersweet"), and a person of any age is "young" and "old" at the same time (depending on the reference frame along the life course: "old" in relation to birth date, "young" in relation to a possible death date).

2. The man depicted in the biblical story—Holofernes—was an Assyrian warlord whose troops were surrounding the village of Bethulia (a fictional place). Judith—a beautiful widow and a citizen of Bethulia—used her charms to enter the tent of the enemy leader, managed to get him drunk, and then cut off his head that she subsequently carried off as a trophy. The headless enemy as a result failed to capture the village, and the danger was averted. This incident is presentable as an act of heroism in war, duty of a citizen in time of war, as well as *de facto* an act of killing a drunken man. The story—attributed to the period from the 3rd century BC to the 1st century AD is considered fictional with the aim of promoting patriotic duties. The story received much attention in 16th- and 17th-century European art, with almost all major artists depicting the decapitation scene, usually presenting realistic details of the act.
3. Invented in 1858 in parallel by German mathematicians August Möbius and Johann Benedikt Listing.
4. The efforts to "preserve" the affective moments in one's life—the good taste of food (in slow eating) or drink, the lazy relaxation on a beach, the reverberation of bodily pleasures to be continuing on from orgasms, or in the appreciation of sensual moments of body contact are similar moments of extending the experience of the moment.
5. The Fado Houses of Portugal are places of "intense interiority," which allows for deep expression of the interior self through the act of singing. The singer and musicians are deeply enmeshed in the "pouring out" of the interior of the soul (Nielsen, Soares, & Machado, 2009, pp. 300–301).
6. For example, "ambivalence is *not necessarily negative*..." (Lüscher, 2002, p. 587, emphasis added). Lüscher explicitly considers it a "sensitizing concept" (Lüscher, 2002, p. 585) that guides researchers' attention to phenomena, acknowledging, however, that this notion does not suffice ("Yet the notion of a 'sensitizing concept'—granted its pragmatic plausibility—is not fully appropriate for studying intergenerational ambivalence inasmuch as it overlooks the need for coherent theoretical foundations"; Lüscher & Hoff, 2013, p. 53).
7. However, Katarzyna Lubiewska (Chapter 14, this volume) cautions us that when assessing ambivalence through self-reports, questioning could trigger the coming to mind of ambivalences for the individual.
8. We can locate such efforts in the context of psychology in the Soviet Union in the 1920s that ended with the elimination of the discipline in 1936 (Valsiner, 1988), efforts by Klaus Riegel (1975) in the United States in the context of lifespan development research in the 1970s, and those by Irwin Altman (1993) in the area of environmental psychology in the 1980s. The absence of such efforts over the 19th century—the last effort was that by Karl Rosenkranz (1843)—can be explained by the social politics of the "war" for *Naturwissenschaft* in the German language areas (see Valsiner, 2012) that involved an overturn of Hegelian excesses. The failures of the efforts in the 20th cen-

tury can be explained by the social fixation of methodological norms in psychology from 1930s onward (Toomela & Valsiner, 2010), which is currently undergoing a period of *perestroika* through restoring the value of qualitative methods in science (Michell, 2004). In all of these efforts, the key value of the dialectical focus—on that of overcoming the previous state of contradiction (*Aufheben*) into a new dialectical opposition—has remained undeveloped. The "dialectical perspective" in the international scholarship of the second half of the 20th century, if present at all, has been considered as equaling the transactional perspective.

REFERENCES

Abbey, E. (2012). Ambivalence and its transformations. In J. Valsiner (Ed.), *The Oxford handbook of culture and psychology* (pp. 989–997). New York, NY: Oxford University Press.

Abbey, E., & Diriwächter, R. (Eds.). (2008) *Innovating genesis: Microgenesis and the constructive mind in action.* Charlotte, NC: Information Age.

Albert, I., & Barros Coimbra, S. (2017). Family cultures in the context of migration and ageing. *Integrative Psychological and Behavioral Science, 55,* 205–222.

Altman, I. (1993). Dialectics, physical environments, and personal relationships. *Communication Monographs, 60,* 23–34.

Barni, D., Rosnati, R., & Ranieri, S. (2013). Value transmission between parents and their adolescent children: The process and its outcomes: A psycho-social perspective. In I. Albert & D. Ferring (Eds.), *Intergenerational relations: European perspectives in family and society* (pp. 101–117). Bristol, England: Policy Press.

Bergson, H. (1913). *Time and free will.* London, England: George Allen & Co.

Bleuler, E. (1910). Vortrag von Prof. Bleuler über Ambivalenz. Aus Vereinen und Versammlungen. Ordentliche Winterversammlung des Vereins schweizerischer Irrenärzte in Bern. 26–27 November 1910. *Zentralblatt für Psychoanalyse (1911), 1,* 266–268.

Bleuler, E. (1914). Die Ambivalenz. In *Festgabe zur Einweihung der Neubauten der Universität Zürich 18.04.1914* (pp. 95–106). Zürich: Schulthess.

Branco, A. U., & Valsiner, J. (1997). Changing methodologies: A co-constructivist study of goal orientations in social interactions. *Psychology & Developing Societies, 9*(1) 35–64.

Cabell, K. R., & Valsiner, J. (Eds.). (2014). *The catalyzing mind: Beyond models of causality: Vol. 11 of Advances of Theoretical Psychology.* New York, NY: Springer.

Connidis, I. A. (2015). Exploring ambivalence in family ties: Progress and prospects. *Journal of Marriage and Family, 77,* 77–95.

Diriwächter, R., & Valsiner, J. (Eds.). (2007). *Striving for the whole: Creating theoretical syntheses.* Somerset, NJ: Transaction.

Ferring, D. (2017). The family in us: Family history, family identity and self-reproductive adaptive behavior. *Integrative Psychological and Behavioral Science, 51,* 195–204.

Hermans, H. J. M., & Hermans-Konopka, A. (2010). *Dialogical self theory: Positioning and counter-positioning in a globalizing society.* Cambridge, England: Cambridge University Press.

Janet, P. (1921). The fear of action. *Journal of Abnormal and Social Psychology, 16,* 150–160.

Janet, P. (1928). Fear of action as an essential element in the sentiment of melancholia. In M. Reymert (Ed.), *Feelings and emotions: The Wittenberg Symposium* (pp. 297–309). Worcester, MA: Clark University Press.

Josephs, I. E., & Valsiner, J. (1998). How does autodialogue work? Miracles of meaning maintenance and circumvention strategies. *Social Psychology Quarterly, 61,* 68–83.

Lehmann, O. V., Chaudhary, N., Bastos, A. C., & Abbey, E. (Eds.). (2018). *Poetry and imagined worlds.* Melbourne: Palgrave Macmillan.

Lüscher, K. (2002). Intergenerational ambivalence: Further steps in theory and research. *Journal of Marriage and Family, 64,* 585–593.

Lüscher, K. (2013). Das Ambivalente Erkunden. *Familiendynamik, 38,* 238–247.

Lüscher, K., & Hoff, A. (2013). Intergenerational ambivalence: beyond solidarity and conflict. In I. Albert & D. Ferring (Eds.), *Intergenerational relations: European perspectives in family and society* (pp. 39–63). Bristol: Policy Press.

Michell, J. (2004). The place of qualitative research in psychology. *Qualitative Research in Psychology, 1,* 307–319.

Nielsen, C. S., Soares, A. M., & Machado, C. P. (2009). The cultural metaphor revisited: Exploring dimensions, complexities and paradoxes through the Portuguese Fado. *International Journal of Cross-Cultural Management, 9,* 289–308.

Riegel, K. F. (1975). Toward a dialectical theory of development. *Human Development, 18,* 30–64.

Rosenkranz, K. (1843). *Psychologie, oder die Wissenschaft vom subjektiven Geist.* Königsberg: Bornträger.

Schönpflug, U. (2001). Intergenerational transmission of values: The role of transmission belts. *Journal of Cross-Cultural Psychology, 32,* 174–185.

Siegler, Robert S. (1996). *Emerging minds.* New York, NY: Oxford University Press.

Silva, Z. B. (2012). Saudade: A key Portuguese emotion. *Emotion Review, 5,* 203–211.

Smelser, N. (1998). The rational and the ambivalent in the social sciences. *American Sociological Review, 63,* 1–16.

Stern, W. (1935). *Allgemeine psychologie.* Den Haag: Martinus Njihoff.

Surgan, S., Pfefferkorn, A., & Abbey, E. (2018). Knowing ourselves: Dances of social guidance, imagination and development by overcoming ambivalence. In A. Rosa & J. Valsiner (Eds.), *Cambridge handbook of socio-cultural psychology* (2nd ed.). Cambridge, England: Cambridge University Press.

Toomela, A., & Valsiner, J. (Eds.). (2010). *Methodological thinking in psychology: 60 years gone astray?* Charlotte, NC: Information Age Publishers.

Valsiner, J. (1988). *Developmental psychology in the Soviet Union.* Brighton: Harvester Press.

Valsiner, J. (2001). *Comparative study of human cultural development.* Madrid: Fundacion Infancia y Aprendizaje.

Valsiner, J. (2012). *A guided science: History of psychology in the mirror of its making.* New Brunswick, NJ: Transaction Publishers.

Werner, H. (1954). Change of meaning: A study of semantic processes through the experimental method. *Journal of General Psychology, 50,* 181–208.

Wohlfahrt, E. (1932). Der Auffassungsvorgang an kleinen Gestalten. Ein Beitrag zur Psychologie des Vorgestalterlebnisses. *Neue Psychologische Studien, 4,* 347–414.

ABOUT THE CONTRIBUTORS

Emily Abbey is a professor in the Department of Psychology at Ramapo College of New Jersey. Working from an explicitly present-to-future developmental orientation, she is generally curious about the role imagination plays in guiding the transformation of thoughts and feelings over time. Recently, she has published her second edited volume, *Emerging Methods in Psychology* (Transaction Publishers) as well as made contributions to the *Oxford Handbook of Cultural Psychology* (Oxford University Press) and the *Cambridge Handbook of Socio-Cultural Psychology* (Cambridge University Press). E-mail: mimuspolyglottus@gmail.com

Isabelle Albert is a post-doctoral research scientist at the University of Luxembourg in the area of generations and development across the life-span. Her main research interests are in the field of life-span developmental psychology with a special focus on intergenerational transmission of values, intergenerational family relations in the context of migration as well as personality and family development across cultures. Her teaching activities include courses in psychology and gerontology. She is PI of the FNR-funded project on "Intergenerational Relations in the light of Migration and Ageing (IRMA)", MC Member of the COST Action IS1311 INTERFASOL ("Intergenerational Family Solidarity Across Europe") and Member of the EFPA Board on Cultural and Ethnic Diversity. She is editor of the volume *Intergenerational Relations: European Perspectives in Family and Society* together with Dieter Ferring (Policy Press). E-mail: isabelle.albert@uni.lu

Trans-Generational Family Relations, pages 333–338

Daniela Barni is Associate Professor of Social Psychology at the Department of Human Sciences, LUMSA University of Rome. She is a member of the Advisory board of the Family Studies and Research University Centre (Università Cattolica del Sacro Cuore, Milan). Her main research topics are values and intergenerational transmission of values, family relationships and adolescence. She is author or co-author of many scientific publications on these topics. E-mail: daniela.barni@unicatt.it

Stephanie Barros studied psychology at the Free University of Brussels (ULB, Belgium) and later joined the University of Luxembourg as a research associate on the FNR-funded IRMA-project (2013–2016) within the INSIDE unit. She is currently a PhD student at the University of Luxembourg, focussing on the concept of cultural identity and value transmission processes within Luxembourgish native compared to Portuguese migrant families all living in the Grand Duchy of Luxembourg. Her research interests focus on intergenerational family relations, family dynamics, identity & personality and transmission of values in a cross-cultural perspective and a life-span developmental perspective. E-mail: stephanie.barros@uni.lu

Thomas Boll is a senior researcher in life-span developmental psychology and geropsychology at the University of Luxembourg, Integrative Research Unit on Social and Individual Development (INSIDE). His research interests include inter-generational relationships, subjective well-being in adulthood, and caregiving for older people. He is a member of the editorial board of *GeroPsych: The Journal of Gerontopsychology and Geriatric Psychiatry* and of the Scientific Board of *Human Arenas. An Interdisciplinary Journal of Psychology, Culture, and Meaning*. E-mail: thomas.boll@uni.lu

Marlis Buchmann is professor of sociology and former director of the Jacobs Center for Productive Youth Development at the University of Zurich. She is also one of the two General Editors of *Emerging Trends in the Social and Behavioral Sciences* published by Wiley Online. Her research interests include social inequality, life course and competence development in children, youth, and young adults as well as labor market dynamics and social mobility across the life course. E-mail: buchmann@soziologie.uzh.ch

Kevin R. Carriere is a PhD candidate at Georgetown University where he examines the political psychology of perceived threat and its effects on support for human rights violations. His research focuses on how individuals understand, apply, and negotiate human rights and their violations through self-affirmation, education, and activism. His most recent co-edited book is entitled *Imagining Collective Futures: Perspectives from Social, Cutural, and Political Psychology*. E-mail: krcarriere@gmail.com

Silvia Donato is researcher in social psychology for the faculty of psychology at the Università Cattolica del Sacro Cuore–Milano. She is a member of the advisory board of the Family Studies and Research University Centre. Her research focuses on the study of stress and coping in couples, the intergenerational transmission of coping, partners' interpersonal perceptions, partners' support in response to positive events, scale psychometrics, preventive psychosocial interventions and their evaluation. E-mail: silvia.donato@unicatt.it

Dieter Ferring (†) was a Professor of Psychology and the co-founder and longtime director of the "Integrative Research Unit on Individual and Social Development" (INSIDE) at the University of Luxembourg. His main research interests were in the field of life-span developmental psychology, geropsychology, and cultural psychology.

Eugenia Gouvedari is an independent researcher interested in the development of theoretical concepts and their metaphorical, transdisciplinary transfers. After her studies in Linguistics and in Learning and Development, what currently inspires her scientific imagination is the meta-reflective perspective on the process of research *in the making* mainly refracted through her encounter with cultural psychology. E-mail: egouvedari@gmail.com

Mogens Jensen, MSc Psychology, PhD, associate professor at Aalborg University, Denmark. He has worked as psychologist in social work and residential care. Presently he is researching within these fields and in professional competence both within a cultural psychology tradition. E-mail: mogensj@hum.aau.dk

Kairi Kasearu, PhD is currently an Associate Professor at the Institute of Social Studies, Faculty of Social Sciences, University of Tartu in Estonia. She is also the head of the "Human resource-related sustainability of the Estonian Defence Forces" research project. She has participated in several European Commission FP projects. She has specialized in the fields of family studies (e.g., family structure, process of family formation, family relations etc.), work–life balancing and intergenerational relations, the evaluation of family policies, and carried out research on social well-being and inheritance of social inequalities. She has recently published articles in the following journals: *European Societies, Journal of Early Adolescence, Ageing and Society, Journal of Contemporary Family Studies, Children and Youth Services Review.* E-mail: kairi.kasearu@ut.ee

Dagmar Kutsar, Phd (Psychology) is an associate professor of social policy of the Institute of Social Studies at the University of Tartu in Estonia. Her research interests are around family, childhood and welfare research and policies (incl. poverty and social exclusion/inclusion, childhood relative deprivation and poverty, changing family structures and family decision-making), social indicators and social reporting (problems of international comparability). Currently she is a principal investigator in the project "Children's subjective well-being in comparative perspective: methodological challenges and practical contributions". E-mail: dagmar.kutsar@ut.ee

Katarzyna Lubiewska is a postdoctoral researcher at Warsaw University and Kazimierz Wielki University in Poland. Her scientific interest is focused on developmental psychology, namely attachment, parenting, and intergenerational relations in a cross-cultural perspective. She took postdoctoral internships at University of Konstanz (Germany) and Tilburg University (the Netherlands). She took part in world-wide international projects on family relations as the team-leader in Poland (e.g., "Value of Children and International Relations") or as the primary investigator ("Combination of emic and etic approach to parenting and attachment" carried out in Turkey, Netherlands and Poland). E-mail: lubkat@ukw.edu.pl

Maliina Lyberth gratuated from Aalborg University and is currently living and working in Greenland as a psychologist. She works in a government based project to help minimize the fallout of students in general and among other things treat them therapeutically to help optimize their quality of life. This issue is one of Maliina's first public writing with the help from her former teacher Jaan Valsiner from Aalborg University and other amazing contributors affiliated with this project. She is also co-author of *Maintenance of Family Networks: Centrality of Peripheral Communication* (2015). E-mail: maliina88@gmail.com

Elsa de Mattos, PhD in Developmental Psychology (Federal University of Bahia–2013). She participates in the Research Group in Development in Cultural Contexts with emphasis on psychosocial development of children and adolescents at urban poor communities. She teaches Forensic Psychology and works as a family mediator. Main areas of interest: adolescence, transition to adulthood, youth, psychotherapy, psychosocial interventions, family mediation. E-mail: e.mattos2@gmail.com

Vívian Volkmer Pontes, PhD, is clinical psychologist and a university professor. Her studies are situated in the psychological perspective of semiotic-cultural constructivism, based on the qualitative and idiographic methodology, and focused especially on the experience of recurrent ruptures in the life course and the semiotic strategies of dynamic repairing of the self. Currently, she is part of the national post-doctoral program linked to the Federal University of Bahia, Brazil, with CAPES funding. E-mail: vvolkmer@yahoo.com.br

Kadri Raid is currently a sociology PhD student and a junior research fellow at the Institute of Social Studies Faculty of Social Sciences, University of Tartu in Estonia. In her recent article she focuses on the changing gender role expectations in the family formation process through the lens of ambivalence. E-mail: kadri.raid@ut.ee

Gaby Marinho Ribeiro works as a psychologist at the Service national de la Jeunesse in Luxembourg. She studied psychology at the Universities of Luxembourg, Paris (France), Louvain-la-Neuve (Belgium) and Maastricht (Netherlands). Her main interests are in the fields of developmental psychology, educational psychology and cultural psychology with a special focus on processes of identity construction in young immigrants. E-mail: gaby.marinho.002@uni.lu

Lívia Mathias Simão, PhD, is Associate Professor at the Institute of Psychology of the University of São Paulo, Brazil, where she coordinates the Laboratory of Verbal Interaction and Knowledge Construction. Her main research interests concern issues embracing the ontological construction of human subjectivity in I-Culture-Other relationships from the perspective of the Semiotic-Cultural Constructivism in Psychology, with emphasis in the issues regarding the notions of Alterity, Temporality and Disquieting Experiences. E-mail: limsimao@usp.br

Annekatrin Steinhoff received her PhD in sociology from the University of Muenster and is currently a postdoctoral research collaborator at the Jacobs Center for Productive Youth Development at the University of Zurich. Her research interests include the interrelations between young people's social and emotional development and characteristics of the social environment, particularly in the realm of family and peer contexts. E-mail: steinhoff@jacobscenter.uzh.ch

Luca Tateo is Associate Professor in Epistemology and History of Cultural Psychology at Aalborg University. His research interests are the study of imagination as higher psychological function, the epistemology and history of psychological sciences. He is editor in chief of the book series *Innovations in qualitative research*, Information Age Publishing, and co-editor of the Springer journal *Human Arenas. An Interdisciplinary Journal of Psychology, Meaning, and Culture.* E-mail: luca@hum.aau.dk

Jaan Valsiner is a cultural psychologist with a consistently developmental axiomatic base that is brought to analyses of any psychological or social phenomena. He is the founding editor (1995) of the SAGE journal *Culture & Psychology*. He is currently Niels Bohr Professor of Cultural Psychology at Aalborg University, Denmark. He has published and edited around 40 books, the most pertinent of which are *The Guided Mind* (Harvard University Press, 1998), *Culture in Minds and Societies* (SAGE, 2007), and *Invitation to Cultural Psychology* (SAGE, 2014). He has been awarded the Alexander von Humboldt Prize of 1995 in Germany, and the Hans-Kilian-Preis of 2017, for his interdisciplinary work on human development, and Senior Fulbright Lecturing Award in Brazil 1995–1997. He has been a visiting professor in Brazil, Japan, Australia, Estonia, Germany, Italy, Luxembourg, United Kingdom, and the Netherlands. E-mail: jvalsiner@gmail.com

Printed and bound by CPI Group (UK) Ltd, Croydon, CR0 4YY

15/09/2026

14962371-0001